Reader's Digest Book of the
GREAT BARRIER REEF

Reader's Digest Book of the

GREAT BARRIER REEF

Devised, edited and
designed by
Mead & Beckett
Publishing

Frank Talbot
Scientific consultant

Roger Steene
Major photographer

Reader's Digest, Sydney

Reprinted with amendments 1990
Published by Reader's Digest Services Pty Limited
(Inc. in NSW)
26-32 Waterloo Street, Surry Hills, NSW 2010
© 1984, 1987, 1990 Reader's Digest Services Pty
Limited
© 1984, 1987, 1990 Reader's Digest Association Far
East Limited
Philippines copyright 1984, 1987, 1990 Reader's Digest
Association Far East Limited

National Library of Australia
cataloguing-in-publication data
The Reader's Digest book of the Great Barrier Reef
Includes index.
ISBN 0 949819 41 7
1. Geology – Queensland – Great Barrier Reef.
2. Geomorphology – Queensland – Great Barrier
Reef. 3. Coral reef biology – Queensland – Great
Barrier Reef. 4. Natural history – Queensland –
Great Barrier Reef.
551.4′24′09943

Typeset by Asco Trade Typesetting Ltd, Hong Kong
Reproduction by Bright Arts (H.K.) Ltd, Hong Kong
Printed by Dai Nippon Printing Co. (H.K.) Ltd,
Hong Kong

Endpapers: This mushroom coral, Fungia, *is a free-living animal which grows in the shape of a dome. It is found throughout the Indo-Pacific region.*

Page one: The sun rises over the waters of the Great Barrier Reef, streaking them a shimmering, liquid gold.

Page two: This prolific genus of stony coral, Acropora, *with its herd of blue damselfish, is the dominant coral on most reefs. The growth form varies from delicate branches to plate-like formations.*

Page three: The male blue-headed wrasse, Thalassoma amblycephalus, *is found throughout the reef waters. The female has a white belly and a dark blue back, covered with thin black bands.*

Page four: Just inside the gaps in the long ribbon reef of the northern outer barrier are great eroded coral blocks, with crevices, channels and caverns, favourite haunts of the black snapper, Macolor macolor. *These outer barrier reefs, and the channels between them, have a grandeur reminiscent of the great game parks of Africa.*

Page seven: A pink and white ovulid cowry eats a colonial growth of soft coral Dendronephthya. *These corals consist of polyps embedded in the fleshy body mass, which contains small chalky granules. Unlike this species, many soft corals can completely withdraw the polyps into their bodies.*

Contents

Contributors

P. N. Alderslade, BSc
Curator of Coelenterates, Northern Territory Museum of Arts and Sciences, Darwin.
Corals

Gordon R. V. Anderson, BSc, MSc
Principal Project Officer, Australian National Parks and Wildlife Service, Canberra.
Conserving for the future

J. T. Baker, OBE, MSc, PhD, FRACI
Director, Sir George Fisher Centre for Tropical Marine Studies, James Cook University of North Queensland, Townsville.
Conserving for the future

A. A. Benson, PhD
Professor of Biology, Scripps Institution of Oceanography, University of California, San Diego.
Symbiosis

R. Alastair Birtles, MA
Tutor in Marine Biology and Zoology, James Cook University of North Queensland, Townsville.
Echinoderms

A. J. Bruce, BSc, MB, BS, DSc
Chief Curator, Division of Natural Sciences, Northern Territory Museum of Arts and Sciences, Darwin.
Crustaceans

M. Y. Chaloupka, BSc
Management Officer, Queensland National Parks and Wildlife Service, Rockhampton.
Algae and sea grasses

Harold G. Cogger, MSc, PhD
Deputy Director, Australian Museum, Sydney.
Marine reptiles

Peter J. Davies, BSc, PhD
Chief Research Scientist, Bureau of Mineral Resources, Canberra.
The greatest reef on earth

Alistair J. Gilmour, BSc, PhD, FTS
Executive Officer, Great Barrier Reef Marine Park Authority, Townsville.
Conserving for the future

Barry Goldman, BSc, PhD
Director, Lizard Island Research Station, Great Barrier Reef.
Fishes
Conserving for the future

Harold F. Heatwole, BA, MSc, PhD, DSc
Associate Professor in Zoology, University of New England, Armidale.
Island plant and animal life

David Hopley, MA, PhD
Director, Sir George Fisher Centre for Tropical Marine Studies, James Cook University of North Queensland, Townsville. The greatest reef on earth

P. A. Hutchings, BSc, PhD
Senior Research Scientist, Australian Museum, Sydney.
Marine worms

D. W. Kinsey, BSc, PhD
Executive Officer, Great Barrier Reef Marine Park Authority, Townsville.
The greatest reef on earth

Patricia Kott, PhD, DSc
Senior Curator, Higher Invertebrates, Queensland Museum, Brisbane.
Ascidians

Edward R. Lovell, MSc
Experimental Officer, Australian Institute of Marine Science, Townsville.
Corals

H. D. Marsh, BSc, PhD
Research Fellow in Zoology, James Cook University of North Queensland, Townsville.
Marine mammals

G. L. Pickard, MA, DPhil, DMS (Hon.)
Emeritus Professor of Oceanography, University of British Columbia, Canada.
The greatest reef on earth

I. R. Poiner, BSc, PhD
Research Scientist, Division of Fisheries Research, CSIRO, Brisbane.
Algae and sea grasses

H. Reynolds, BA, MA
Associate Professor in History, James Cook University of North Queensland, Townsville.
Man on the reef

W. B. Rudman, BSc, MSc, PhD
Senior Research Scientist, Invertebrate Division, Australian Museum, Sydney.
Molluscs

P. Saenger, BSc, PhD, FLS
Research Fellow, Department of Zoology, University of New England, Armidale.
Mangroves
Diving and snorkelling

Frank H. Talbot, MSc, PhD, FRZS, FLS
Executive Director, California Academy of Sciences, San Francisco.
24 hours on a coral reef
Fishes
Dangerous animals of the reef
Conserving for the future

M. Suzette Talbot, BSc, MSc
Life in the plankton

Carden C. Wallace, PhD
Research Fellow, Department of Marine Biology, James Cook University of North Queensland, Townsville.
Corals

R. E. Wass, BSc, PhD
Senior Lecturer in Geology, University of Sydney, Sydney.
Bryozoans

C. R. Wilkinson, BSc, PhD
Senior Research Scientist, Australian Institute of Marine Science, Townsville.
Sponges

E. J. Wolanski, BE, MScE, PhD
Principal Research Scientist, Australian Institute of Marine Science, Townsville.
The greatest reef on earth

We extend grateful thanks to the Australian Institute of Marine Science for granting permission to use their material.

We also gratefully acknowledge the assistance of the Australian Museum, and the following people: Janice Aldenhoven, Dustin Chivers, Phil Coleman, Paul Dixon, Dr William Eschmeyer, Linda Gibson, William Gladstone, Dr Andrew C. Heron, Dr Doug Hoese, Dr James Lowry, Dr John McCosker, Paulette McWilliam, Susan Middleton, Randolph Olson, Dr John Paxton, Dr Stuart Poss, Dr Frank Rowe, Dr Peter Sale, Dr Roger Springthorpe and Hugh Sweatman.

Photographers

(Abbreviations: a = above, b = below, c = centre, l = left, r = right, t = top.)

P. Alderslade: 98 br, 99 bl and r. **Kathie Atkinson:** 139 br, 165 t, 166 tr, 167 l, r and b, 168 r, 171 l and r, 356 c. **Australian Museum, Roth Collection:** 361a, b and r. **Australian Survey Office:** 79, 80. **D. Bellwood:** 123 r. **A. A. Benson:** 149 t, r and bl. **G. Biddle:** 133, 333, 362 l. **A. Birtles:** 234 tr. **Arthur L. Bloom:** 76 t. **Sandy Bruce:** 200 tl, ca, c and r, 202 l and r, 210 r. **M. Bryden:** 301 bl. **Harold G. Cogger:** 350 l. **Neville Coleman:** 123 tl, 177, 179 bl, 182 t, l and r, 185 l, 188 br, 189 r, 190 b, 196 bl and r, 197 l, 226 br, 227 c and r, 228 br, 235 l, 236. **David Colfelt:** 298. **Ben Cropp:** 303. **P. Davie:** 312 tr, 315 b. **Peter Davies:** 75 t, 78 tr and br, 87 t. **Z. Dineson:** 118 br. **Paul Dixon:** 143 tr. **T. Done:** 126 l and br, 331 l. **James Elsol:** 323 tl and bl. **D. Fisk:** 122 tr. **Keith Gillett:** 294 l. **Barry Goldman:** 18 r, 75 b, 324 r. **GBR Marine Park Authority:** 300 l, 321 b. **Bill Hamner:** 143 br. **P. Harrison:** 112 tr and br, 114 bl, 115 tl, 116 l and br. **Harold Heatwole:** 329 bl, 330 bl, c and t, 331 l, 332, 335 c, 336 l, 338 l, 339, 340 b, 341 tl, 342 tr, 343 bl, 344 l and br, 345 bl, 346 l, 347 r, 348 b, 353 r. **George Heinsohn:** 300 r. **Andrew C. Heron:** 137 l, 141 l and r. **A. Heyward:** 114 t. **David Hopley:** 66 l, la, and r, 67 a, c and b, 69 la, l, ra and r, 70 l, r and b, 71 l and r, 72 l, ar and r, 73, 76 b, 83 l, 88, 89 a and b, 90 b, 91 l and r. **Russell Hobbs:** 353. **Jim Hudnall:** 299. **P. Hutchings:** 165 b, 166 l, 356. **Shirley Jeffries:** 137 bl. **James M. King:** 135 tl and bl, 142, 143 l, 144 br, 145 bl and r, 355 l. **Jiro Kikkawa:** 340 t. **D. Kinsey:** 82 c, r, 83 r, 84 l,

ar and br, 85 al. **LANDSAT:** 65, 68 **E. Lovell:** 98
bl, 103 bl, 104 l, 106 la, l, ra, and r, 107 tl, tr, cr, bl
and bc, 108 ct, c, cr and br, 110 la and br, 117 bl and
br, 118 tr, 119 bl, 120 br and tr, 121, 122 l, 123 bl,
124 r, 125 bl, 126 tr, 127 b, 128 b, 129 r, 130 l and
r, 131 tl, cl, bl and r. **C. MacDonald:** 301 r.
Mitchell Library: 359, 360, 363, 365. **John H.
Moverley:** 318 a and b, 319. **National Geographic:**
148. **M. Nowak:** 153. **J. Oliver:** 112 la and lb.
Oxley Library: 367, 368 a and b. **D. Parer:** 302 t.
Oxford Scientific Films: 140 lb and tr, 168 l, 170
l. **Ian Poiner:** 153 l. **Gordon Praik:** 154 l, 155 r.
Bill Rudman: 174 al and l. **Peter Saenger:** 305 l,
ra and rb, 306 l and r, 308 l, ra and rb, 309, 311 tr,
rb and lb, 312 rb and lb, 313, 314 tl, and bl, 315 t,
316 bl, c, tr, br and tl, 317 r, 319 t, 320 tl, bl and br,
322 a and b, 325 b, 328 b, 335 bc, 336 tr. **Howard
Spero:** 145 tl. **W. A. Starck:** 82 l, 362 r. **Roger
Steene:** Cover, endpapers, 1, 2, 3, 4, 7, 8, 9, 10,
11, 20 l and r, 21 l and br, 22 l and r, 23 a, l and r,
24 a, l and r, 25 l and r, 27 b, 28 l and lb, 29 r, 30 l
and r, 31 al, l, ar and r, 32 al, l and r, 33, 34, 35 a
and b, 36, 37 bl and r, 38 b, 40 bl and r, 41 la, l and r,
43, 44 l and r, 45 tl, tr and br, 46 tr and br, 47 l, 49 a
and b, 50 l, cb and br, 51, 52 tl and br, 53 la, l and r,
54, 56 la, lb ra and rb, 57 a and b, 58 br, 59 la, lb, ra
and rb, 60 bl and r, 61, 63, 78 b, 82 b, 85 bl and r,
86 a, b, 87 a, b, 90 t, 94, 95, 96 b, 97 l, r and b, 98 l
and ar, 99 l, 100 l, c, ar and br, 101 a and b, 102 l, a
and b, 103 al, cb and r, 104 tr and br, 105 a and b,
107 al, cl, bl, c and br, 108 l, cb and tr, 109 l, ar
and r, 110 bl and ar, 111 l, al, r and ab, 113 tl, tr, c
and b, 114 br, 115 bl and br, 116 tr, 118 l, 119 tl
and r, 122c, 124 l, 125 r, 127 t, 128 t, 129 l and al,
132, 134, 136 l and r, 138 t, c and b, 139 tr and l,
140 tl, cr and br, 144 l and ar, 146 l and r, 147, 150,
151, 154 t, 155 l, 156 r, 158 l and r, 159 l, la and r,
160 r, 161 l, c and a, 162 l, 163 r, 164 l, c and r,
166 br, 169 t, 170 r and br, 173 br, 174 r, 175 t, 176 l
and br, 178, 179 tl and r, 180 r, 181 t, 183 r, 184 bl
and r, 186 a and b, 187 bl, 188 l and ar, 189 bl, 191 bl,
192, 193, 194 a and b, 195, 196 t, 198, 199 a and b, 201,
203 a and b, 204 l, 205 l and r, 206 l and r, 207 r, 208,
210 tl and b, 211, 212 l, 214, 215 tl, tr and br, 217 bl
and r, 218, 219 al, b and r, 220, 221, 222 l, t and r,
223 a and b, 224 l, a and b, 225, 226 c and r, 227 l
and la, 228 l and ar, 229 l and r, 230 a and b, 231 l
and r, 232, 233 l, r and b, 234 l, c and r, 235 r, 237,
238 l and r, 239 tl, 241 l and r, 242, 243 l, 244 l, t, bl
and br, 245 t, c and br, 246 l, t and c, 247 t, l and r,
248 l, al, r and ar, 249 l, al, r and ar, 250 l, t and r,
251 a and b, 252 bl and tr, 253 tl, ac and r, 254,
255 tl and bl, 256 l, t and r, 258, 259 tl and r, 260 l
and r, 261 a and b, 262 a and b, 263 t, l and br, 264 a
and b, 265 tl, cl, bl and r, 266 r, 267 bl and r, 268 a
and b, 269 a and b, 270 l and br, 271 l, 272 b, 273 l
and r, 274 b, 275, 276 l and r, 277 t, bl and br, 278 l,
r, and br, 279, 280, 281 a and b, 282 l and tr, 283 t,
bl and r, 284 tl, tr, cl, cr and b, 285 t, c and b, 286 tl,
cl, r and br, 287 a and b, 288 a and b, 289 al, l and r,

290 t, c and b, 292 a and b, 293 tl, l, tr and r, 296,
297 r, 301 tl, 302 b, 304, 309, 310, 311 tl, 314 tl, r,
317 tl and bl, 320 tr, 321 a, 323 br, tl and cl, 326 r,
334 a and b, 335 l and r, 337 l, 344 tr, 345 t and b,
346 r, 350 tr and br, 351, 352, 354, 356 l, 357 l, bl
and r, 358, 364, 366 a and b, 370, 371 l and r, 373,
375. **Frank Talbot:** 18 t and bl, 19 a and b, 62, 96 t,
215 bl. **Sue Talbot:** 369. **Valerie Taylor:** 257 t. **R.
Wass:** 212 br, 213 r. **Clive Wilkinson:** 156 l, 162 r,
163 tl, bl and bc. **B. Willis:** 117 t. **Leigh Winsor:**
169 b. **Eric Wolanski:** 92, 93. **Bill Wood:** 16, 17,
21 tr, 26, 27 t, 28 l, 29 l, 37 tl, 38 t, 39, 40 tl and br,
42, 45 bl, 46 l, 47 r, 48 tl, c, b and r, 50 tr and c, 52
tr, 55 a and b, 58 tr and l, 60 tl, 86 t, 107 ca, 125 tl,
152, 153 tl and r, 172 l and r, 173 l and tr, 175 b, 176
tr, 180 l, 181 b, 183 l, 184 tl, 185 r, 187 tl and r, 189
tl, 190 t, 191 r and tl, 197 r, 204 tr and br, 205 c, 206
tl and c, 207 l, 209 al, ar and c, 212 tr, 213 tl and bl,
214, 217 tl, 238 c, 239 bl and r, 240 l, ac, c, ar and r,

243 r, 245 bl, 246 br, 252 tl, br, 253 bl, 255 r, 257 b,
259 bl, 266 l, 267 tl, 270 tr, 271 r, 272 t, 274 t, 291,
294, 295 l and r, 297 l, 324 bl, tl, 325 t, 326 l, 327 al,
l and r, 328 t, 329 r, 330 b, 336 br, 337 r, 338 r, 341 bl
and r, 342 l and br, 343 tl and r, 345 cr, 347 l, 348 t,
349 a and b, 355 r. **Liz Yeoman:** 329 tl, 335 ca.
Len Zell: 137.

Diagrams

Leonie Bremer-Kamp: 76, 78 al and bl, 81 l, 95 r,
96 l, 216. **Pam Brewster:** 160 l, 307, 321. **Bureau
of Mineral Resources, Geology and
Geophysics:** 77, 81 r.

Maps

Mercury-Walch: 12–15. **Paris Match** and
Mitchell Beazley International: 74.

Shrimp, *Rhynchocinetes*

An introduction to the Great Barrier Reef

There are a few places in the world which fulfil the meaning of the word 'enchantment'. They not only delight the senses, but they cast a spell which can even affect the behaviour of human beings. Most of us are monsters to whom self-interest is the main motif of life. Only beauty and power of a remarkable order can charm us into forgetting our interests and doing battle on its behalf. The Great Barrier Reef is one place which has that power.

The reef survives today, without the industrial threat of oil rigs and mineral exploitation and consequent killing pollution, because of this power. The years in which people first took on the battle to have the reef protected from unsympathetic exploitation and declared a Marine National Park are long ago now, and some of those who worked on its side are old or dead. But the remarkable factor in its rescue was the near-unanimity of Queenslanders, and indeed most other Australians, that it should not be spoiled. Once the issues were made clear, many who had never seen it or scarcely knew more of it than reports and photographs joined in the public outcry on its behalf. It would not now be politically possible to reverse the decision that the reef will be protected from the grosser forms of exploitation as a Marine Park – though there are many other threats to its continuing existence, it will not be thrown to the modern dragons quite so carelessly. It has cast a spell, and the people who know it and whom it has enchanted will continue to work on its behalf.

The Great Barrier Reef is perhaps the only such place which lies mainly under water and is therefore not accessible except at certain times and seasons. This is part of its mystery. Also, it is alive – the summits of those underwater mountains teem with life of an unbelievable variety of colour, pattern, form, function and interaction. It is this *livingness* that makes the reef so much more than a mere 'place'. Every isolated cay and shore, the barrier ramparts and the tidal pools, move and sway and dart with living creatures. The beauty of the earth – mountains, forests, cultivated landscapes, icefields, deserts – is not like this; such places are static, accessible, inhabited by warm-blooded creatures like ourselves for the most part and therefore familiar sharers in our breathable atmosphere. But the underwater world is still alien. Its inhabitants live on different terms from ours, and we have only recently been able to explore it in comparative safety. The lives of its inhabitants are unsharable – we have nothing in common with them except life itself. This gives to the reef a strangeness which adds a special dimension to its beauty.

My own knowledge and experience of the Great Barrier Reef is comparatively small – a holiday on Heron Island, and a much earlier few weeks in the immediate postwar years on Lady Elliott Island, the reef's southernmost coral cay, then inhabited only by a little colony of lighthouse keepers. It is Lady Elliott Island which has left the deepest memory with me, though even then it had been devastated by the visits of guano-seeking ships and by a herd of goats kept as a meat supply for the lighthouse staff. Yet its fringing reef had survived all this and the sea which surrounded the island was brilliantly clean and dazzling-clear. 'When I remember it', I wrote more than thirty years later, in *Australia's Natural Heritage*, 'my inner eye is flooded with those marvellous blues and greens of unpolluted water; and the coral pools at low tide held millions of little fishes, anemones, stars, urchins, holothurians, shellfish, crabs, sponges and coral species, all apparently trying to outdo each other in elegance and beauty of pattern, form and colour'.

On calm days we could row out over the fringing reef to look down the crags of coral into valleys and down walls where dim, many-coloured seaweeds and branching growths of coral harboured thousands of other organisms, and shoals of larger fishes, squid, octopus, manta rays and sharks swam. Farther out, whales still blew great fountains on the horizon, dolphins somersaulted and undulated in cheerful processions, and everywhere sea birds hunted the skies – from the big white-breasted sea eagles to the little terns.

All these teeming and changing lifescapes – to coin a term – visible under and over the glowing blues of a tropical sea, seemed to demand interpretation in terms more accessible than the Latin nomenclature most of them were saddled with. But the only poet who has specifically tried to write in and of the reef and its non-human inhabitants – Mark O'Connor, who has lived on it, dived on it, and been instructed in terminology by scientists working on its research stations – has almost despaired of the limitations of an English language evolved in cold northern latitudes and of a Latin system of nomenclature to express the life of the reef. It is hard to find a way of conveying, say, the character and beauty of a spectacular creature whose name is *Euborlasia quinquestriata*, which has been seen by few people, and which has no common name except 'ribbon worm' – and there are many different species of ribbon worms. Roses and nightingales, even waratahs and magpies, are easier poet-fodder. It may be a long while before the reef has a literature of its own.

Since my own first visit to the southernmost part of the reef, there has been much change. Where in 1949 few people visited it and tourist resorts were few and far between, the accessibility of much of the area by petrol-driven launches, tourist ships and helicopters has brought it into the ambit of world tourism. Diving and spearfishing equipment, big-game fishing and the rest of the modern introductions whose impacts on the reef and its waters are still unknown, have thrown it at our mercy, and its days of peace are not likely to return. While zoning plans and educative projects will help, the future of the reef lies with *people*. A rising population, a rising tourist industry, onshore pollution and many other factors threaten it. How to educate for reverence and respect? Our record is not good; but at least we have made a start. The Great Barrier Reef is perhaps the most important, certainly one of the most beautiful and significant, gifts Australia has given the world by nominating it as a World Heritage possession.

JUDITH WRIGHT

Aboriginal cave painting

△ *Aborigines have lived in Australia for more than 40 000 years. From their earliest occupation of the continent they had a knowledge of the sea and its inhabitants, which they recorded in cave paintings.*

◁ *This colourful shrimp is a member of a diverse family found throughout the Indo-Pacific region. Many forms live within the corals and are active mainly at night.*

Discovering the world of the reef

This book has been written by coral reef specialists, each intrigued by an aspect of the Great Barrier Reef. Knowledge of their subjects is only in its beginnings, but over the past two or three years the information has started to fit together. In the past, researching on the reef has been like working on isolated pieces of a jigsaw puzzle without the benefit of a picture on the box. Then suddenly, small bits link up and the first picture, whole though still patchy, emerges. Individual research has contributed to an understanding of fish and bird, fossil reef and water current, but the combined knowledge brings a broader discovery – a discovery of the reef itself.

Man has been studying coral reefs for a long time – in the Great Barrier Reef region probably for

Orange fairy basslet, *Anthias squamipinnis*

△ *The orange fairy basslets are the most common fairy basslets on the reef. They are seen on coral heads, bommies, dropoffs and reef edges. Highly territorial and aggressive, each male maintains a harem of females.*

40 000 years, and even longer in the seas of southeast Asia. These thousands of years of study were undertaken originally by hunter-gatherers and then later by more settled village people who cultivated crops but also fished the reef. They, too, must have wondered at its richness and beauty, but their concern was primarily to learn which creatures were good to eat and which were poisonous, and when one could catch certain fish. Only recently have scientists started to explore this wonderful store of knowledge accumulated by people living on coral reefs. They have found that in some cases the folklore far exceeds the written scientific

information, particularly on the migration and breeding behaviour of many edible fishes.

Compared with the land, the sea is still a place of discovery. Early scientists rarely put their heads under water. In 1843 J. Beete Jukes, the naturalist on the British naval vessel HMS *Fly*, landed on One Tree Island and wrote of his disappointment in his first coral reef – he saw only its surface. For a long time scientists' visual knowledge of the Great Barrier Reef came from looking through glass-bottomed boxes or observing lagoons and low-tide pools on windless days; collecting in anything but shallow water was extremely difficult. Now, scuba equipment and compressors provide the freedom to spend hours under water observing reefs, or to glide 30 metres down the reef face to collect and study.

Recent research has begun to indicate how old the reef is, how it grows and at what rate, and what makes it decay. We now know how some of its creatures live, and how the great water movements driven by tides, trade winds and distant low-pressure systems carry nutrients and planktonic food to the reefs and transport larvae.

Hundreds of reef scientists and other scholars have added to our information since the naturalists Joseph Banks and Daniel Carl Solander sailed along the reef with James Cook; thousands have studied reefs on a worldwide scale. This work has helped to form the present body of reef knowledge presented here.

Classification

Faced with the bewildering array of forms and living patterns in the world of nature – over two million species are already named, and at least as many again are not – mankind has always attempted to put organisms in groups that seemed similar, starting with 'plants' and 'animals'.

Some logical way of giving names to each species was also needed, and not long before Captain James Cook sailed along the Great Barrier Reef the Swedish naturalist Karl von Linné developed the binomial, or 'two name' system we now use: firstly the 'genus', usually denoting a small group of very similar organisms, and secondly the 'species', denoting one particular kind of organism of that group. For example the genus *Chaetodon* comprises a number of very similar butterfly fishes, but the name *Chaetodon auriga* applies only to one, the threadfin butterfly fish (see page 255). That scientific name separates the threadfin butterfly fish from all other animal species in the world, and it also indicates its closeness to the other butterfly fishes of the genus *Chaetodon*. Linné used Latin names because at that time it was the international scientific language. He also Latinised his own name to Carolus Linnaeus!

Common names vary from place to place – the

same fish, mangrove or worm in Queensland may have a different name in Western Australia, Indonesia, the Philippines and so on. But the scientific name is the same everywhere.

The study of the classification of the living world is called taxonomy, and taxonomists name and describe species and classify them in groups. A grouping that seems obvious and sensible at first is the division of the living world into the plant and animal kingdoms. Some taxonomists further divide plants into three kingdoms because of the great differences between, for example, fungi which are not green and don't make their own food, and other plants which make food by photosynthesis in sunlight. But a closer investigation of these groupings uncovers some single-celled organisms that are different from either plants or animals. In bacteria and blue-green 'algae' (which are not in fact algae) the individual cell has no separate internal nucleus containing the deoxyribonucleic acid (DNA) molecules – the genetic engineering plan which is responsible for the organism's design. Most modern classifications place bacteria and blue-green algae in a separate major kingdom.

No classification is perfect; we can only estimate the evolutionary past of species and therefore cannot know precisely which species was derived from which ancestor. The following modern classification attempts to place together species that are closely related:

Kingdom Monera

The first great division or kingdom consists of organisms that do not have their genetic material (DNA) in a separate nucleus within the cell (the procaryote condition). These are the bacteria and the blue-green algae, the earliest recognised living forms. Fossils of some of them have been found preserved in rocks formed over three billion years ago. The Kingdom Monera is then divided into two phyla – the next subdivision down from a kingdom – the bacteria and the blue-green algae. The bacteria are abundant in the ocean, and do much of the breaking down of dead organic matter, releasing the basic chemical elements back into solution for plants to reabsorb into the food chain. Blue-green algae are able to photosynthesise carbohydrates and many also incorporate nitrogen from the atmosphere – a useful ability in the coral reef habitat where nitrogen is scarce. They occur as symbionts with some species like the ascidians, and may form masses in shallow lagoons.

Kingdom Plantae

The next great evolutionary step included the separation of a nucleus within the cell containing genetic material (the eucaryote condition), found in both plant and animal kingdoms. With some

Sea fan, *Subergorgia mollis*

exceptions, the plants, like blue-green algae, use photosynthesis to create food for their own growth and energy needs – and provide the basic food source for animals. The plant kingdom is divided into ten phyla, of which seven include many marine forms: the dinoflagellates, green algae, brown algae, red algae, diatoms, fungi and vascular plants.

Kingdom Animalia

The animal kingdom has a fascinating diversity of structure and behaviour with species varying from single-celled animals to man. The cell has a nucleus, as in plants' eucaryote condition, and most species do not make their own food, depending instead on plants. Much of this book concerns the many great marine phyla of animals without backbones, or invertebrates (22 phyla); and the backboned animals and their relatives (one phylum, the chordates). Examples of the marine invertebrate phyla are

the sponges, coelenterates (corals and jellyfish), bryozoans (lace corals), molluscs, annelids (segmented worms), and echinoderms. The chordates include groups like the ascidians (sea squirts) in which the juveniles have a backbone-like supporting rod or 'notochord', and the vertebrates – all the backboned animals.

The phyla are further divided into classes. The cartilaginous sharks and rays form one class in the chordate phylum; the bony fishes form another; the reptiles another, and so on. And classes are divided into orders – the turtles are one order of reptile, the crocodiles another. And orders are further divided into families, which may have many genera, and each genus has one or more closely related species.

By such classifications we have taken the two million or so described species on earth, and put them in groups, first large, then smaller and smaller – kingdoms, phyla, classes, orders, families, genera

△ *Gorgonians are horny corals attached to the sea bed, vertical walls or overhangs. Their interlacing branches provide an ideal habitat for other invertebrates such as echinoderms and crustaceans.*

and species. The final group, the species, consists of very similar individuals that can interbreed successfully in the wild. Taxonomy attempts to take into account the evolutionary past, and present relationships. And it leads us to the obvious questions: how a species lives and behaves, and how it relates to its neighbours and its physical environment. This book tries to answer these questions as they relate to life on the Great Barrier Reef. We have learnt much in a relatively short time but there will always be more to discover. □

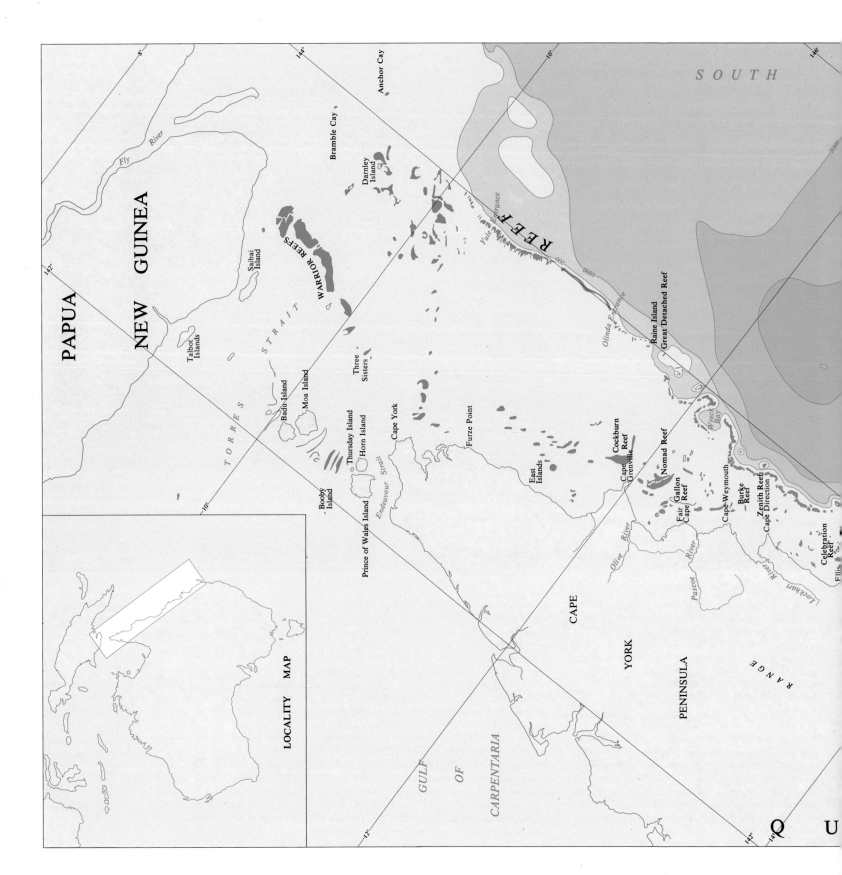

SOUTH

PAPUA

NEW GUINEA

Fly River

Saibai Island

WARRIOR REEFS

Talbot Islands

TORRES STRAIT

Badu Island

Moa Island

Bramble Cay

Anchor Cay

Darnley Island

Yule Entrance

Tidal Entrance

REEF

REEF

Olinda Entrance

Raine Island

Great Detached Reef

Three Sisters

Thursday Island

Horn Island

Prince of Wales Island

Booby Island

Endeavour Strait

Cape York

Furze Point

East Islands

Cape Grenville

Cockburn Reef

Nomad Reef

Wreck Bay

Fair Cape

Gallon Reef

Cape Weymouth

Burke Reef

Zenith Reef

Cape Direction

Celebration Reef

Ellis

Olive River

Pascoe River

Lockhart River

RANGE

CAPE

YORK

PENINSULA

GULF

OF

CARPENTARIA

LOCALITY MAP

QU

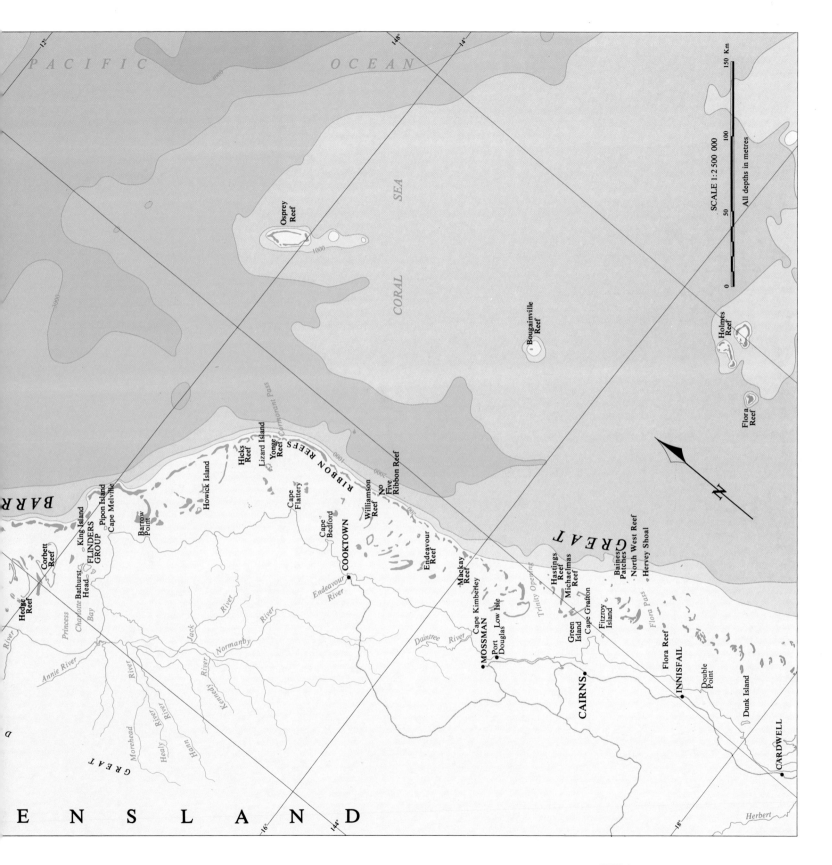

PACIFIC OCEAN

CORAL SEA

Osprey Reef

Bougainville Reef

Holmes Reef

Flora Reef

SCALE 1:2 500 000

All depths in metres

150 Km

100

50

0

N

QUEENSLAND

GREAT BARRIER

Corbett Reef

Hedge Reef

FLINDERS GROUP

King Island

Bathurst Head

Pipon Island

Cape Melville

Barrow Point

Howick Island

Hicks Reef

Lizard Island

Yonge Reef

RIBBON REEFS

Cape Flattery

Cape Bedford

COOKTOWN

Williamson Reef

No Five Ribbon Reef

Cormorant Pass

Endeavour Reef

Mackay Reef

Endeavour River

Cape Kimberley

MOSSMAN

Port Douglas

Low Isle

Daintree River

Trinity Opening

Hastings Reef

Michaelmas Reef

Green Island

Cape Grafton

Baines Patches

North West Reef

Hervey Shoal

GREAT

Fitzroy Island

Flora Pass

Flora Reef

CAIRNS

INNISFAIL

Double Point

Dunk Island

CARDWELL

Herbert

Princess Charlotte Bay

Annie River

Jack River

Normanby River

Hann River

Kennedy River

Healy River

MoreHead River

Morehead River

12°

14°

16°

18°

144°

146°

148°

1000

1000

2000

2000

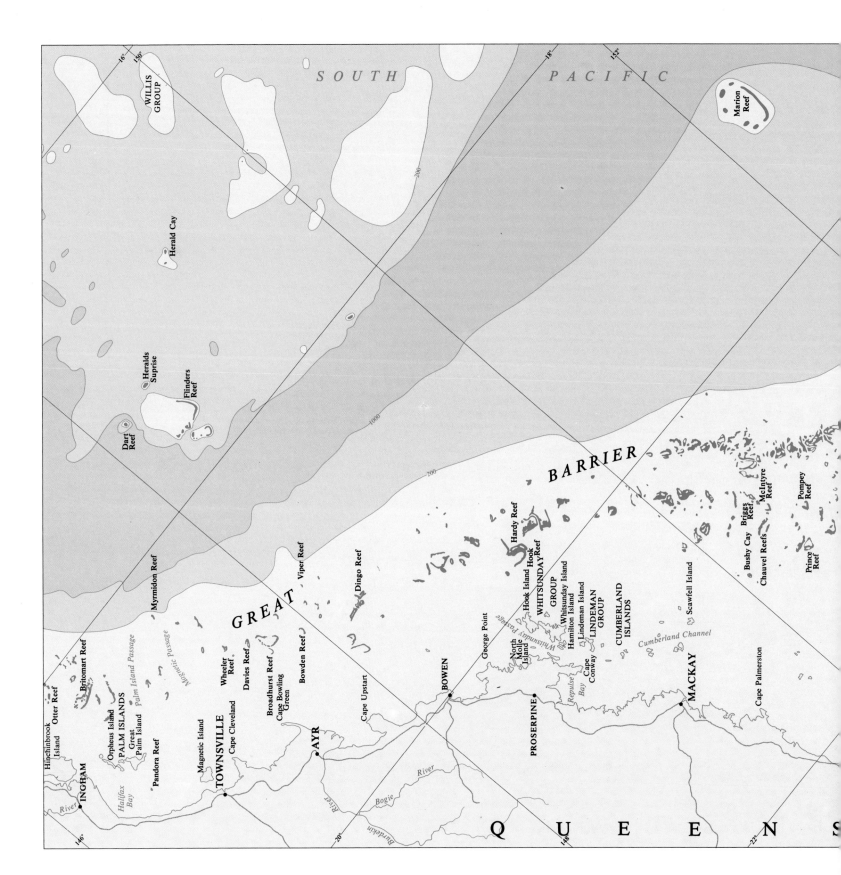

SOUTH PACIFIC

WILLIS GROUP

Marion Reef

Herald Cay

Heralds Suprise

Flinders Reef

Dart Reef

Myrmidon Reef

BARRIER

Hardy Reef

Hook Island Hook Reef

WHITSUNDAY GROUP

Whitsunday Island

Hamilton Island

Lindeman Island

LINDEMAN GROUP

CUMBERLAND ISLANDS

Cumberland Channel

Scawfell Island

Bushy Cay Briggs Reef McIntyre Reef

Chauvel Reefs

Pompey Reef

Prince Reef

Viper Reef

Dingo Reef

GREAT

Hinchinbrook Island

Otter Reef

Britomart Reef

Orpheus Island

PALM ISLANDS

Great Palm Island

Palm Island Passage

Pandora Reef

Magnetic Island

Magnetic Passage

Wheeler Reef

Davies Reef

Broadhurst Reef

Cape Bowling Green

Bowden Reef

Cape Upstart

George Point

BOWEN

North Molle Island

Whitsunday Passage

Cape Conway

Repulse Bay

PROSERPINE

MACKAY

Cape Palmerston

INGHAM

Halifax Bay

River

Cape Cleveland

TOWNSVILLE

AYR

Bogie River

Burdekin River

QUEENS

146° 16° 150° 18° 152° 20° 148° 22°

200 1000 200

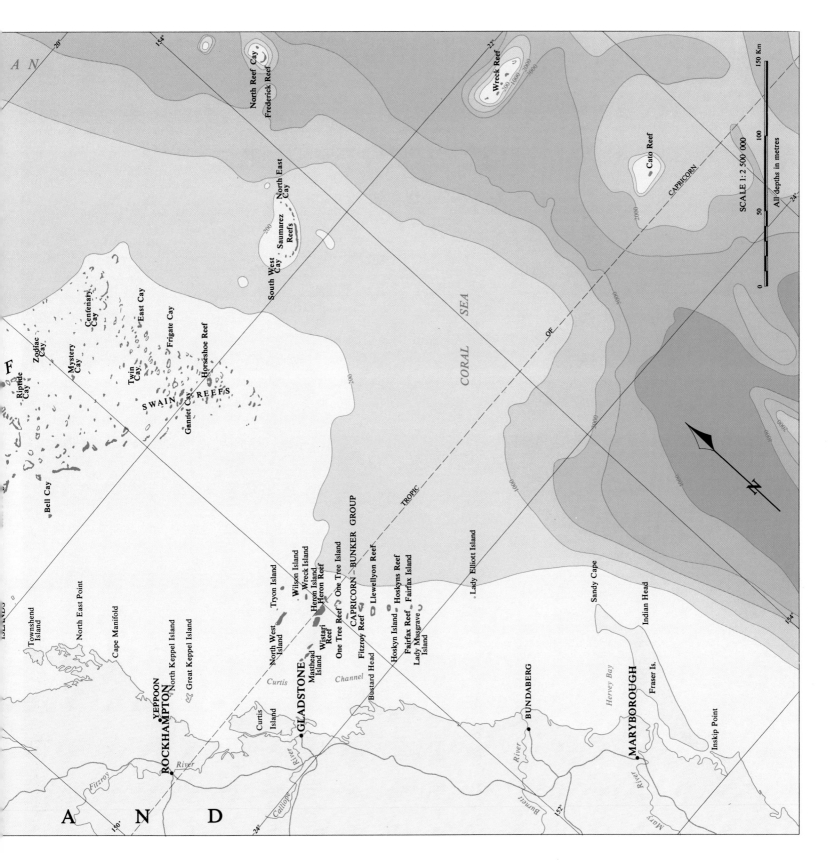

A N

F

Riptide Cay

Zodiac Cay

Mystery Cay

Centenary Cay

East Cay

Twin Cay

Frigate Cay

Gannet Cay

Horseshoe Reef

SWAIN REEFS

Bell Cay

North Reef Cay

Frederick Reef

North East Cay

Saumarez Reefs

South West Cay

200

Wreck Reef

200 1000 2000 2000

Cato Reef

CAPRICORN

200

CORAL SEA

TROPIC OF CAPRICORN

200

2000

1000

3000

4000

4000

N

ISLANDS

Townshend Island

North East Point

Cape Manifold

Tryon Island

Wilson Island

Wreck Island

Heron Island

Heron Reef

Wistari Reef

One Tree Reef

One Tree Island

CAPRICORN – BUNKER GROUP

Llewellyon Reef

Hoskyns Reef

Hoskyn Island

Fairfax Reef

Fairfax Island

Lady Musgrave Island

Lady Elliott Island

Sandy Cape

Indian Head

North West Island

Fitzroy Reef

Masthead Island

YEPPOON

ROCKHAMPTON

North Keppel Island

Great Keppel Island

Curtis Island

Curtis

GLADSTONE

Channel

Bustard Head

BUNDABERG

Hervey Bay

MARYBOROUGH

Fraser Is.

Inskip Point

Fitzroy River

Calliope River

Burnett River

Mary River

A   N   D

150°

154°

152°

20°

22°

24°

24°

SCALE 1:2 500 000

All depths in metres

0   50   100   150 Km

Silver gull, *Larus novae hollandiae*

Part one: 24 hours on a coral reef

The underwater world of the Great Barrier Reef follows a unique day and night pattern, influenced by the coming and going of the high tropical sun and the twice-daily rise and fall of the tides. Reef organisms of breathtaking colour and variety have evolved a delicate balance of hunters and prey, camouflage and brilliant display, competing with each other for space and feeding time, yet accommodating themselves to the reef's great rhythms. A morning dive, and then another at dusk, enable us to watch an amazing cycle of change and re-formation.

The morning dive
It is dawn over the Great Barrier Reef. We carry our gear over smooth, cool sand and load the boat just as the sun breaks through a layer of those little cotton-wool clouds, now grey below and tinged with gold above, that seem to be always on the horizon and seldom above you in the tropical sky. The tide is very low and the surface so still that it reflects the green hill on the island and the clouds sailing high above it.

Everywhere the reefs are above the surface, and the reef crest makes a long line at the outer edge of the lagoon with only a few gaps where the water gently sucks in and out. The exposed reefs will shelter us from even a hint of the coral sea swell. Out on the reef flat a heron is already hunting on his low-tide territory, white plumes tinged yellow by the sun and its reflection in the still pools.

▷ *Hungry after a night's sleep, a grey reef heron waits for the falling tide to expose its feeding places on the reef flat. This species of heron – either slate grey or pure white – searches for food over the whole area exposed at low tide, each in its own territory, often using its wings to shade the pool so that its sharp eyes can see the fishes and shellfish below without reflections. Though it roosts in groups, each bird occupies and vigorously defends its own territory on the reef at low tide. It often stands motionless by the water with its head sunk onto its shoulders.*

◁ *A scavenging silver gull, the opportunist of the reef's islands and cays, pauses in the dawn light. During the breeding season the gulls steal eggs or chicks from careless birds of other species. The hatching period of young turtles is also a feast time, for gulls wait in noisy groups and take the youngsters as they make their dash for the sea. But at low tide they also hunt the sands and the exposed reefs for scraps, perhaps of some predator/prey battle of a few hours before, or for small dead animals from the plankton that have washed ashore.*

'Early dawn on the reef. The air is cool and clean with the city far away. The scene is so untouched and splendid that it could be pre-man.'

Reef heron, *Egretta sacra*

▷ *More than a few hours of exposure will kill the corals. They produce heavy mucus that helps to prevent dehydration and that can be easily seen as a surface slick floating away with the rising tide. A giant clam lies completely exposed but comes to no harm. This has happened many times before and the slow-growing clam has probably been here for a hundred years or more.*

Giant clam, *Tridacna gigas*

Δ *At extreme low tide on the reef on a lovely morning the water is crystal clear and the exposed coral shows wonderful sculptured shapes and colour. A day like this is ideal for diving or just wading through the shallows watching the life in and about the corals.*

◁ *Still pools at the reef crest. Even in this protected reef the water at the outer edge of the reef flat is usually turbulent. A combination of very low tide and lack of wind results in a glassy surface, with exposed shrub, staghorn and plate or tabular corals. As the tide rises this area will be grazed by surgeon and parrotfish, for there is much algal turf at the bases of and between these corals. At present these grazers are over the reef crest, waiting and feeding in deeper water.*

Shrub, staghorn and plate coral, *Acropora*

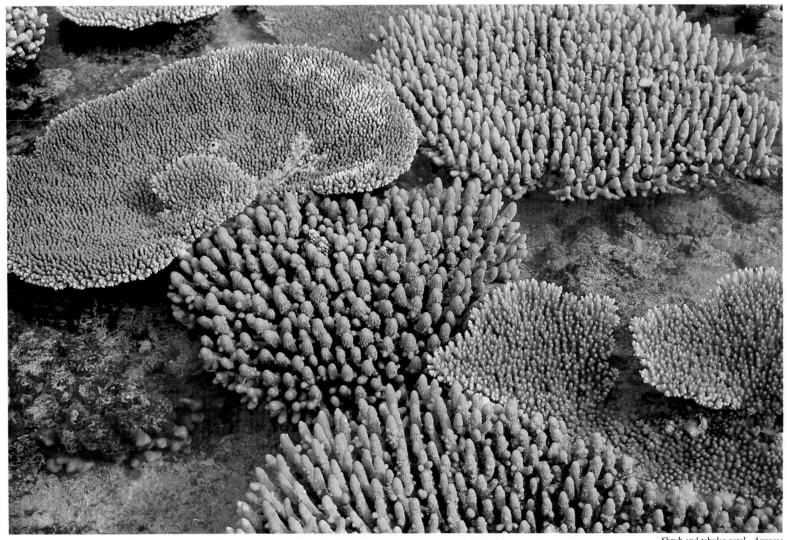

Shrub and tabular coral, *Acropora*

Splendour at low tide

'Exposed reefs at extreme low tides are rare and offer danger to the coral that will be harmed by long exposure. At certain times of the year, large areas of reef may be exposed to atmospheric conditions for some hours each day.'

Shrub and tabular coral, *Acropora*

△ *These corals, above and left, seen so clearly in the low tide show a variety of growth patterns. Some are tabular, plate-like structures while others show typical branching shrub forms. The Acroporidae encompasses more species than any other family of corals. They have varied growth forms, porous skeletons and tiny polyps, rarely more than two millimetres in diameter. These corals grow well in shallow water.*

▷ Large sponges are also more abundant on the reef base, apparently able to find a foothold where the light-loving corals start thinning. These tall tubes have small pores on the outer walls of the tube through which they draw water. This is filtered for food as it passes through the body, then enters the central tube and is exhaled through the open top. The process is aided by the currents that sweep along the reef and draw water out of the sponge tube.

Sea whips, *Junceella*

△ At the bottom of the reef sea whips dominate. Black coral, sea whips and sea fans of different types inhabit the deeper water of the reef. The scenery differs from the reef above and there is a new fauna of shrimps and small transparent gobies living on the sea whips.

Even without wind the temperature is cool. Although we know that the water temperature over the outer reef edge changes little from night to day, a morning dive always seems cold at first. The small outboard motor pushes the boat across the shallow lagoon and through a gap in the reef crest to the open water beyond, where we look for a convenient place to explore on the rich slopes of the outer reef. The air is cool and clean and the city seems far away. As we stand with bare feet on crisp sand, it seems that no one else has ever been here, and the reef is utterly deserted.

Tubular sponge

Sea whip country

Clumsy in the boat in diving gear, we become weightless as we sink down the sloping face of the reef past a great jutting coral, to rest on soft sand twelve metres below. Here we are in sea whip country where the long whip-like horny corals spiral outwards from the coral rock above us. They have their own fauna: specially adapted, minute fishes – some of the smallest vertebrates in the world – cling to their stalks, along with shrimps. The little gobies are transparent and difficult to see, but if we put our hands round the base of a sea whip and gently move it, we will probably find a small goby skimming along in front of it.

Down below on the sandy slope a few feathery sea pens are visible, but the surface has mounds and small holes; it is a burrowing annexe of the reef, with many worms, crustaceans and molluscs living on the base. We now see a burrowing sea anemone with delicate tentacles trailing in the slight current. At the slightest touch it will draw back into its fibrous tube and disappear.

The coral slope

The cold greyness of the early dawn is slowly lightening and the soft, warm colours of the corals start to show. We rise a little off the sea bed, adjusting our compensators to be able to hang motionless above the reef slope. Like the heron on the reef flat, the great mass of fishes that have rested overnight deep in the coral are hungry now and are leaving their 'beds' to start the day's foraging. Small sleepy fishes hang above the coral heads, wrasses and goatfish begin searching for food between the coral and the coral trout appear. Along the whole reef face there is movement. Looking up we can see the pale green-blue undersides of the small waves and their lazy splash where the reef breaks the surface.

'Along the whole reef face there is movement – clinging, spiralling and drifting.'

▷ From below water the waves breaking on the reef crest create patterns of reflection and translucence, with colours of sky blue, turquoise and foam white, that constantly change and fascinate. Wave action during cyclones can be damaging to the reef. Large portions of branching coral colonies can be broken off, and sometimes whole blocks of coral are removed.

Sea pen, *Pteroides*

△ Below the reef is a steep sandy slope full of worms, crustaceans, molluscs, sea pens and anemones. Minute copepods shelter near rubble from the reef above, and schools of tiny, translucent possum shrimps, each about five millimetres long, can be found in hollows. Further down the slope wonderful feathery sea pen plumes, bravely held at right angles to the current, sift the water for small plankton.

▷ This sea anemone lives on the sandy mud below the reef. It has a tube into which it can withdraw with lightning speed if touched. Looking like a gentle flower, its long delicate tentacles waft with the current. But the stinging cells in the animal's tentacles are for serious food gathering and cause instant death to any small creature that sweeps into them.

Sea anemone, *Cerianthid*

A tangle of corals

'Huge, rounded corals with eroded,
undercut bases form holes and caverns
that afford shelter for fishes. The
seaward slopes of reefs are where the
greatest and most virile coral growth
occurs, but in deeper water, erosion is
faster than growth.'

△ *Early morning on the reef base, above and right. The
water here is too deep for a rich growth of sun-loving
corals. They are replaced by a number of sea whips, sea
fans and black corals with flexible skeletons that wave
when the water is disturbed, unlike their stony shallow-
water counterparts. Black corals are not black for, when
alive, their flesh is actually yellow, orange, brown or
grey. The 'black' skeleton, which is really very dark
brown, is visible only after the animal's flesh is scrubbed
off. Black coral is sought after for jewellery.*

Siphonogorgia, sea whips and sea fans

Gorgonian, sea whips, sea fan and feather star

◁ *A tangle of horny corals is found with a large sea fan that has grown at right angles to the current flow along the reef, and strains microscopic food from the constantly washing water. A feather star clings here for its own feeding. Most sea fans, black corals and sea whips favour deeper levels where the water is cooler and the sunlight greatly reduced.*

Plate coral, *Acropora hyacinthus*; feather star, *Comatulids*

Δ *Plate corals found in channels and protected areas, or in moderately deep water below the worst of the wave action, will sometimes grow to over two metres in diameter. But they can never live too deep; they need light strong enough for those algal food factories, the zooxanthellae, to produce enough food for vigorous coral growth. Here many species live permanently or shelter temporarily under a plate coral. Several feather stars are perched under this plate coral, but at night may be seen on top of it, arms extended, to net their fill of plankton.*

◁ *Nocturnal fishes return to shelter under their protective overhang after the night's feeding. The entrance of this cave is dominated by a rich growth of black coral.*

Black coral, *Antipathes*

Corals, *Porites*

Branching and plate coral, *Acropora*

'The great mass of fishes that have rested overnight deep in the coral are hungry in the morning and leave their beds to start the day's foraging.'

◁ *On the coral slope the early morning light is reflected through the small waves. A full cover of living coral is on the slope, and a mass of small daylight plankton feeders seek food after the fast of the night.*

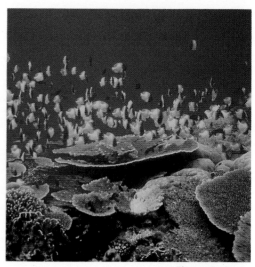

Plate coral, *Acropora*

△ *A school of harlequin-coloured fishes fin gently above the coral at the base of the slope. These plate-like corals are some of the most beautiful on the reef. Related to the spectacular staghorns, they often occur together.*

◁ *It is still not fully understood what environmental subtleties create the varied patterns of the reef. Here the shrubby Acropores and their plate-shaped relatives have given way to species of solid boulder form. Some of these may grow over hundreds of years to colonies three to five metres in height.*

Anthiids

△ At the base of the slope there may be small cliffs, overhangs and caverns. The erosive forces of the reef have overtaken reef growth, aided in some cases by wave action at earlier lower sea levels. Fishes of the night may shelter, sometimes in huge numbers, in these caverns.

◁ Where conditions of light or current are less suitable for stony corals, the surface is covered with other life – soft corals, encrusting algae, sponges and sea squirts. These small pink anthiids, relatives of the big rock cods, usually prefer deeper water.

A solid, colourful mass

The corals on this outer slope are spectacular. Sweeping up to the reef crest is a great bank of shrub, staghorn and plate-like corals – many species of soft blues, pinks and greens forming a solid colourful mass. Total coral cover of the bottom is unusual, for normally the coral shrubs are separated by dead compacted coral rock, covered in either a fine algal turf or a hard, cement-like pink surface – also, surprisingly, encrusting algae. Here, this full coral cover is probably due to many factors, including currents, food and a wave action that is never great because of the shelter given by nearby reefs. The sloping bank of coral is punctuated by huge, rounded *Porites* corals with eroded, undercut bases that form holes and caverns large enough for us to enter. It has taken hundreds of years for the coral to grow to this size.

Colours of daylight

At full light, all the day species are about. Hundreds of fishes hang above the coral slope, a bewildering kaleidoscopic display of colour and form – large and small, elongated and chubby, with colours from hard black to translucent pink, yellow, orange, red, purple, blue and shimmering silver. There is nothing on land to compare with this variety:

Population explosion

'Daylight brings out an enormous variety of fish species – sometimes as many as 150 different kinds can be seen within the space of 100 square metres.'

Puller fish, *Chromis atripectoralis*

White stinging hydroid, *Lytocarpus philippinus*

△ *Growing on the lower slope is a hydroid with striking sprays of white fronds. This is one of the most beautiful of the soft hydroids, but it stings!*

▷ *A large school of young fishes on the reef edge are silhouetted against the morning light. Sometimes fishes settle from their planktonic phase in very large numbers.*

▷ △ *Small damselfish or pullers sleep deep in the coral branches at night, but even while feeding during the day they stay close to their coral shelter.*

Damselfish

Sweetlip emperor, *Lethrinus chrysostomus*

△ Sweetlip emperors start to feed actively at dusk and are an angler's favourite. They grow up to 900 millimetres in length and their alternate name is 'tricky snapper'.

◁ Paddle-tail hussars school, keeping very close to the sea bed, and seem to pour over the surface following each hummock or dip. They live in shallow waters, feeding at dusk and in the early morning.

'There are more species of fishes on a coral reef than in any other place in the sea.'

Paddle-tail hussar, *Lutjanus gibbus*

Football trout, *Plectropomus melanoleucus*

Hawkfish, *Parachirrites forsteri*

Yellow-banded hussar, *Lutjanus amabilis*

△ *A hawkfish sits firmly on the coral. This little predator never hangs above the sea bed as most fishes do, but is always on the surface or tucked into a fork of coral.*

△△ *The colours of this close relative of the coral trout, the football trout, are similar to a football jersey. Its habits are like those of the coral trout, and it has sometimes been considered merely a colour variant. But it is not as common as the coral trout.*

schools of damsels like delicate moving clouds, wrasses, butterfly fish, parrotfish, hussars, sweetlips, small groupers and triggerfish. Where else does one find a hundred and fifty living species within a hundred square metres?

Feeding on the reef

Three large coral trout also hang over the coral slope, seemingly in harmony with the other fishes, but they are waiting for an unwary move by one of their prey – a fish too close, or too far from coral shelter. The potential prey go normally about their feeding, but with one eye on the big-mouthed trout. When a coral trout takes a fish, it happens in a flash – not a long rush, but a swift lunge and a suck – while the rest of the school continue feeding as though nothing has happened.

About fifty large yellow-banded hussars laze quietly around a huge undercut coral, resting. They

are night feeders, but there is little doubt that if a tasty small fish came too close they would snap it up regardless of the time of day. Many night-hunting and dawn-and-dusk hunting species will find rest and protection in a school, quietly swimming to and fro near good shelter.

The outer slope is a rich area for plankton feeders. The ocean water, carrying its living load of minute plankton, washes through the reefs, restlessly pushed and pulled by tide and wind. A number of species of fusilier feed off the reef edge above the coral, sometimes in small groups, but often in large schools. And tiny damselfish pick the minute animals in the plankton. They leave their sheltering coral for food but never go far. There must always be the temptation to move further out from shelter upstream to get the drifting morsel before your neighbour. But go too far, and you will end in a trevally's maw.

'A large coral trout may stay around one area of coral for weeks, or even months, and then move off somewhere else, where the feeding is better.'

Parrotfish, *Scarus frenatus*

◁ *Yellow-banded hussars often school on the outer reefs during the day and hunt singly over the lagoon floor at night, protected by the darkness.*

▷ *A school of grazing parrotfish works, heads down, bumping at the coral and at each bump scraping the surface with their strong beaks. They keep the whole reef cropped, and seem to cover any dead rock or coral base each day. The drab-coloured individuals are in their female phase, and the brightly coloured fish are in the male phase. Parrotfish begin life as females and have at least one reproductive season before turning into males.*

▽ *The island coral trout is a wily predator, swimming out in the open with its prey, seemingly harmless and drifting slowly over the coral. But this one may well be about to attack. It has distinctive, bright blue markings on the head, cheeks and gill cover, with the rest of its body being reddish brown or grey. At least five species of coral trout are found on reefs in northern Australia.*

Island coral trout, *Plectropoma maculatum*

Hungry algal feeders

The grazers, chiefly schools of variously coloured parrotfish and sombre dark surgeons, are still being kept from the reef crest by the low tide and are scraping the algal-covered bases of the living corals and dead coral rock just below the gentle surge at the reef's edge. The parrotfish – a mixed school of different species and different colour phases – hang, with their tails up, bumping the surface as they take algae and dead coral with their hard beaks. The bristle-toothed surgeonfish eat more delicately, not leaving the bare scrape marks characteristic of the parrots. These fish grazers seem to cover every part of the surface daily – if we protect a piece of rock with wire mesh, its algae grow several centimetres long within a few days. Little of the algal turf along the reef's two thousand kilometres is untouched by the hungry algal feeders.

As we get close to the reef an aggressive black damselfish guarding its territory rushes at us, a goliath twenty thousand times its weight. On top of a rock a blenny, with comical face and swivelling eyes, watches us as it hops about its small territory. While most fishes have a gas-filled swim bladder that keeps them buoyant, others, like the blennies and moray eels, lack one and actually 'sit' on the coral. A small hawkfish also props itself between two coral twigs, quietly watching us go swimming past.

Moving fast along the edge of the reef is a hunting school of trevally or horse mackerel, six of them, and a mass of yellow-striped fusiliers race away for refuge in the coral. The reef edge is the hunting place of many larger fishes such as lesser tuna, a number of species of barracuda, trevally and turrum, and big red bass. They patrol great distances of the reef edge, feeding on unwary or isolated fishes, some of them crossing to other reefs.

▷ A school of yellow-striped fusiliers is silhouetted against the surface as dusk approaches. During the day they live in schools for protection, and hover in the water column off the front edge of reefs where ocean currents are strong and there is a good supply of plankton in the water. As dusk approaches they can quite often be seen feeding actively on the rising plankton before they retire singly, and settle deep into the coral for the night.

▽ This school of yellow-tailed fusiliers feeds on plankton. During the day they can be seen patrolling anywhere up to fifty metres off the front of a reef. But as darkness approaches, the schools become tighter, and the fish seek the protection of the reef. As darkness falls, they change colour to a drab blue with a mottled appearance and the belly takes on a reddish tinge. At night they rest motionless deep in caves and among the branches of the coral for protection.

Yellow-tailed fusiliers, *Caesio cuning*

Sharks drift by

A large shark may drift by off the reef edge – majestic, powerful and very beautiful. A sick or disabled fish sends out unusual swimming 'signals' and if these are picked up by the sensitive pressure receptors of the shark the fish is chased and eaten immediately.

Attacks by sharks on swimmers and divers on the reef are rare and the sharks we see may be curious, but are usually timid. Occasionally, territorial sharks may be aggressive. A rush by a grey reef shark seems more a warning than an attack, but all sharks should be treated with care. Unpredictable, and potentially dangerous, they sometimes become too curious, but they seldom affect the enjoyment of diving in the waters of the Great Barrier Reef.

The shark's eye seems particularly adapted to dim light, and most sharks are active at dusk and after dark. They also have pressure sensitive pores on the

Yellow-striped fusiliers, *Caesio chrysozonus*

Trevally, *Caranx melampygus*

White-tipped reef shark, *Triaenodon obesus*

Trevally, *Caranx sexfasciatus*

Whaler shark, *Carcharinus*

△ *The six-banded trevally is said to reach a weight of 40 kilograms or more. Here a school of young trevally search for small fishes along the reef base.*

△△ *Big trevally hunt the edge of the reef during the daylight hours, but seem most active at dawn and dusk. Here a blue trevally drifts past two pennant coral fish off the edge of the reef.*

'There is tension at dawn and dusk, when large swift-swimming fishes appear out of the gloom.'

body and any unusual movements in the water around them are sensed. They have little difficulty in picking up the movement of a prey, and can also sense its direction. A shark with covered eyes has still been able to catch prey in an experimental tank. In the dark of night a shark will both sense and see a diver long before the diver even becomes aware of the shark.

A fish hooked on the reef by an angler after dark is often immediately pounced on by a shark, suggesting that those canny scavengers are actively searching in the dusk for disabled fishes sending out unusual swimming signals. Divers often see sharks at night by torchlight, but aggression towards humans seems to be extremely rare. Sometimes a small-toothed shagreen or tawny shark, two to three metres long, may be seen over the reefs, showing two large equal-sized fins clear of the water in front of the tail fin. It is not known to attack man.

△ *Sleek and streamlined, big sharks drift effortlessly along the reef. Sometimes they seem timid and flee from divers, but often they ignore them, moving majestically by, as though aware that they have few effective enemies. There are many species of shark on the reef and one of them, the whaler shark, can be fiercely aggressive to divers. Threatening behaviour includes hunching of the back, and rapid opening and shutting of the mouth, which may occur before an attack.*

△△ *The white-tipped reef shark is a common sight off the edge of the reef and over coral beds and seems to live in one area, occupying a territory. It is not usually aggressive and seldom exceeds one and a half metres in length.*

Oval spot butterfly fish, *Chaetodon speculum*

Blue-patch butterfly fish, *Chaetodon plebeius*

Blue-spotted boxfish, *Ostracion cubicus*

△ *The beautiful, small blue-patch butterfly fish is abundant on most reefs in sheltered areas of living coral. Blue-patches are easy to approach underwater and are not alarmed by divers.*

△△ *The oval spot butterfly fish has a very distinct false eye spot. It is thought that this false eye makes a predatory fish strike incorrectly, with the fish swimming off in the 'wrong' direction. The true eye is concealed by a dark bar. There have been many theories as to why coral reef species are so colourful. One of the more likely explanations is that individuals within a species can more easily recognise their own kind from among the bewildering array of similarly shaped fishes.*

Carnival time

The sun is now higher and the colours show to their best advantage. So many fishes are swimming above and around the coral that the reef is gay with colour and movement. It has a carnival atmosphere. The butterfly fish, true pierrots of the reef, move merrily over the living coral, taking small nips of coral flesh as they move from shrub to shrub. If we watch them for some time, we can see that they are following a pattern. They travel over roughly the same path, never taking too much from any one coral clump, and cover a 'home range', an area of a few metres for some species, a hundred metres or more for larger butterfly fish. They know these areas in minute detail – the best feeding spots and every coral channel, shelter hole and crevice in which to hide.

If you are dangerous you do not need to hide. Fire fish and some poisonous puffers flaunt bright

△ *This little boxfish releases a poisonous mucus from its skin and is distasteful for predators. It swims using its side fins and often tucks its tail to one side. Boxfish are common on coral and mainland reefs. The juvenile form is bright yellow with black spots.*

▷ *Striped butterfly fish move over the coral, taking small nips at coral polyps. They usually cover a fairly wide area, but other species may defend a small territory and they often travel over roughly the same path. These magnificent fish are common on coral reefs, especially on the upper slopes and near the reef edge.*

Striped butterfly fish, *Chaetodon trifasciatus*

Staghorn coral, *Acropora nobilis*

△ *When the gloominess of the early morning has gone, the reef is friendly and colourful and numerous small fishes can be seen swimming over the coral. Most of the zooplankton leave the surface at this time of day and move just above the sea bottom or even in the sand. As a result the water is dazzlingly clear – sunlight is able to penetrate to greater depths, and visibility is good.*

A friendly reef

Most of the plankton have left the surface, some species swimming just above the sea bed sand, or even burrowing in it. Many are in the coral crannies, and the open-sea species are many metres deep. With sparse zooplankton and the sparkling sunlight, visibility is very good and the reef seems bright and friendly.

The tension of dawn and dusk, when big fishes appear out of the gloom, is over. The diver, and perhaps the fishes, feel safer at this time and the corals show their soft colours to best advantage. They have drawn in their dart-filled tentacles and

warning colours which say, 'You have touched me once and it was unpleasant, don't you remember?' The comical little boxfish swims by, using only its side fins like a paddle-wheeler. The skin exudes an unpleasant mucus, making it fairly safe from attack.

closed their polyp mouths because they feed when the rich night plankton cover the reef, and may now be digesting plankton caught during the previous night. The small symbiotic plants, zooxanthellae, in the corals' cells are rapidly making food, using the sun's energy by the chemical process called photosynthesis. Some of this food 'leaks' to the corals. Larger algae and algal turf also use the sun's energy to make food and to grow, and the water over the lagoon bubbles with oxygen, a by-product of photosynthetic food production.

Many reef animals, including some sponges, sea squirts and molluscs, have come to a useful arrangement with zooxanthellae during evolution. The giant clams expose their beautifully coloured and patterned fleshy lips, filled with algae, to the sunlight, supplementing their plankton diet from the constant stream of water they filter. As we swim slowly over one, it convulsively jerks its two shells;

Giant clam, *Tridacna gigas*

'In its mantle the giant clam has sensitive eyes that respond to shadows. It is a fully protected species, which grows to a great size.'

◁ *The giant clam is said to weigh up to 260 kilograms, and to reach a hoary age of hundreds of years. It is open to the sun during the day, and the minute algae in its lips produce carbohydrates using the sun's energy, and provide some of the clam's food. Water passes through its mantle, providing oxygen and plankton.*

▽ *In the noon sun the colours of the corals are at their best showing delicate blues, mauves, pinks, yellows and fawns. The combination of the colours and their varied shapes of turrets, plates, delicate shrubs and solid boulders makes magical underwater landscapes.*

Corals

Grey-and-white puller, *Acanthochromis polyacanthus*

Swimming in the shallows

'When two goatfish spar with their barbels it is difficult to tell whether they are males fighting or a pair fondling each other.'

◁ ◁ *Grey-and-white pullers are very common in the lagoon. They seem to be the only species that cares for both eggs and young. During the day they are all out seeking plankton above the coral, but at dusk the parents will chase the young down into the coral to sleep.*

◁ *The harlequin tuskfish, one of the wrasses, is common all over the reef. It is easy to pick out with its brilliant colouring as it searches the lagoon floor for crustaceans and molluscs.*

Harlequin tuskfish, *Choerodon fasciatus*

Anemone fish, *Amphiprion perideraion*

△ *Anemone fish are only found with large anemones and seem immune to the batteries of stinging cells in their tentacles, although other small fishes will die if they strike the anemone. But it seems that when an anemone fish first settles it is not totally immune, and will touch the anemone, move away, and repeat this performance many times, apparently slowly building up resistance, probably by covering itself with mucus from the anemone, until it is unaffected.*

◁ *Below the chin, bicolour goatfish have very sensitive barbels that can be folded away in a groove or brought forward to use for tasting. Goatfish often follow other larger fishes digging and blowing on the lagoon floor, sweeping the disturbed surface with their barbels and sensing small edible items, such as small animals missed by the larger fishes.*

Bicolour goatfish, *Parupeneus barberinus*

Damselfish

Coral cod, *Cephalopholis miniatus*

it has small eyes that respond to our shadows and are probably necessary to save its exposed flesh from hungry fishes.

Activity at its highest

The water has risen high enough for the grazers to swim over the reef edge into the shallow lagoon, and we can comfortably follow. The day activity is at its highest. A tuskfish is digging on the lagoon floor, followed by a goatfish that wriggles its two chin bristles across the turned-over sand to sense tasty morsels too small for the tuskfish. Clouds of damselfish are above every coral shrub, feeding on the sparse day plankton, and a pair of anemone fish plough into the protective tentacles of their anemone as we come close.

The one species of fish that carefully guards its young, the grey-and-white puller or spotty-tail, is common here. A pair of adults watch over their swarm of two dozen young, ready to chase off any predator who takes too close an interest, then shepherd their young to the shelter of the coral. The parental drive is strong, and if a swarm of young loses its parents other grey-and-white pullers have been known to add them to their brood.

An object of interest

As we swim over the coral we are not only the observers; we are objects of interest to some fishes and of fear to others. Some of the smaller ones watch and follow, and we attract a swarm of fishes from nearby corals. But the bigger fishes – four large blue surgeonfish and a large Maori wrasse – just drift away. A predatory fish of human size would probably be a threat to the larger fishes but ignore the smaller ones, and they respond accordingly.

If we should sit beside a coral without moving for a long time, the scene would slowly revert to its normal pattern. Aqualungs emit a noisy stream of bubbles every half minute or so, which initially disturbs the fishes. Living underwater in a habitat for two weeks, and using a rebreather that does not emit bubbles, we can get so close to a large bream that its scale rows can be counted to check its identification.

Rest for the night feeders

A small group of spangled emperors, their bodies pale and merging with the sand, drifts past in a lagoon channel beside a coral patch. They will become active at dusk. Many of the other nocturnal species are now taking their rest. In coral caves we can see scores of fifty-millimetre cardinal fish schooling all day in shelter, ready to spread out in mid-water at nightfall. By looking through the entrance to a deep cavern and becoming accustomed to the dim light, we can also see squirrelfish and soldier fish. Both groups are red and almost invisible when they come out to feed at night. The scarlet-fin soldier fish shows a brilliant scarlet dorsal fin as it turns in its cavern.

Scarlet-breasted Maori wrasse, *Cheilinus fasciatus*

◁ △ *Staghorn coral often forms dense thickets in slightly sheltered water. A patch in the lagoon makes an ideal habitat for a myriad of small fishes, providing perfect shelter from large predators. The tiny damsels can easily slip down into the deep recesses of the thicket. The upper portions of the staghorn branches are alive and grow rapidly. The lower portions may be dead and algal-covered, providing food such as worms, molluscs and crustaceans that attracts a mass of different kinds of fishes over the staghorn beds.*

◁ *A number of small species of rock cod live among the corals of the lagoon, pouncing on any dead or disabled fish and feeding on small invertebrates. One of these is the coral cod, an opportunist who takes almost anything it can find. This is the fish most likely to be caught by an angler dangling a bit of fish bait over a coral reef.*

'As a diver swims past, smaller fishes come to investigate and larger ones drift away. A fish of human size would be a threat to larger fishes, but would ignore the smaller ones. They respond accordingly.'

△ *The scarlet-breasted Maori wrasse is a relative of the harlequin tuskfish and is widespread over the reefs of the Pacific and Indian oceans though it does not reach Hawaii. It is common in the lagoon and grows to about a third of a metre in length, unlike its close relative the giant wrasse which reaches over two metres and weighs about 200 kilograms.*

Leopard sea cucumber, *Bohadschia argus*

Textile cone, *Conus textile*

Crown-of-thorns starfish, *Acanthaster planci*

△ Many of the cones hide in rubble or coral crevices during the day, but some can usually be seen in the shallows of the lagoon. They should be treated with caution because the venom apparatus at the tip of their snouts can inject poison. Some species, like the geographer cone, have caused fatalities. This textile cone is also considered dangerous.

△△ Sea cucumbers are common on the lagoon floor. The leopard sea cucumber is one of the most striking in colour, and the most common is the black sea cucumber, an almost inert form of life 200 to 300 millimetres long. Lying in hundreds in the lagoon, they are very slow growing. Oral tentacles sweep the surface for food particles and sand that are passed to the mouth and through the body. They seem to be safe from predators and, if threatened, exude sticky, toxin-containing threads.

Spider shell, *Lambis lambis*

△ It is common in many lagoons to find a few crown-of-thorns starfish and to see where one has fed on a coral. The crown-of-thorns feeds by turning its stomach outwards, pressing it against the coral and digesting it. When, the next morning, the stomach is withdrawn and the starfish moves under the coral for daytime shelter, a round, white, dead patch of coral is left.

◁ The spider shell is a large and colourful shell quite common in the lagoon. Unlike many molluscs, spider shells do not hide during the day and are often seen in the shallows. This one has been turned over to show its lovely colouring. It has eyes on long stalks and a strong and mobile foot, tipped with a hard horny end, with which it moves. The horny tip is stuck into the sea bed just ahead of the shell, and pulled down and back, lifting the whole shell, which falls forward a few millimetres as the foot gets past the balancing point. Primarily herbivores, they are also scavengers.

On the lagoon floor

'The sea cucumber and blue sea star seem immune to predation while the crown-of-thorns starfish is the most notorious predator of the reef. All are echinoderms.'

◁ *A few stony corals, such as this one, have their polyps out and feeding during the day. It is fairly common in lagoons, and there are colonies of about 300 millimetres across, although it grows to three or four times this size. With its stinging cells it feeds on plankton. But it is quite safe for humans to touch the soft polyps, which draw back into the solid skeleton for safety.*

Stony coral, *Montipora*

Slate pencil urchin, *Heterocentrotus mammilatus*

△ *The slate pencil urchin is not very common and is rarely seen. It is not known what its long and very strong spines are for – perhaps they provide protection through strength, for it is certainly difficult to pull one out of the coral if it is wedged in by its spines. Some islanders thread them to make necklaces.*

◁ *The blue sea star is one of a number of sea stars on the reef, but because of its abundance and distinctive colour it is one of the easiest to see. Like the sea cucumbers this species seems to be immune to predation and lies in the open. Perhaps it is distasteful to hungry fishes.*

Blue sea star, *Linckia laevigata*

Black-tipped reef shark, *Carcharinus melanopterus*

△ *The black-tipped reef shark is one of the most common sharks in shallow water over the coral and fortunately is harmless to man. This pair, which are hunting just behind the reef crest, are likely to race off in fear if they are disturbed.*

A prickly plague

We see a white patch of dead coral the size of a soup plate, and know that a crown-of-thorns starfish must be close by. It is found after a few minutes' search under coral ledges, but is left untouched because its spines are sharp and covered with an irritant mucus that will cause pain and then itchiness for a week. When there are only a few, as on this reef, the crown-of-thorns feed by night and hide by day. But when they build up to the huge numbers that have been seen in some areas of the reef over the past twenty years, they feed actively during the

day as well and can be seen in great masses on the coral in the bright sun, looking like a brown and prickly plague.

Life in the shallows

Black sea cucumbers lie everywhere in the warm water of the lagoon shallows and in reef-flat pools, spending their lives passing surface sand through their gut and absorbing food from it. Some of the molluscs are also out in the day. The ring-shaped, annular cowry is common in the shallow water, as is its close relative, the money cowry. We can also see the big common spider shell with its seven large spines, deep red colouring on its underside, and strange habit (common to all its relatives in the Strombidae family) of moving by lifting itself with its horny-tipped foot and falling forwards a few millimetres or so. Other non-spined strombus – the red-mouthed stromb and the flower stromb – lie in

the open in the shallows, as do many of the cones. Beware, some of these cones are very poisonous. Most of the molluscs, however, are not visible. We shall see many of them at night, but now they are under rocks or in coral.

Most of the corals, both hard and soft, withdraw their tentacles and close their polyps during the day but there are species open in the sunlight. One of the very few hard corals open is called *Goniopora*, and if we smooth our fingers across its waving tentacles it steadily withdraws into its skeleton.

Some of the soft corals use their tentacles to grab continuously, like small hands. We pass by the fire coral, or fire weed, with caution, because even the brush of an ankle, exposed between wet suit and flipper, against the creature's feathery fronds, can be painful and cause irritation. It is wise not to scrape corals of any kind, for many will remind you of it for the next few days, and deeper cuts often fester.

'The tenseness of 20th century living ebbs when looking over the pale green sea and feeling at one with the great rhythms of the sun, the moon and the winds.'

Noon on the reef

As we swim slowly back to the boat, two small black-tipped reef sharks swim towards us. They can be fierce predators to the reef fishes, and we have seen a pair chase a school of fishes to a small sandy beach and strand themselves as they rushed the school. But they were unconcerned by the beaching, flapping from side to side in strong swings and slowly working down the wet sloping sand till the next surge caught them. They then herded the school for further attacks. They are harmless to us and fun to watch as they lazily and sinuously swim in our direction, not yet seeing us. When one spots us, in a panic the two turn and rush away.

At noon the colours are bright, but there is markedly less activity. The urgency of feeding seems to have decreased, and the large predators are swimming more languidly. The reef is in a restful mood.

△ *On the island in the noonday sun, life is still. Few birds sing and the reptiles have crept into the shade. It is time to relax in the heat of the day, for animals both above and below the water. In the deep shade of the rainforest patches lovely butterflies still flit about, but even here there is a feeling of a slowing of time. A peaceful world seems content to wait for the noon sun to ease, and then resume the daily battle for existence.*

The reef at night

There is real excitement about a night dive, perhaps because there is a touch of danger. A large shark might not be seen before it strikes, and though thousands of daylight swims and dives have been made safely, the number of night swims attempted is far less. But as yet no one has been harmed. Night diving is also exciting because the search through coral holes and caves, finding sleeping fishes and lovely cowries, is a bit like a treasure hunt.

When studying the night behaviour of certain fishes, an observant colleague with good night vision said that on each dive he saw small reef sharks behind us, a few metres beyond our feet. In a dozen dives we did not see a single shark. We found it more comfortable to concentrate on the fish we were watching and not look back at our legs on the sand behind us.

The changeover begins

At five in the afternoon we take the boat to the spot where we made our morning dive to watch that last hour of light and see the great changeover of the day to the night shift. As we sink down in the water the light is already soft, and the changeover has begun. This is a confused time, and the reef edge predators seem to profit from the confusion. The big trevallies and mackerel are feeding energetically, and every ten minutes or so one or two come racing along the reef, setting up a scurry for shelter among the reef residents with audible thumps made by the power of the tails of the larger species as they take off in fright. Many species are now entering the coral as the light fades. A pair of spotty tails chase their reluctant young down into a coral. A school of small damsels is now nestling among the twigs of an *Acropora*, and the coral is alive with them.

The butterfly fish are disappearing, and one blue-patch butterfly fish is going to sleep in the same branch of coral that it used when we were here last year. When the fish was small the branched coral offered some protection; now it has grown and lies in the fork with its head out at one end and most of the rest of its body out of the other, no longer protected.

The big school of hussars is disappearing, one by one, and we shall find them later, singly working over every metre of the reef. The parrotfish are moving slowly about and entering the coral; the coral trout have gone. With all these fishes now in shelter the scene at dusk has a deserted feeling. Looking up we can see a school of ten or so drummers outlined against the last light in the sky – they are plant feeders, and have come back to rest from their day's foraging. All the fish vegetarians are day workers, although many of the invertebrates prefer to graze at night.

△ *Sunsets from the lagoon can be spectacular, with richly coloured clouds over the mainland. At this time, the nocturnal feeders come out from their daytime hiding places and begin to feed. This is also the time of maximum activity for the plankton, on which many of these creatures feed.*

▷ *Under a flashlight in the last light of day a number of species of small damselfish are beginning to settle into the coral for their night's sleep. This coral is their home, and during the day they forage away from it, but usually only for a metre or so. At night they nestle inside its twigs and seem quite safe from predators. Damselfish are perhaps the most abundant small fishes on the reef.*

Damselfish

Sea urchin, *Diadema setosa*

◁ Long-spined sea urchins with their needle-sharp spines would seem to have no fear of being preyed upon, but this is not true. Some triggerfish feed on them, and are not deterred by being pierced around the mouth by spines. Perhaps because of this the sea urchin often stays under corals during the day, where the moving spines can often be seen pointing out of a crevice. At night they move in the open, scraping the surface with their sharp beaks.

▽ Some of the most beautiful molluscs feed at night, and often the colours and patterns on their bodies rival those on their shells. The cowries are particularly beautiful and their shells are among the most popular in the world. There are many different shaped and coloured cowries, including this tiger cowry.

Baler shell, *Melo amphora*

Tiger cowry, *Cypraea tigris*

The black-spined sea urchin moves actively about, and many molluscs slide out of shelter or, like the creepers on the lagoon floor, emerge from the sand and feed over the surface. The huge baler shell, a giant mollusc with a foot over six hundred millimetres long, ploughs its way out of the sheltering sand to feed, and if we are lucky we may also find a massive helmet shell. This species also buries itself but often leaves just the tip of the strong shell exposed in daylight, and the result is a little green cap of algae that manage to grow there. The thickness of these tips makes it quite safe from even the strongest toothed wrasse.

The reef by torchlight

Now it is time to use the torch because we can no longer see detail. The beam shows a sight that is always fascinating: a small school of shrimp fish swims head down among the black spines of a

△ A giant among molluscs, the baler shell has a body and foot growing to 600 millimetres in length. At night the underwater animal world changes and many creatures are out that are not seen by day. Some are small, but some, like the baler shell, are large and conspicuous. During the day the baler buries in the sandy lagoon floor and in daylight it is rare and delightful to find the large majestic mollusc steadily moving over the lagoon floor. The night diver has a chance to see balers searching over the sand for the molluscs that they prey on.

▷ On the base of the reef the feather stars are catching their nightly plankton. Most species are on the coral slope, but one feather star is out on the sand, squatting firmly on its long arms by bending some of them to form 'elbows'. The arms use a poisonous mucus to trap drifting plankton that are then passed down food grooves on the upper surface of the arms to a central mouth.

Feather star, *Comatula rotolaria*

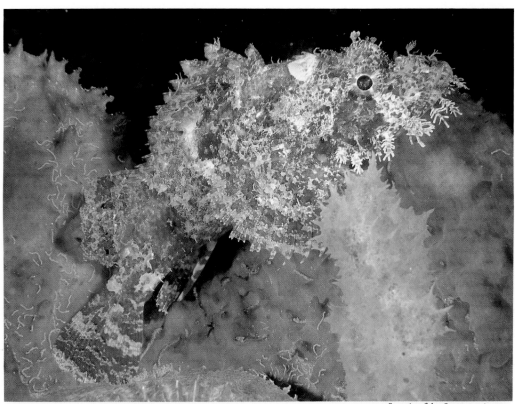

▷ This scorpion fish is out on the coral at night, and presumably is waiting to catch one of the small cardinal fish that are feeding in the water column or any other delectable shrimp or fish that comes its way. Some of this family catch their prey by day, but the majority seem to be nocturnal. As with most fishes, however, little is known of the detail of their daily lives.

Scorpion fish, *Scorpaenopsis venosa*

Spanish dancer, *Hexabranchus sanguineus*

Δ This beauty can sometimes be seen in the day, but it is more active at night. The Spanish dancer is a mollusc with brilliant colouring and the ability to swim by making strange undulations of the body. It has also been called, very appropriately, the 'magic carpet'.

▷ A nudibranch (meaning 'naked gilled') mollusc is caught by the camera as it moves over the coral at night. This group has scores of species with lovely colour patterns, and there are many species still undescribed. 'Sea slug' is a popular name for nudibranch, a name that does not do justice to the splendid appearance of this green-spotted creature.

Green-spotted nudibranch, *Nembrotha nigerrima*

'Night diving is rather like a treasure hunt, searching through coral holes and caves, finding jewel-bright molluscs and glimmering fishes. Many species, such as the butterfly fish, have different day and night colour patterns, usually adding spots or blotches at night.'

▽ *The quaint little shrimp fish swims head down, moving around at night. It is found in the long-spined sea urchin where it is well camouflaged with its transparent body and black stripe. Here shrimp fish are in the coral, feeding on small crustaceans from the sea bed. The shrimp fish is encased in a hard transparent box, wafer-thin, elongate, with a tubular snout, and swimming on its head: yet it is superbly adapted to existing successfully in its own particular way on a coral reef.*

Shrimp fish, *Aeoliscus strigatus*; coral, *Porites cylindrica*

Red-backed cardinal fish, *Archamia fucata*; blue-striped cardinal fish, *Apogon cyanosoma*

sea urchin. The shrimp fish is a strange creature: as thin as a wafer, only twenty millimetres deep, and a hundred and twenty millimetres long, seemingly made of transparent plastic, with a black stripe down each side. An extraordinary fish, but when swimming in its usual head-down position between the long black needle-sharp spines of a sea urchin, it is both beautifully camouflaged and well protected by the waving spines. Our torches find an eyed cowry, large and beautifully coloured with bright red rings. Why should a nocturnal mollusc – that covers beauty with its mantle during the day – display such a wonderful and seemingly useless pattern to the dark night? The colouring must have a significance we have not discovered.

Clawed crabs are also about, seeking molluscs. They are unlikely to be able to attack shells the size of an eyed cowry, but are quite capable of breaking open strong shells of smaller size.

△ *Two species of cardinal fish school in a coral cavern, awaiting the darkness before moving out to feed. The cardinal fish take over the damsels' daytime role, moving out from their day shelter deep in coral caverns to hunt little planktonic animals in the water above the reef. Unlike the damselfish, cardinals do not stay in schools near the sheltering coral. Instead, they move out, protected by darkness and their own ruddy colouring.*

Squid

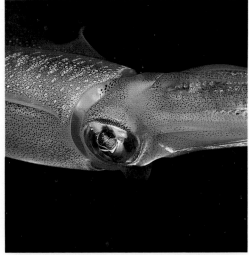

Cuttlefish, *Sepin* sp.

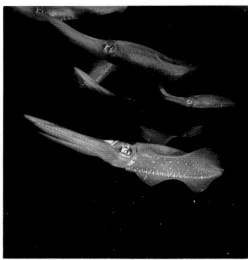

Cuttlefish, *Sepin* sp.

△ *Distinctive colouring marks this young squid, but like its relative, the octopus, it is able to change colour rapidly. Large elastic cells contain coloured material and when at rest the coloured fluid is concentrated in a small spot. Around and attached to the cells is a series of small muscles which can pull the cell flat, spreading the colour out and making it much more visible. The result can be spectacular, and an excited squid can send waves of blue, gold, russet and many other colours flushing swiftly across its body.*

△▷ *Cuttlefish are not fish at all but molluscs, related to the squid and octopus. They are active over the reef all day long and hunt for prey in the waters off the reef at night. They have excellent vision with eyes very similar in structure to human eyes, and a fantastic ability to change colour to camouflage themselves. Not satisfied with good vision, speed and the ability to change colour, this creature also practises trickery, or 'sleight of hand'. When threatened by a predator, it may suddenly go very dark, then eject a blob of ink into the water which takes a similar shape to its body. The cuttlefish then goes light in colour and swims off rapidly leaving the predator to lunge unsuccessfully at the 'blob'.*

△▷▷ *A school of cuttlefish stays just long enough to give us a questioning look, then decides we are too large, or too uninteresting, and shifts off in high gear. These fast-swimming predators use jet propulsion and are very effective at catching fishes moving through the water.*

▷ *Soldier fish, unlike their gentler cousins the squirrelfish, have a strong spine at the bottom of the gill cover. Handle with care if you ever catch one. This species has a blood-red colouring and strong white markings that help to disguise its shape. Red is not easily seen in the water as water filters out the red end of the light spectrum. Presumably the red colouring of the soldier fish would then look black and be good camouflage in the dark of night.*

Soldier fish, *Adiorax ruber*

Squirrelfish, *Myripristis vittatus*

△ The squirrelfish and the soldier fish are true members of the night shift. They are sturdy spiny fish, invariably red in colour, that school secretively in caverns during the day but come out to feed at night. This pretty squirrelfish, 200 millimetres long, is a common sight during a night dive on the reef.

◁ A school of two species of squirrelfish at the mouth of their cavern at dusk, just before they take the plunge into the hazardous outside world to feed through the night. There are at least 13 species of squirrelfish in Australian waters.

Members of the night shift
'Even at night all shades of the colour spectrum are shown by the reef fishes. Some also change their marking.'

Squirrelfish, *Myripristis*

Rare sights and fatal arms

'Feeding on plankton are the corals, whose many small mouths surrounded by tentacles wait for the tiny drifters to touch them and be rapidly impaled.'

Mushroom coral, *Fungia*

▷ *Strange bulb-like tentacles of a mushroom coral out at night. The mushroom coral is a single, very large polyp that as an adult lies loose on the surface. Here it waits for some worm, or other small nocturnal creature, to touch the tentacles, whose groups of coiled stinging cells will instantly pierce and poison the prey. The mushroom coral is always found with tentacles extended. When picked up it will still display its tentacles.*

▷ *The tentacles of this coral are out and ready for action. They have been successful in catching and paralysing two small red bristle worms.*

▽ *A school of flashlight fish, below, below centre and below right, is one of the rarest sights for night divers. This amazing fish has a light organ under the eye, which is a large gland made of parallel tubes that contain luminous bacteria. The bacteria get their food from the fish, and in return give it light. Muscles can turn the light organ down into a black-lined pocket and the light is switched on and off, every five or ten seconds. The light is important for recognition of the individuals of the school, but it also may be used for seeing food.*

Hard coral, *Symphyllia*

Flashlight fish, *Anomalops katoptron*

Flashlight fish, *Anomalops katoptron*

Flashlight fish, *Anomalops katoptron*

Soft tree coral, *Dendronephtha*

Hard coral, *Porites*

Coral and feather star

△ *Fully distended, a colony of soft coral, which lacks zooxanthellae, fully extends its polyp tentacles in order to optimise its chances of capturing planktonic food. White skeletal elements called sclerites are clearly seen in the transparent surface tissue, while red sclerites colour the contrasting polyps.*

◁ *It has been said that the reef at night is just one mass of waiting mouths and, it could be added, a bed of waving fatal arms. The tentacles of corals and the outspread arms of a feather star compete for the tiny swimming and drifting creatures of the night.*

◁◁ *The colonial corals may have very different-sized polyps. The polyps of this coral are small and, although it is feeding and its polyps and their tentacles are expanded, it looks similar to its daytime appearance.*

Soft coral, *Eleutherobia*

Hard coral, *Tubastraed aurea*

△ *Feathery tentacles surround the soft coral's mouth, each with stinging cells to paralyse small zooplankton drifting or swimming in the dark. Expanded in the dark to long, delicate tubes, these polyps will withdraw in daylight.*

▷ △ *The polyps of this coral expand considerably and have several rings of tentacles. Reef overhangs are a typical spot for a coral colony of this type, as well as caves and other sheltered locations.*

▷ *This hard coral often grows in huge domes in sandy situations. The polyps are extremely large and each one has a separate mouth.*

Hard coral, *Goniopora*

Expanded polyp mouths

'Night-time plankton pour in
hundreds of thousands from the reef
crevices, the sandy floor and the deeper
water off the reef. This is the time that
the coral polyps feed on the rich
banquet nature provides.'

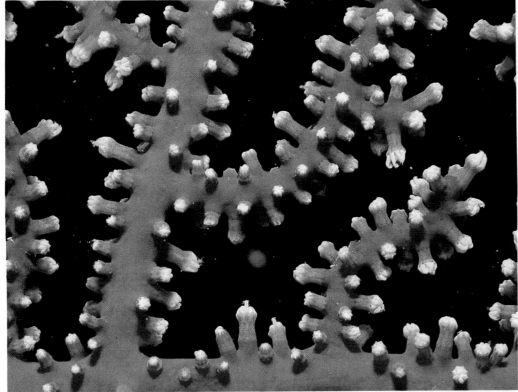

Sea fan, Gorgonian

Sea fan, Gorgonian

△ Sea fans usually grow at right angles to the current,
and here one grows out of the reef face with polyps
expanded. The tentacles of the polyps almost touch each
other across the spaces, and any small drifting creature has
little hope of passing through without getting caught.

◁ The expanded polyps of a sea fan have feathery
tentacles with stinging cells, left. Touching the stem of a
sea fan causes the polyps to retract, above left, showing
the red surface of the stalk.

Sea fan, Gorgonian

'The liveliest and rarest of shells come out to feed at night, better protected then than during the day but still sought by nocturnal predators.'

▷ *A reef crinoid, more like an exotic crimson plant than an animal, is often prominently located, showing a bewildering array of brilliant colour patterns. Feather stars generally select sites that provide a good flow of water because they are passive suspension feeders, filtering minute plankton from the current.*

Feather stars

△ *Although feather stars may be seen during the day, many hide in the coral. At night they are much more obvious, moving to prominent positions and holding up their feathery arms to make their nightly catch. Many species are revealed in the torch light, and some of them have very varied colouring. The reason for this phenomenon is not known.*

▷ *Basket stars impale their prey on tiny hooks on the undersides of their arms. The stars feed on fish and crustacean larvae, shrimps and worms. From time to time, the catch is transferred to the mouth by scraping the entire arm over comb-like oral spines. Remaining hidden during the day, this basket star will mount the same exposed perch to feed each night.*

Feather star, *Himerometra robustipinna*

Basket star, *Astroboa*

As we shine the torch beam into the water its rays are reflected by small silvery cardinal fish that have left their caves and have spread out to feed on the mass of night-time plankton that has poured in hundreds of thousands from the reef crevices, the sandy floor and the deeper water off the reef. The cardinal fish replace the damsels of the day, but unlike them do not stay in schools near sheltering coral. Instead they move boldly out, protected by the darkness and their pink or red colouring.

Also feeding on the plankton are the corals themselves, many small mouths surrounded by tentacles, waiting for the tiny drifters, perhaps a worm or crustacean, to touch them and be rapidly impaled by the stinging darts that the corals, jellyfish and their relatives use to such effect. Other plankton feeders are also netting this harvest. A big basket star has climbed up a whip coral and is spread out against the current, a living plankton net. Scores of feather stars have their complex 'feathers' held up above the coral, also sifting for their nightly plankton meal.

Every now and then a larger fish flits over the sand at the base of the coral, chasing the molluscs, shrimps and crabs that feed on the sandy slope. Among these are many of the hussars, sweetlips and sea bream, as well as a huge trevally. If we search now behind the reef crest, on the reef flat and lagoon, we will see many of the liveliest and rarest of shells. Cowries, olives, volutes and mitres come out to feed, better protected at night than during the day, but still sought by the nocturnal predator.

The day-feeders rest

We are engrossed by the holes and caverns in the coral, for here all the fishes that we saw during the day are resting, and many of them are so sleepy that we can pick them up in our hands. Under a ledge is a big coral trout that moves slowly away from the torch beam, bumping the coral. But as we reach out and touch it, the trout suddenly takes off, wildly blundering past. We are always very careful of unicorn fish for their long spike is hard, and a large

▷ △ *Rare and beautiful molluscs are out at night. Spindle cowries feed on gorgonians and soft corals, and may be coloured to match their hosts, thus avoiding becoming prey themselves. This spindle cowry has the colour of its sea fan, and white spots simulating its polyps.*

▷ *A colourful crayfish out on the coral at night. By carefully looking under coral caves and crevices on most reefs, a crayfish, even if only a juvenile, can usually be found. But they are tucked well away. At night they come out to feed, scavenging over the reef. Although they are delicious eating they are too sparsely spread to be the basis of an effective industry.*

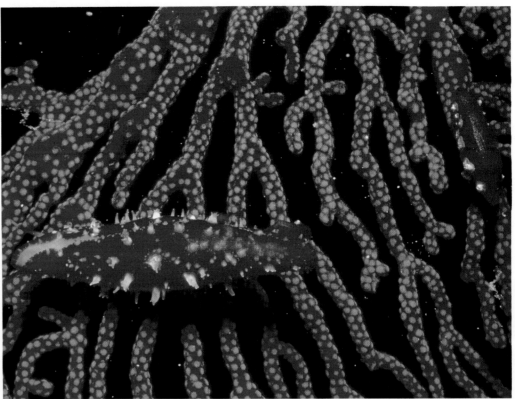

Spindle cowry, *Volva*

Crayfish

▷ *Many of the butterfly fish have different colours for night and day. They are typically day feeders, and at night hide away in the coral, often resting in the same branch of coral or small cave. In the day the little citron butterfly fish is a light yellow, with fine spots and a black stripe camouflaging the eye. But at night, below right, it darkens to a brownish hue, and two strong white blotches appear on its side. Presumably this colouration gives better nocturnal protection.*

▽ *The Moorish idol looks like a different species at night, far below, with its large white central bar blacked out. This makes it more difficult to see.*

Citron butterfly fish, *Chaetodon citrinellus*

Moorish idol, *Zanclus cornutus*

Moorish idol, *Zanclus cornutus*

Citron butterfly fish, *Chaetodon citrinellus*

Chevron butterfly fish, *Chaetodon trifascialis*

fish could drive its sharp horn into a human chest if it blundered into one in a panic.

Beautiful butterfly fish are now showing their night colours. The right-angled butterfly fish has a dark bar along its body with two brilliant white patches that are not visible in its daytime pattern. Most of the butterfly fish have night patterns differing from those of the day, usually adding spots or blotches. Presumably this breaks up the body shape further and deceives the occasional nocturnal predator such as a large eel. During the day most of the butterfly fish are not territorial, but at night they are, and fight hard over their resting places. A threadfin butterfly fish tried to settle down to a sheltered spot between two coral rocks that it had used previously, only to find it occupied by a small grouper. After swimming in and out of the spot for some time, clearly disconcerted, it swam firmly in front of the grouper, which could have eaten it whole, and then backed into the grouper's head with its sharp anal fin spines erect. The grouper left.

Nocturnal activity

Yellow-striped fusiliers are in many of the crevices. They are no longer in the large schools of the day but are now single, and they have changed colour from blue with distinctive yellow stripes along the body to pink with four or five pale crossbars. They move sluggishly in the beam of light, snuggling deeper into the coral.

We see three large red-and-white-banded shrimps moving in the coral, and one is picking over a small blue-spotted rock cod, taking off parasites. It also feeds on the sea bed, but has in part the role of a nocturnal fish parasite picker.

Among the rock cods the pretty black-spotted barramundi cod always seems to be moving about the corals at night and must be a nocturnal feeder. One rock cod slips away from the light beam through a coral channel.

◁ *At night the chevron butterfly fish develops a strong black bar running along its body with a pair of dense white patches quite unlike its day colours, above left. This is a fiercely territorial species, unlike many of the other butterfly fish, and guards its coral home, often a platform Acropora coral, against all comers.*

'Camouflage is one reason why the reef fishes are so highly coloured – it is the only way to fit into an environment where the other flora and fauna are far from drab.'

Chevron butterfly fish, *Chaetodon trifascialis*

The colours of night

'If the base of a sea whip is gently shaken a small goby will probably be disturbed and shoot quickly away.'

▷ *At night many anemones close and enfold their commensal anemone fish. Here a pair of anemone fish peep out from their nocturnal home. They are usually found in pairs, with the female larger than the male.*

▷ ▽ *Some small gobies make their homes on sea whips. This one is almost transparent above, but the lining of the body cavity contains red pigment, helping to camouflage it on its chosen sea whip. They are very difficult to see under water.*

▽ *Head down in the coral is a vibrantly coloured surgeonfish. It does not change its brilliant colours as it rests through the night. Although this fish is alone, it occurs more often in small schools. It should never be handled as a wound from its caudal blades can be serious.*

Anemone fish, *Amhiprion perideraion*

Surgeonfish, *Acanthurus dussumier*

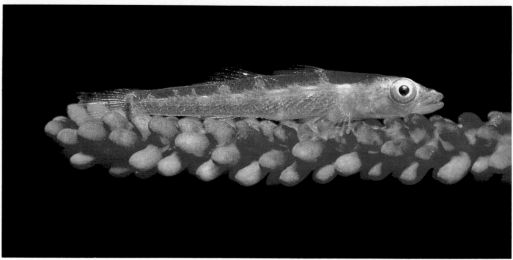

Goby, *Cottogobius yongei*

Blunt-headed parrotfish, *Scarus gibbus*

Blunt-headed parrotfish, *Scarus gibbus*

△ *A parrotfish, top, lies in its night dress, above, a cover of mucus that it produces each night before sleeping in the coral, perhaps to confuse predators that hunt by smell. It is often so transparent that it can only be seen by the specks of sand that have washed on to it.*

▷ △ *In the coral crannies fusiliers are common. One rests quietly, now pinkish-red with four pale crossbars, no longer the bright blue with two gay yellow stripes of the daytime. And at night it hides singly, not in groups.*

▷ *Awake in the coral is the beautiful young wrasse. The adult of this species loses the red and black spots and is less lovely with its green colour and pale crossbar.*

Fusilier, *Caesio chrysozonus*

Wrasse, *Coris aygula*

▽ The blue-spotted stingray is widespread in tropical coral reefs of the Indian and Pacific oceans. On the Great Barrier Reef it is one of the most common rays that the diver sees, and often flits from one coral clump to another in the shallow water of the lagoon during the day. At night it may partially bury itself in the sand. Be careful you do not kneel or stand on it. Its one or two needle-sharp barbs on the tail have a coating of poisonous mucus that can hurt badly.

Damselfish, *Pomacentrus popei*

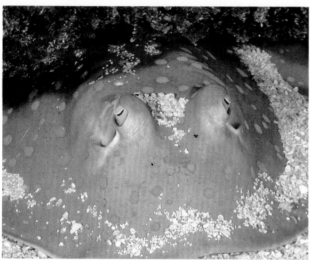

Blue-spotted stingray, *Taeniura lymna*

Barramundi cod, *Chromileptes altivelis*

△ The lemon damsel is tucked in among sponges at night, while feather stars feed around it. Damselfish are sometimes found alone but are more frequently seen in groups. They move under the light of a torch and, unlike some fish, do not seem to sleep soundly.

◁ The pretty barramundi cod is so often out in the coral at night that it must surely be a night feeder. It is a delicious eating fish, but it is a pity to hunt such a beautiful creature for food. This specimen is a juvenile. The adults are darker and have more numerous spots. Barramundi were once common in northern waters, but commercial fishing has seriously depleted their numbers.

'So many species live together, each in its own way, in this great structural mass of corals like an underwater city. At times the reef seems so crowded it's like rush hour.'

Banded coral shrimp, *Stenopus hispidus*

Resting and sleeping

We see a sight that never fails to amaze. A large parrotfish, weighing about two kilograms, is lying on its side, completely encased in gelatinous mucus. The coating is so transparent that it is visible only because a thin scatter of sand has stuck to the envelope, showing its outline – an extraordinary habit. Fish of the same species can be found with or without the cover at night, and sometimes with a partial cover. Perhaps its presence prevents the scent of the fish being picked up by a nocturnal predator, some of which, such as certain eels, hunt by smell.

A number of stingrays are now feeding on the sea bed and, while peering into the coral, we must be careful where we put our legs. The most common stingray is the small blue-spotted ray and its sharp tail barbs can be extremely painful.

Although some fishes are asleep in the coral, many seeming to become fully unconscious, but damsels move under the torch beam, as do the butterfly fish, and seem to rest rather than sleep.

As we swim slowly just under the surface, back to the boat, we ponder on the fishes we have seen in the beam of our torches; the few making their living in the night, and the much larger number of species resting in the coral for the activity of tomorrow. The richness of these different forms must surely be partly due to the tremendous capacity of coral to create such extensive reefs, from thousands of small patches to single reefs many kilometres long, all with an infinite variety of shelter places for invertebrates and fishes. The reef is an evolutionary laboratory, in which hundreds of thousands of different species have been developed, tested, and discarded if found wanting, or added to the huge throng of species if successful. But the greatest puzzle is how so many species can find food and shelter, and co-exist in such close communities.□

△ A pair of banded coral shrimp or cleaner shrimp delicately feeds during the nocturnal round. Small animals are picked from the surface, but the coral shrimp has also developed the specialised role of a nocturnal fish cleaner and can sometimes be seen walking over a sleeping fish, picking off external parasites. Growing up to sixty millimetres long, the shrimps are white with deep red bands across claws, head, abdomen and tail. Each of the long antennae are three-branched and their size is designed to attract customers to their cleaning station.

Staghorn coral, *Acropora*

Part two: the reef's origins

The Great Barrier Reef is situated off the eastern coast of Queensland, in relatively shallow waters rarely more than 60 metres deep. This is the world's largest coral reef province, and it extends over an area of 230 000 square kilometres from the Gulf of Papua along 2300 kilometres of coastline to just beyond the Tropic of Capricorn. Over 2100 individual reefs make up the main barrier, with a further 540 high continental islands closer inshore having significant fringing reefs.

Single coral reefs may cover an area of over 100 square kilometres; massive structures that have been built almost entirely by marine plants and animals. The material of the reef is calcium carbonate: limestone derived from the surrounding waters by the reef organisms. The living reef forms merely a veneer, adding new limestone to these massive structures at rates that can be annually measured in kilograms for every square metre of the reef surface.

Corals are probably the most obvious life forms of the reefs. Their intricate and colourful shapes are colonial structures made up of thousands of individual polyps, each secreting its small cup of coral limestone. Not surprisingly, until the middle of the 18th century corals were regarded as plants, not animals. However, these flower-like creatures provide the building blocks for reef construction.

Plants are also important in the development of the system, as many secrete limestone. Coralline algae in particular form cementing crusts that act as 'mortar' for the coral 'bricks'. Innumerable other plants and animals also contribute, forming fine sand and coarser skeletal material which ends up as either sediments on the reef surface or as infill in the many cavities that develop within the reef.

Coral reefs have existed in the earth's shallow seas for a long time, probably in excess of 450 million years; a clear indication of how successful a life form they are. Although the original corals, called rugose corals, became extinct about 200 million years ago, the reefs they formed were probably very similar to modern coral reefs. The scleractinian corals that succeeded the rugose forms probably evolved in the warm waters of the Tethys Sea, a massive ancient ocean which originally existed between the northern European and Asian land masses and the southern African and Indian continents. It was eventually closed by the gradual northward migration of the southern continents, a process known as continental drift. The closing of the ancient sea was earliest in the west and latest in the east, so that the evolving corals were slowly pushed eastwards into the shallow peninsulas and island-studded seas of the western Pacific. It is this area which has by far the greatest diversity. Over 500 coral species are known in this region.

At the same time as the Tethys Sea was closing and the modern corals were evolving, the Australian continent was also on the move, slowly drifting northwards from the cold polar latitudes into the warmer waters of the tropics. By chance, its migration took it into this area rich in coral growth. Its northeastern shores in particular were bathed by oceanic waters passing through the coral-rich seas.

The Great Barrier Reef is thus relatively young, having started to grow probably no more than 18 million years ago, with many parts little more than one million years old. However, this was a period of great environmental fluctuation in the earth's history. Sea levels in particular have oscillated from positions slightly higher than present to at least 150 metres below the present level.

Corals and associated life forms were able to survive these massive environmental changes, and this is indicative of how resistant to natural disturbances this ecosystem is. The coral reef has a very high order of internal organisation, greater even than the tropical rainforests of the adjacent humid landmasses, with which coral reefs are frequently compared. Both environments receive high levels of solar radiation, the ultimate source of all ecosystem energy.☐

▽ *The coral formations of the Great Barrier Reef make up the most extensive structure ever built by living creatures. At low tide the reefs extend to the horizon.*

◁ *Hardy staghorn coral thrives in areas with plenty of water movement and sunshine. Many* Acropora *species regenerate from broken pieces.*

The greatest reef on earth: created by plants and animals

Reefs in tropical waters

Corals occur in the relatively cool waters of southern Australia, but it is only in the warmer tropics that coral reefs form. Here the rates of deposition of the corals' calcium carbonate skeletons increase, combine with other organisms and become sufficient to exceed the rate of destruction by physical, chemical and biological processes. The result is the slow development of a coral reef.

The southernmost reefs in the world are found in the northern Tasman Sea, around the shores of Lord Howe Island (31°33′S). Incipient fringing reefs occur around the Solitary Islands off northern New South Wales, but apart from some small reefs within the protection of Moreton Bay, off Brisbane, the waters of southern Queensland are generally devoid

▷ *A total impression of the Great Barrier Reef can only be gained from space. Since the 1970s the American* LANDSAT *satellite system has provided this overview. The system records each scene in a number of ways, including infrared. Each of these forms is shown in a different colour. This* LANDSAT *false colour image shows the north Queensland coastline from Temple Bay to the northern part of Princess Charlotte Bay, where the large reef flats can be seen. The red on the mainland and islands indicates the presence of rainforest and mangroves. The amount of fresh water entering the sea here is limited, so reefs can develop even closer inshore; small reefs can be seen in the inner shipping channel, located close to the shore. In the middle-shelf area are very large hard-line crescent reefs, and in the north are the narrow crescents of Eel and Gallon Reefs. The apparently reefless area in the south in fact has extensive shoals at depths of about 20 metres. The ribbon reefs form an almost continuous outer barrier; the largest shown is Tijou Reef, which is 27.8 kilometres long. White patches are clouds, which often form along the lines of the reef. Waves breaking form spray, which in turn forms nuclei for the condensation of droplets that make clouds.*

'An enormous regional diversity exists: no two reefs are the same, but some regional patterns can be recognised.'

of modern reefs. It is not so much temperature control or even the effect of fresh water runoff from the mainland that prevent the formation of reefs, as the effect of a massive transport of sand up the eastern Australian coast, reflected in the huge dune complexes of southern Queensland, the most northerly of which, Fraser Island, extends across the continental shelf – the sea bed surrounding the continent. A change in the orientation of the coast causes the sand to be directed seawards and into deep water. Immediately to the north, at Lady Elliott Island, the world's largest coral reef region, the Great Barrier Reef, commences.

In 1842, Charles Darwin devised a scheme to describe coral reefs that still dominates their classification. He described them as fringing reefs attached to a mainland or island, barrier reefs, or open ocean atolls. Fringing reefs, the simplest reef landforms, are built upwards and outwards in shallow seas adjacent to islands or continents. Barrier reefs occur further offshore, separated from the mainland shore by a shallow lagoon. In contrast, atolls are found in the deeper oceans, having usually developed over volcanic foundations that have subsided beneath the sea. Coral growth in this case produces saucer-like reefs with central lagoons.

Barrier reefs, Darwin suggested, developed from the upward growth of fringing reefs as the sea level rose. But this is not the way the Great Barrier Reef has evolved. It is not a simple barrier, as envisaged by Darwin, but an intricate and varied series of reefs. Built entirely by animals and plants from calcium carbonate drawn from the sea water, it has existed in its present form for a relatively short time in geological terms.

The sea level, which limits the upward growth of the reefs, has fluctuated during the period of construction of the Great Barrier Reef, sometimes falling more than 100 metres below its present level and exposing the earlier precursors of the modern reefs to the atmosphere. The sea has been at its present level for little more than 6000 years, and it is during this short time that the present form of the Great Barrier Reef has developed.

Fringes, lagoons and ribbons

The Great Barrier Reef covers an enormous area of over 230 000 square kilometres. From its southernmost outpost at Lady Elliott Island, it extends off the coast of Queensland for 2300 kilometres to the Gulf of Papua, where fresh water and sediment from New Guinea's Fly River prevent reef growth. The outer reef is generally close to the edge of the continental shelf, and is unprotected from the powerful or high energy waves from the ocean. The outer reef varies greatly in distance from the mainland: it approaches within 32 kilometres off Cape Melville to a maximum of 260 kilometres off

Mackay. In the south, the reefs generally occupy only the outer third of the shelf, and even the innermost reefs may be more than 50 kilometres from the mainland. Northwards from Cairns, however, the continental shelf is narrower and the reefs are much closer to the mainland shores. Further south, fringing reefs are relatively common around the high continental islands close to the mainland, particularly from the Whitsunday Islands northwards. Most of the tourist resorts are located on the continental islands and so it is the fringing reefs that most visitors see. Nonetheless, these reefs have a great diversity of coral species.

A fragile ecosystem

The size of the reef and its distance from the mainland, particularly from the more highly populated areas of central and southern Queensland, protect the reef from many potential hazards. Over the years the reef's fragile ecosystem has been under increasing recreational and commercial pressure, and in 1975 the Australian Government passed the Great Barrier Reef Marine Park Act, which became effective in October 1979, when the southernmost Capricornia section of the marine park was declared. By the end of 1983, the entire reef had been declared a marine park, although detailed planning and zoning of large areas has yet to be carried out.

The marine park extends only to Cape York and thus excludes about 400 reefs in Torres Strait; nevertheless the park area is an impressive reef province. It contains over 2100 reef complexes, many consisting of more than a single reef; the coral area, including related submerged coral shoals, that is, reefs that do not reach sea level, covers 20 300 square kilometres. Reefs occupy about nine per cent of the continental shelf waters of the region. The individual reefs average seven square kilometres in area, although they range from small isolated coral pinnacles to massive complexes of over 125 square kilometres. As well as outer reefs, over 540 continental islands have well-developed fringing reefs and another 200 have at least some corals around their rocky shores.

Not surprisingly, in an area extending so far, an enormous regional diversity exists in the reef. The incidence and severity of tropical cyclones, the numbers of coral species, and even rates of growth of the corals, for instance, change from north to south. Equally important differences exist across the shelf from west to east, with decreasing influence of the mainland in the form of freshwater runoff, sediments and mineral nutrients. In addition to variations in conditions today, the geological history of the reef is varied: some parts began to develop up to 18 million years ago, and others began little more than one million years ago. No two reefs are the same, but some regional patterns can be recognised.

Temple Bay to Princess Charlotte Bay

Ribbon Reef

Pipon Reef

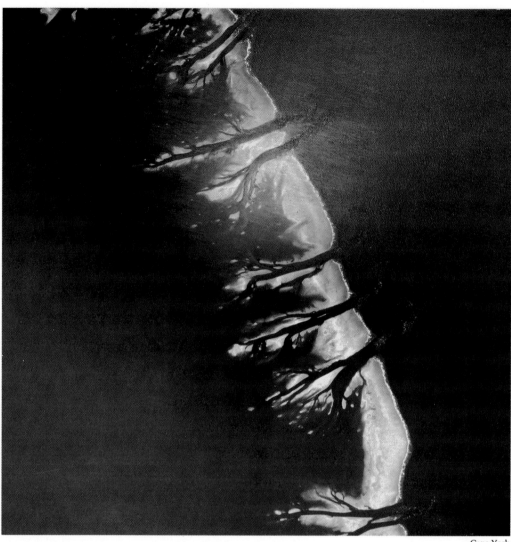

Cape York

△ *Pipon Reef is a typical platform reef of the inner shelf. It is protected by the outer reefs and wave energies, except during cyclones, are low. Its high and extensive reef flat has been developing for over 6000 years and is ringed by ramparts of shingle thrown up during tropical cyclones. In the lee of the ramparts are extensive mangroves. A small vegetated sand cay also occurs on the reef's leeward side. These are the components of the low-wooded island reefs.*

△◁ *Ribbon Reef, over 35 kilometres long, is the largest of the outer linear reefs. It is a very high energy reef, and water depths of over 1000 metres are found within a few hundred metres of its windward edges. Long, low swell waves continuously break on the outer edge and during cyclonic conditions waves up to eight metres high may break on this bastion. The reef is no more than 500 metres wide. The outermost part of the reef flat is formed by coralline algae. Behind this is a narrow coral area aligned into 'windrows' by waves passing over the reef. The light-coloured water in the lee of the reef is a sand slope made up of sediments swept over and from the reef flat. Numerous small patch reefs, including massive Porites coral heads five metres or more in diameter, are found on the lee sides of the ribbon reefs.*

△ *For about 80 kilometres opposite Cape York, the outer barrier is made up not of long linear ribbon reefs, but of deltaic reefs. They closely resemble deltaic sand banks which build up at the mouths of rivers, and their origin is probably similar. Opposite Torres Strait the tidal range is greater than three metres and strong tidal rips of more than eight knots occur. Because the tides of the Gulf of Carpentaria and the northern Coral Sea, on either side of the Strait, are out of phase, the tidal streams can become even stronger. Sediments produced by the outer reefs have been swept westwards by the currents to form deltas at each break in the outer barrier. And the deltas themselves have formed the foundation for reef development so that, although they are like sand banks, and many contain broken rock and coral, they are true coral reefs.*

The northern Great Barrier Reef

The northern reef has developed on a narrow shelf, generally no more than 50 kilometres wide, south of Torres Strait. Its most distinctive feature is the development of linear or ribbon reefs running parallel to the edge of the continental shelf, which extend as far south as Mossman. The ribbons, up to 25 kilometres long and rarely more than 500 metres wide, are separated by narrow passes, most of which are less than 1000 metres in width. Most of the reefs are very close to the shelf edge, and depths of more than 1000 metres may occur only a few hundred metres in front of the reefs. Their linear form is thought to be due to their growth from shorelines that existed when sea level was lower than today's. Some detached reefs rise from the deep water in front of the ribbons.

Inside the ribbon reefs, a variety of extensive, flat oval reefs, or platforms, occur. Some platform reefs are very large, especially opposite Princess Charlotte Bay, where the reefs – Magpie, Hedges and Corbett – are more than 25 kilometres long; the largest in the province. The distribution of platform reefs may be entirely random, but as most corals readily colonise a hard substrate, in many cases the foundations of platform reefs may originally have been rocky outcrops, similar to the present continental islands. The most extensive reef flat – the part of the reef at sea level which is periodically exposed at low tide – is often developed on the western side of the reef, and the well-defined edge of the reef, or hard line, occurs on this side or where it is open to the prevailing southeasterly trade winds. The main shipping channel is in the more open waters close to the mainland, although even here small reefs, many of them capped by distinctive low-wooded islands, are common.

In Torres Strait this distinctive regional pattern breaks down and the middle section of the shelf in particular is dominated by a mosaic of small reefs. On the outer edge, ribbon reefs become smaller, altering to deltaic reefs with more numerous and complex passages. A well-defined line of larger reefs occurs northwards from Cape York, including the Warrior Reefs with high, sea grass-covered reef flats. In Torres Strait the reefs are aligned east-west – streamlined by the high velocity tidal currents that rip through the Straits.

Apart from the islands of the Straits, high islands are not common in this region, although the few that do exist have large fringing reefs, such as those at Lizard Island or in the Flinders Group. Occasional small outcrops of continental rocks occur in the main reef masses of the middle and outer parts of the shelf.

The central Great Barrier Reef

The ribbon reefs and inner low-wooded island reefs extend south to just north of Cairns. As the continental shelf widens towards the south, the Great Barrier Reef occupies only the outer third,

Three Isles

Barnett Patches

Davies Reef

'The Great Barrier Reef is not a simple barrier, as envisaged by Charles Darwin, but an intricate and varied series of reefs.'

◁ *The reef flats of the inner northern reefs are distinctive. Large rubble banks or ramparts made up of coral shingle are characteristic of the outer reef flat, and sandy sediments may even extend over the whole reef top. Three Isles has outer shingle ramparts, in the background, with occasional mangroves. At low tide, the shingle banks impound shallow, moated pools, and flat disc-like coral colonies, called micro-atolls, grow up to the water level of the moat, which may be up to a metre higher than the low tide level on the outside of the reef.*

◁ *On the central Great Barrier Reef there are no vegetated reef islands, but some of the younger reefs may have sufficient reef-flat areas for small, highly mobile, unvegetated sand cays to develop. Many of the reefs in this region are patchy, with no continuous windward rim. The reef flat consists of living coral and a shallow sandy lagoon. The algal pavement and rubble flats associated with the higher energy reefs north and south are almost completely absent from younger and lower energy reefs.*

◁ *Because of their younger age and lower energy conditions, open sandy lagoons with numerous reef patches and irregular reef edges are common on the central Great Barrier Reef. Davies Reef, off Townsville, like many others in the region, has a secondary reef front – a series of coral pinnacles growing from a deeper terrace. Eventually, the gutter between these pinnacles and the main reef will fill with sediments to create the typical hard-line margin.*

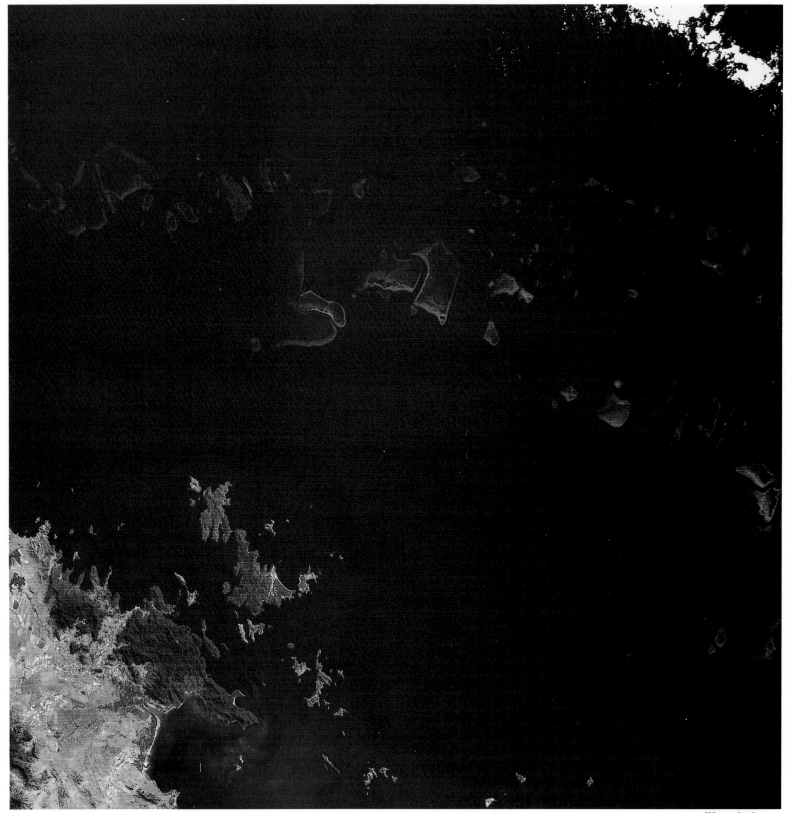

Whitsunday Passage

although the numerous island chains between Cairns and Mackay have well-developed fringing reefs.

Reefs of the central Great Barrier Reef are younger and are thus less densely distributed over the shelf, and they have lower and less extensive reef flats. Many reef complexes are made up of irregular reef patches, some with a narrow crescent of well-defined hard line reef only on the windward southeastern side. These are young reefs, for whereas the reefs to north and south grew up to modern sea level by 6000 years ago, many of the reefs of this region reached sea level less than 3000 years ago.

Many of the reefs are large, and the shallow internal lagoons are choked with sand. Recent drilling of some of the reefs has indicated that a large proportion of the modern reef may have accumulated as unconsolidated sediments with little reef framework.

From Bowen southwards, narrow passages 30 to 70 metres deep, with steep side walls, cut through the larger reef complexes. Tidal currents of six or seven knots rip through these channels and are undoubtedly responsible for keeping them open, and possibly even for their origin, although during low sea level phases in the past they would also have contained drainage channels that crossed the exposed continental shelf.

A continuous barrier of ribbon reefs does not occur on the outer shelf, but set back a few kilometres from the shelf edge is a continuous set of submerged linear shoals, rising from depths of about 70 metres and in places reaching within 10 metres of the surface, although most of them lie at depths greater than 20 metres. Reef growth is continuing on these shoals, and they may eventually evolve into ribbon reef systems.

Pompey Complex and Swain Reefs

Opposite the Whitsunday Islands, the continental shelf is 120 kilometres wide, but to the south it rapidly widens to about 300 kilometres, so that even the inner reefs of the Swain Reefs lie 150 kilometres from the mainland and are separated from it by the Capricorn Channel. Although remote and rarely visited, this is one of the most spectacular areas of the Great Barrier Reef. A series of submerged reefs occupies the shelf edge, but ten kilometres back is an area containing some of the largest and most

◁ *A LANDSAT false colour composite shows how distant the reef is from the mainland and how scattered and irregular is the reef development, limited to the outer shelf, opposite the Whitsunday Passage. Although not visible on this scene, most of the Whitsunday Islands have narrow fringing reefs around many of their shores. The outer reefs have large open lagoons. The tidal range in the narrow passage between Hook and Hardy Reefs, upper left centre, is about four metres, and sediment-laden lighter blue water can be seen spiralling around the Whitsunday Islands.*

Dingo Reef

Pompey Complex

△ *Individual reefs of the Pompey Complex can be up to 20 kilometres long and over 100 square kilometres in area. The most distinctive reef flat, made up mainly of hard algal pavement, occurs alongside the channels separating individual reefs. Elsewhere, meandering ridges covered in branching corals divide the reef top into intricate lagoons up to ten metres deep. Because of the high velocity tidal current over even the reef flat, sediments are rapidly moved into the lagoons, which have sandy bottoms.*

△ △ *The lower level of the reef tops of the central Great Barrier Reef, where they rarely extend higher than the average low-water level of spring tides, allows for extensive cover of living corals, including low, branching forms that are resistant to wave action on this reef edge but more intricate corals leewards. These reef tops, with their living corals, contrast with the older reefs north of Cairns and at the southern end of the Great Barrier Reef, with their algal pavements and rubble-covered flats.*

△ *The effects of the tidal currents are obvious in this detail of the reef tops. Sand is being swept from bottom right to top left and can be seen trailing from the brownish coloured living corals of the reef flat. Distinctive coral rims form around many of the reef patches.*

△ △ *In the south central Great Barrier Reef, the reefs, such as the Dingo Reef Complex, off Bowen, are larger than those further north and tend to have grown as complexes separated by narrow tidal channels. In many other respects the reefs are similar to those of the central region as a whole, with the reef flat developed only along the margins of the channels, and lagoons being shallow and sandy.*

Pompey Complex

Hoskyns Reef

△ Deep circular lagoons, called 'blue holes', are found on many reefs around the world. They are generally considered to have formed when cave systems that developed in the reefs during periods of low sea level have collapsed. Only three blue holes are known in the Great Barrier Reef province, all of them in the Pompey Complex, including this one, which is almost 300 metres wide and 33 metres deep.

▷ South of the Pompey T-line, the change in reef morphology is quite remarkable. Massive reefs with numerous lagoons separated by tidal channels give way to smaller, ovoid platform reefs, some with deep central lagoons, others with flat surfaces. Numerous unstable sand and shingle cays are found on the Swain Reefs, which contain over 430 individual reefs.

△ Hoskyns Reef, with its sand and shingle cays, is an example of a reef in which a former lagoon has been filled with sediment. Like other reefs of the Bunker–Capricorn Group it is a high energy reef, open to the continuous swell from the Tasman Sea and particularly susceptible to cyclonic storms in summer. A large area of the reef flat around the windward shingle cay is covered in coarse rubble, which has been derived from the reef front. In high energy situations, however, the reef-building corals may respond by building their own baffle – the spur and groove system which can be clearly seen in the foreground. It is an area of luxuriant coral growth on the spurs or buttresses, with narrow intervening sand chutes. The spur and groove system both reduces the power of the waves on the reef front and increases the surface area available for coral growth.

Swain Reefs

'Tidal currents of six or seven knots rip
through the steep-sided channels cut
through the larger reef complexes.'

◁ *Heron Island and Wistari Reef are among the best
known reefs in the Great Barrier Reef region. Wistari has
a completely enclosed lagoon with a mosaic of patch reefs.
Heron's lagoon is shallower, especially around the cay.
The artificial boat channel cut into the reef adjacent to the
cay can be clearly seen. The channel has accelerated the
ebb currents draining the reef flat near the island, resulting
in the removal of sediment and serious erosion problems
around the resort located on the far end of the cay.*

Heron Island; Wistari Reef

Pompey Complex

intricate reefs in the world. Individual reefs of the
complex are over 100 square kilometres in area, but
in a belt about 20 kilometres wide the massive reefs
are almost continuous for a distance of 200
kilometres, separated only by narrow channels that
split into intricate deltaic systems on both the ocean
and landward sides of the complex.

The high tidal range and high velocity currents,
which exceed 10 knots, are major influences on
these systems. The tides and currents have scoured
the channels to depths as great as 90 metres between
the reefs (far deeper than the depth on either side of
the reefs). Sediments produced by the reefs have
formed tidal deltas, similar to those in Torres Strait,
at both ends of the channels. Intricate lagoon
systems and mid-reef coral ridges characterise the
Pompey Reefs; the lagoons become deeper and
more open towards the south. The southern extent
of the Pompey Complex is a distinctive T-line

junction of reefs where it meets the contrasting
Swain Reefs, with their myriad of small but closely
spaced reefs with numerous sand cays.

The tidal range on the adjacent mainland reaches
over ten metres at Broad Sound but declines rapidly
out towards the reefs, and in the outer reefs it only
just exceeds four metres. The innermost reefs,
however, experience tidal ranges of between five
and six metres, among the highest in the world for a
coral reef area. As a result, many of these inner reefs
have massive, terraced algal rims, which isolate
lagoons nearly three metres above the level of the
surrounding ocean at low tide.

The Bunker and Capricorn groups
To the south of the Capricorn Channel, where the
continental shelf narrows to less than 100 kilometres
wide, is the southernmost region of the Great
Barrier Reef – the Bunker and Capricorn groups of

△ *The channels through the Pompey Complex are
spectacular. Up to 100 metres in depth, they have almost
sheer sides and flat bottoms. The water remains still in
these channels for only very short periods at the turn of
each tide. The reversing flood and ebb currents of ten
knots cause great turbulence. Major channels can be up to
one kilometre wide, but at both oceanic and mainland ends
they tend to split between wedge-shaped reefs. The
channels and tidal deltas on each end, which provide the
foundations for reef growth, are the response to the tidal
currents although the channels may also have acted as
surface drainage ways during times of low sea level. The
reef flat adjacent to the channel is hard, algal pavement.*

'During cyclones, fringing reefs may be extensively damaged by freshwater runoff and wave action.'

▷ *Smaller, isolated islands may have extensive leeside fringing reefs, such as Holbourne Island off Bowen, which is 500 metres wide. The reef flat is made up of coarse rubble and shingle, which impounds small pools in which micro-atolls form. This reef was devastated by a major tropical cyclone in 1918, and it has still not fully recovered. During high energy storms, the more fragile corals are broken and transported to the island shores to form coral shingle beach ridges like the one that makes up the low area of the island in the foreground.*

Holbourne Island

Great Palm Island

△ *A young and narrow fringing reef has developed on the windward side of Great Palm Island. Windward reefs are generally less extensive than their leeward counterparts, but the reef slope in particular has a rich species diversity. The island is fringed alternately by boulder beaches from the rocky slopes and white coral shingle beaches.*

▷ *Fringing reefs are particularly well developed around the Whitsunday Islands, varying from uneven fringes around the shores of the larger islands, such as Hook Island in the background, to wide flats, such as on Hayman Island, in the foreground. This reef started to grow from older reef foundations about 8500 years ago. The modern reef flat started to develop about 5000 years ago, initially forming an offshore barrier, which was later attached as the lagoon filled with sediments from the island and coral debris from the evolving reef.*

Whitsunday Islands

Carlisle and Brampton islands

22 reefs and 11 reef shoals. The reefs are not large and many, particularly in the central part of the region, have enclosed lagoons; those to north and south have more extensive reef flats. Many have vegetated coral cays, and two of the southernmost – Hoskyns and Fairfax reefs – have two islands, a windward shingle cay and a leeward sand cay.

The fringing reefs

Chains of high continental islands are common off the Queensland coast, and over 540 of them have fringing reefs. On the windward sides of islands, exposure to the southeasterly winds results in narrow ledges of coral no more than 20 metres wide because the corals cannot advance in the face of the winds. On sheltered leesides, extensive reef flats of more than one kilometre form. The main difference between these and the outer reefs is the extent of influence from the land. In the wet season, these

reefs are often within the influence of freshwater runoff and sediments from the mainland, as well as from the adjacent island. Fresh water floats over the denser sea water, and if salinity falls too low for a long enough period, it can affect the reef tops, because corals need salinity levels similar to those of the open oceans. But the slopes may not be so vulnerable as the tops, and the variety of coral species found on the fringing reefs may be little different from that of the outer reefs. Many fringing reef flats closely resemble those of the low-wooded island reefs of the north, with extensive rubble cover and cemented deposits.

Close to the island shores are sand beaches and massive boulder foreshores. Dead coral-heads on the inner reef flat are the result of a slight fall in sea level over the past 6000 years. The fringing reefs began to develop from about this time, when sea level first stabilised at about a metre above its present position.

△ *In bays and in the lee side of larger islands the reef flats are wider, a feature that may have resulted from them evolving as thin coral crusts over sands and silts swept into the bays during the rise of the sea level at the end of the ice age. The reefs may join individual islands, as in this example of Carlisle and Brampton islands in the Cumberland Group. Carlisle's fringing reef has also formed the foundation for a series of windward dunes and a boulder beach on the northern side in the foreground, which together impound a small saltwater lagoon.*

Pacific basin

Reef systems past and present

The world's coral reefs are strikingly distributed in relation to the structural development of the tropical oceans and adjoining continents. Areas of reef growth are centred in the Pacific, the Indian and West Atlantic oceans, but their distribution is not random. Their location is in many ways determined by plate tectonics. Plate tectonics is a theory concerning the nature of the earth's crust, suggesting that the outermost layer of the earth is made up of a number of plates that are moving in relation to each other. Where plates meet, the edge of one slides under the other. In the oceans, this results in ocean trenches, earthquakes and arcs of volcanic islands; at the edge of continents, in mountain building. Reefs grow at areas of volcanic activity away from the main active plate boundaries – hot-spots in passive areas at plate margins, along island arcs at active plate margins, along rifted margins and along transform faults. In the west Pacific, the Great Barrier Reef, the reefs of New Caledonia and those of the South China Sea were formed along passive rifted continental margins.

The Great Barrier Reef, on the northeast Australian continental shelf, is unique in being the largest reef province occupying one particular structural setting. Similar modern reefs are the north Caribbean plateau reefs and the reefs of the South China Sea, but the Great Barrier Reef is the largest, the most morphologically interesting, and the most biologically diverse. Although in some other aspects it is equalled or even bettered by reefs in other areas, the forms of the reefs here show the greatest adaptation to the environment imposed by the southeast trade winds that blow over most of the region for much of the year. There are, therefore, distinct differences between windward and leeward reefs.

The world's modern reef systems began to develop in the Tertiary period, about 25 million years ago. Reefs have existed and grown successfully many times in the past. In Australia, a barrier reef system, comparable in many ways to parts of the modern Great Barrier Reef, grew in what is now the Canning area of Western Australia about 350 million years ago. But the Great Barrier Reef is much younger than most of its counterparts throughout the world.

The long voyage north

The reefs of the Great Barrier Reef are relatively thin and a geologically recent phenomenon. Studies of the structure of the continental margin and elsewhere in the southern oceans have provided not only reasons for the apparent late development of the Great Barrier Reef but also a clear indication of events leading up to its formation.

Between 75 and 65 million years ago, Australia and Antarctica were joined, and almost all of Australia lay south of latitude 40° S; that is, well south of the present latitude of Tasmania. About 65 million years ago, Australia began to split from Antarctica and move northwards. Slightly later, northeastern Australia was formed by rifting between the Australian and Pacific plates. By the time the sea invaded the land, Australia had drifted northwards until north Australia lay between 30° and 40° S, still well south of the tropics. No coral reefs formed at this time, probably because water temperatures were too low.

Thirty million years ago Australia continued to move north when ice sheets first developed in Antarctica, and sea levels fell nearly 100 metres throughout the world. Layers of rock beneath the Great Barrier Reef show that major rivers, such as the Burdekin, flowed on to the shelf, building it upwards and outwards over nearly 15 million years. The following melting of the Antarctic ice cap and rise in sea level occurred at the same time as the northwest drift of Australia, which carried its northeast margin into the tropics. No coral reef formed, except in the area between Australia and New Guinea. This period, the Miocene, lasted between 25 and five million years ago.

It was not until about two million years ago, when northeastern Australia was firmly ensconced in the tropics, that most of the Great Barrier Reef started to grow. The reason for this late development is not known. It is clear, however, that throughout much of its history, northeastern Australia lay in latitudinal areas too cold for the growth of coral reefs.

◁ *In the central Pacific, chains of reefs and atolls that grow around subsiding volcanic peaks form the main reef types. These volcanic coral reef chains and associated submerged seamounts are distinctive features of the area. Successive volcanic peaks formed as the Pacific plate drifted over a hot-spot in the earth's mantle. After passing over the hot-spot, each volcano becomes extinct and subsides. Coral reefs then grow around its shores as fringing reefs and eventually form atolls as the volcano subsides further below sea level. The reefs of the western Pacific occupy two contrasting tectonic environments. Most occur around the arcs of volcanic plates thrown up by collision of the Pacific with the Australian and Philippine plates, and most are fringing reefs. In contrast to these tectonically active areas, the stable, passive margin platform areas with shallow seas and little earth movement have formed ideal environments for reef growth for many millions of years. In areas such as in the Great Barrier Reef and the South China Sea, the form of the reefs is dependent on substrate shape and local oceanographic conditions, and reefs of all shapes and sizes abound. The Indian Ocean reefs occur as a series of atolls. They have formed around stable passive continental margins, hot-spot volcanoes, or volcanic eruptions associated with earth movements around ocean ridges.*

▽ *A well-preserved, former great barrier reef is visible for about 350 kilometres in limestone ranges along the northern margin of the Canning Basin in Western Australia. The reef may have extended for 1000 kilometres around the west and north sides of a shoreline which existed in the area about 350 million years ago. The sinuous line of the outer barrier separates what was ocean on the left from back reef and lagoon on the right. Small patch reefs occur within what was originally the lagoon. A similar formation occurs along the ribbon reefs of the outer Great Barrier Reef to the northeast of Cairns. The sinuous line of the ribbons, bottom, separates ocean, left, from lagoon, right.*

Canning Basin

Yonge Reef

Huon Peninsula

▷ *Coral reefs in uplifted areas, such as the Huon Peninsula in New Guinea, have provided much of the evidence for sea level changes in the Quaternary period (the past 1.8 million years). The peninsula has been rising by as much as four metres per 1000 years. Each high sea level has seen the growth of a fringing reef, and even when the original sea level was many tens of metres below present sea level, the uplift rate has been sufficient to elevate the reef above present sea level, making it easily available for research. Each sea level stage can be calculated from the present height of the reef terrace; its age is established by radiocarbon and other dating techniques, and the rate of uplift has been relatively constant through time.*

Levels of reef growth

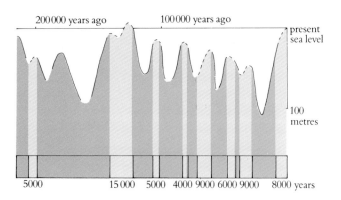

△ *The sea level curve for the past 200 000 years shows the periods of high-sea-level reef growth in light green and low-sea-level reef destruction in dark green. Individual periods of reef growth have lasted only 5000 to 15 000 years; the time of total growth amounts to less than 20 per cent of the past 200 000 years.*

△ ▷ *For much of their history, coral reefs have been elevated above sea level and have been exposed to the atmosphere. This section of barrier reef at Sabari Island, in the Louisiade Archipelago of Papua New Guinea, which has been raised by earth movements, may be typical of many reefs at an intermediate sea level. At a full glacial stage, sea level would have stood against the sharp drop-off at the edge of the continental shelf, and reef development would have been very limited. Most of the present reefs would have been high and dry.*

Sabari Island

Sea level changes

Coral reefs can only grow up to about the level of a low spring tide, and reefs (as opposed to individual coral) will probably not develop in water more than 40 metres deep. Reefs are, therefore, very strongly influenced by sea level. Over the time that most of the world's reefs have grown, there have been major changes in sea level. There are two main reasons for sea level changes. One is that the world's ocean basins have changed in size and shape because of sea floor spreading and plate tectonics. There have also been more rapid fluctuations due to the effects of the ice ages. Sea level first fell more than 30 million years ago, when glaciation began in West Antarctica and was intensified by the first glaciation of Greenland shortly afterwards. It is uncertain what set this off, but it was probably both changes in the amount of heat being received from the sun and the drifting of the continents, which placed them in positions where climatic conditions were suitable for ice accumulation. The growth of these two ice sheets was sufficient to cause lower temperatures throughout the world and to initiate glaciation in some parts, tying up a considerable part of the earth's water. At the height of glaciation more than 2500 metres thickness of ice lay over much of northern America and Eurasia, sufficient to lower sea level by 150 metres. Today, 2.24 per cent of the world's water is locked up in the ice caps of Antarctica and Greenland, which, if melted, would raise sea level by up to 100 metres.

Over the past two million years, major changes in sea level have occurred as a result of the growth and decay of ice sheets. During high sea level stages, reefs have flourished and grown on the continental shelf, only to be exposed to the atmosphere when the glaciers advanced and sea level fell. When sea levels rose once more, when ice sheets melted, the older reefs often formed the foundations for new coral growth, producing layers of old reef beneath the modern ones.

Two million years' growth

It is a paradox that the growth of coral reefs, normally associated with the tropics, has occurred in northeastern Australia in the past two million years at a time dominated by glaciation. Changes in sea level caused by glaciation had a greater effect on the growth of the Great Barrier Reef than most other factors.

The reasons for coral reefs suddenly beginning to grow on the Queensland coast are unknown. A particularly rapid rise in sea level probably 'cleansed' the surface of the continental shelf of the muds and sands deposited there during the previous low sea level and produced clear shallow water conditions – the kind that allowed coral larvae, perhaps originating on reefs of the Coral Sea, to settle and gradually form niches, from which reefs eventually grew. The sites first colonised were probably the banks between river channels, and perhaps even the bars and islands that remained when old river channels were drowned by the rising seas. The channels themselves were probably unfavourable sites for the corals to establish themselves for two reasons: the thick muds and sands would have formed unstable foundations, and the channels would also have been scoured by rapid and strong currents.

The growth of coral reefs during high-sea-level phases was periodically interrupted by a rapid fall in sea level. Death of the reefs ensued, only to be followed by development of new reefs on the sites of the old when sea level rose again. The Great Barrier Reef as we know it today is a series of high-sea-level growth phase layers separated by erosion surfaces representing the death and destruction of the reef during low sea levels. In fact, coral reefs have grown during a mere 200 000 to 400 000 years of the past two million years. During the rest of the two million years, sea level was low; then erosion destroyed the reef and rivers crossed the shelf to the low-sea-level shoreline, near the present-day shelf edge.

Are the shapes of the reefs of the Great Barrier Reef caused by growth during the short periods of high sea level, or by the erosion that occurred during the long periods of low sea level? There can be little doubt that low-sea-level erosion of the reefs did occur; up to 15 metres of reef may have been removed during 100 000 years of the last low-sea-level period. But the erosion rarely produced large scale collapse structures like those in the Pompey Reefs. Normally it caused the formation of smaller scale cave systems and soil development on and around most reefs. In most areas, erosion by atmospheric forces, such as heat, wind and rain, seems only to have modified the shape of the earlier reefs. The shape of the new reef is determined by a combination of factors, including the shape of the earlier reef, the river patterns during low sea level, and erosion of the reef during low sea level. These processes ensured that the reefs grew in more or less the same places during the succeeding high-sea-level phases, and that reef shapes were inherited largely from the shape of the earlier reef, modified by erosion.

Reefs have grown rapidly over short periods: individual periods of growth have probably only lasted for 5000 to 15 000 years. The present period of reef growth has already lasted 8000 years – more than half of its maximum expected duration.

Zones of the modern reef

The intricate and varied reefs of the Great Barrier Reef have grown during the past 8000 years, in the time since the most recent rise in sea level flooded the continental shelf. The reefs have grown from the older reef platforms, which lie at an average depth of 15 to 20 metres. The modern reefs are relatively thin and their shape reflects quite accurately the shape of the surface over which they are growing. The most obvious growth features of modern reefs are those visible on the surface in both outer-shelf ribbon reefs or mid-shelf platform reefs. To understand the growth of modern reefs it is best to begin at the surface, where five easily defined zones can be identified: the reef front, the reef crest, the coral flat, the sand flat and the lagoon.

The upper slope of the modern reef front extends from mean low-water level of spring tides down to a depth of 10 to 20 metres. Fairly steep, sometimes vertical, sometimes terraced, and often serrated by coral-covered spurs and channels, the area has a lot of coral cover, often of the plate-like or branching *Acropora* species. On some reefs, the front is protected by a line of patch reefs, many of which join to form an outer front.

- coral framework
- pavement and boulders
- sand zone with patch reefs
- algal flat
- encrustations
- algal pavement and framework

'Throughout much of its history, northeastern Australia lay in latitudinal areas that were simply too cold for the growth of coral reefs.'

▽ *Ribbon Reef No. 5 is formed at the edge of the continental shelf in the northern Great Barrier Reef, northeast of Cairns. It is a long, sinuous reef which does not enclose a lagoon. It is a high energy reef – affected by strong waves from the oceans – so that coral growth is restricted to the upper slope, a narrow coral flat on the lee side and prolific growth on the leeward margin. Much of the upper surface consists of algal pavement.*

Ribbon Reef No. 5

One Tree Reef

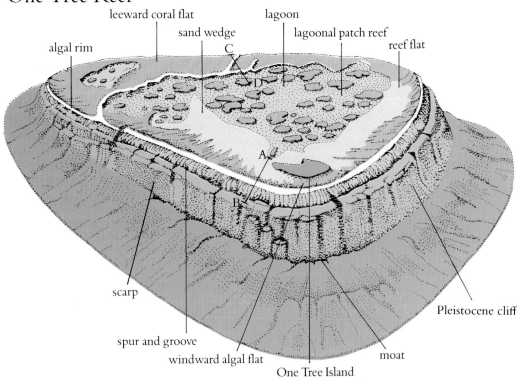

algal rim
leeward coral flat
sand wedge
lagoon
lagoonal patch reef
reef flat
scarp
spur and groove
windward algal flat
One Tree Island
moat
Pleistocene cliff

Hard coral, *Pocillopora*

△ One Tree Reef is an outer shelf platform reef in the southern Great Barrier Reef, east of Gladstone. It has all the classic surface features of the platform reef, including a lagoon. The island on the windward margin is built up of rubble. Cross sections of the reef, below, show growth characteristics at profiles of the windward margin (A–B) and the leeward margin (C–D). The reef has grown on a Pleistocene foundation, following its shape.

One Tree Reef, cross section

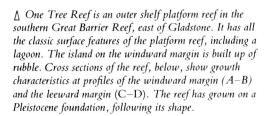

A
sea level
bombies
branching and massive corals
coralline algae
B
rhythmic intertidal sediments
branching corals
10 metres
rhythmic subtidal sediments
massive corals
coarse subtidal sediments

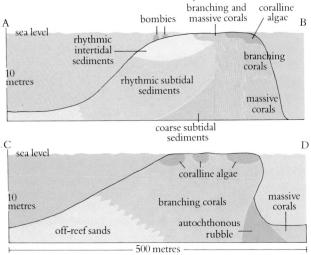

C
sea level
coralline algae
D
10 metres
branching corals
massive corals
off-reef sands
autochthonous rubble
— 500 metres —

△ These small patches of Pocillopora, two metres across, grow on the sand flats. The patches coalesce through growth along their windward and leeward ends and gradually extend the coral flat across the sand flat.

△△ The outer reef crest may be stepped and highly consolidated coralline pavement. These pavements may be 200 to 300 metres wide on the Great Barrier Reef. The boulders on the surface are remnants of much larger accumulations tossed up during storms.

◁ A serrated surface of coral-covered spurs and grooves may develop on the windward margin of the reef front. These long spurs and grooves generally extend to a depth of about 20 metres.

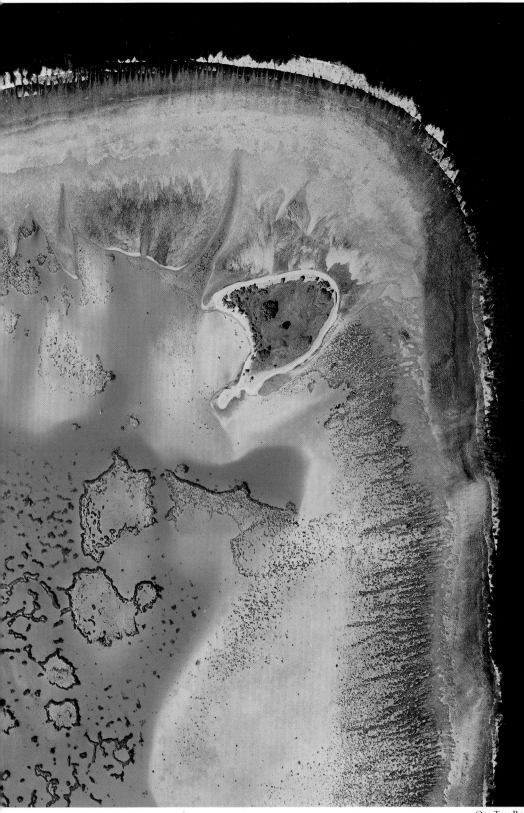

One Tree Reef

The exposed windward reef crest, or outer reef flat, lies above the mean low-water level of spring tides. It is composed of either a seaward, stepped surface encrusted with coralline algae and devoid of corals, or a flat coralline-encrusted surface that may reach half a metre above the mean low-water level of spring tides, as on the ribbon reefs. The upper surface of the reef crest is sometimes covered by a green turf of fleshy algae, which provides a home for countless small organisms, particularly foraminifera. Throughout the Great Barrier Reef, these algal pavements are 200 to 300 metres wide. They form in response to the high energy conditions typical of windward edges. Exposed outer reef flats with predominantly algal surfaces are often replaced in lower energy or more leeward parts of the edge of the reef by extensive coral development that is contiguous with that forming the coral flat.

The coral flat, or reef flat, occurs on the sheltered or lee side of the algal flat. It usually consists of an aligned coral zone, where *Acropora* and *Pocillopora* species are dominant, along with *Porites*, *Favites* and *Goniastrea* species; most corals are encrusted by corallines. The aligned corals occur in patches one to two metres wide and 20 metres long, formed by coral growing parallel to the direction of waves refracted across the top of the reef. The water movement is thus channelled through the grooves between the aligned assemblages of coral, and in this way, coral growth on the reef top controls the backward flow of water across the reef. Nutrients and sediments are carried back through these channels to the sand flat and lagoon areas.

Platform reefs, such as Fitzroy Reef, have a leeward coral flat built of stubby, branching corals and some coralline algae. The leeward reef slope is, however, characterised by well-developed spurs and grooves. The growth of spurs, composed of diverse and often delicate branching and massive corals, indicates that the leeward edge of the reef is being extended.

The aligned coral zone is usually separated from the lagoon by a sand flat, which may be up to 500 metres wide. The sand flat is made up of the broken skeletons of corals, coralline algae, and other reef organisms derived from the reef front and coral flat and transported towards the lagoon as sands and gravels. Foraminifera from the algal turf of the reef crest also form part of the sediment.

Colonising a sand flat

Sand flats have been built by the prevailing swell and waves that continually destroy the reef front and transport the broken products backwards. The

◁ *The sand flat may engulf patch reefs, as on the southern margin of the lagoon on One Tree Reef in the southern Great Barrier Reef. A yellow camera filter accentuates the colour contrast of different water depths.*

surface of the sand flat, covered by one half to two metres of water, depending upon the tides, is often sparsely covered by small colonies of branching corals, such as *Pocillopora* and *Acropora* species. The small colonies grow from fragments brought from the coral flat; the first migrants are *Acropora* tips, which grow where they come to rest. These first colonisers are quickly followed by other branching forms, such as *Pocillopora damicornis*, which occupy niches in the framework created by *Acropora*. Eventually, however, *Pocillopora* takes over and expands the colony to several metres in size. A small, solid patch is eventually formed after larvae of massive corals, such as *Goniastrea*, *Favites*, *Goniopora* and *Porites* species, settle and grow. In this way the coral flat extends backwards across the sand flat. The buried outlines of lagoonal patch reefs indicate that the sand flat is filling the lagoon, just as the coral flat is spreading across the sand flat.

The lagoon is best seen in platform reefs, such as Fitzroy, in the southern Great Barrier Reef. Such lagoons are commonly five to ten metres deep, with the deepest part occurring on the leeward side of the reef. Lagoons are sometimes open, with very few patch reefs rising from the floor, or closely crowded with patch reefs that make navigation in the lagoon difficult. The patch reefs, whether they form discrete circular or network-like structures, usually rise vertically from the lagoon floor. They are made up of many species of branching and massive corals, the dead parts of which are encrusted by coralline algae. The lagoon floors consist of coral sand, which becomes finer away from the windward margin, and patches of mud sometimes occur in the quiet water of the leeward margins. The lagoons are the repositories for sediment and organic material created on the windward margin, and so they are slowly filling up.

Reefs growing to sea level

The surface zonation of the reefs has risen through growth of the reefs at sea level. Growth at and growth to sea level must be distinguished because growing reefs have not always been at sea level.

Sea level at first rose rapidly, so that up to ten metres of water covered the previously exposed surface before corals started to colonise the substrate. About 6000 years ago, sea level established and maintained a position close to its present level. In ten metres of water corals grow upwards towards the light, so that the reef surface grows upwards from the deeper, quiet water to the high-energy surface environment characterised by heavy pounding of the surf. The types of corals that make up the reef change as the environment changes.

The composition of the reef also varies with the position of the reef on the continental shelf. The structure of outer-shelf reefs generally reflects the influence of powerful waves, and here most of the reef consists of coral skeletons forming a porous, but relatively stable, framework. Reefs in the middle

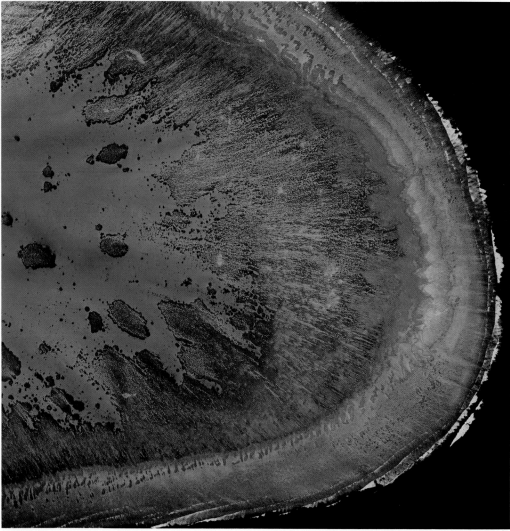

Fitzroy Reef

and inner parts, particularly those of the central and northern Great Barrier Reef, are dominated by accumulations of sand, and the coral framework forms a much smaller proportion of the reef, reflecting the calmer sea, or lower energy conditions compared with the more exposed outer shelf. Reefs such as Orpheus and Wheeler, in the middle and inner shelf off Townsville, are little more than coral veneers on sand and rubble piles.

These reef growth features, incorporating limited colonisation, vertical growth to sea level, and lateral growth and destruction at sea level, reflect the influence of three important determinants of growth: the depth of the colonising substrate, sea level history, and reef growth rates. Once the roles of these three factors were recognised, it could be seen that different reefs have reached different stages of development which could be defined as juvenile, mature or senile.

△ *An aerial photograph of Fitzroy Reef in the southern Great Barrier Reef, taken with a yellow filter to accentuate the colour contrast of different water depths, shows the aligned coral zone of the coral flat, the sand flat and part of the lagoon.*

A reef growing slowly from a deep substrate may not yet have reached sea level or may only recently have reached sea level; the reef will be characterised by vigorous growth of free-standing branching or massive corals upwards to sea level. Such a reef is termed juvenile, and examples occur in the shoals forming the northern Capricorn reefs, or parts of Pith Reef on the northern side of Magnetic Passage.

A reef growing from a relatively shallow substrate, or one growing rapidly from a deeper substrate, will reach sea level quickly and will be subject to the influences of shallow water for a long

Evolutionary growth stages

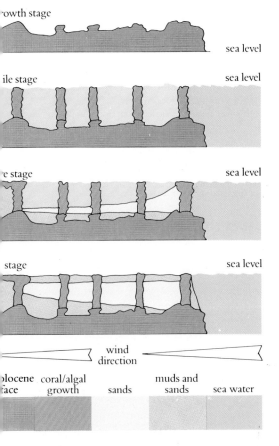

owth stage   sea level

ile stage   sea level

e stage   sea level

stage   sea level

wind
direction

| olocene | coral/algal | | muds and | |
| :ace | growth | sands | sands | sea water |

Viper Reef

time; many reefs have been at sea level for 4000 to 6000 years. Swell, waves and currents will have helped develop the classic morphologic features already described, and such reefs are called mature.

Reefs growing from very shallow substrates, or small reefs that have grown rapidly from deeper substrates, may have been at sea level even longer than the mature reefs, and because such a long time in the surface environment leads to destruction of the reef, lagoons will have been filled in and the typical zonation destroyed. Erosion is thought to exceed production, and such reefs are called senile.

It is believed that reefs progress through the growth stages from juvenile to mature to senile. Different reefs require different lengths of time to follow this progression, the time being dependent on depth and size of substrate, the rates of growth, length of time at sea level, and the intensity of the processes operating at sea level. As reef growth has

◁ *The growth stages of these southern platform reefs are very similar to most reefs of the Great Barrier Reef. In the pre-growth phase, sea level has not yet risen above the old land surface. In the juvenile phase, sea level has risen above the old surface to its stabilised position, and a reef has grown, particularly around the margins. In the mature phase, the reef has been at sea level for some time; the zonation has developed and the lagoon has begun to fill. In the senile phase, the reef has been at sea level several thousand years; the lagoon has filled in and the zonation pattern is becoming obliterated.*

seldom lasted for more than 5000 to 15 000 years, some of the large lagoon reefs may not have had sufficient time to progress through the complete cycle in one high-sea-level growth phase. They may require more than one growth phase to reach a senile condition.

△ *Viper Reef lies on the edge of the continental shelf to the east of Townsville in the central Great Barrier Reef. It has no enclosed lagoon, but exhibits both a reef crest and a detached outer rim. The modern reef has grown from the first terrace, the depth of which varies from windward to leeward. The structure of the windward margin is similar to that at One Tree Reef.*

'Modern reefs are relatively thin and their shape reflects quite accurately the shape of the surface over which they are growing.'

Maintenance and destruction

Coral reefs come in a vast array of shapes and sizes, and they display many differences in physical details. Many of these large-scale differences result from erosion that occurred when the reefs were periodically exposed by low sea levels during the great ice ages, rather than from differences in the growth of the reefs when they were submerged and alive. In fact, today's reefs are often little more than a veneer of new growth on older eroded reefs. In spite of these differences in large-scale physical characteristics, there are startling similarities in the seemingly organised roles of the living communities of the growing reef.

Reefs epitomise biological complexity with their myriad plants and animals, yet they also elegantly demonstrate ecological organisation, with a series of zones across the reef, each serving a specific role in providing food, consuming wastes, recycling nutrients, and creating and maintaining the limestone structure that is the reef. It is tempting to see this order, which occurs in most reefs, as the result of a single purpose for the whole reef. In reality, it is no more than a demonstration of the inevitable result of interactions between organisms; and many combinations of organisms can lead to this predictable order.

Coral reefs are dramatic examples of the natural order of things because of their relatively clear boundaries and apparent isolation as oases in what has been assumed to be the desert of tropical oceans.

Many of the world's tropical oceans have few plant nutrients, which results in little plankton growth, the absence of which accounts for the beautiful blue colour usually associated with tropical seas. However, coral reefs show no particular preference for the most barren areas of the ocean.

They can occur in a wide range of oceanic and coastal environments, from water very low in plant nutrients and plankton to water that is quite enriched. In enriched environments, however, reefs cannot always compete with other marine systems; for example, dense beds of large algae populated by filter-feeding animals such as barnacles. Coral reefs do not prefer to struggle for nutrition, but they have developed the ability to thrive in barren areas of the ocean more effectively than other marine systems. They do this by creating and recycling their own internal food supply. So coral reefs, in their most pure forms, frequently occur in waters that are very low in nutrients.

The genuine article

It is difficult to establish a simple boundary to separate the true coral reef community of blue oceanic waters from ecosystems that contain many

△ *Typical reefs of the Great Barrier Reef complex, like most other coral reefs in the world, occur in beautiful, blue, barren tropical waters. The colour of this water is an indication of the lack of plankton and coastal influences. Because coral reefs frequently occur in these oceanic deserts, they have evolved communities that maximise the use of the available nutrients in the ocean. This requires that all material grown, whether plant, animal or microbial, is, as far as possible, recycled within the system.*

Princess Charlotte Bay

△ *Reefs such as those in coastal waters over the wide continental shelf east of Cape York and in Princess Charlotte Bay appear distinctly different from the reefs of clean oceanic waters. These reefs have modern reef limestone surfaces and should be described as coral reefs. Nevertheless, they have conspicuous larger plant components, including extensive sea grasses, indicated by the green coloration over the filled reef flat. Such reefs are also surrounded by green water enriched with both nutrients and plankton, which allows them the relative luxury of free exchange with the ocean. Hence, the communities that develop do not have the same rigid constraints for efficient recycling that are typical of the more oceanic reefs.*

Pandora Reef

△ *Pandora Reef, an inshore reef in Halifax Bay, indicates a development that has always been a mixture of the growth of true reef limestone builders, such as corals, with the long-term build-up of sediments of mainland origin. The communities on these reefs have poor zonation and only passing similarities to the more typical oceanic and outer continental shelf reefs. They do not exhibit the tight nutritional organisation so essential to the survival of reefs in the low nutritional environments of the outer shelf.*

of the typical reef organisms in association with organisms of strictly coastal origin. Many structures in coastal waters are limestone of predominantly coral origin, and their living communities appear to be in a stable condition of continuing development in a fertile environment. Many other inshore structures clearly originated as reefs but no longer seem to function as true coral reefs. They have been overgrown by communities typical of rocky and muddy coastlines. This may be the result of the natural evolution of reefs during 6000 years of relatively constant sea level over the continental shelf, or perhaps it reflects the impact of sediment and chemical runoff from intensive agriculture in the northern coastal plains and river valleys. Chemicals in runoff can either be destructive, such as herbicides and insecticides, or enriching, such as fertilisers. In either case, the viability of a coral reef community is threatened.

Inshore reefs, whether they be stable or in decline, do not develop the structured zonation and precisely balanced biological communities of the outer reefs. This is because they exist in enriched and biologically active waters, and internal recycling of the food supply is not essential.

A balanced diet

The creation and maintenance of a coral reef requires not only the provision of a food supply for the entire community but also the building of the reef structure itself. The classic outer shelf or oceanic reef produces most of its own food supply. It is also totally dependent on the limestone structure it has created for its habitat and for substrates on which its biological community can grow.

Sunlight provides the basic energy for a coral reef's food production and the creation of its vast limestone structure; plant photosynthesis maintains

the reef. Reefs, therefore, are restricted to areas where the penetration of light is sufficient for plants to carry out photosynthesis. At depths with a light intensity of one per cent of that of sunlight, little photosynthesis occurs. Most active growth of corals, algae and other reef animals and plants occurs in regions where light intensity is considerably higher. The reduction of light intensity is a function not only of depth within the water but also of its turbidity. Reef growth can thus continue at greater depths in clear oceanic water, but it is nowhere very significant below about 50 metres.

A coral reef requires only the basic plant nutrients plus a copious supply of calcium for the construction of the calcium carbonate of coral skeletons and the other limestone-forming materials of the reef. Carbon dioxide and calcium are abundant in sea water. Nitrogen, phosphorus and some trace elements, however, may be present in very limited quantities in clear oceanic water, and the reef must recycle these materials to maintain its intense biological activity. All plant and animal matter grown must be totally consumed or fully degraded within the reef community to prevent the loss of any nutrients.

Reefs have evolved an alternative to the absolute need to conserve nitrogen, involving extensive mats of blue-green algae. These algae are able to convert the abundant nitrogen gas of the atmosphere into soluble inorganic nitrogen nutrients. Although these algal mats are frequently extensive in the shallow reef flats, it is not yet clear whether they produce enough inorganic nitrogen to satisfy the reef's requirements.

Self-sufficiency and recycling are vital, but there are very small but very important losses and gains from any reef system. There is the exchange of larval forms with other reefs. This ensures that excessive periods of inbreeding within species will not occur and that any species seriously depleted by localised disease or other stress will be replaced by larval input from anywhere within a series of reefs, which could be as large as even the whole Great Barrier Reef complex. There may also be small but significant inputs of oceanic plankton, and reef plankton and fragments of reef organisms can be lost in the ceaseless flow of water over the reef. The total of such gains and losses in an oceanic reef is less than one per cent of the total food turnover. They can, however, be vital factors in maintaining the community structure and the balance of nutrition.

All working together

About three-quarters of the carbon dioxide that is removed from the sea water by a coral reef in each 24-hour period is used directly in photosynthesis within the reef algae. Each day, this creates about 20 grams of new organic matter for every square metre of shallow, reef-flat environment, and as much as 50 grams a day may be created in areas of intense biological activity. This is the reef's food supply.

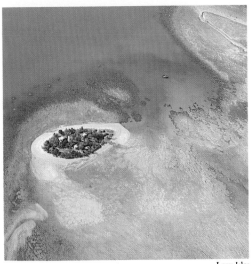

Low Isles

△ *The Low Isles reef system off the Daintree River is an example of an inshore reef that seems to have degraded from the status of a relatively classical coral reef community. From 1928 to 1929, when used by the British Association as the base for the early Great Barrier Reef Expedition scientific studies, the reef was a rich and typical coral reef system despite its proximity to the mainland. Today it shows substantial degradation, with many of its earlier rich coral communities largely dead and overgrown with soft corals and algae. Although it is not certain that this decline is exclusively the result of human influences, intensive agriculture in the region has been a contributing factor.*

Blue-green alga

△ *Extensive mats of blue-green algae may form over many parts of the reef flats and intertidal rubble, here alongside a small clump of colonial ascidians. Sometimes it looks like little more than an unattractive black or reddish stain. This alga is able to convert nitrogen from the atmosphere into a vital inorganic nitrogen supplement to help in the total nutrition of the reef community. This inbuilt supply of fertiliser probably means that few, if any, coral reefs are limited by the availability of nitrogenous nutrients. But there is no equivalent means of providing the phosphates and other trace nutrients so essential for reef growth and maintenance in the more sterile ocean environments. Consequently extreme conservation measures have evolved in all but inshore reef communities.*

▷ Most of the limestone making up the solid underlying mass of the coral reef consists of skeletons of once-living corals. This material may remain where it grows, though it is perhaps more commonly broken off and redeposited in other parts of the reef. One thing is certain: corals cannot cement their skeletons together in a solid reef structure, they merely form a vast quantity of limestone. They provide the aggregate of the reef concrete. At least some of the corals in this rich surface growth are likely to add to the structural framework of their own reef when they die.

▽ Large areas of most reefs consist of the nondescript mixed communities of the reef flats. These zones, loved by shell collectors, often form the largest area in small non-lagoon reefs. They typify the balanced reef community and generally produce as much photosynthetically derived algal food material as they consume, so they are in fine balance. The ubiquitous algal fuzz or turf is seen on the reef flat at Lizard Island.

Lizard Island

▷ Encrusting coralline algae hold together the sand and framework materials of the reef to create a solid structure. These bright pink, hard films occur on most reef surfaces, including dead coral branches. They belong to the extensive group of red algae and are frequently much more brightly coloured when they occur at depth. They have a vital role in building a real reef rather than a pile of uncemented coral debris and sand. Once the reef has been totally consolidated by these algae, chemical precipitation of more carbonates in the reef structure provides additional cementing of the remaining loose calcium carbonate materials. This process is slow, but it makes the entire structure more rigid. The final reef material is a porous but strong limestone, though it frequently contains uncemented regions.

Encrusting alga

Almost every gram of organic matter created by a coral reef is consumed and eventually finds its way back into the sea water as carbon dioxide. This is a delicate nutritional balance. Before most of the organic matter is finally degraded back to carbon dioxide, it may move through all or part of the complex and finely balanced coral reef food web.

What is the result of the reef creating and totally consuming so much food material? First, it allows the continuing maintenance by reproduction of the coral reef community by feeding the sun's energy into the system. Second, and perhaps most significantly, it provides the energy needed to remove the other quarter of the total carbon dioxide used by the reef in a 24-hour period. This additional carbon dioxide is used in the biological formation of calcium carbonate or limestone. The limestone created is mostly retained by the system, giving rise to the physical growth of the reef structure.

We may think of coral reefs as assemblages of beautiful animals, but in fact they are dominated by the activities of plants. The whole system is driven by the photosynthetic activities of plants, just like most ecosystems existing in the light. Even corals function principally as plants, deriving as much as 90 per cent of their total food and energy requirements from the tiny algae, known as zooxanthellae, contained within the coral tissues. Their remaining requirements are met through feeding on reef plankton.

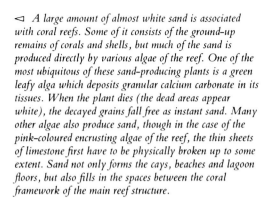

◁ A large amount of almost white sand is associated with coral reefs. Some of it consists of the ground-up remains of corals and shells, but much of the sand is produced directly by various algae of the reef. One of the most ubiquitous of these sand-producing plants is a green leafy alga which deposits granular calcium carbonate in its tissues. When the plant dies (the dead areas appear white), the decayed grains fall free as instant sand. Many other algae also produce sand, though in the case of the pink-coloured encrusting algae of the reef, the thin sheets of limestone first have to be physically broken up to some extent. Sand not only forms the cays, beaches and lagoon floors, but also fills in the spaces between the coral framework of the main reef structure.

Green alga, *Halimeda*

△ The outer, high-wave energy areas of the seaward reef flats are typically dominated by algae. The area has the lowest percentage consumption of food produced of any zone, as much of the algal matter is broken off by waves and turbulence, finding its way into the calmer inner flats and lagoons. Thus, the area functions as the principal 'source' zone of the reef. The underlying limestone pavement is largely cemented by the action of encrusting coralline algae. When limestone forms at higher levels, such as in beach rock and rubble ridges, the cementation is largely chemical.

◁ Whenever reef coral debris accumulates as rubble below about the half tide level, it is bound together and stabilised by soft organisms such as zooanthid mats or masses of small bead-like green algae. When the accumulation is below the low tide level, as it is here, algal cementation also occurs and appears as a pink encrustation.

Green alga, *Caulerpa*

▷ *Not all lagoons are simple, deep areas waiting to be filled. Many shallow lagoons, such as those on Wistari Reef in the Capricorn Group, have an elaborate and frequently interconnected structure of patch reefs. Each of these is zoned on a small scale, just like the reef as a whole: there are small, outer reef flat perimeters of active growth surrounding mini-lagoons being filled with sediments produced by the perimeters. The whole careful balance and conservation of materials that occurs in the reef system is mirrored here, with exchange between local sources and sinks. Each patch reef, therefore, acts like a miniature of the complete reef, though self-sufficiency in the generation of a food supply is not so necessary.*

Apart from the corals themselves, the major plants providing the food supply of the reef are the fine, inconspicuous, filamentous algae that form a rapid growing fuzz or turf over almost all available surfaces within the reef. The algal turf is grazed by animals, which in turn are preyed on by larger predatory animals, and so the food web expands.

All living materials die and undergo microbial decay. These microbes form the basis of yet another component of the complex food web. The coral reef also creates and consumes its own plankton. Each animal and plant serves a vital role in the reef's finely tuned balance. Brief population explosions may occur for particular groups, but over a full year everything returns to a balance.

The reef factory

The 10 to 30 grams of calcium carbonate or limestone created every day for each square metre of the active parts of the reef are usually retained somewhere within the general reef environment. The reef thus exhibits real, measurable growth over hundreds of years. The energy to enable the creation of all this limestone comes into the system through algal photosynthesis. Much of the limestone originates as growing coral but other organisms, such as many algae, tiny single-celled forams and shells make major contributions. The cements in the limestone rock are partially deposited by algae and are partially chemical precipitation.

Perhaps the most obvious of all the reef-destroying processes are storms. They not only break up immense amounts of the growing corals and other reef organisms but also move around the resulting debris, reorganising the reef shape and filling in lagoons. Storms also occasionally fracture the cemented reef structure itself.

▷ *Living corals and reef limestone are always under attack from a large array of boring organisms. These often colourful worms, filamentous algae, bivalves and sponges frequently cause substantial collapse. They also produce acid secretions which dissolve some of the reef materials.*

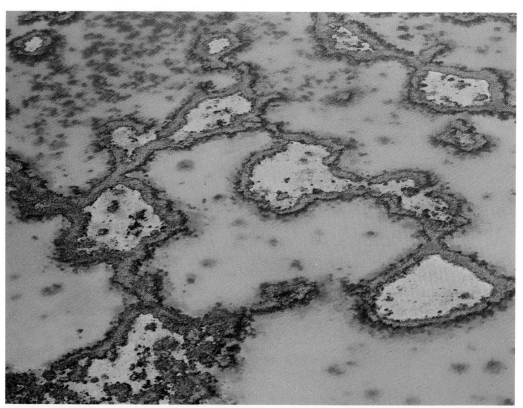

Wistari Reef

Christmas tree worm, *Spirobranchus giganteus*

Lady Musgrave Reef

Producer and consumer societies

A zonation of function exists within the total reef, and particular parts of the reef may not be representative of the whole.

The upper part of the seaward reef slopes of the typical reef is a region of very high biological activity: the highest levels of photosynthesis and calcium carbonate skeleton formation. This rather turbulent area is a source zone; that is, much of the organic matter created here is broken away and redistributed to other areas of the reef. And much of the calcium carbonate deposited is broken away in coarse pieces by wave surge and storms to tumble deeper down the slope, to be washed up on to the reef crest to form shingle banks, or even washed right over into the lagoon. There is little biological activity on the debris-littered lower slope.

The outer areas of the reef flat or reef crest are the areas exposed to highest physical energy from waves and storm impact. Biological activity is only moderate, but most of the plant matter made here is broken away or grazed by fishes, making the area the principal source zone of the reef. The only carbonate materials deposited here are by encrusting coralline algae and a few small stunted corals. Most of this production is also broken and ground away to finish at the back edge of the reef flat as a sand sheet gradually filling in the lagoon.

The main reef flat has a balanced, mixed community, with quite high levels of photosynthesis and calcium carbonate deposition. Most of the food created in the area is also consumed here, making the reef flat an area of near self-sufficiency. Little of the calcium carbonate formed here is retained, however, as the reef flat is essentially at the low-tide sea level, allowing no room for further upward

◁ *Typical reef zonation is seen most easily in a reef of uncomplicated shape, such as Lady Musgrave Reef in the southern Bunker Group. The outer, seaward slope is just visible beyond the white breaker zone. The algal-dominated outer reef flat, itself clearly separated into three zones, is the seaward half of the brownish area of the reef. The inner reef flat, with its self-sufficient mixed communities containing many small corals, is the inner half of the brownish area terminating on the lagoon side with a typical, scalloped edge. The shallow sand flat of sediments moving away from their site of production on the reef flat into the lagoon is clearly visible behind the active reef flat. The deeper blue of the lagoon is the part of the reef that is still available for filling by sediments produced elsewhere and contains discrete patch reefs.*

◁ *Major storms may cause the fracture of large pieces of the cemented limestone of the reef structure itself. Cyclones may be so violent that these massive pieces of limestone do not tumble down the reef slope but are actually lifted up to the top of the reef, where they can be a hazard for boats.*

Not all reef destruction is caused by physical forces. Many animals and even some algae live out their lives inside the reef structure and even inside the skeletons of still-living corals and other organisms with hard skeletons. Some, such as chitons and many fishes, graze off the reef surfaces, removing considerable amounts of the limestone at the same time. These boring and grazing organisms weaken the structure of their host or the reef itself by physically disrupting the limestone materials. This in turn creates more fine sand and calcium carbonate detritus in the reef system. But the boring organisms also dissolve, with acid secretions, much of the calcium carbonate they remove. This means that not all of the carbonate deposited by the reef limestone makers is retained; it is thought that this loss is probably between five and 25 per cent of the total deposited. Hence a lot of limestone and sand are collected by the average reef over the year.

growth. The reef flat is, therefore, self-sufficient in food, but it is a major source zone for sand and limestone gravels. This material mostly moves back with the sand sheet along with the material from the more seaward zones.

The back reef or lagoon environment acts as the major sink zone for the whole reef system: it is the dumping ground for the excess organic matter broken away in the turbulent, seaward source areas. It is also the final resting place for much of the calcium carbonate sands and gravels from all other areas of the reef. This results in the progressive filling in of lagoons and the gradual physical growth or accretion of the reef in a down-wind or down-current direction. The patch reefs, so common in the lagoon environments, function as self-sufficient miniatures of the main reef flat.

The net result of the integration of excess production and consumption within all reef zones over a full annual cycle is that there is a zero balance for the production of organic matter but a substantial gain in the production of carbonates. Some of the carbonate increase leads to extension of the main cemented reef limestone structure and the creation of further intertidal ramparts and islands. Most of it results in the filling in of lagoons and the leeward extension of unconsolidated reef sediments.

On average, over all zones, a coral reef produces each year about two kilograms of organic matter for every square metre. All of this organic matter is consumed and respired back to carbon dioxide. By contrast, about 1500 grams of calcium carbonate sands, gravel and cemented limestone are produced, most of which remain as accretion to the reef, except in very 'senile' reefs, which have been at sea level for a long time. Here, erosion may dominate.

It is often easy to forget that this coral reef is not a beautifully organised, controlled production machine, but the natural result of the interaction between a complex set of living organisms and the physical forces of their environment.

Cays: the sediment storers

A coral cay is an accumulation of sediments derived from the carbonate-secreting plants and animals of the reef. All reef flats have these sediments, but a cay forms when the wave pattern, as it bends around the margins of the reef, concentrates the material in particular areas. During storms, large reef blocks and coarser shingle may be deposited on the windward side of the reef, but sand-size material is generally carried to the leeward side. On many reefs, the sand is carried into the deeper water behind the reef or into a central lagoon but, especially on oval platform reefs, sediments tend to be concentrated on a particular point, where an embryo sand cay may evolve.

The cay is initially very unstable: it disappears and reappears with changes in weather patterns, and

Tryon Island and Reef

vegetation is unable to establish itself. As a cay becomes larger, its rate of movement decreases. Storm waves may build it to heights not normally reached by tides, and wind may add more sand to the top. It becomes a haven for sea birds, which themselves add phosphatic guano to the sand and carry in seeds in their plumage and through their digestive tracts. Other seeds float in, and a colonising vegetation of low creepers can grow and help stabilise the cay.

Waters flowing through the sediments may precipitate calcium carbonate within the sands to form beachrock – cemented beach material which, once exposed to the atmosphere, is similar to concrete. Its presence further stabilises the cay. If the area of the cay reaches about two hectares, and if sufficient rainfall occurs, a freshwater lens may form beneath the island. The presence of this ground water and the addition of organic matter to the land

△ *The reef top of Tryon Reef in the Capricorn Group illustrates the way the waves, refracted or bent around the reef top, converge on a lee-side point. Sediment trains, clearly seen focusing on Tryon Island from the coarse rubble zone of the windward reef front, result in the formation of lee-side sand cays.*

by the colonising plants aids development of soil, which will allow the establishment of other forms of vegetation. The variety of plants increases from four or five colonising species to as many as 40 species on older, stable cays. The colonising creepers and low shrubs then become limited to the more recently accumulated fringe of sand around the cay.

Shingle cays, which form on the windward sides of the reef, tend to evolve more slowly, because although they tend to be more stable than sand cays, their coarse open structure provides a very

Redbill Reef

△ *Bushy Cay on Redbill Reef off Mackay is a mature, vegetated reef island. The interior forest is composed of Pisonia trees – Pisonia grandis – but the cay is extending towards the right and the younger sand body has a low vegetation of Pandanus and Argusia argentia, together with ground creepers. Although not obvious, beachrock underlies the beaches of the island and beneath the Pisonia forest are extensive areas of phosphatic cay sandstone.*

'Reef sediments are made up of calcium carbonate in the form of skeletal remains of the carbonate-secreting plants and animals.'

Barnett Patches

◁ *When a reef flat first develops, the point of convergence of the waves may vary according to weather conditions. The sediment body that accumulates in the lee of the reef is highly unstable, changing location on the reef top by up to 15 metres in a single tidal cycle. Although the cay may be only a few tens of metres in diameter and no more than three metres high, it can move over an area of several hectares of reef flat. This cay on Barnett Patches is, for an unvegetated sand cay, relatively stable, and it even has birds nesting on it at times. The sanded reef flat area around the island indicates the area of migration. Very unstable sand cays may disappear completely for years at a time.*

inhospitable environment for the establishment of plants. Some reefs, particularly in high energy environments, may have both sand and shingle cays. On the northern Great Barrier Reef, many smaller inner shelf reefs also acquire an outer perimeter of shingle ramparts, which may sometimes reach a height sufficient for plant colonisation. The bases of the ramparts can then become firmly cemented by precipitation of calcium carbonate from waters passing through them. This not only creates a moat of the inner reef flat, but also provides a sheltered habitat for colonisation by mangroves. These cays become the low-wooded islands that are so typical of the northern reef. Also in the north, some reef flats are so sheltered that they support dense stands of mangroves, forming 'mangrove islands', although these mangrove glades are regularly inundated by the tide.

Low-wooded islands

Although they occur on only the northern Great Barrier Reef, the low-wooded islands are a distinctive type of coral cay. They have been the site of much Great Barrier Reef research: the 1928 to 1929 Royal Society Expedition led by Sir Maurice Yonge was sited on the southernmost example at Low Isles, and the 1973 Royal Society–Universities of Queensland Expedition under David Stoddart examined a large number of these islands, especially Three Isles and the Turtle Islands. The essential

▷ △ *A major stabilising influence on coral cays is beachrock. It forms within the beach or body of the cay when calcium carbonate is precipitated by rain water and sea water flowing through the material, probably due to carbon dioxide degassing of these waters as they approach the surface of the cay sediments. Beach bedding is often preserved, and complete hardening of the beachrock usually occurs after beach erosion has exposed it to the atmosphere. Once exposed, however, the beachrock provides a protective ramp for the cay and slows erosion.*

▷ *The most unstable parts of coral cays are the ends where spits, or narrow strips of sediment, extend out over the reef flat. Unfortunately, these also seem to be the areas where resort buildings or jetties are erected. Green Island, near Cairns, has a long history of erosion, which has intensified over the past 20 years with the growth of extensive sea grass beds on the adjacent reef flat, probably in response to the emptying of sewage on to the reef flat. These beds have enlarged from 900 square metres in 1945 to over 130 000 square metres in 1978. Sand eroded from the island during storms normally moves on to the adjacent reef flat and is returned to the cay in fair weather. But the sea grass holds the sand, which is now lost permanently from the cay. Sand has been artificially pumped on to the cay, causing new growth not where erosion is most severe but on the northwest corner of the cay, a lightly vegetated bulge on the top right-hand corner of the island.*

Green Island

◁ *Vegetated sand and shingle cays occur in Fairfax Reef in the Bunker Group. The larger windward shingle cay is made up of storm ridges. Its vegetation, which was mainly* Pisonia *trees –* Pisonia grandis *– has been severely altered by phosphate mining and by use of the area as a Royal Australian Air Force bomb target. The smaller sand cay has an unstable, elongated sand spit.*

▽ *Beachrock does not always completely protect a cay against erosion. At Ellis Island, on the northern reef, where the remnants of a beacon stand, only the beachrock and a highly mobile spit remain of what was probably once an extensive cay. Tropical cyclones are usually responsible for such dramatic erosion.*

Fairfax Reef

Ellis Island

characteristics of these islands are a leeward sand cay, windward shingle ramparts, cemented rampart rocks and mangroves.

Currents, waves and tides

The waters of the reef form the environment in which marine life exists, just as the atmosphere is the environment for life on land. The water has properties which influence life and growth in the seas, and its movement affects the distribution of fishes and corals and the sediments brought in by rivers or created by coral erosion.

Despite its name, the Great Barrier Reef is not a continuous coral structure; it consists of many individual reefs lying off the Queensland coast. To the north, the coral reefs are densely packed and are almost continuous on the Coral Sea side; in the central region, the reefs are often widely scattered;

in the south, the reefs are again closer together and cover a wider area. Between the reefs and the shore is the main Great Barrier Reef Lagoon where waters may be up to 50 metres deep. North of latitude 14° S, this coastal channel is studded with reefs and shoals, but these are relatively rare further south. The Great Barrier Reef Lagoon also provides a channel for ships and water movements along the mainland side of the reef.

The waters of both the coastal channel and the reef area are quite shallow and the turbulence, generated by currents around the reefs and over the sea bottom, and by the effects of wind waves, causes them to be generally well-mixed from top to bottom. The main exception occurs during the summer, when rain brought by river waters and the prevailing northwest monsoon in the north and central parts of the reef, creates a stable layer of fresh water in the upper top five to ten metres of the sea.

This in turn traps the sun's heat. The reduction in salinity can significantly limit the growth of corals, which do not tolerate fresh water.

Water temperature

The temperature of the reef waters varies with the seasons. The lowest temperatures occur in July at the middle of winter, when southern waters are about 20°C and northern waters 25°C. In January, in the middle of summer, the highest temperatures occur: 27°C in the south and 29°C in the north. Satellite observations show that the distribution of sea surface temperature is very patchy in both time and space.

The variation in temperature throughout the year is lowest in the north, as solar heat varies least towards the equator. There is generally a temperature difference of about 3° in the central zone of the reef, with the coastal channel waters being colder than the outer reef waters (Coral Sea side) in winter, and warmer in the summer. In the north, where the reefs are more dense and mixing is, therefore, greater (due to the complex eddy-like water circulation around coral reefs), the temperature difference across the reef is much smaller – about 0.5°C.

How salty is the sea?

The salinity of sea water is a measure of the concentration of dissolved salts in it. This is expressed as a number, with fresh water having a salinity of zero and ocean waters having an average salinity of about 34.7.

The sea water for the Great Barrier Reef comes from the oceanic water of the western Coral Sea, the salinity of which ranges from 34.5 to 35.5. The rain and river waters flowing into the Lagoon have salinities of zero, although river waters may include some dissolved materials such as fertilisers and pesticides, as well as much sediment.

Salinity also varies during the year. In all regions of the reef, salinity is increased at the end of the dry season from September to November, because of evaporation. The lowest values occur during the wet season, because fresh water from rainfall and river runoff dilutes the coastal channel waters.

Although both rainfall and runoff vary considerably from year to year, the input of fresh water each year is only a small fraction of the total volume of sea water in the region. In addition, the reduction of salinity is often limited to the top few metres of water, so that the effect on reef organisms is usually slight on the outer reef, but can be dominant inshore.

Rainfall is likely to be distributed fairly uniformly across the reef, but runoff from rivers is confined to areas near the shore. As it flows north this river runoff tends to stay close to the shore. Water from the Burdekin River does not cross the coastal channel reefs in significant quantity until near Innisfail, about 300 kilometres north of the river, by which time the water from the river has been well diluted by sea water.

The optical transparency of the water is important both for underwater studies and because corals will only grow where there is sufficient sunlight. Visibility in calm weather is usually one to five metres near the shore and 15 to 25 metres among the reefs. However, when winds are strong, waves will stir up sediments that may reduce visibility to a few metres, even among the reefs. Disturbances, such as feeding parrotfish scraping corals, may also affect water transparency.

Drifting back and forth

Some of the motions of reef waters, such as the waves generated by the wind and the rise and fall of the tides, are easily seen. Others are not so obvious but they may, nonetheless, be of great importance to the biology and geology of the region.

Some motions are periodic, in which the

Britomart Reef

directions of motion alternate back and forth at intervals ranging from a few seconds to days, or even weeks. Others are net drifts, in which the flow is in one direction for a longer time, at least for a few months.

Waves generated by the friction of the wind on the sea surface move for only a few seconds. Although only the movement of the sea surface is noticeable, there is some motion below the surface. In shallow water, the water particles move in vertical ellipses; the vertical motion diminishes as the water depth increases, but the horizontal motion persists unchanged until, on the sea bed, the water movement is just back and forth. This stirs up sediments that may then be moved by net drift. The swell from the Coral Sea, with intervals of ten to 15 seconds, does not penetrate far into the shallow waters of the reef, where short wind waves with intervals of about five seconds prevail.

△ *A dye-cloud, from a self-recording wave-averaging current meter suspended from a frame over the reef flat of Britomart Reef, shows the direction of water motion and provides an estimate of the rate of mixing into neighbouring waters. Records indicate that seiching (rapid wind-driven oscillations at water level) can occur in the coral reef lagoons, and that wind-driven currents over the reef flat are the result of a balance between the wind stress at the surface, which drives the flow of water, and the bottom friction, which opposes it. The friction is increased by the (darker) coral outcrops in the smooth (white) sand bottom. Data from such current meters also show that tidal and wind-driven currents contribute to the exchange of the reef lagoon waters with surrounding sea waters, with an exchange time of about four days in the case of the 15-kilometre Britomart Reef lagoon.*

The tides, caused by the varying gravitational forces of the moon and sun, are also periodic motions. In any locality, tides are strongly affected by the underwater topography: the shape of the continental shelf, the reefs, the channels and other features. However, the continental shelf in this region is little known, and tides and tidal currents are still not clearly understood.

Travelling tides

Tide waves from the oceans, as they approach from the Coral Sea, run mainly parallel to the coast so there is not much difference in the times of high and low water along most of the Great Barrier Reef. The tide takes one to two hours to travel from the outer reefs to the mainland shore, and it rises by half to one metre in this distance. These tides have two high and two low waters each day, known as semidiurnal tides, but the successive high waters are of different heights. This feature took Captain James Cook by surprise when his ship, the *Endeavour*, ran aground near present-day Cooktown at the higher high water and was unable to float off at the next, lower, high water.

Along most of the Queensland coast the tide range is about half a metre at neap tides – the lowest tides, which occur in the first or last quarters of the moon, when the gravitational pull of the sun and moon are almost in balance – to three metres at spring tides, which occur at the full or new moon, when the gravitational pull of the sun and moon is in the same direction and the highest tides are produced.

The tidal currents among the reefs and in the coastal channel are largely influenced by the topography of the sea bottom. In the deep passages from the ocean through the outer reefs, the flood inward and the ebb outward reach speeds of up to seven kilometres an hour (four knots), forming tidal jets flowing out into the Coral Sea. Cook observed, when he was trying to re-enter the reef at latitude 12.5° S, 'to our surprise we found the tide of ebb gushing out like a millstream so that it was impossible to get in'.

Oceanographic studies have revealed the existence of continental shelf waves with wave lengths (the distance between the same point on two consecutive waves) of more than 1000 kilometres caused by wind variations. These waves travel north along the reef at speeds of about 400 kilometres a day. Their height does not exceed 350 millimetres at the shore, and it decreases offshore. They have periods (the interval between the peaks of two waves), of about ten days, so a person standing on a cay or island would be unaware of the existence of these waves, since a 350-millimetre change over ten days is hard to detect when tidal changes of 3.5 metres are also involved. This long period means that they can cause extensive north and south water movement – a bottle floating in the water might be swept as far as 300 kilometres along the reef by one wave, and

then be swept back on the return flow. The return flow is primarily due to the composite effect of the wave return flow and the southward flowing East Australian Current in the Coral Sea. Fish eggs, or larvae about to settle, can thus be transported considerable distances from their point of origin and pollutants are carried great distances from where they were discharged.

The internal waves or tides below the surface along the eastern boundary of the reef are similarly not visible, since they do not change the sea level. But they have an important indirect effect on the reef ecology because they may draw nutrients into the upper layers of reef waters. The upper layer of the Coral Sea outside the reef is depleted of nutrients, but they are concentrated at depths of over 150 metres. The vertical motions of the reef's internal tides can raise this nutrient-rich water from the floor of the passages through the outer reefs

Hinchinbrook Island

⚠ *Mangrove swamps, such as those of Hinchinbrook Island, may be important to the coastal waters because they provide nutrients for the reef's food chain. Material, such as mangrove leaves, floats to the surface and is carried offshore, where it sinks and decomposes.*

(50 to 70 metres depth) so that it can be carried by the flood tide to supply the needs of reef organisms. The inflowing tide in reef passages may also draw this deeper water from the passage floor and then carry it to the reef.

The long-term or net motions of the reef waters are the least known because the process of measurement extends over a very long time. The two likely sources of net motion are the wind on the sea surface and the influence of the East Australian Current below the surface, flowing towards the South Pole.

Since the southeast trade winds prevail for much of the year, a northward flow would be expected, at least near the surface. There is a northward drift of 20 to 50 kilometres a day north of latitude 20° S, and less to the south of this. In the northern zone, the northwest monsoon from December to February generates a weak southward drift. At greater latitudes, in the central and southern zones, there is a southward drift of about five kilometres a day at the coastal channel side, ranging to 17 kilometres a day near the Coral Sea side. These drifts are attributed to the influence of the East Australian Current on the continental slope outside the reef.

Tides cause regular variations of sea level, but abnormal variations occur during cyclones. Then, the reduction of atmospheric pressure causes sea level to rise by ten millimetres for each millibar of atmospheric pressure drop. In addition, cyclone winds of up to 150 kilometres an hour can whip up the water and raise the level another one or two metres near the coast.

These extremes last for a few hours only, although if they occur near normal high water at spring tides they can cause serious coastal flooding. The large storm waves can also damage ships and make major changes to the size and shape of cays and sandbanks by moving large quantities of sand and shingle and breaking up the coral structures of the reefs.

Wakes and eddies

Tidal jets from narrow reef passages are often visible, mainly in turbulent waters. In areas where the currents are weaker, the presence of coral outcrops in reef lagoons can impede the flow of water, and interfere with the general flushing of the lagoon.

Satellite photographs of the northern reef zone, where there is sediment in the shallow Torres Strait waters and the waters from Papua New Guinea rivers, show evidence of wakes and eddies downstream from reefs. Although these wakes are only readily visible in the muddy continental shelf waters, they can occasionally be seen in the clearer water of the outer reefs. They are thought to be present wherever strong currents and sharp topography such as steep coral reefs occur. These wakes may affect the distribution of water properties and marine life. Eddies in the lee of reefs trap waterborne detritus and populations of plankton and larvae. These eddies can break free from their natal reefs and drift with the prevailing currents, enabling in this manner an interaction between individual coral reefs. The communication between reefs is thus patchy and intermittent in nature, making the precise assessment of the degree of interdependence of reefs a vital issue in the present and future management of the Great Barrier Reef Marine Park; a question that remains, for the most part, unanswered. □

Hydroid coral, *Distichopora violacea*

Corals: animal, vegetable or mineral?

The reef builders

Corals are an extraordinary group of animals that provide the framework, both living and dead, of the reef. They are responsible for much of the reef's scenic beauty and provide shelter for its more mobile occupants. Corals are strange, puzzling creatures. With shapes that are solid and unyielding, or soft but firmly attached to the reef, formed into mounds, plates, branches and crusts, they seem more like rocks or plants than animals.

The true nature of corals can best be appreciated if three things are kept in mind. Firstly, they are positioned between sponges and various worm-like groups on what biologists call the 'evolutionary scale'. With jellyfish and sea anemones they belong in the phylum Coelenterata: animals with special prey-catching cells called nematocysts and a simple body plan in which one opening is used for the passage of materials both into and out of the body.

Secondly, and more remarkably, corals are for the most part modular organisms, occurring not as a single animal with a single set of bodily characteristics, but as a special kind of colony. A coral colony is not a group of related individuals living and working together for the common good. Rather, it is the result of a single founder individual dividing to replicate itself over and over again, repeating the set of organs vital for its maintenance and reproduction. This modular characteristic provides corals with an array of special features and abilities. The entity that is the colony has a form of its own, with a base attaching it to the reef, a growing edge zone, an upper surface exposed to the light and a shaded under-surface. It also has hundreds of individual units – the polyps. These are genetically identical and are united by common tissue connections, and as a result are in constant beneficial communication.

The third and most remarkable feature of corals is

◁ *Corals are like an art form with endless variations of shape and wonderful subtleties of colour. Small colonies of the Hydrozoan coral,* Distichopora violacea, *are extremely common, usually in situations sheltered from sunlight. Hydrozoans are more akin to jellyfish than to the true corals,* Scleractinia.

Hard coral, *Favia favus*

Hard coral polyp

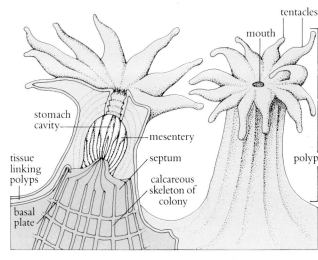

◁ *Within its setting in the modular colony, the coral polyp of* Favia favus, *left and above, displays the simple coelenterate body plan – essentially a cylinder with a ring of tentacles at the top, surrounding an opening that serves as both mouth and anus. Inside, the cylinder is partitioned by sheets of tissue extending inwards from the cylinder wall – the mesenteries. On these, the sex cells ripen each year to produce the eggs and sperm that will give rise to the next generation, so their appearance is constantly changing. The walls of the cylinder have three layers, the middle one being the equivalent of the 'jelly' layer of jellyfish. Cells within the outer layer produce the skeleton, in this case of limestone which, by a complex system of foldings of the coral wall, forms struts or septa extending, like the mesenteries, into the centre of the polyp. The patterns produced by the combination of polyp wall and septa are unique for each species.*

the presence of millions of zooxanthellae – tiny single-celled plants – within the animal's tissues. These obtain nourishment from photosynthesis, where the energy from sunlight is used to convert carbon dioxide and water into carbohydrates and oxygen. The presence of zooxanthellae in the coral colony enhances its capacity to grow and lay down skeleton. Quite a number of corals do not have them and some of these, with no need to live in the light, cling to caves, crevices and the underside surface of boulders.

What's in a name?

Like 'worms', 'shellfish' and 'bugs', the word 'coral' can be applied loosely to a variety of animals. They come from several groups with different kinds of polyps, but corals can also be distinguished by the kinds of skeletons they build.

Soft coral polyp

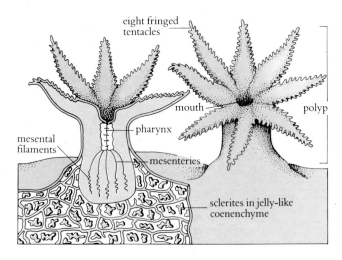

eight fringed tentacles

mouth

polyp

pharynx

mesental filaments

mesenteries

sclerites in jelly-like coenenchyme

Stony coral, *Acropora*

△ Soft corals do not have a solid limestone skeleton. They do, however, have hard parts in the form of tiny limestone crystal structures called sclerites embedded in their tissues. Their polyp structure is similar to that of hard corals, but they have eight fringed tentacles.

▷△ The stony corals are the only animals capable of building massive geological formations. Reaching up to the surface of the ocean, these solid limestone cliffs withstand the buffeting of waves and harness the resources of sunlight and sea to grow ever more solid.

▷ Daisy corals often oblige the daytime diver with an excellent view of expanded polyps. Two rings of smooth tentacles surround the disc with the mouth at its centre. The little yellow dots on the tentacles contain stinging cells for catching prey.

Daisy coral, *Tubastrea*

Daisy coral, *Tubastrea*

Soft coral, *Eleutherobia*

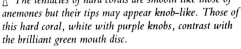

Hard coral, *Catalophyllia jardinei*

The strictest use of the term applies to hard corals, which have a white skeleton of limestone (calcium carbonate) and belong to the order Scleractinia, which comprises the 'hard', 'stony' or 'true' corals. These are the creatures that, with the hidden help of their zooxanthellae, create limestone so successfully that they are responsible for the reef's existence.

In contrast to the hard corals, the soft corals and gorgonians from the order Alcyonacea appear not to have a rigid skeleton. In fact, they have tiny, hard, elaborate crystalline structures called sclerites in their tissues. These are limestone but of a different crystal structure from the limestone of stony corals.

The fan and whip corals, gorgonians, have a second skeleton which is made of a hard but flexible material called gorgonin, and their appearance differs markedly from that of the soft corals. Sometimes occurring in yellow or orange, with the polyps appearing as tiny, fragile white flowers scattered over the surface, sea fans often live in deeper waters down the face of the reef.

Fringed polyps

Polyps of both these groups (and also a few other small groups) have eight tentacles that are fringed rather than smooth. Corals with this formation of polyps are called octocorals, as distinct from hexacorals, which have smooth tentacles in rings of six and multiples of six.

△ The tentacles of hard corals are smooth like those of anemones but their tips may appear knob-like. Those of this hard coral, white with purple knobs, contrast with the brilliant green mouth disc.

◁△ When the polyps retract, the daisy coral reveals that it is a stony coral with a hard skeleton. It does not have single-celled plants in its tissues, however, so its brilliant orange colouring does not have the brown veneer that these cells impart.

◁ Night falls and this soft coral expands its polyps, their transparent walls revealing the details of their anatomy. The gonads (sex organs) are situated just below the white cylinder of the muscular pharynx. Surrounding the mouth is a crown of eight tentacles fringed with feathery pinnules.

'Formed into mounds, plates, branches and crusts, corals seem more like rocks or plants than animals.'

CORALS 97

Soft coral, *Nephthea*

Soft coral, *Dendronephthya*

△ *Some soft corals have the astonishing habit of wandering about on the reef, extending the tissues in their bases in the direction they wish to travel; not the speediest method of transport, but nevertheless remarkable for a coral colony. Sometimes the dead trails of moving soft corals can be seen on the surface of living hard coral tables. This soft coral has settled on the tip of a colony of black coral, Cirrhipathes. Only the skeletons of black corals are actually black or dark brown. Their flesh can be yellow, orange, brown or grey.*

▷△ *The prettiest of the soft corals must surely be* Dendronephthya. *This is because no zooxanthellae mask the brilliant pink, purple and orange sclerites of these translucent colonies.*

▷ *Not all soft corals are beautiful. Some are leathery, dull coloured and lacking in symmetry. Many of these excel at occupying space. The sea squirt in the centre, black with blue tips, has so far repelled the soft coral.*

▷▷ *Like cut-glass miniatures the tiny polyps of an undescribed species of* Dendronephthya *wait patiently for their meal. The minute red sclerites of the polyps are dwarfed by the large white ones which, when the colony is contracted, present a porcupine exterior.*

Soft coral, *Sinularia*

Soft coral, *Dendronephthya*

Soft coral, *Anthelia*

△ *United only by a thin membrane, the tall and relatively large polyps of this soft coral have no body mass into which they can retract. Eager for light, they flourish in unshaded areas and prefer sheltered and shallow parts of the reef.*

Soft coral, *Heteroxenia elizabethae*

△ *Distributed mainly in the surface tissues, the minute oval sclerites of the soft coral family Xeniidae diffract the light, giving the colonies an opalescent sheen. This female colony has two types of polyps: the eggs ripen in the polyps shown and tiny ones on the surface of the colony maintain water currents through it.*

The crystal palace

'Soft corals have tiny, hard, elaborate crystal structures in their tissues which are called sclerites.'

Soft coral, *Sinularia flexibilis*

◁ *Species of this soft coral genus have spindle-shaped sclerites, large enough to be seen by the naked eye. These are packed densely into the tissue, and leave behind a kind of skeleton when the coral dies. This material, known as 'spicularite', can form a considerable part of the reef's substance in some inshore reefs where this genus is common. The species vary enormously; this one has extremely soft and flexible snake-like branches that waft to and fro with the water movement.*

'A single coral reef province stretches 2000 kilometres from Capricorn to the low tropics, with reefs of every conceivable shape and size, high islands and low, rough seas and calm.'

Organ pipe coral, *Tubipora*

▷ *The organ pipe coral has characteristic feather-like polyps that are expanded even during daylight hours. Large and closely arranged, they overlap to cover as much area as possible to catch detritus and other food particles efficiently. Pieces of the strange, bright red, internal skeleton are commonly found in many coarse coral sands. They look like small vertical tubes with cross platforms.*

Soft coral, *Sarcophyton trocheliophorum*

Soft coral, *Sarcophyton trocheliophorum*

△ *Many soft corals, in particular the large fleshy forms, are able to alter their external appearance, often with dramatic effect. They achieve this through two processes. If a colony with all of its polyps expanded is gently disturbed, it may partially retract its polyps and immediately alter its appearance. Further disturbance will result in complete retraction of the polyps and a feathery Sarcophyton may take on sharp lines. The main body of the colony, however, is still expanded with sea water, and on further irritation it will gradually deflate. Sarcophyton trocheliophorum excels at this: the fully expanded colony is capable of deflating until portions of the colony pucker into weird contortions.*

▷ *The blue coral is not a true hard coral, but a unique octocoral with no close relatives, placed in a group of its own. When cleaned of its tissues and dried, its skeleton is a beautiful blue, caused by the presence of iron salts. This colour is hidden in the live coral by its dull brown tissues. Blue coral is confined to warm waters, and on the Great Barrier Reef it is an uncommon sight on reefs south of 19 degrees latitude.*

Blue coral, *Heliopora caerulea*

Gorgonian fan coral

Fans and whips

The beautiful fans and whips belong to the Gorgonians group, which also includes the precious red coral from the Mediterranean Sea, as well as various other corals whose dense skeletons are cut and polished or carved into tiny sculptures for coral jewellery. Their solid skeleton is a complex mixture of protein, limestone and minerals. However, most reef Gorgonians do not have this hard skeleton: the protein, sometimes with and sometimes without sclerites, forms a flexible core with a colourful 'skin' surrounding it.

Fans grow at right angles to the current, and when the polyps are expanded their tentacles almost touch, forming a very efficient plankton collector. Some whips form long, unbranched stems, slender and waving in the current. Others are branched, forming bushy tangles to trap food.

Organ pipe coral, *Tubipora musica*

△ *An opportunistic black and white feather star, utilising a tall Gorgonian fan, gets itself up into the food conveying tidal flow away from the eddy currents of the reef surface. The correct generic name of this Gorgonian, often mistakenly called Muricella, is still uncertain.*

◁ *Some of the polyps in this organ pipe coral have withdrawn into their 'pipes', exposing the unmistakable red skeleton. Little pieces of this skeleton are a common sight among the white sands on coral beaches.*

'Corals are carnivores and catch food from the surrounding waters by extending tentacles armed with stinging cells.'

Gorgonian coral, *Ctenocella pectinata*

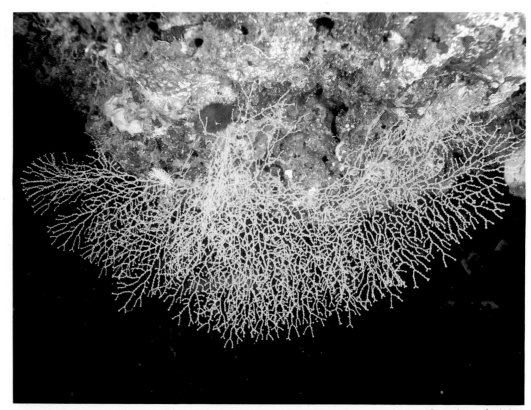

Gorgonian coral, *Acabaria*

△ This Gorgonian coral may incorporate alterations into its geometry as it grows, often with startling, bizarre or even superb results. This ability is the special prerogative of modular organisms.

▷ △ Noted for their bright colours, these Gorgonian coral colonies are commonly found under ledges or attached to cave roofs, indicating possible light avoidance behaviour of the planktonic larvae.

▷ This common Gorgonian is also one of the strongest, belonging to the Holaxian group, which have a continuous axis of hard protein ('gorgonin'). This gives the colony flexibility and strength. The branches are covered by a thick cork-like layer containing lots of zooxanthellae, and it is to the coral's advantage to grow in areas of high light intensity. It is one of the few species of Gorgonians that survives close to the water surface in areas with strong water movement.

Gorgonian coral, *Rumphella aggregata*

Expensive corals

'The Gorgonian whips and fans, and the Antipatharian black corals are beautiful alive, and some are very precious dead.'

◁ *Usually confined to depths below 20 metres, black corals may vary from dense bushy growths to long thin whips. Large, very old colonies are sought for the manufacture of black coral jewellery. A very thin veneer of tissue covers the hard black skeleton, which is adorned with fine thorns. The dense yet flexible nature of the axis, a horn-like material similar to the skeletal axis of Gorgonians, lends itself to shaping and bending and takes a high polish.*

Gorgonian coral, *Subergorgia mollis*

Black coral, *Antipathes*

△ *The largest of the reef Gorgonians spreads its net into the current. The strength of the water flow determines the size of the mesh. A floppy fan with a wide mesh taken to a place with stronger currents develops a smaller mesh to give it greater rigidity to cope with its new conditions.*

◁ *In close-up view, a portion of a branch of the black coral whip shows the unusual six-tentacled polyps expanded to capture their prey – the tiny animals which are floating by in the plankton.*

◁◁ *Most Great Barrier Reef Gorgonians are highly coloured, the colour coming from tiny sclerites in the surface tissues which overlay the brown rod of flexible material within. Shades of red and yellow predominate for the sclerites, and different mixing of sclerites allows the spectrum of colony colour to include oranges and rich browns. White, delicate lilacs, pinks and rich purples, however, are not uncommon.*

Gorgonian coral, *Paramuricea*

Black coral, *Cirrhipathes*

Fire coral, *Millepora*

△ *The fire coral delivers a burning sting as a sharp reminder of its relationship to the stinging jellyfish. The sting comes from well-loaded nematocyst cells, carried by hollow, mouthless polyps arranged in little circles around a central polyp with a mouth. Fire coral can occur as elegant lacy plates or as sheets and mounds. Divers soon get to know its tell-tale yellow colouring and to remember to wear gloves when diving in the reef front areas that it seems to favour.*

▷ △ *Coralliomorphs are a mysterious little group of anemone-like creatures very closely related to corals but having no skeletons. Their thin, rainbow-coloured discs, covered in clubbed tentacles, are quite often encountered among corals on the reef.*

▷ *Zooanthids are commonly mistaken for soft corals, but they are closer to hard corals. They are colonial, anemone-like animals in which the individual polyps are connected by creeping tubes. These creatures sometimes cover huge tracts of reef flat pavement, and they are very quick to move to parts of the reef that have been cleared of live hard corals.*

Coralliomorph bead coral

Zooanthid; pavement coral

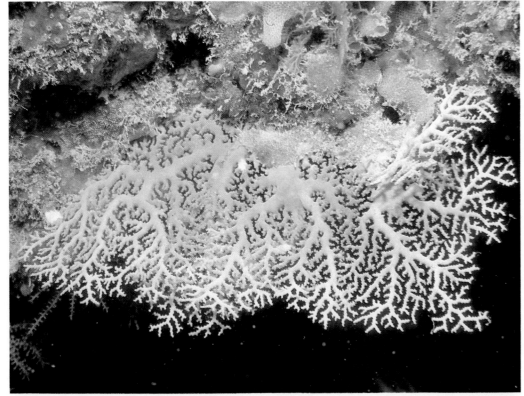

Hydroid coral, *Stylaster*

A valuable skeleton

Black coral, from the small subclass Ceriantipatharia, is more familiar in the form of a polished stone than the prickly tree-like formations or corkscrew twists of the live colonies from which it originates. This is because black corals are deep-water animals: even colonies near the bottom of a reef slope do not have the density of skeleton that is prized for cutting and polishing, since the colonies seem only to grow old enough, and hence solid enough, in deeper waters.

Complex hydrozoans

A few coral-like animals belong to the class Hydrozoa, an enormously varied group that includes such animals as the Portuguese man-of-war or bluebottle. These hydrozoan corals are only remotely related to true corals, but they have some characteristics in common with jellyfish.

Their polyps are not divided internally, like the true corals, and individual polyps can specialise in different duties – feeding, defence, reproduction. The feeding polyps have a mouth, but those specialised for defence or prey-catching make no pretence to any function except stinging; these have lots of stinging nematocyst cells, and no mouth. For this reason hydrozoans are to be avoided on the reef.

Hydrozoans live a more complex life than their coral kin. In order to reproduce sexually they must first produce little male or female jellyfish (medusae), which then produce reproductive cells.

◁ △ *Stylasterines are elegant and sometimes beautifully coloured hydrozoans with hard skeletons. They are sometimes called 'lace corals', which is confusing because this name can also be applied to the bryozoans, animals not remotely related. In* Stylaster, *and also in* Distichophora, *the dead colony skeleton retains the strong colouring.*

◁ *The distinctive fronds of this hydroid deliver a nettle-like sting. The colony contains zooxanthellae and grows much larger than other species of its group, many of which can barely be seen as tiny hairs on the reef waters.*

'Hydroids and fire coral are more closely related to jellyfish than to all the other kinds of coral kin because they produce tiny medusae as the sexual phase in their life cycle.'

Fire coral, *Aglaeophenia cupressina*

Form and pattern

The hard corals have been aptly described as the architects of the reef. The limestone of their skeletons is in the form of needle-shaped crystals that fit together in fan-shaped tufts. These sit one upon another in rods called sclerodermites – the girders that form the basis of the reef's architecture.

Girders placed in different formations give different structures. A basic polyp 'house' has outer walls (theca), floor (basal plate) and internal divisions (septa); sometimes there is also a centre pole (columella).

As the coral colony grows, new polyps are added, either from outside old polyps or from divisions within – sometimes with the formation of common walls. In some corals, when the colony grows, the polyps with their connecting tissues pull upwards and lay down new basal plates, so that a living colony has living tissue and skeleton on top, and untenanted skeleton underneath. The empty skeleton has an architecture that shows the history of the building of the colony.

Reading the plates

The depositing of basal plates is done faster or slower at different times of the year, and in different weather conditions. This gives different densities of basal plates, which show as light and dark bands in the empty skeleton. The age of these corals – like trees – can be ascertained from the calendar of events that occurred during the building process. Some corals on the reef are hundreds of years old, and they carry valuable documentation of meteorological and other events, which scientists are now learning to read.

One enormous polyp

The variety and nature of patterns in hard coral forms is illustrated clearly in mushroom corals, so-named because they resemble overturned mushrooms with the stalks plucked off. A mushroom coral is one huge coral polyp and the skeleton (called a corallite) it has constructed. The dent in its centre is the position of the polyp mouth, and the struts radiating from this are the septa. When the polyp is not withdrawn into its skeleton, dozens of tentacles cover the top of the coral. Unlike most polyps, those of the mushroom coral do not divide and repeat themselves to form colonies.

They are also an exception to another rule in that they do not cement themselves to the reef, but rather live as individuals, unattached to the surface. Very young corals are attached by a stalk that joins the polyp, not where it would on a mushroom, but on the other side, so that the mouth of the polyp is uppermost. When the polyp gets too big for the stalk, it drops off and begins its solitary existence. Mushroom corals usually prefer the quiet waters of pools or lagoons or the deeper water.

Mushroom coral, *Fungia fungites*

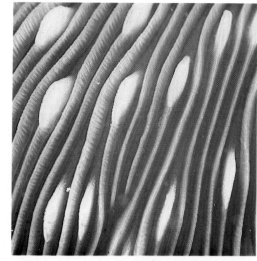

Mushroom coral, *Fungia scutaria*

Mushroom coral, *Diaseris distorta*

Mushroom coral, *Fungia klunzingeri*

▵ *This acrobatic mushroom coral has two remarkable habits which allow it to live in parts of the reef not suitable for most other corals. It is a tiny coral with great powers of movement, using its tentacles and a considerable expansion of its body size to lift itself off the mud, even to flip itself over if it finds itself wrong-side up after a disturbance. It can also break into several pieces, each piece then becoming a separate coral. The white skeletons, some of them in the process of dividing, can be seen through the distended tissues.*

▵ ▵ *A big old mushroom coral, one of several species, shows the form that gives the group its common name. They are free-living species found in quieter waters.*

▷ *The extraordinary variety of coral shapes and patterns has intrigued the curious since mankind first walked the coral shore.*

▵ *The mushroom corals have enormous skeletons in which the features can be seen easily, above and top, whereas in small polyps a microscope is needed. These skeletons show the structural differences between species.*

Separate walls

When polyps divide, the connections that remain between old and new contain an extension of the stomach cavity, so that nutrients can be passed from one polyp to the next. Even when polyps are well separated by an expanse of skeleton, this connection remains. Many different hard corals have a 'separate but connected' structure. Most of these grow as mounds, but some are sheets, plates or branches. Such corals come from different families and they do not have a uniting common name. The polyps can be very large and easily seen, or so tiny that they cannot be seen without a microscope.

Mushroom coral, *Heliofungia actiniformis*

Acanthastrea echinata

Galaxea astreata

Oxypora lacera

Diploastrea heliopora

Turbinaria peltata

Echinopora lamellosa

Favites chinensis

Brain coral, *Leptoria phrygia*

Turbinaria frondens

Pectinia paeonia

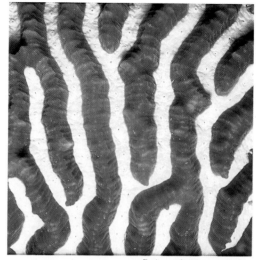

Brain coral, *Platygyra daedalea*

Pachyseris speciosa

Pavona minuta

'Stony cups, plates, brains and branches with tapers, ridges, struts and beams, are different architectural responses to stress from wave and current, need for light for the zooxanthellae plant food factories, and direct competition with neighbours for space.'

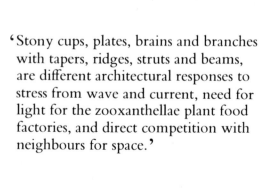

Pectinia lactuca

Pavona decussata

The mighty brains

The fitting common name 'brain coral' belongs to several different species from two families whose colonies look much like the human brain. Long lines are formed by dividing polyps that form walls along their sides but not between their mouths. These colonies are formed in the shape of mounds; they have a thin veneer of living coral over empty skeleton, and all contain internal calendars in the form of light and dark bands.

Some brain corals can be up to two metres in diameter, and have patterns of maze-like intricacy.

Doing their own thing

The coral's modular lifestyle places few limits on the structure of colonies. Some species have drafted blueprints that are unique and sometimes a little bizarre. In these it is sometimes difficult to see where

Brain coral, *Symphyllia radians*

one polyp ends and another begins: walls are eliminated or the centre pole exaggerated; some patterns are streamlined, and some are elaborate.

The branching strategy

In almost every hard coral family there are some branching forms. Branching gives more access to space and allows all the polyps good exposure to the water currents carrying their food. Branching is achieved in various ways, and it has been perfected by corals of the genus *Acropora*. These are the only hard corals known to have two different kinds of polyps (though one kind can change into the other). The first kind – the axial polyp – forms the axis of the branch, and it grows longer and longer, without bothering to pull itself up and lay down basal plates. As it grows, it buds off radial polyps. The axial polyp is a cylinder, but the radials have a distinctive wall structure.

Pocillopora eydouxi

Staghorn coral, *Acropora gemmifera*

Acrhelia horrescens

Needle coral, *Seriatopora hystrix*

Staghorn coral, *Acropora nobilis*

'Branching gives more access to space and allows all the polyps good exposure to the water currents carrying their food. It has been perfected by corals of the genus *Acropora*.'

Staghorn coral, *Acropora tenuis*

◁ *Branching is a common coral form, but there are many variations of the branching habit, from small shrubs with needle-like branches (some* Seriatopora *species) to large thickets two metres high and 50 metres long, with basal branches as thick as a human leg. Growth of branches may be rapid – often 50 to 100 millimetres or more per year. This allows avoidance of competitors for sunlight, or growing clear of a silty lagoon floor. Although branches may break off in violent storms, they often re-grow from the pieces and spread the colony.*

Euphyllia divisa

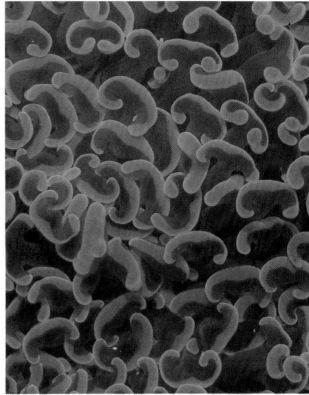

Euphyllia anchora

In their true colours

Because hard corals are nocturnal in their habits, the daytime observer sees little more of them than a skeleton with a fine overlay of tissue colour. A few, however, extend their polyps, or at least some part of their surface tissues, during the day, and these offer a different view of hard coral form. While most of the clues to relationships among corals are built into their skeletons (a feature that has led to an excellent fossil record), idiosyncrasies of species or genus are apparent in the tissue; however, these are lost when the coral dies.

△ *The skeletons of these two species of* Euphyllia *are almost identical but their special tentacle shapes separate them immediately. The tentacles of* Euphyllia divisa, *above left, have rounded caps and little branchlets while those of* E. anchora, *above, end in scroll-like expansions.*

◁ *In the daytime, this coral has bubbles of expanded tissue covering a beautifully sculpted skeleton. The tentacles are only expanded during the night, projecting out among the bubbles.*

◁◁ *All the polyps of this coral remain continuously extended and these can be many millimetres long. The same phenomenon is seen in its relative,* Alveopora, *which has six tentacles rather than the twelve which are found in* Goniopora.

Hard coral, *Goniopora*

Bubble coral, *Plerogyra sinuosa*

Sexual reproduction

For a few nights every year, the Great Barrier Reef puts on a spectacular display when corals of many different species, both soft and hard, participate in synchronised mass spawning. Those who have witnessed this spawning describe it as being 'like a fireworks display' or 'an upside-down snowstorm'.

During the months before the event, the gonads (sex organs) of the individual polyps ripen in readiness. The eggs begin their development first, at least six months ahead of time. The testes, with their maturing sperm, usually take less time to ripen. This process is called 'gametogenesis'.

As the sea water warms rapidly in spring, the sex cells also develop rapidly. Eggs become coloured: pink, red or orange, sometimes even purple, blue or green. The sperm in the testes change from simple tadpole-like forms to elegantly shaped heads with long, beating tails. In some corals, the sexes are separate, every polyp in a colony being female or male. More often, the polyps contain both male and female gonads; a condition known as 'hermaphrodite', from the names of the Greek god, Hermes, and the goddess Aphrodite.

On cue with the moon

Once gametogenesis is complete, the corals have only to wait for their cues to spawn. The major cue is provided by the moon. Spawning seems to begin one or two nights after a full moon in late spring or early summer, but activity is greatest on the fourth, fifth or sixth night.

After dusk on the chosen night, the coral colonies ready themselves for spawning. The eggs and/or sperm are gathered beneath the mouths of the polyps. Soon after, the mass is expelled, and the waters above the reef begin to fill with the tiny reproductive cells.

The significance of this occurrence has yet to be explained. For many members of one species to spawn at once ensures a very high rate of cross-fertilisation. Because a coral is fixed and cannot go hunting for a mate, it must cast its seed at the most appropriate time for the maximum production of offspring. However, to do so at a time when the seeds of so many other corals are abroad would seem to involve a great deal of extraordinary confusion.

Synchrony of timing suggests a strong selective advantage, but what can this advantage be? By 'swamping' predators with an over-abundance of food for a short time, a high level of survival is assured. Perhaps the arrival of a night when tidal amplitude is lowest and various other unknown factors are at their most suitable, overwhelms the consideration of bumping into the wrong mate's offspring. Some corals spawn a different way: their eggs are fertilised while still in the polyp, and the polyps brood the developing larvae (called planulae). They are released over long periods.

Staghorn coral, *Acropora*

Staghorn coral, *Acropora formosa*

◁ *Festooned with pink baubles, the common staghorn coral awaits the right moment for its annual spawning. Each bauble is actually a bundle of about eight pink eggs, with the testes wrapped among them. Only some young polyps around the growing tip have not produced an egg-sperm bundle.*

◁ ▽ *In the days before the spawning night, the gonads (sex organs) of the polyps are fully developed and waiting for their cue to spawn. This staghorn coral has been broken open to reveal the long cream testes attached at their tops to the mesenteries. Behind them can be seen a number of bright pink, mature eggs arranged singly along other mesenteries.*

▽ *The egg-sperm bundle held within the open mouth of* Goniastrea palauwensis *is suddenly released, and it will float quickly to the surface. The exact moment of release is captured in the two photographs below.*

Goniastrea palauwensis

Goniastrea palauwensis

Galaxea fascicularis

Galaxea fascicularis

△ Before they spawn, the corals can be seen 'setting': all the polyps show a brightly coloured distension beneath the mouth disc. About fifteen minutes after this stage the egg-sperm bundles are pushed through the polyp mouths. Then the moment of release comes. Sometimes an entire colony will release within seconds, sometimes patches of the colony go in bursts. Frequently, all polyps release within about fifteen minutes.

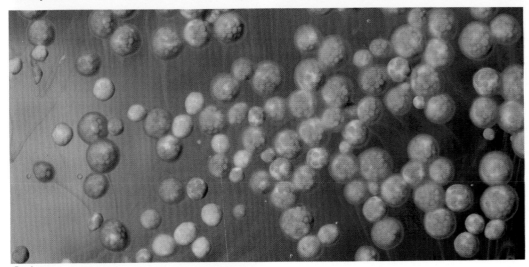

Coral eggs

◁ The egg-sperm bundles are large enough to be seen in the light of a torch directed at the water surface. At the peak of spawning the sea surface is dense with these brightly coloured little balls. Soon after reaching the surface, the bundle breaks up and the melee begins. Sperm streams out over the water, thousands from each bundle. Propelled by their long tails they travel, hopefully to collide with an egg of their own species, which they will fertilise. The fertilised egg will develop into a tiny swimming larva which will drift in the plankton for a few days before descending into the water column.

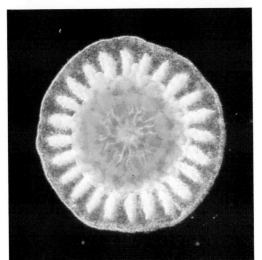

Coral planulae

◁ A little polyp, about ten days old and two millimetres wide, already shows its affinity with the huge corals of the reef. Through its transparent tissues the beginnings of the white limestone skeleton can be seen. The fertilised coral larvae are called planulae, and mature corals are known to produce thousands of them at a time. When released by the parent, they swim upwards towards the sunlight. Then, before attaching themselves, they alter their behaviour and swim away from the light towards the sea bed. There they settle and build new colonies. Some settle near their parent colonies, but others are capable of floating for months in the surface waters. These are of great importance in distributing the species over a very wide area; the mortality rate during this early stage of the coral's life is extremely high.

'*Acropora* polyps usually have four strings of eggs and two or four testes, each on a separate mesentery. All of these are gathered to make the egg-sperm bundle that will be released later.'

Montastrea

△ *In this coral, spawning is underway. The polyps at the bottom right are empty; in the centre the round egg-sperm bundles have been ejected and are rising; and at left they are still held in the polyp.*

▷ *Not all corals have male and female gonads together in the one polyp. In the mushroom corals, each individual is either male or female. This male mushroom coral is releasing a cloud of white sperm, which will have to find the eggs of a nearby female.*

▷▷ *Most egg-sperm bundles are buoyant, but this is not the case for* Goniastrea favulus, *where the sperm travel alone upwards as a white cloud. The eggs are sticky and negatively buoyant, falling to remain around the base of the colony, seemingly making it difficult for the two to get together.*

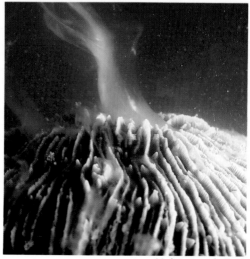

Mushroom coral, *Fungia*

Goniastrea favulus

Favites halicora

Mass spawning

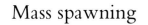

'As the reef waters warm in the spring the coral sex cells develop rapidly. Eggs become coloured: pink, red or orange, sometimes even purple, blue or green.'

◁ *When there are too many eggs and testes for a single bundle, several bundles may be released. This is the case with* Favites halicora, *where eggs and testes can be seen in each of the little packages coming out of the polyp mouths. Many more await release, and appear as pink shading underneath the mouth discs.*

◁ ▽ *Many soft corals spawn at the same time as the hard corals. This unidentified species has released individual eggs, which are clinging to the surface of the green polyps.*

▽ *The separate mouths of the joined polyps of a brain coral still release their separate egg-sperm bundles. The tentacles of this brain coral have retracted because of artificial lighting.*

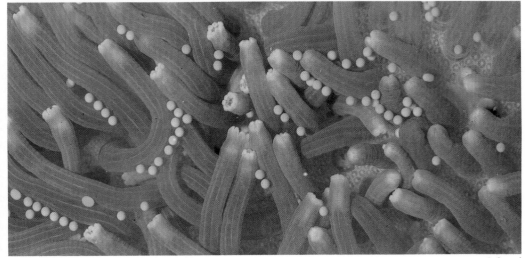

Soft coral

Brain coral, *Platygyra sinensis*

Staghorn coral, *Acropora florida*

Staghorn coral, *Acropora listeri*

△ *Closely related animals or plants usually reproduce at different times of the year and thus avoid the possibility of hybridization. However, many species of staghorn coral spawn on the same night of the year releasing egg-sperm bundles. The evolutionary pressures to do such a paradoxical thing must be very powerful.*

'Scientists are puzzled about how a coral sperm manages to find the right mate. Perhaps the answer lies in the chemical make-up of the eggs.'

Staghorn coral, *Acropora secale*

New life for old

The reef has seasons of change and constancy, and these can be seen in the reproductive patterns of corals and the settling patterns of their larvae. Other changes are less regular. Rough weather can bring big changes, causing the branches of tree-like corals to snap and large coral tables to tumble down the reef slope, destroying and taking with them an avalanche of other corals.

Such movement will cause the death of some corals that cannot withstand the effects of the change of position. For others, the movement is an opportunity for asexual reproduction by breaking into many parts. For many reef organisms, shifting coral means a piece of cleared space, and those who are in the right place at the right time then compete for its occupancy.

The nature and scale of possible changes are almost limitless. A population explosion of the crown-of-thorns starfish, *Acanthaster planci*, for example, may leave thousands of corals dead, and much clear space. One fast-growing coral plate may expand and block out the space in the light for the slower growing species below it. Perhaps such changes benefit corals, whose primary aim in life seems to be to find, maintain and if possible expand upon, a suitable place in which to live.

◁ *Ripe coral eggs are usually brightly coloured in shades of pink or red, but this species spawns bundles of brilliant blue eggs.*

◁ ▽ *This big plate of table coral was over a metre across and about ten years old when it snapped from its stalk and fell 12 metres from the reef top to a bed of staghorn coral on the sandy reef floor. It did not survive the fall, and its dead tissues sloughed away, leaving a clean limestone surface full of nooks and crannies – just the spot for tiny larvae and algae spores to settle. Little yearling corals, mostly about 15 months old, can be seen on its surface. The staghorn corals that broke its fall are now beginning to grow up around it.*

◁ *Twenty months after the first picture, the corals, now three years old, have grown large enough to make their presence obvious. Many have not survived, being eaten in their first, second or third year by grazing animals, being overgrown by other young corals or expanding organisms, or simply suffering the consequences of having settled in the wrong place. They now face another growing problem: competition for space from the surrounding staghorn corals that are thriving and winning back the space that was previously theirs.*

Favia favus

Table coral, *Acropora cytherea*

Table coral, *Acropora cytherea*

Whip coral, *Junceella fragilis*

△ *Some of the most novel methods of asexual reproduction are shown by Gorgonians and soft corals. This whip coral is usually found in clumps – a good clue for asexual reproduction. As the whips grow, small pieces are pinched off at their tops. This is done by degeneration of the tissues along a small portion of the whip, until only the central horny rod remains. This is broken by the slightest water movement, and the bud drops to the reef floor, where it cements itself before commencing growth into a new whip. Some buds land upside down, and have to change their direction of growth, leaving a record on the base of the whip of their asexual origin.*

'The most successful corals in seemingly inhospitable places are those which can produce new colonies by asexual means, cloning from one originally settled larva.'

Hard coral, *Acropora*

Soft coral, *Efflatounaria*

△ *Coral larvae require a hard surface on which to settle. Such sites abound on the solid reef, but on the sandy reef floor they are restricted to bits and pieces of dead coral and shells. Lots of staghorn and bottle-brush forms of the hard coral genus* Acropora *settle these areas. As the colonies grow, parts of them become buried in the sand and the polyps die. Those parts become weakened by the action of various boring animals, but the parts beyond them are still living. The final outcome is a mass of many colonies that may cover several square metres of reef floor.*

◁ *Soft corals very commonly employ asexual reproduction. This soft coral produces a long stolon like a strawberry runner, which grows out and away from the colony. Once this finds an agreeable piece of surface it stops extending, attaches itself, and proceeds to grow a new daughter colony. This process can be repeated many times and little groups of parent and offspring like this are a common sight on some areas of the reef.*

Asexual reproduction

Corals have another recourse, apart from spawning, to ensure the continued survival of their own types. Because they are modular organisms, with polyps replicated many times over, some corals break up in various ways so that one colony creates more colonies, without the complicated process of producing juveniles.

There are many beneficial consequences of such behaviour: more colonies mean more chances that the organism will survive; asexual reproduction can take place at any time of the year; and the offspring, sometimes known as 'daughter colonies', do not have to face the vicissitudes of planktonic life in a larval stage.

Other benefits are less obvious: in places that are too silty or too crowded for the settlement of tiny larvae, such problems can be avoided by producing offspring that are already adult.

The modes of asexual reproduction vary from relatively unsophisticated means, such as pieces snapping off in storms, to ingenious devices such as the colony pinching off small portions or sending out runners. One of the features of this kind of reproduction is that the offspring stay close to the parent colony, so that a group of similar colonies – a clone – results.

Feeding

Corals are carnivores and catch food from the surrounding waters by extending tentacles armed with stinging nematocyst cells. Microscopic floating animals – zooplankton – trigger the firing of these barbed darts, which paralyse and hold them. The tentacles then pass the morsel to the mouth of the polyp with a graceful bending motion. The prey is broken down in the polyp stomach and becomes part of the nutrition for the whole colony.

Black coral, *Cirrhipathes*

Soft coral, *Sarcophyton*

Most hard corals feed in this way at night, while many other coral kin feed at any time, night or day. They take a variety of small animals: shrimps and their relatives; eggs and larval stages of many reef invertebrates; even, in the case of some large polyps, tiny reef fishes. Some corals also ensnare bacteria and zooplankton in nets of mucus, a slimy substance manufactured by the polyps. Organic materials dissolved in sea water passing through the polyps also supply some of the needs of the polyp tissues. When a soft coral feeds, this process can sometimes be seen in many polyps at once, with a half dozen plankton being caught and moved into the mouth. Some of the common soft corals of the family Xeniidae open and close their large polyps, which look like tiny grasping hands. However, as these animals rely almost entirely on their symbiotic zooanthellae for nourishment and do not feed on plankton, the reason for this pulsating is still a mystery.

△ *This young soft coral feeds during the day with polyps expanded and tentacles unfolded to ensnare the minute zooplankton floating past in the water currents.*

◁ △ *The coiled spring of the black coral waits for planktonic organisms to drift into the clutches of its yellow polyps. Water turbulence around the coil may cause the plankton to linger momentarily, giving the coral a feeding advantage over its straighter relatives.*

◁ *Hard corals feed at night with tentacles expanded, displaying the little clumps of concentrated stinging cells that will immobilise prey.*

Hard coral, *Trachyphyllia geoffroyi*

Association and conflict

The interaction between corals and other organisms is many and varied. Mobile reef animals seek shelter and food within and around the boundaries of a coral colony. However, since corals are modular organisms with many polyps in each colony, interference with parts of the colony does not represent the calamity it would to unitary organisms. Individual polyps, or even groups of polyps, can be eaten, damaged or nudged aside without destroying the rest of the colony. Few predators are large enough to eat entire colonies.

Corals have various ways of dealing with the intrusion of other colonial animals, including other corals, sometimes drawing up 'battle lines' with their neighbours, sometimes growing up or away in another direction.

For mutual benefit

In many cases the nutrition that corals obtain by feeding is sufficient for their existence. It is supplemented, however, through a remarkable association with their inhabiting zooxanthellae, which in effect creates super-corals from what would otherwise be insignificant, small animals. The relationship between the two is complex and not yet fully understood. Each seems to complement the nutritional needs of the other, and the zooxanthellae significantly enhance the coral's ability to build skeletons. The mutual benefits to coral and algae make this special association a symbiosis, and the reef-builder that results from the association is called a hermatype.

Zooxanthellae are algal cells of a species *Gymnodinium microadriaticum*, which is also able to exist independently in the sea water. In their free-living state these cells are moved by two long fine tails called flagellae, but those living in the coral have no flagellae. They live inside cells in the coral tissue, where they are able to take in carbon dioxide (a byproduct produced as the cell uses oxygen). This is used in photosynthesis: the process by which plants absorb the energy of sunlight and manufacture materials needed for growth and continued existence. Some of these materials are passed to the coral, and other products from the coral are also used by the algae.

Solar cells

Many of the habits of corals are explained by the presence of zooxanthellae. Since they are little solar cells, requiring exposure to sunlight for their operation, they only perform during the day and they can only function in shallow regions where sunlight penetrates. Their hosts, the reef-building corals, thus restrict themselves to shallow, well-lit waters – living coral reefs are therefore only a shallow-water phenomenon. Another consequence is seen in the shape of coral colonies. Many corals that form various shapes in shallow water are

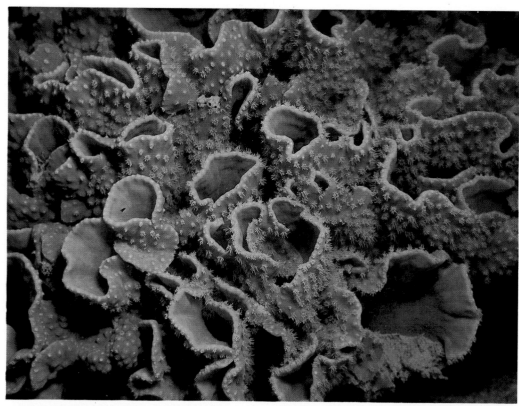

Hard coral, *Turbinaria mesenterina*

▽ *When the tissues of a reef-building coral are magnified, thousands of the little algal cells, zooxanthellae, can be seen. These are the non-motile or encysted stages of certain species of algae. These tiny plants obtain shelter from their life in the coral cells. In return they act as a solar powerhouse for the coral and endow it with the special ability to play a part in the construction of a coral reef. However, the proportion of a coral's nutritive requirements provided by zooxanthellae is not known.*

△ *The polyps of this hard coral are arranged on the upper surface of thin plates. It abounds on muddy inshore reefs where light cannot penetrate far through the murky water; a difference of about a metre in depth makes a striking difference to the amount of light energy reaching the coral surface. By its growth form this coral is able to position zooxanthellae to catch the sun's rays. Where there is an unlimited supply of sunlight, the plates are folded into extravagant patterns that place the polyps and their tissue connections in variously shaded positions.*

▷ *In deeper water, where available light is at a premium, colonies of this hard coral grow as spreading plates, with the polyps and tissues fully exposed to take every possible advantage of the waning sunlight. The difference in colony shapes is so striking that they appear to be two different species. However, a convoluted colony, transferred to deeper water, changes its style of growth in an attempt to flatten out into a plate. This is a slow process because the coral cannot alter skeleton that was existing before the move.*

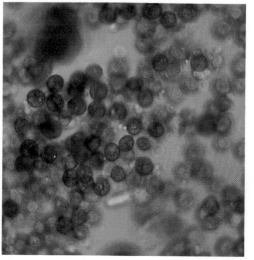

Zooxanthellae

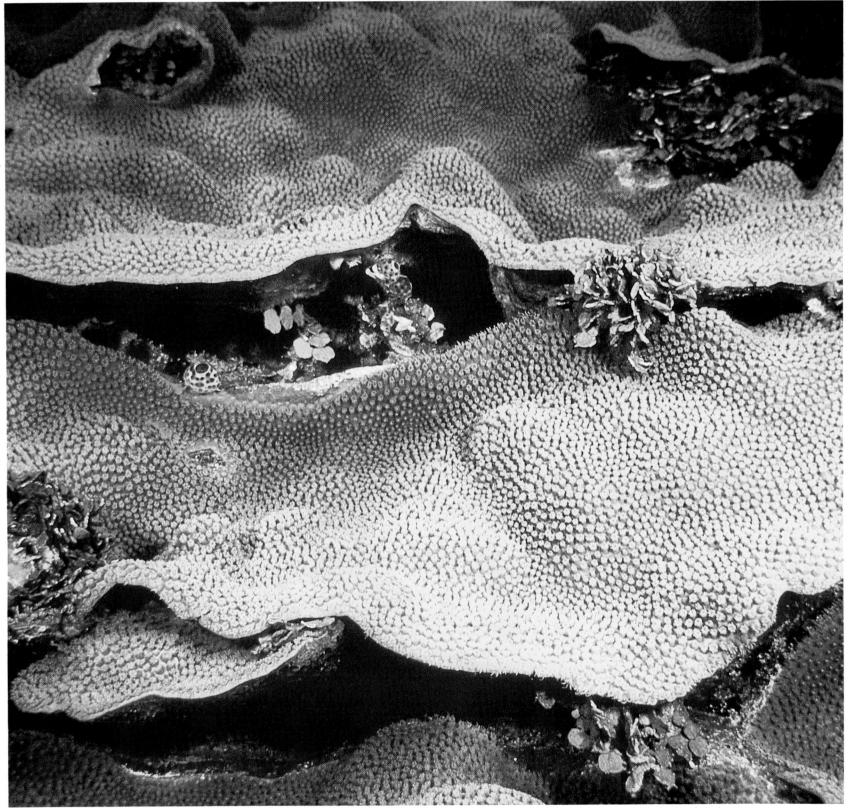

Hard coral, *Turbinaria mesenterina*

Hard coral, *Porites*

Button coral, *Heteropsammia cochlea*

flattened out when they occur in deeper water, demonstrating the importance of light-capturing in the life of a reef-building coral.

A coral resident

Heteropsammia cochlea is a little coral with a unique life style. It has only one or two polyps and lives unattached on the sandy inner-reef floor. Every specimen of this coral has a sipunculid or peanut worm, *Aspidosiphon corallicola*, inhabiting its skeleton. The foraging activities of the peanut worm keep the coral from becoming buried in the reef sediments and stabilise it in an upright position. The coral invariably occurs in association with the worm, which seems to be fundamental to its existence on the soft, unstable sea floor.

The peanut worm settles from a floating, planktonic existence to become a bottom dweller by inhabiting a tiny snail shell. As it grows it sheds smaller shells for larger ones. About this time the larva of *Heteropsammia cochlea* is metamorphosing into an adult coral by attaching itself to the shell inhabited by the worm. The peanut worm now has no need to seek further accommodation, which is often a problem for larger worms. Instead, it modifies the developing coral skeleton to maintain an entrance hole and a series of small holes around the coral's periphery. The entrance allows the worm to extend from the skeleton for foraging and for moving its coral house along. The small holes

Needle coral, *Stylophora pistillata*

△ This solitary little coral lives on the sandy inter-reef floor with a tenant peanut worm. The tenant's dimple-like 'windows' (for the passage of water currents) are along the side of the coral, which is digesting a yellow fish, seen through the swollen transparent mouth disc.

△ ◁ Corals can play host to a large number of tenants, without appearing to suffer from their presence. This mound of small-polyped hard coral is inhabited by tubes of the Christmas-tree worm, Spirobranchus giganteus, which occurs in many colours and will withdraw its feathery feeding appendages at the slightest disturbance.

◁ Coral skeletons are often modified to grow around small animals such as crabs, shrimps and barnacles. This needle coral forms elegant little shell-shaped cysts around its guests, the crabs Hapalocarienus marsupialis.

'The hard corals have been aptly described as the architects of the reef. The limestone of their skeletons is in the form of needle-shaped crystals that fit together in fan-shaped tufts.'

are used for drawing in water for respiration and expelling it again.

This coral can occur in huge populations, and each coral is either male or female. After it settles it becomes dependent on the peanut worm; the worm, however, can exist without the coral.

Being eaten

Few animals kill a whole coral colony when they feed on it. Exceptions are the crown-of-thorns starfish and the buffalo fish, avid predators. The crown-of-thorns starfish can eventually kill even large coral plates as a single specimen sometimes returns to the same colony nightly until the entire plate is eaten; during population explosions, many starfish may feed on one colony. Other animals, particularly some small gastropod molluscs, feed on coral tissues and can damage large areas of them when feeding in big groups.

Crown-of-thorns starfish, *Acanthaster planci*

Buffalo fish, *Bolbometaphon muricatuin*

△ *Buffalo fish bite large chunks from corals, leaving characteristic wounds. Both tissue and skeleton are taken, but sometimes part of the colony survives the attack. The wounds are often colonised by algae that remain as patches on the surface of the coral.*

◁ △ *The crown-of-thorns starfish is a persistent coral predator. When present in large numbers, this species kills whole colonies by digesting the coral tissue and leaving a clean skeleton.*

◁ *When a coral encounters another coral or colonial organism as it grows, a number of alternative strategies are available to it. If it is a branching coral it may grow up and over or away from its neighbour. If it is an encrusting coral, such as the purple* Montipora *and grey* Hydnophora, *it may grow over its neighbours.*

Encrusting corals, *Montipora and Hydnophora*

'On the reef there are no hard and fast rules about which coral should appear where and what blendings of species may occur.'

▷ *Various mobile animals, like this sea slug,* Chelidonura inornata, *may often be found crawling over living coral colonies.*

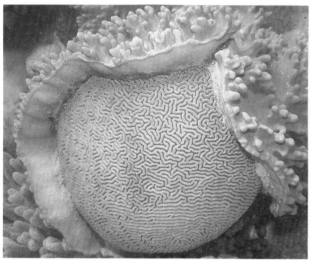

Hard coral, *Leptoria phrygia*; soft coral, *Sinularia densa*

Δ *For many hard corals, confrontation with neighbours involves the formation of a no-man's-land by the action of long sweeping tentacles or extended stomach filaments, which kill and sometimes devour coral tissue. Many soft corals have the added advantage of toxic chemical defences. The outcome of such encounters depends on the relative skills of the contenders. This hard coral appears to be succumbing to the invasion of a soft coral.*

Hard coral, *Diploastrea heliopora*

Visual dominants

Every coral reef has unique features, but some patterns are repeated in similar circumstances. There are plateaux – the reef flats – where the top of the reef is exposed to full sunlight, where temperatures may fluctuate greatly, and where the watery environment may come and go with the flow of the tide. Sometimes the reef encloses a lagoon – a protected pool with sandy bottom and scattered patches of coral. At the edge of this flat the waves break, especially on the 'weather side' where the reef faces the prevailing winds. From the reef top, the slope descends to the sea floor: sometimes gently, sometimes as a steep cliff face. Strong currents may run along this face, and deep channels may intercept it at regular intervals. The effects of wind and sea play a part in the sculpturing of the reef, thereby influencing the suitability of areas for the settlement of coral larvae or for the survival of different shapes and types of colonies. Sometimes the effects of wind and sea even determine the form taken by modular colonies as they grow.

The corals inhabiting the reef change from place to place, influenced by many things: some obvious, some understood only after years of research, most still unknown and mysterious. Differences in life cycles, the ability to tolerate environmental conditions, the practicality of shapes for different physical situations and the plasticity employed in shaping a colony to suit the location all play a part. So, too, do influences beyond the control of the corals – the chance occurrence of a 'good' or 'bad' year for reproduction and settlement; the unexpected devastation of a cyclone, or the dilution of reef waters by flooding. Sweeping changes and small influences, working locally on a single portion of the reef, all play a part in making the completion of its pattern a game of chance as well as strategy.

Exposed coral head

Exposed corals

Ridge coral, *Acropora palifera*

△ *Any reef, no matter how rich and luxuriant its overall coral composition, has places where few corals grow. Other parts of the reef flat, where water flows freely, may support coral cover so rich that a reef walker might be well advised to avoid them. During some of the very low spring tides, these corals are exposed to the air for some hours, above and left. While they will usually be able to tolerate this, any added difficulty, such as a heavy rain squall or unusually hot or cold conditions, can cause massive local death to exposed corals.*

◁ *Reef fronts exposed to the influences of prevailing winds and full ocean swells support a coral community which resists these forces with sturdy, stunted growths. This ridge of staghorn coral has blunt blades aligned perpendicularly to the reef edge, despite the fact that it can occur with long branches on more sheltered parts of a reef.*

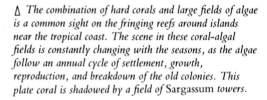

Plate coral, *Montipora foliosa*

Coral microatoll, *Porites*

△ The combination of hard corals and large fields of algae is a common sight on the fringing reefs around islands near the tropical coast. The scene in these coral–algal fields is constantly changing with the seasons, as the algae follow an annual cycle of settlement, growth, reproduction, and breakdown of the old colonies. This plate coral is shadowed by a field of Sargassum towers.

▷ △ Corals growing on the reef flat encounter a barrier – the water surface at mid-tide level – above which coral tissue simply cannot survive. The presence of this barrier has led to a fascinating form of coral growth in which the colony continues to expand around its radius, but is dead on top. As the colony gets older, the dead patch may become hollowed out, and other corals may settle in the shallow lagoon so formed. These formations resemble miniature coral atolls and they are referred to as 'microatolls'. Many coral species can grow this way and on some parts of a reef flat there are hundreds of microatolls to be found.

▷ This mound-like outline is achieved by branching colonies. Some parts of reefs, whether due to accidents of history or to special characteristics of the environment, support a coral assemblage that is predominantly marked by one shape. As far as the eye can see, this patch of sandy reef lagoon is dominated by colonies of a single species of Porites coral.

Coral mounds, *Porites cylindrica*

Branching coral, *Porites cylindrica*

Suiting the location

'Some parts of reefs, whether due to accidents of history or special environmental characteristics, support a coral assemblage where one shape of coral colony predominates markedly.'

Reef slope, Myrmidon Reef

△ *Some corals have great plasticity of form, being able to vary the colony shape from mounds to sheets or from branches to plates. Something has caused considerable death within this acid-yellow colony of branching coral, exposing the white skeleton of the dead portions. The remaining live patches of the colony have spread out as plates around their bases.*

◁ *Hard and soft corals living on the reef slope must cling to the reef surface and at the same time must spread out their surfaces to catch the light. This steep slope supports a large variety of species.*

The protean staghorns

Acropora, the staghorn coral, has more species, grows faster, and occupies more reef than any other coral. The most beautiful reef scenes are set against a backdrop of a luxuriant covering of *Acropora*.

Its shapes range far wider than the general name implies: table, plate, bottle-brush and shrub are among them. Some individual species cover the whole range, varying their colony shapes to suit their particular location. Others are rigidly confined to a single shape. *Acropora* has been described as 'the protean coral genus' – an allusion to Proteus, the god fabled for his habit of changing his form to confuse and elude.

Acropora species seem to thrive in areas with plenty of water movement and sunshine. It is quick to colonise places where corals have been damaged, and many of its species regenerate from broken fragments. It appears to be a very hardy coral, but paradoxically it is very difficult to keep most species alive for more than a few days in aquaria. □

▷ *Staghorn coral growing in two of its starkly contrasting forms: below,* Acropora nobilis, *in the form that gives the coral its common name; above, a magnificent table of* A. cytherea. *The tables begin as small compact bushes, the branches growing first upwards to form the stem, and later outwards and upwards so that an intermediate 'vase' shape is formed. The top of the table bears little branchlets on which the polyps are densely packed.*

▷ *Tables or plates of staghorn coral thrive and grow in abundance on the very shoulder of a reef. Paradoxically, as they grow, their vulnerability increases. Strong waves whipped up by high winds can snap them from their stalks, and they go crashing to the reef floor below, sometimes taking an avalanche of other corals with them. The reef shows the scars of such events in patchy patterns of distribution of large and small plates.*

'A branch of *Acropora* coral has a large, cylindrical polyp as its axis, and other polyps are budded from around the tip of this as it grows.'

Staghorn coral, *Acropora nobilis, A. cytherea*

Staghorn coral, *Acropora*

Staghorn coral, *Acropora listeri*

◁ One colony or many? This huge old colony shows the versatility of Acropora growth. Portions of the colony resembling sturdy hands die off around their bases, so the colony effectively has many separated parts. This growth form is seen in places with strong currents, such as channels between outer reefs, where many species of staghorn coral may take the same shape.

◁ ▽ This coral has close relatives in the Montipora genus, which mainly occurs as thin plates. Rarely is a reef seen which does not include one or other of these genera.

▽ Staghorn coral is a familiar sight to reef walkers who venture to the reef's edge, where the genus reigns supreme. Low tables, bushes and shrubs of staghorn thrive in the well-aerated waters provided by the breaking of waves on the reef.

Bottlebrush coral, *Acropora echinata*

Staghorn coral, *Acropora*

Diverse and beautiful

'One of the most remarkable features of *Acropora* corals is the fact that so many species occur together. In the animal world "close relatives" generally spells competition for food resources.'

▷ *Few divers are treated to the sight of low, dense* Acropora *cover, which is characteristic of high current banks on outer reefs.*

▽ *The intricate branching patterns of staghorn corals make them excellent shelters for tiny fishes, which feed in and around the colonies, retreating into the branches when danger approaches. Towards dusk, staghorn patches become clouded by these fishes as they come out to feed in their thousands.*

Staghorn coral, *Acropora yongei*

Staghorn coral, *Acropora monticulosa*, *A. listeri* and *A. gemmifera*

Staghorn coral, *Acropora horrida* and *A. lovelli*

Christmas coral, *Acropora elseyi*

Staghorn coral, *Acropora grandis*

Staghorn coral, *Acropora*

△ Some of the prettiest reef scenes are those completely dominated by staghorn corals. Their beauty and variety make these 'coral garden' sites favourites with divers.

◁ △ It is an axiom of animal ecology that two species with exactly the same resource requirements cannot co-exist; however, the requirements of many Acropora appear to be very similar, and most species reproduce at the same time. The co-existence of so many species is a fascinating puzzle.

◁ △ Bottlebrush Acropora abound in the more protected waters of the reef, where they may occupy huge tracts of sandy reef floor. This large colony of Christmas coral shows the typical elegant form that makes it a favourite of the coral curio trade.

◁ Some reef sites support dense groupings of colonies of many Acropora species, but in other places single majestic colonies grow in splendid isolation.

Giant clams

Part three: life above and among corals

Strange are the stories told about the animals and plants that live in the different kinds of habitats on the Great Barrier Reef and its wild islands, seemingly timeless, yet constantly changing. Strange indeed – and difficult to believe – but very real. Many hundreds of new species are yet to be described, and for scientists or the casual observer there is still much to learn.

A lot of the activity in the water above the reef is invisible, except to the sharp-eyed observer. One small floating animal builds a large, gossamer fishing net to trap fine plankton, and drifts with its net in the tropical waters. Boring sponges chemically digest the limestone skeleton of corals during the search for living space, using a mechanism resembling an ice-cream scoop. As the sponges bore they weaken the coral skeleton, which then crumbles during storms.

Sponges and ascidians constantly filter vast quantities of water through their tissues. A small ascidian, only 30 millimetres long, can filter water at the rate of approximately one litre an hour.

The lowly worm is abundant on the reef. Who would guess that one coral head, 450 millimetres across, would contain over 1200 individual small burrowing worms of over 100 different species. The peanut worm, so-called because of its shape, lives in the skeleton of a little coral with only one or two polyps, and carries it around on its foraging expeditions. This keeps the coral from becoming buried in reef sediments and keeps it upright. Many creatures on the reef live in similarly supportive relationships.

Down in the coral city are thousands of crustaceans – the insects of the sea. One strange little crustacean finds a salp with a firm, gelatinous home, about 10 to 20 millimetres long, and lives on the salp until it has eaten it away; the crustacean is left with a useful, barrel-shaped house, open at each end.

In the David and Goliath category is a very small shrimp that will attack the crown-of-thorns starfish, a hundred times its size, tearing into one after the other of its soft tube feet and often forcing the giant to leave the coral it was about to consume.

On land, too, much is not as it seems. The coral cays, with their lovely *Pisonia* trees and silver *Argusia* shrubs, are not inhabited by a stable set of animals and plants. Many of the smaller species are changing constantly; a different set of insects and spiders may be present, or a new herb may cover the sparse soil, from year to year. A delicate balance exists between a constant stream of immigrants and a continuous series of extinctions, as animals and plants fail to build stable populations on a small and often harsh terrain. Perennial visitors are the turtles; as many as 10 000 may leave the sea to lay eggs at the same time on an island.

So little is known about the animals and plants of the reef as yet; the life histories of only a few score of the tens of thousands of species have been studied. But with each detailed exploration, new and strange living patterns are found.☐

◁ *Giant clams, corals and tropical fishes are the trademark of the coral reef. The jumbled profusion of life which stuns the visitor to the reef is a fragile ecosystem dependent on clear, clean water for its continued existence. Unless the tropical sun can penetrate to the microscopic plants living in the tissues of the corals and giant clams, they are unable to grow and provide the places for other reef animals to live and hide.*

▷ *A whale disturbs the surface of the calm clear waters of the reef as it rises to breathe. Although some whales are awesome divers and can reach depths of hundreds of metres, they are mammals and must breathe air. Marine reptiles – sea snakes and turtles – must also surface for air, unlike most animals living in and around the corals.*

Pilot whale

Copepod, *Sapphirina*

Life in the plankton: riding the open water

Transparent and inconspicuous

The seas of the Great Barrier Reef contain millions of creatures that live afloat in open waters. Swarms of globular jellyfish pump along beneath the waves while flotillas of Portuguese men-of-war may drift by, relatives of the jellyfish and so named because they look like tiny blue galleons on the water.

But much of the life teeming just below the surface of the sea is invisible. Many of the organisms carried in the currents of the open sea are too small to be seen, and the larger ones are nearly all so glassily transparent that only the experienced eyes of a skilled diver would be able to distinguish them from the surrounding water. Arrow-worms and comb jellies (with eight rows of iridescent combs formed of fused cilia), salps and 'wing-footed' sea snails, or pteropods, are among the many marine creatures whose transparency makes them inconspicuous in an environment devoid of shelter.

Most members of the group are gelatinous; some are predators; some secrete delicate nets or lassoes to collect their food; others construct elaborate mucus houses in which they live and feed, consuming the very small plankton. This underwater glass menagerie is part of the community of floating animals known as the zooplankton.

Separate floating cells

The world of plankton is generally investigated by the use of nets hauled through the water. A very fine meshed net is needed to obtain a sample of the

◁ *The most conspicuous creature accompanying a salp swarm is the male of the copepod, Sapphirina. Often present in large numbers, they are brilliantly iridescent and glitter like small jewels as they swim through the water. Their flashing blues, reds and yellows probably alert females to their presence and attract them out of the salps in which they are living and feeding. Although the male will often attach itself onto the surface of a salp, it is too large to make its way inside and the female has to emerge to mate with it. Because she can easily see a brightly coloured male clinging to her salp, she does not have to spend time searching for a mate and, once fertilised, she can quickly move back inside and continue feeding. In mature Sapphirina males the gut is reduced or missing, so once they become adult they probably do not feed but devote their lives to attracting females.*

▷ *In these sea snails, the foot is reduced and two shelves of tissue at its upper edge are greatly enlarged to form muscular swimming 'wings', hence the popular name, 'sea butterflies'. Several groups of small free-swimming gastropod molluscs have this type of adaptation, and they are collectively referred to as pteropods, because of their 'winged' feet. The body of herbivorous pteropods is protected by a hard transparent shell, which may be elongated, as in Creseis virgula, above, or rounded and keeled, as in Cavolinia, below. They harvest phytoplankton by secreting a large food-collecting mucus web; they then swallow lengths of the sticky strands together with adhering plant cells and other nutritious particles. If disturbed, they will jettison their webs and swim away.*

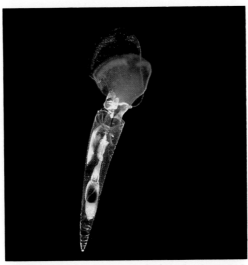

Sea butterfly, *Creseis virgula*

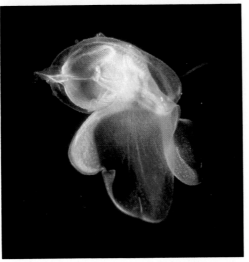

Sea butterfly, *Cavolinia*

Portuguese man-of-war, *Physalia utriculus*

△ *The most venomous and noticeable of the surface drifters is the Portuguese man-of-war. It is a siphonophore hydrozoan colony, consisting of a crested balloon-like float, 50 or 60 millimetres in length, and a set of specialised individuals, or zooids, that hang beneath it and include one or two long thick elastic tentacles, ribbed with batteries of powerful stinging cells. These are the fishing zooids of the colony and they dangle below it to a depth of several metres, ready to seize and kill small fishes or other prey. Shorter tentacles secure the captured animals close to the float and the tubular feeding individuals are then able to tackle them with flared mouths. Between the bases of the other zooids are bunches of pale gonozooids that produce eggs or sperm.*

myriads of floating plants that make up the phytoplankton. Although they are the dominant green organisms of the ocean, the phytoplankters (plant plankton) are microscopic in size. Each plant usually consists of only one separately floating cell, but sometimes the cells are linked together to form fine strands or filaments.

To capture the smallest members of the zooplankton, the tiny animals that ride the currents of the sea, a net with a slightly coarser mesh is used. Every haul of zooplankton usually includes hundreds of copepods – ubiquitous crustaceans, one or two millimetres long, usually tinted pink or orange. There might also be single-celled, star-like radiolarians, minute, newly hatched fishes and, especially in near-shore waters, bizarre invertebrate larvae, sporting cilia, spines or bristles, or a combination of these.

Almost all the major groups of animals are represented in the plankton. Some spend their entire lives afloat, while others hitch a ride in the currents, as eggs or young stages. Many plankters are herbivores, feeding on the phytoplankton, but some are carnivores that prey on their smaller fellows. The plankton community also has opportunists that live on whatever they can find in the form of food, including drifting organic debris.

Not all the inhabitants of the open water can be caught in plankton hauls. Agile creatures with acute vision often avoid the nets; gelatinous zooplankters tend to be damaged and fragmented; and the delicate structures some of them make are destroyed. Other organisms are so small that they pass through the meshes of even the finest nets. This category includes many minute green plant cells, known collectively as the nanoplankton. These are the smallest of the phytoplankton and are only a few thousandths of a millimetre in diameter.

The ocean's small plants

Only while they are floating in the upper waters penetrated by sunlight can the microscopic green plants of the ocean use their chlorophyll to manufacture the food necessary for life and growth. They have evolved ways of slowing their rate of sinking, and their small size is probably a contributing factor. Because they consist of only single cells, phytoplankters can easily take up nutrients from the surrounding water and excrete wastes into it. If provided with suitable conditions for growth, for example, when nutrient-laden water wells up from deeper parts of the ocean, they can multiply rapidly, giving rise to phytoplankton blooms and colouring the water green or red.

Among the most numerous of the phytoplankters are the diatoms. Each diatom is encased in a silica-impregnated capsule, consisting of two porous valves that fit together like a box and its lid. Diatoms often occur singly, but in some species the cells adhere together as strands or spirals. This may help flotation, especially when the diatoms are embellished with hairs or spines, or when each cell is compressed, so that the strands are flat and ribbon-like. Diatoms usually store the food they manufacture as oil. This, too, helps keep them from sinking beyond the reach of the sun's rays.

Armour-plated and bare
The dinoflagellates make up the second major group in the phytoplankton. Unlike diatoms, they are equipped with flagella: whip-like growths that they use to move about in the water. Every dinoflagellate has two flagella, usually with one inserted in a shallow longitudinal groove and trailing in the water and the other lying in a transverse groove girdling the cell. Most of these dinoflagellates also have an armour made up of three or more sculptured cellulose plates. These armoured forms are known as the thecate dinoflagellates. As well as these, there are a few species of naked dinoflagellates that lack any type of plating.

Like diatoms, dinoflagellates need to keep in the upper sunlit part of the sea. Their flagella enable them to swim upwards towards lighted regions, but in addition many of them have structures like long spines, or projecting collars that may serve to keep them afloat.

Dwarf plankton
Although the nanoplankton, or dwarf plankton, is an important part of the plant life of the ocean, it is only relatively recently that it has been investigated in detail. It was first discovered through the agency of the appendicularians, the little house-builders of the zooplankton, whose homes made of mucus contain extremely fine filters, capable of trapping organisms less than five micrometres (five-thousandths of a millimetre) in diameter. The appendicularians can catch a variety of single-celled

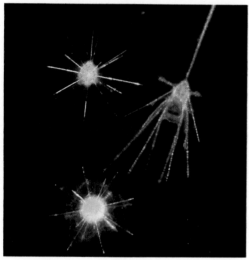

Radiolarian protozoa; heart urchin larva

△ *On the right are two permanently planktonic radiolarian protozoans. Their spines serve as aids to flotation and traps for prey. Each radiolarian has a dense central capsule housing its nucleus and an outer translucent layer of protoplasm that extends over its spines and gives them an adhesive surface. Minute organisms drift against these spines, become stuck, and are eventually engulfed. To the left of the radiolarians is a tiny echinoderm larva. It is a stage in the development of a sea urchin, called the heart urchin. This larva lives only temporarily among the plankton, feeding and slowly developing as it drifts in the water. It has six pairs of elongated arms, supported by calcareous skeletal rods. Its mouth lies between the arms and opposite is a single long projecting spike, that may act as a stabiliser, keeping the larva with its mouth pointing upwards. After a planktonic period of several weeks, the larva settles and metamorphoses into a young urchin.*

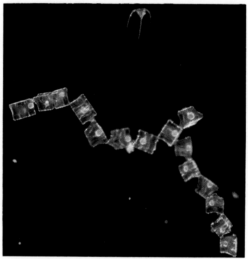

Diatoms; dinoflagellate, *Ceratium*

△ *Plant life in the meadows of the sea. Plant plankton grow and divide in the sunlit upper layers of the sea. These microscopic, single-celled floating organisms make up the dominant part of the plant life in the oceans. They are grazed by tiny, herbivorous animal plankters and form the basis of most of the marine food webs. Here diatoms float in a skein and above them is suspended a minute three-pronged dinoflagellate. Its projecting prongs probably help to keep it afloat, and they may also deter small planktonic grazers from making a meal of it.*

plants, all of them too tiny to be trapped in the meshes of even the finest plankton nets. These minute plants called nanoplankton include the smallest of the diatoms and dinoflagellates, naked green flagellates, flagellates with a silicate framework and the coccolithophores, tiny cells with an armour of very small calcium carbonate plates.

Diatoms and dinoflagellates are both widely distributed in the oceans of the world, but diatoms are more common in cold regions; dinoflagellates and coccolithophores are often prevalent in the tropics.

In the waters of the Great Barrier Reef diatoms appear to be the major component of the phytoplankton during most of the year.

Sawdust of the sea

A striking phenomenon periodically transfigures the surface of the sea in the reef province. Especially in the later part of the year, between August and October, golden brown or rust-coloured streaks often appear in the water. These may be only a few metres across, or they may extend over an entire seascape. Sometimes they drift together to form great spirals and swirls that give the impression of a vast abstract painting. The painter, however, is a small planktonic organism whose name, *Oscillatoria erythraea*, can be roughly translated as 'little hairy red bundle'. Seen from the deck of a boat the windrows of *Oscillatoria* have a smooth, gleaming, almost oily sheen and a bucket of water taken from one of these slicks will have a distinctive, rather rank smell. It is common to see streaks of *Oscillatoria* stretching to the horizon while travelling in the small planes to and from the resort islands. Most of the algae are invisible below the surface, but this gives an indication of the reproductive ability of minute, single-celled plants to produce great tonnages of living matter.

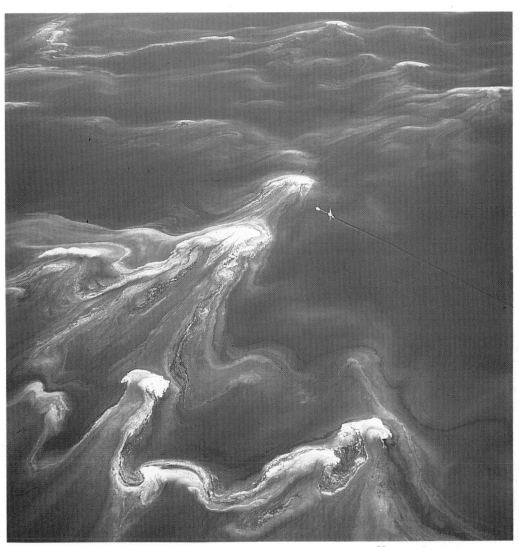

Blue-green alga, *Oscillatoria erythraea*

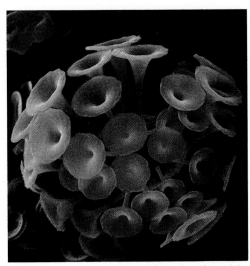

Nanoplankton, *Discosphaera tubifera*

◁ This calcareous member of the nanoplankton, or dwarf plankton, is one of the smallest of the single-celled planktonic plants. Nanoplankters are often abundant, but as they are only a few thousandths of a millimetre in diameter, they usually pass through the meshes of even the finest plankton nets. The electron micrograph of this member of the nanoplankton reveals a corona of minute, flaring trumpet-like projections radiating from the central cell. They greatly increase its surface area and buoyancy.

△ Oscillatoria is one of an ancient group of photosynthetic organisms – the blue-green algae. Its cells are associated in mucus-sheathed filaments and are capable of a gliding movement. Each cell contains a minute bladder that enables it to control its buoyancy and regulate the depth at which it floats. The filaments tend to clump together to form bundles or sheaves. Periodic large-scale blooms of Oscillatoria in reef waters culminate in the sheaves floating to the surface and streaking the water with their rusty colour. These surface windrows appear to be made up of dead or moribund cells whose buoyancy-regulating gas bladders have burst or no longer function. The sheaves are visible as red-brown specks; they feel slimy and give the water an oily sheen and a rank smell. Oscillatoria is widespread in tropical waters with high salinity, and it probably causes the colour that gave the Red Sea its name.

'There are reports of fishes dying because their gills become clogged with sea sawdust.'

▷ *This colonial hydrozoan grows attached to coral boulders in sheltered subtidal areas. It buds off tiny medusae into the plankton. The colony resembles a small upright feather, with a main shaft and side branches. Along each branch is an evenly spaced row of feeding individuals that seize and engulf minute prey organisms as they drift past them in the water. Because they are connected to each other by a common digestive tube, these feeding polyps are able to share their food.*

▷ *This branch of a colonial hydrozoan colony has three feeding polyps towards its tip. Minute jellyfish or medusae grow out from between the tentacles at the base of the polyps and eventually break off to become free-swimming members of the plankton. Two of these microscopic elongated medusae have already left the parent colony and two more are attached to the polyp at the tip of the branch. The medusae produce eggs or sperm. Once fertilised, the eggs develop into larvae that settle out of the plankton, attach themselves to the lower surface of suitable boulders, and grow into new branching colonies.*

▷ *This hydrozoan medusa is one of the common jellyfish of the Great Barrier Reef. It is the mobile, sexually reproductive phase in a hydrozoan life cycle. The asexual phase is a small shrub-like bottom-dwelling colony that buds off the free-swimming medusae. In most hydrozoans these medusae are so small as to be barely visible, but in this species they are relatively large and can reach about 100 millimetres across the disc. The jellyfish is almost completely transparent, and its many unbranched digestive canals can be seen, radiating out from the central gastric cavity above the fringed mouth to a ring at the edge of the umbrella. It swims vigorously, rhythmically contracting a shelf of muscular tissue on the underside of its disc, while trailing long fishing tentacles from its rim.*

Colonial hydrozoan, *Pennaria australis*

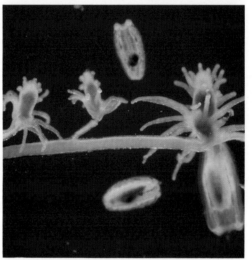

Colonial hydrozoan, *Pennaria australis*; medusa

Hydrozoan medusa, *Aequorea pensilis*

Floating bundles

The cause of the rusty colour is the presence of many thousands of reddish brown specks in the water. Filaments of *Oscillatoria* clump together in floating bundles or sheaves, each about a fifth of a millimetre long and visible to the naked eye as small dark grains. They have been given various names, such as 'sea sawdust' and 'coral spawn'. The latter is an unfortunate misnomer, because *Oscillatoria* is not produced by the corals. It is a member of the phylum Cyanophyta, an ancient group of plant-like organisms, commonly known as the blue-green algae, but more closely allied to the bacteria than to other forms of life. In *Oscillatoria* the blue-green colour is masked by a red pigment.

What triggers the population explosions of *Oscillatoria* is not fully understood. They may occur when nutrient-laden deep water wells up into the sunlit zone and allows the cyanophyte to start multiplying, or they may be linked to rainfall on the nearby coastal strip bringing enrichment in the form of runoff from the land. *Oscillatoria* blooms are not as toxic as the blooms of dinoflagellates, called red tides, although there are reports of fishes dying because their gills have become clogged. Some fishes, such as the milk fish, *Chanos chanos*, avoid these areas as adults, but in their young stages they may feed on the sheaves.

Zooplankton: small voyagers

Most of the zooplankton depend directly or indirectly on the phytoplankton for their food, and like the phytoplankters, they have a variety of devices that help make them buoyant. A few of the floating animals, such as some of the jellyfish and their allies, can grow fairly large, but most are only a few millimetres long. Their small size means that they have a large surface area relative to their volume, an advantage in their life afloat.

In many, an array of protuberances, bristles, hairs, or spines also counteracts the tendency to sink. In some of the gelatinous zooplankters, the salts of the body fluids are so adjusted that the animals have the same density as sea water. Some zooplankters have gas bladders that act as floats; others store food as oil globules, also an aid to buoyancy. Almost all of them swim actively and maintain their level in the water, but they are not powerful enough to move effectively against currents and tides.

The surface of the open sea is the living place of a distinctive group of colonial coelenterates, such as *Porpita* and *Velella*, which are related to the jellyfish, corals and sea anemones. Usually bright blue in colour, they have gas-filled floats that buoy them up. Periodically they are driven towards beaches by onshore winds, and large numbers may be stranded and dry out in the lines or wrack at the water's edge. They are often accompanied by the gastropod molluscs that feed on them and live at the surface with them.

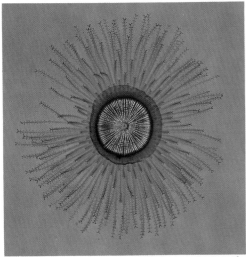

Hydrozoan, *Porpita pacifica*

△ Porpita, *a surface drifter that lives at the junction of sea and air, is a small chondrophoran hydrozoan colony in which the individuals, or zooids, are suspended from a supporting circular disc about 20 millimetres in diameter. The disc contains air chambers and acts as a float. Around its rim is a fringe of knobbed, tentacular zooids that capture prey and pass it to a central feeding individual, whose large mouth lies on the underside of the float.*

▷ △ *This scyphozoan jellyfish is sometimes called 'the lion's mane jellyfish', because of its thick mane of long tentacles and the tawny colours of its bell. It can occur in large numbers in the northern part of the Great Barrier Reef and is most likely to be prevalent in the muddy water close to the coast during the wet summer season. It is a large jellyfish with a bell that may be one metre in diameter and tentacles that may reach a length of ten metres. It has about 800 tentacles, which are hollow, strongly contractile, and armed with densely packed stinging cells. They are capable of injuring humans that encounter them. Like other coelenterates, the lion's mane jellyfish is a predator. It captures and paralyses its prey with its tentacles and their stinging cells. Schools of small fishes, however, shelter among its tentacles. Some of these fishes, such as juvenile trevally, seem to be able to come into contact with the tentacles and not be harmed.*

▷ *Another colonial chondrophoran hydrozoan is the by-the-wind-sailor. It is similar to Porpita, but it has an oval disc, surmounted by a small sail, which is set at an angle along its axis. The sail enables it to harness the wind to drive it across the surface of the sea in search of prey. Both Velella and Porpita are hosts to symbiotic dinoflagellate algae. Their surface-living habit guarantees the algae a place in the sun where they can pursue their photosynthetic activity, while providing the host with extra food. This Velella is being eaten by the eyeless violet sea-snail, a floating gastropod mollusc.*

Lion's mane jellyfish, *Cyanea capillata*

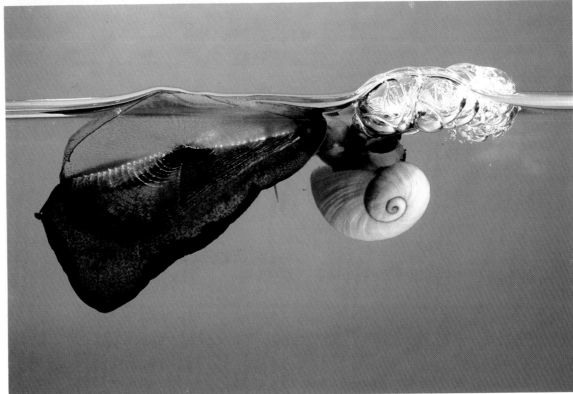

By-the-wind-sailor, *Velella*; violet sea snail, *Janthina*

LIFE IN THE PLANKTON 139

Pagurid larva

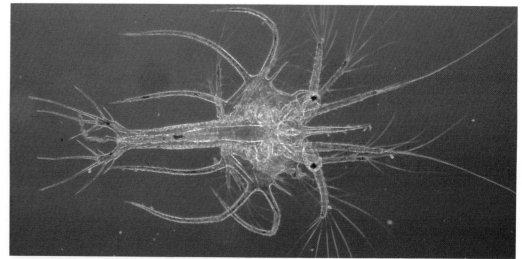

Sergestid larva

△ *Decapod crustaceans, such as crabs, crayfish and shrimps, spend a period of their early lives adrift in the plankton. While there the larvae feed and as they grow, they pass through a series of developmental phases, punctuated by moults. The late larvae begin to look somewhat like the adults. Early larvae of a pagurid – a hermit or stone crab – above; a sergestid shrimp, above right; and a hippolytid shrimp, right, only remotely resemble their adult forms.*

▽ *This aeolid nudibranch is also a surface dwelling gastropod about 20 millimetres long that preys on some hydrozoans. It lives an upside-down life, as it creeps about the surface-film with its foot, mouth and undersides facing upwards. It gulps in air and swallows it, and the bubble in its stomach helps to keep it afloat. Its colour is similar to that of its prey but is even more intense. The deep azure and brilliant silver-blue of its foot and underside make it difficult for predatory birds to distinguish from the blue sea.*

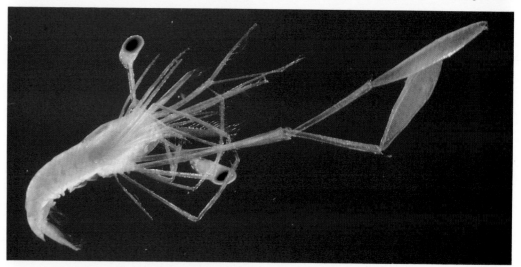

Hippolytid larva

Aeolid nudibranch, *Glaucus atlanticus*

Porcellanid larva

Vertical commuters

Salps and appendicularians are the inner-city dwellers of the zooplankton. Like their human counterparts, they live and work for their food in the same place. For herbivorous zooplankters, this place is the sea's sunlit upper waters, where phytoplankton can grow. Some of the animals remain here throughout their lives: the salps and appendicularians tend to stay in this zone, filtering the water continuously for its small plants. Like humans, the salp belongs to the phylum Chordata. By sucking a current of water into its mouth, passing it between the strands of a delicate internal mucus net and squirting it out of a rear pore, the salp both propels itself forward and collects food. Driven by rhythmically contracting muscle bands encircling its body, the salp pulses through the water, feeding as it goes. Salps can grow and reproduce more rapidly than almost any other animal. When blooms of phytoplankton occur, they take advantage of the abundant supply of their microscopic plant food and quickly build up into dense swarms, far outnumbering all the rest of the animal plankton.

Most zooplankters are commuters, with a pattern of daily movement not unlike that of city workers who travel to and from the shelter of their suburbs each day. Among the plankters, the direction of the daily migration is vertical, and it is during the hours of darkness that they venture into the upper layers – the herbivores in search of phytoplankton and the carnivores in pursuit of prey.

Going down

At dawn, with the first faint sign of light, they move quickly downwards. The open-water plankters are able to descend to depths below the sunlit zone. Those that inhabit lagoons and the shallow seas of the back reefs take refuge in a variety of ways. Some mysid and copepod crustaceans swarm in dark caves or beneath the shaded overhangs of the coral ramparts of the reef. Shrimps may burrow in the sand of lagoon floors. Many other crustaceans retreat to crevices in dead coral rubble. Some even shelter in living corals, while others hover in sea-grass beds or algal mats. At sunset, with the coming of darkness, they emerge and start swimming upwards.

This vertical migration is not a simple mass exodus towards the surface. Each species has its own timing and moves to its own level, with juveniles sometimes behaving differently from adults, but in most cases it is the reduction in the amount of light that apparently triggers the start of the upward excursion. The zooplankton tend to concentrate in the surface waters in the dark periods just after sunset and just before dawn. In the middle of the night there is often a 'midnight sinking' when the animals disperse and descend to a greater or lesser degree. In some instances this may be a response to the light of the moon or a bright night sky.

An energetic dive

Many of the deep-water plankters undertake extensive vertical journeys each day. The crustaceans are particularly active; copepods only a few millimetres long are known to migrate over a distance of several hundred metres, swimming upwards at speeds of more than 15 metres an hour; going downwards, they have been recorded as achieving bursts of over 100 metres an hour. The planktonic commuters of lagoons, back reefs and coastal waters have a similar daily routine.

For all these animals, the benefits of this way of life must outweigh its considerable costs in energy and time spent away from the productive sunlit

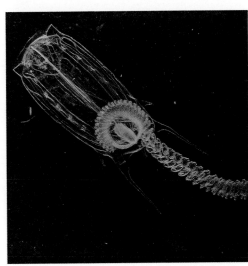

Copepod, *Sapphirina angusta*

Salp, *Thalia democratica*

△ *Wherever there are dense swarms of salps, large numbers of small cyclopoid copepods of the genus* Sapphirina *also occur. Females and juveniles prey on the salp by invading its body cavity and eating it from the inside. The copepod hitches itself onto the surface of its potential victim, clinging to it with hooked antennae. It then works its way towards the pore through which the salp expels its water current. If it manages to avoid being swept away by the force of the current, it enters through this pore and starts to feed on the salp's internal tissues. Small juveniles live in salps as parasites. Just before they become adult, male juveniles leave their salps, but females remain inside. Only when they are ready to mate do they emerge; after mating, the females go back inside.*

◁ *The young zoea larvae of porcelain crabs can be recognised by the extremely long rostrum, which projects like a lance from the front of the carapace.*

△ *This salp is a solitary individual giving birth to a chain of sexual salps. The chain is about to break free of its attachment to the loop of embryos still inside the parent's body. In the loop itself there are two distinct sets, each at a different stage of development. One consists of larger salps, approaching birth size, and the other is made up of tiny embryos, newly formed by the parent.*

'Most zooplankters are commuters, just like city workers who travel to and from their dormitory suburbs.'

layers. The deleterious effect of bright sunlight on the animals themselves may be one reason for avoiding it. It has also been suggested that, because surface and deep currents often move in opposite directions, animals migrating regularly between one and the other would be able to maintain their overall position in a favourable environment, instead of being swept beyond it. And differences in the rate or direction of movement of the upper and lower water layers would allow them to venture up each night 'to fresh fields and pastures new'.

Reacting to light intensity

Variations in temperature, salinity and oxygen levels may modify behaviour in particular situations, but in the main it is the change in light intensity that gives the animals their cue to start out on their vertical journey twice a day. The level of illumination also seems to have a strong influence on their choice of daytime depth. Their tendency to retreat from lighted areas lends support to the idea that vertical migration is chiefly a way of hiding from predators that hunt by sight. On the Great Barrier Reef, about a quarter of the fishes are planktivores, ready to snap up any animal morsel in view. Those that are slow to retire at dawn or quick to emerge at dusk are those most likely to be seen and eaten by their vigilant predators.

The hours of darkness are not without hazards for the plankton. Some of their predators, like the squirrelfish, are active at night, and this is also the time when the coral polyps stretch out their tentacles to snare their diminutive quarry. Small animals that spend their day at the bottom of reefs or lagoons are less likely to be captured by the corals if they move up into the mid-water at night.

The travelling city

In the three-dimensional world of the plankton, a range of living patterns exists. Some permanent plankters have specialised life styles, like the herbivorous salps and pteropod molluscs and the carnivorous arrow-worms. Then there are the moonlighters: some copepod and mysid crustaceans collect phytoplankton in the upper waters at night, and when they descend to their various shelters during the day, they may eat detritus, faecal pellets and 'marine snow': the floating specks of mucus produced by the corals and other organic fragments, all with their accompanying bacteria. Other plankters alter their way of life as they develop. Very small planktonic larvae usually begin their careers feeding on the nanoplankton, but as they grow, they may become predators, like many fishes.

Communities on the move

The microcosm of the plankton is a community on the move, with both long-term and temporary inhabitants. In the waters of the Great Barrier Reef

it may be transported through the coastal channel over coral patches, into the lagoons of the islands and cays, and perhaps even through the passages in the ribbon reefs out to the open sea, where it might enter one of the great spiralling ocean currents that periodically wheel down the Pacific Ocean and through the Tasman Sea.

The community travelling in deep water differs from that of shallow reefs and inshore areas. It tends to be less diverse and to contain a greater proportion of permanent gelatinous zooplankters, such as scyphozoan jellyfish, siphonophores, comb jellies, pteropod and heteropod molluscs, appendicularians, as well as copepods and arrow-worms.

A great range of animals live in the shallow waters of the reefs and lagoons, particularly crustaceans. Many of them spend the hours of daylight in or close to their own characteristic type of shelter, be it a coral cave, an algal mat, or a sandy

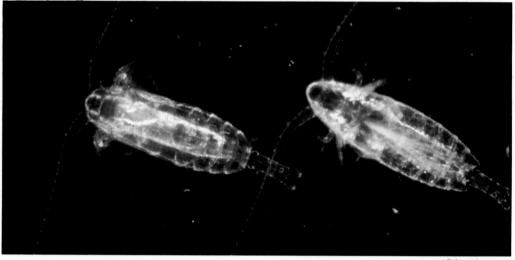

Calanoid copepod

floor. At night some of them venture only a short distance into the mid-water, while others bravely make the full trip to the surface.

Swarming to breed

Crustaceans with this way of life include copepods, mysids, amphipods, ostracods, isopods, cumaceans and shrimps. Among the cumaceans, females lack swimming legs and remain buried in the sand. Cumacean males are equipped to swim and it is they that take to the water at night. In this community parasites are common. Among them are monstrilloid copepods, whose early stages parasitise other invertebrates, such as worms, molluscs or echinoderms, but whose free-swimming planktonic adults lack mouthparts and do not feed.

At times, usually during the summer and especially in the shallow-water community, transient members of the plankton swarm up into

the mid-water. Some of these are adults, ripe for sex, such as the nereid polychaete worms. A few polychaetes are permanently planktonic, but for most of their lives the nereids crawl about in the crevices of corals and the cavities of the broken rubble of the reef. When they are about to breed, they grow a projecting row of paddles on their sides and become packed with ripe eggs or sperm.

Cycles of the moon

Usually on dark nights at a particular time of tide and phase of moon, the nereids swim up clear of the coral and expel their eggs and sperm into the water, flashing with a fiery red luminescence as they dart and twist in the gyrations of their nuptial foray into the plankton. The fertilised eggs develop into microscopic larvae that look like minute transparent tops, with a tuft of cilia, short threads used in movement, at the apex and a ciliated girdle. As they

△ *Calanoid copepods are only a few millimetres in length, but they make up the largest part of the zooplankton in the oceans of the world and they are the major consumers of the phytoplankton. They have a pair of large first antennae, equipped with sensory hairs, stretching out on either side of the front of the head. In these specimens, a single small red eye can be seen on the top of the head as well. By using their projecting second antennae and mouthparts, these copepods set up feeding currents, and with the help of chemoreceptors they are able to detect the presence of algal cells in the flow. Water that contains cells is selectively directed towards the meshed bristles of a pair of special mouthparts that then entrap the cells. Calanoids are active swimmers, and many of them perform extensive daily vertical migrations. In swimming they propel themselves by using rapid strokes of their second antennae and a set of thoracic limbs.*

drift with the currents, these larvae begin to grow into tiny worms, acquiring segmented bodies and clusters of bristles. When they reach this stage, they make their way down to the bottom and find themselves a living place among the corals or debris.

Most of the small reef fishes also make a trip into the upper water when ready to spawn. The fish larvae that hatch from their floating eggs remain in the plankton for a matter of days in some species and up to ten months in others, after which they eventually settle out on a coral patch probably some distance from their parents' reef.

Colonising new areas

Many of the bottom-living invertebrates of the reef broadcast their eggs and free-swimming sperm into the water. The larvae that result travel in the plankton for a while before moving down to begin their adult life below. For animals that lead fairly sedentary lives, such as sea stars, sea urchins and sea cucumbers, or are fixed to rocks, such as oysters, or embedded in coral, such as clams, this planktonic larval phase provides a way in which their progeny can colonise new areas. The planktonic larvae of molluscs are equipped with a pair of ciliated lobes, with which they swim and feed. Echinoderm larvae are also ciliated, and those of sea urchins and brittle stars have long slender arms supported by spicules.

The young stages of crustaceans make up a large part of the temporary plankton. Crustacean males produce sperm that are not free-swimming. Usually they are packaged, and during mating the males attach them directly to the females, who then carry their fertilised eggs until they hatch. In the peracarid crustaceans, the female has a brood pouch in which she keeps the developing young throughout their entire larval life. The mysids belong to this group, and when juveniles emerge from the pouch and swim away, they are small versions of the adult.

Growing in steps

Among other crustaceans, such as crayfish and crabs, the larvae join the plankton as soon as they hatch from their eggs, and they bear hardly any

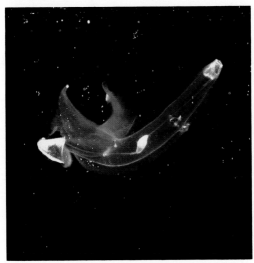

Heteropod, *Carinaria cristata*

△ *The heteropods are wholly planktonic gastropod molluscs. Almost totally transparent, heteropods swim upside down, with their fin-like foot held above the body. Their keen eyesight enables them to detect prey at a distance and they rush it from below, seize it, and swallow it; this heteropod has its body arched upwards, ready for action. Below it hangs its small cap-like shell, with gills projecting from its lip. Although usually much smaller, this species may reach a length of 250 millimetres. When not swimming, some heteropods float passively, suspended with their bodies in a loose ball.*

▷ *This small crustacean is a highly specialised carnivorous copepod that inhabits the waters of the Great Barrier Reef. The female shown here is nine-tenths of a millimetre long, and she is carrying two egg sacs. Her green eggs are protected inside the sacs, and as she swims along a constant flow of water passes over the eggs, supplying them with oxygen and removing wastes. The eggs hatch within a few days. The second antennae of this cyclopoid copepod are large and used for grasping prey. It has well-developed eyes and can spot prey animals, such as other copepods, at long distances. Cyclopoids swim in a 'hop-and-sink' manner and usually become aware of the approach of prey while they are sinking.*

▷ *The mysids occur in great numbers in Great Barrier Reef waters. During the daytime, large schools hover over the pale sandy floors of the shallow seas between the back reefs. They strictly avoid going near anything dark and leave a 'mysid-free zone' around each coral head. The specimens shown here are in an aquarium at the Lizard Island Research Station. The bottom of the aquarium is lined with black and white plastic strips, and the mysids are swimming above the light strips and shunning the vicinity of the dark ones. A smaller mysid species, Anisomysis australis, is at a higher level in the water. Mysids belong to a group of crustaceans in which the female keeps her developing young in a bulging pouch slung below her and made up of plates that grow at the base of a number of her thoracic legs. She ventilates her pouch by moving the plates rhythmically. The period the larvae spend in the pouch is usually two or three weeks. They emerge at night; the female spreads her plates, the larvae fall out, moult and swim away as miniature adults.*

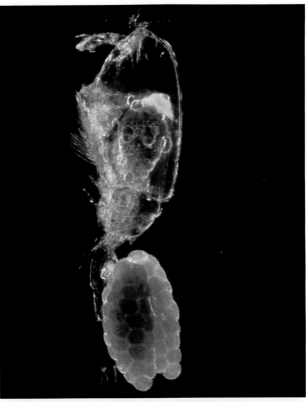

Cyclopoid copepod, *Corycaeus catus*

Mysids, *Promysis orientalis*, *Anisomysis australis*

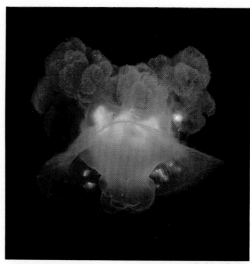

Jellyfish, *Cephea*

△ *Named after Cepheus, the legendary king of Ethiopia, this jellyfish has a crown of rounded tubercles on the top of its bell. Like Mastigias, it is a scyphozoan jellyfish of the rhizostome type, and it is characterised by having many very small mouths set on elaborately branched and frilled mouth-arms. In this jellyfish, the swimming muscles of the bell are relaxed and a network of digestive canals can be seen running outwards to its lifted edge.*

▷ *Eels are among the many reef fishes that release floating eggs into the plankton. Most of them spawn on summer evenings at sunset. Inside the transparent egg, the backbone of the embryo can be seen curled over the bulge of the yolk sac, so that the tip of the tail almost meets the head. While it is in the egg, the developing eel absorbs the yolk into its gut and it hatches as an active larva that feeds and grows in the plankton for about two weeks, before moving to the sea bottom as a young eel.*

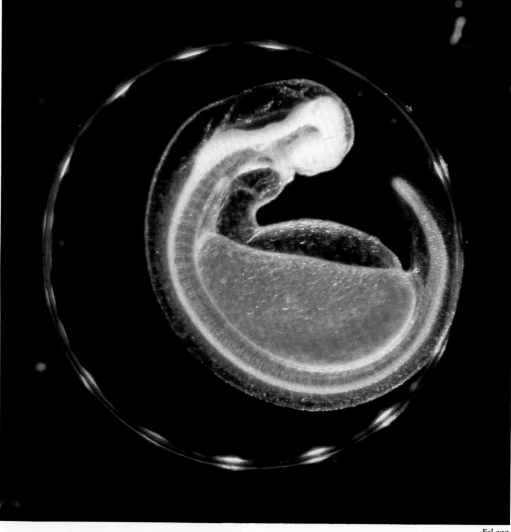

Eel egg

▷ *The 'sea gooseberry' is a small, transparent, globular ctenophore, usually less than 20 millimetres in diameter. It is often found in large swarms and sometimes washes ashore in great numbers. It swims with its mouth forward and carries the specialised cells that seize and hold its prey on two long, fringed, highly elastic tentacles that can be retracted inside the pockets from which they trail.*

Stingers *par excellence*
'Spring-loaded stinging darts are common weapons in the plankton.'

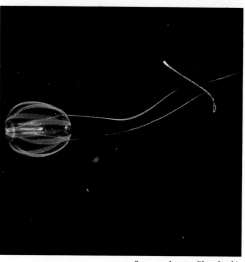

Sea gooseberry, *Pleurobrachia*

△ ▷ *Orbulina belongs to a group of protozoans known as the foraminiferans or 'forams'. It secretes a many-chambered calcite shell, adding progressively larger chambers as it grows. A few days before it reproduces it adds a spherical chamber surrounding the others. Its long delicate projecting spines are sheathed with sticky cytoplasm and they entrap any small organisms that may bump into them. These are then digested.*

▷ *Like the Portuguese man-of-war, this siphonophore is a coelenterate colony made up of a group of specialised individuals. Suspended beneath a small apical float is a set of transparent swimming bells which, by their contractions, drive the colony through the water. They are attached to a central stem, from the lower part of which hangs a collection of different specialists. Among them are central clusters of reproductive zooids and, reaching out around the edge, long, finger-like gastrozooids that engulf planktonic prey and supply the colony with food.*

Protozoa, *Orbulina universa*

▷ *This scyphozoan jellyfish is one in which, instead of a single central mouth, there are innumerable tiny openings carried on a set of mouth-arms that hang below the bell. The enormously subdivided feeding surfaces of the rhizostome, or 'root-mouthed', jellyfish provide an efficient means of screening the water for small planktonic prey. The species is widely distributed in the Indo-Pacific. It is about 50 to 100 millimetres across the bell.*

Jellyfish, *Mastigias papua*

Physonect siphonophore

▷ This crustacean belongs to an oceanic group known as the hyperiid amphipods. They are almost always found in association with the animals of the gelatinous deep-water plankton. They feed on them, shelter in them, and deposit their developing young in their recesses. Phronimids often live inside the bodies of salps and pyrosomes, invading them as juveniles and proceeding to eat away their tissues, until nothing is left but the barrel-shaped tough outer coat. The female phronimid cares for her offspring in the shelter of her eaten-out barrel. She brings food to them and prevents them from escaping by herding them inwards away from the open ends. A strong swimmer, she is able to propel her floating nursery through the water until the young amphipods are ready to leave; it is thought that she then places them separately on new hosts.

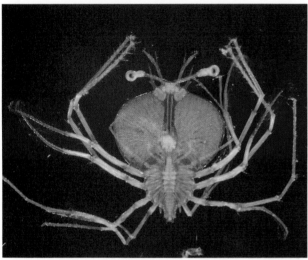

Scyllarid larva

Amphipod, *Phronima*

△ *Crayfish and allied species have flattened, leaf-like early larvae, known as phyllosoma larvae. They often ride on the umbrellas of jellyfish, clinging to them with the hooked tips of their spindly legs. This phyllosoma is a close relative of the Moreton Bay bug.*

'As crustacean larvae grow, they moult at intervals, becoming more and more like the adult form with each succeeding moult.'

resemblance to their adults. The early larvae of crayfish have flattened leaf-like bodies, and they are sometimes found clinging to the top of small jellyfish, on which they are thought to feed. Crab larvae have projecting spines; in the case of the porcelain crabs, these spines may be several times the length of the body. As the larvae grow, they moult at intervals, emerging from their rigid outer skins, becoming more like the adult with each succeeding moult, until they eventually settle out of the plankton and join the bottom community.

In the case of the acorn barnacles the planktonic larva is the sole means of dispersal. Acorn barnacles are permanently cemented to the rocks as adults, and their distribution depends on the mobility of their larvae. In another group of barnacles, the adults are internal parasites of crabs, and their free-swimming larvae travel in the plankton in search of fresh hosts to invade.

The currents that transport the plankton largely determine its distribution. In the coastal channel of the Great Barrier Reef there is a northerly flow of water for most of the year, but small-scale circulations are also important and their influence often tends to retain the plankton in localised areas, so that it is not simply swept through the system. For instance, steady populations may be maintained in the eddies that form on the lee side of islands, coral cays and sand banks.

In the central and southern parts of the reef, continental shelf waves generate currents flowing along the coast. These travel in a northerly and southerly direction alternately, with the result that the plankton may be carried on an excursion of hundreds of kilometres in one direction, only to be returned many days later. This type of flow would tend to hold the tropical plankton in the area of the Great Barrier Reef, and it would be a dominant

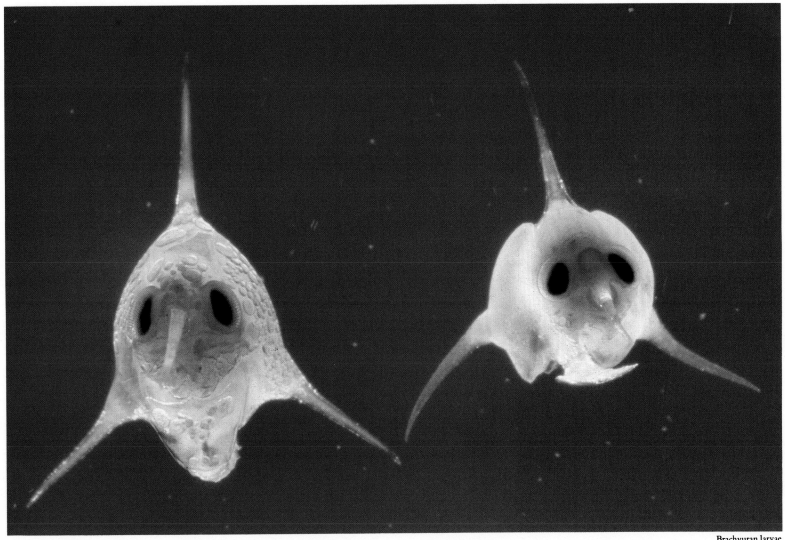

Brachyuran larvae

influence on the distribution of the reef fishes and all the other animals that have planktonic stages in their life cycles.

Home-bodies and the international set
Although local currents may retain their inhabitants, on the large scale the waters of the reef are part of the circulation of the tropical Indo-Pacific, and this is reflected in the widespread distribution of much of the plankton. Study of the planktonic animals of the reef has as yet been too sparse to yield a comprehensive picture of their geographic range, but it is probable that the species confined to the Great Barrier Reef region are among those tied to a bottom-living existence as adults, or those that become planktonic for only short periods at night, or during the mating season.

Many Great Barrier Reef species are found in other parts of the tropical Pacific and Indian oceans and some extend into more temperate waters. Among the crustaceans, for instance, some of the copepods, mysids and shrimps occur off the coast of New South Wales as well as in the waters of the reef; other mysids have tropical distributions extending as far as the Malay Archipelago and the Philippines; and the dominant species of krill on the reef has a range that includes the Tasman Sea, the Bay of Bengal and the Arabian Gulf.

Finally, there are the deep-water 'citizens of the world', a group that includes many of the gelatinous zooplankters, arrow-worms, heteropod and pteropod molluscs, some copepods and hyperiid amphipods. They belong to species that inhabit the warm parts of oceans throughout the globe. All these elements, local, regional and worldwide, contribute, in varying proportions at different times and in different parts, to the total composition of the plankton of the Great Barrier Reef.□

△ *Looking very much like strange creatures from the imagination of a science fiction writer, these two zoea larvae of a reef crab have carapaces that are rounded like helmets and have four prominent spikes projecting from them. The spines may slow their sinking and also deter predatory fellow plankters from eating them. The tails of these zoea larvae are tucked forward under their bodies. A zoea larva is an early larval stage of decapod crustaceans.*

Symbiosis: secret success of the reef

Survival in the desert

The Great Barrier Reef is an oasis in a watery desert – a desert, because almost nothing grows in the low-nutrient waters of most tropical seas. Phosphate, nitrogen, iron and other essential nutrients are barely detectable in the clear, sunlit waters; clear, because so little is growing. A vibrant, living coral reef in such clear water is a miracle of evolution and nature's biological ingenuity.

Coral chemical factory

Collaboration is the secret of success and progress in the reef. The biologist's term 'symbiosis' denotes a special kind of collaboration. To survive in a sea with no nitrogen or phosphate nutrients would be impossible for algae. To survive without a supply of energy-rich food would be impossible for animal life. The corals solved the problem millions of years ago: their animal cells engulfed microscopic algae and confined them; one algal cell in each animal cell in the inner of the coral's two cell layers. The alga is in reality a solar cell that can convert the sun's light energy into chemical energy. This is done through photosynthesis, by which a plant produces food and oxygen. With plenty of light and plenty of carbon dioxide in the water, algae can produce limitless food, provided they have the necessary nitrogen and phosphate to maintain their chemical factory. Inside the animal cell, this is no problem. The animals produce nitrogen in the form of ammonia, which is absorbed by the alga. Instead of trying to survive in the sea, the symbiotic algae of the coral thrive within it. They have no shortage of nutrients, unlike their relatives struggling in the seas outside.

The alga gives up to 80 per cent of the products of its photosynthesis to its host. Ordinary algae cannot do that, nor can coral algae once they are removed from the coral. But when the algae are exposed to the corals' digestive enzymes, the algae become leaky. Glycerol (a sugar-like compound) and nutritious amino acids leak from the alga and are used by the animal. Together, the coral and alga thrive. With much less need for food from the outside, the coral can dominate the reef where independent, less efficient creatures could not.

Coral symbiosis is the major one of many such biological systems operating on the reef – as efficient as the best industrial chemical factory.

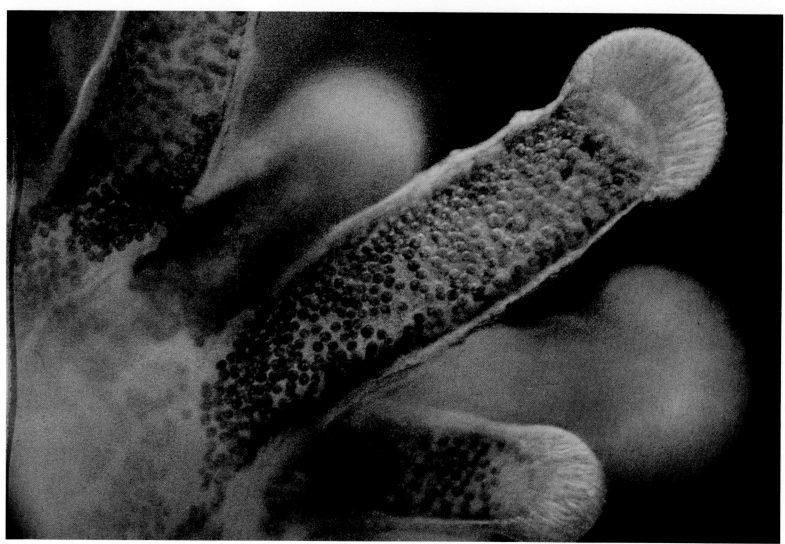

Symbiotic algae, *Symbiodinium microadriaticum*

Adapting to blue light

Algae have also adapted to the blue light that penetrates farthest into the sea. The symbiotic algae of corals appear to be the same species, *Symbiodinium microadriaticum*, although there are probably many subspecies. They are coloured by the golden brown algal pigments that are capable of absorbing blue light. Most undersea photographs reveal this blueness. The algae have adapted to depth and shading from overhanging rock or other corals by increasing the amount of chlorophyll in their chloroplasts. Like sun plants (such as corn and cactus) and shade plants (such as ferns and camellias) algae's apparatus for photosynthesis is well adapted to their light environment.

Almost half of the earth's sedimentary rocks are produced from the calcareous skeletons of surface-living single-celled foraminifera called forams, that settle on the sea floor. Beaches near the Great Barrier Reef are often made of such skeletons. Most of the foraminifera of the upper light zone of the sea contain the same symbiotic algae – the secret of their success.

Living with clams and sponges

Not all successful symbiosis involves algae living within the host animal's cells. The giant clams, *Tridacna*, harbour the same dinoflagellate (red-tide) algae in their often colourful mantles. The mantles extend and contract as light intensity changes, depending upon their need to free their blood of waste ammonia. Unlike the corals, giant clams can harvest their algae as they multiply in the mantle: the clam's faeces contain both digested and still-living zooxanthellae – the symbiotic golden brown algae, so named because they are yellowish brown (xanthos) and living in the animal (zoos). The suffix 'ellae' is typical of many algal names.

Foram, *Marginapora vertebralis*

'Deep sea algae get the blues. Blue light penetrates farthest into the sea, and deep-living algae are well-adapted to exploiting this light environment. Depth and shading from overhanging rocks are accommodated by an increase in the algae's chlorophyll content.'

Foram, *Marginapora vertebralis*

Foram, *Marginapora vertebralis*

◁ In each cell of the coral's inner layer lives a single captive dinoflagellate alga called a zooxanthella. Instead of starving in the nutrient-poor tropical ocean, the zooxanthella thrives on the waste products of the host cell. Its chlorophyll collects solar energy with which the alga builds sugars, amino acids and fats to repay its hosts for its productive environment. This group, known as red-tide when they are growing rapidly at sea, includes the symbiotic zooxanthellae of clams, corals and anemones. These dinoflagellate algae seem to have developed the capability for being selected, invading and thriving within their many hosts.

◁ Forams, left, above and top, are a large class of single-celled animals with calcareous skeletons. This species, which measures five to twelve millimetres in diameter, like most others in tropical waters carries symbiotic algae that use its waste products and the sun's energy to produce sugars and amino acids for its own food requirements. Forams can use their tiny pseudopodia to walk at surprising rates. Their skeletal remains make up many island beaches near the reef, and, indeed, half of the calcareous sedimentary rocks of the earth were formed at the sea bottom from countless skeletons of microscopic forams that lived in the upper light zone of the sea, but whose skeletons ultimately settled to the bottom.

Many sponges of the reef also harbour symbiotic algae and bacteria. The pink algae of the sponges differ from the dinoflagellates of corals and clams, and they, too, have adapted to the blue light. Sponges' algae are the blue-green *Cyanophyta* which possess a red-coloured protein that can absorb energy from the sun and pass it to the chlorophylls of the alga for photosynthesis. The exchange of light energy, nutrients and metabolic products serves the host sponge in its nutrient-impoverished environment.

Transferring goods and services

The inner layer of the two cell layers of a coral contains one algal cell in each animal cell. Just how the coral cell selects and engulfs its alga remains a mystery. Under stress, the coral will spit out the alga. The rapidly growing tips of the staghorn and other corals are often white and devoid of algae. One would think that this part of the coral would most need the energy collected by the algae, but nature has decided otherwise.

Algae absorb ammonia. As the waste ammonia from the animal's protein metabolism increases, the alga absorbs it and, with its copious light energy, reuses it for making amino acids, the building stones for the animal's proteins. The simplest amino acid for the alga to assemble is the compound alanine. The host can use alanine for new proteins, or use it for energy to drive the animal's muscles and pumping system.

Sea water contains an abundance of bicarbonate, a form of carbon dioxide. The algae use bicarbonate and light energy to produce carbohydrates. Glycerol is one of these carbohydrates, a simple sugar-like compound, easily produced from the alga's own sugars. When glycerol leaks from the algal cell, the animal host can use it to provide energy for work and growth. Thus, the coral has a daily supply of energy to drive its pulsating polyps in their quest for more nitrogen and phosphorous compounds from small zooplankton they might capture. The clams need extra energy for pumping the torrents of water that bathe their gills and plankton-collecting cilia.

The secret of coral productivity

The discovery that symbiotic algae leak their products of photosynthesis when living inside their hosts has revealed the secret of coral productivity,

'Coral symbiosis is one of the most efficient biological systems operating on the reef – its efficiency rivals that of the best chemical factory.'

Hard corals, *Stylophora pistillata, Symphyllia radians* and *Aeropora lufkeni*

and has made it clear that symbiosis was the key to the reef's vitality. Without the alga, excess ammonia would suffocate the host. Without the host, the alga would starve; it could barely survive alone on the reef.

A third medium of exchange between host and zooxanthella is acetate, the neutralised form of acetic acid or vinegar. Acetate is produced by both the coral animal and the clam, as it is a nearly final oxidation product of most foods. Algae absorb the acetate and use their energy to reassemble it in long energy-rich chains of fatty acids that stabilise their chloroplasts. The fatty acids are transferred to the outer membrane of the alga, the animal's enzymes take them into its own cells, and it is formed into a product similar to cetyl palmitate, the most common wax of corals. When a small brain coral is immersed in solvent to extract its fats and oils and the solvent is then evaporated, the residue is a mass

△ *The brownish colour of most corals is that of their symbiotic golden brown algae. Apart from their heavy calcium carbonate skeleton, the corals are actually half plant and half animal. Sometimes superficial pigments may conceal the brown colour, resulting from a combination of the chartreuse and red-orange pigments that absorb the blue light penetrating waters of the reef. The deeper the sea and the more blue the light, the darker and browner the corals. The algae, thriving within their colourless coral animal host cells, can contribute over half of the products of their photosynthesis to their host.*

Giant clam, *Tridacna maxima*

of solid cetyl palmitate, which is also an important component of sperm whale oil. If a dried coral had no calcareous skeleton, it could burn just as easily as a candle!

The great energy of the wax of corals at first perplexed biologists because, of all animals in the sea, the coral is least in need of a store of energy. It receives energy from the sun every day. But it is the coral's larvae that will need the wax. The small larva is released, loaded with fuel, for its possibly exhausting search for a suitable site for a new colony. Only then does it accumulate more zooxanthellae and begin to function as an effective symbiotic system.

In the sea, wax wards off starvation. It has the energy of ordinary fats, but it can only be digested one tenth as fast. Animals who live under a threat of starvation, such as the zooplankton and deep sea fish, usually maintain a store of wax in addition to

their usual and readily available energy supplies like fats, protein, and carbohydrates. Wax is a major energy source for animals of the sea.

Small reef fishes often get some of their food in the form of wax from the corals they live with. Corals exude mucus in their quest for small zooplankton and bacteria. This mucus is collected by fishes as they nip at the coral surfaces. The mucus, a protein holding a great deal of water, also contains fats and wax. These lipids are exuded with the mucus, much like a 'primordial milk'.

Nature is replete with symbiotic systems. Human cells interact with each other in co-operative fashion. Trees could hardly survive were it not for their fungal symbionts which collect nutrients for their roots. From human societies to nature's ecosystems, collaboration enhances efficiency for survival, and the creatures of the reef live by this essential rule of life.☐

△ *The blue, green, purple and yellow colours that adorn the extended mantles of the giant clams of this species create a pansy patch effect. The brilliant colours are produced by light diffraction by submicroscopic layers of crystalline non-coloured pigments. Nature's purpose for these colours is perplexing. They conceal the animals' three to ten millimetre-thick layer of photosynthetic symbiotic zooxanthellae, which use the energy of sunlight to produce food and consume waste ammonia for their animal hosts.*

Algae and sea grasses: plants of the sea

Abundant food

Marine plants are forever being eaten and settled upon by an enormous range of reef organisms. Yet despite this exploitation or cover-up, the flora still form one of the most conspicuous, abundant, and important biological components of the coral reef ecosystem.

The seaweeds or algae have been part of the ecological scene for two billion years or more, and they are still thriving. Sea grasses, however, first appeared during the late Cretaceous period, a mere 70 million years ago.

Despite the significance of the seaweeds and sea grasses to the growth and development of the Great Barrier Reef, a thorough understanding of these plants is still in its infancy. Yet they are abundant and are frequently spectacular, with at least 500 species of seaweed and 12 species of sea grasses known from the reef.

Male and female flowers

All marine flowering plants are collectively known as sea grasses, though they are more commonly referred to as turtle grasses or eel grasses. All are dioecious, which means that they have separate male and female flowers, borne on different plants.

A unique feature of sea grasses is their capacity to reproduce by pollination while submerged in sea water – a process known as hydrophilous pollination. The pollen is generally thread-like and is moved from the male to the female flower by water currents, rather like the dispersal of land plant pollens by the wind. Flowering appears to occur periodically, during low spring tides. Fertilisation leads to the production of fruit and seed, the fruit often being transported some distance from the parent plant by water currents before the seeds have been released.

Like the true terrestrial grasses, sea grasses are composed of an underground branching stem with rhizomes, and they bear a series of leafy shoots above the ground.

▽ *Commonly referred to as turtle weed, this green fleshy alga is widely believed to be grazed by the green turtle. The attractive green crab,* Caphyra rotundifrons, *lives among clumps of turtle weed. Other residents of the weed also assume the colour of their algal host.*

Turtle weed, *Chlorodesmis fastigiata*

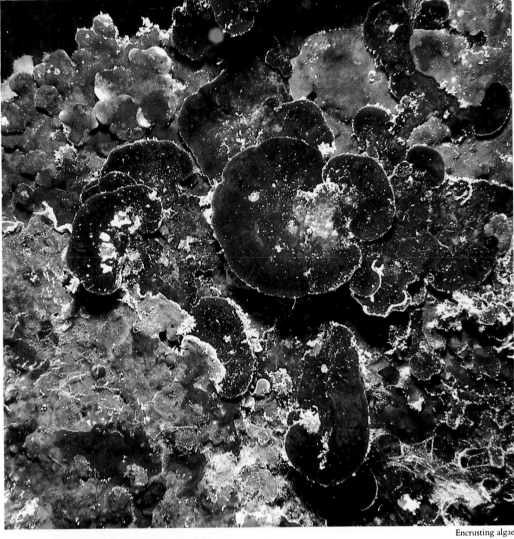

Encrusting algae

◁ *Encrusting or crustose coralline algae are probably the most important calcareous algae on the Great Barrier Reef, and they are especially abundant in areas of high wave action and intense herbivore grazing activity. These algae tend to have a leafy appearance, as well as their more common encrusting habit, in areas of reduced light intensity such as caves, under ledges or in deeper waters.*

▽ *The limy skeletal remains of many algae, such as the encrusting corallines, this alga, and the organisms living on the leaves of sea grasses, contribute much calcareous material to the reef sediments. These sediments, together with the skeletal remains of corals and molluscs, are the basis of the coral cays so prominent in the southern portion of the Great Barrier Reef.*

Calcareous alga, *Halimeda opuntia*

Sea grass

Colour classes

The macroscopic non-flowering marine plants are collectively known as algae, more commonly called seaweeds. All modern algal classification is based on the recognition of four major colour classes: browns, greens, reds and the ancient blue-greens. The reds, in particular, are often heavily calcified, especially the encrusting corallines, which look like pink or red paint spilt on concrete surfaces.

All colour classes exhibit a bewildering array of life forms ranging from delicate, branching plants to robust stony crusts. They also display the fascinating phenomenon called 'alternation of generations', whereby striking differences in form, structure and sex occur during various phases of the life cycle.

Despite its tropical location, seasonality is a common feature of the Great Barrier Reef. The brown algae, for instance, are highly seasonal in nature with *Sargassum* and *Turbinaria* prolific during

◁ *Sea grasses form dense beds or meadows on sandy bases in calm waters. In the reef region 80 to 90 per cent of the plant material is below ground, amounting to more than 200 tonnes per hectare of below-ground roots and stems. Many of these meadows are so extensive that they are recognisable in satellite photographs. The meadows trap substantial quantities of organic and inorganic sediments, creating a nutrient-enriched environment that supports an enormous array of reef fauna and flora, and serves as a nursery ground for many reef fishes.*

'Apart from dugongs, turtles and sea urchins, few reef animals feed on living sea grasses.'

▷ *The prostrate alga, commonly known as grape weed, cascades over the reef substrate, which is encrusted in pink crustose coralline algae. The crustose corallines cement the reef substrate together and hence increase the resistance of the reef to wave erosion.*

Grape weed, *Caulerpa racemosa*

Green alga, *Monostroma*

△ *Beach rock is a common feature of the sand cays, especially in the southern section of the Great Barrier Reef. It usually appears to be devoid of living organisms. This is not the case, however, as beach rock is covered with a thin veneer of blue-green, green and red algae, and marine lichens. The veneer is not obvious and is frequently obscured by a layer of sediment. During winter and spring, and particularly following rain, some green algae grow prolifically and are quite conspicuous. Grazers, such as the prosobranch gastropod,* Planaxis sulcatus, *and chitons, feed on the spores of the beach rock algae. The larger fleshy blades of the emphemeral algae such as* Enteromorpha *are especially vulnerable to grazing fishes.*

summer whereas *Hydroclathrus, Colpomenia*, and *Chnoospora* grow best in winter, especially in the southern section of the reef.

In spring, the winter algae decline and are sloughed from the reef and deposited along the strand line on coral cays during the spring tides. Annual examination of the strand line algal slough on the cays reveals most common species.

The floral connection

Sea grass beds are highly productive, photosynthetic systems comparable with high-yield agricultural crops. Surprisingly, however, few reef animals feed on living sea grasses, the most notable exceptions being dugongs, turtles and sea urchins. Most of the energy produced by the beds of sea grasses is passed on to other reef organisms through bacterial and fungal decomposition of dead plant material via the detrital food chain.

The algae are also highly productive, photosynthetic groups contributing to the construction of the reef and providing the principal food source for an enormous variety of animals such as fishes, sea urchins, crustaceans, turtles, dugongs and many molluscs.

Functioning as the primary producers of the coral reef ecosystem, the flora are the inextricable link between the sun's energy, inanimate nutrients and the organic food source fundamental to the existence of the reef consumers.

Close-up views

From a bird's eye view the algae appear to be more abundant towards the southern end of the Great Barrier Reef. In contrast, the opposite applies for the sea grasses. A closer view shows, from the beachrock of a sand cay, a strip of very fine turf composed of blue-green and red algae. Further seaward is a wide belt of luxuriant fleshy algae on the hard rock substrate, usually composed of dense stands of brown algae such as *Sargassum* in summer and *Colpomenia, Chnoospora* and *Hydroclathrus* in winter.

The bases of many of the corals are covered with encrusting corallines, the red or orange-red encrusting *Peyssonellia*, and leafy brown encrustations of *Lobophora variegata*. The calcareous skeletons of both living and dead corals are invariably riddled with boring algae, especially the green *Ostreobium reineckei* and the blue-green *Entophysalis deusta*.

Outside the belt of fleshy algae, turf algae again predominate, followed by a thick pavement of the pink encrusting coralline alga *Porolithon onkodes* on the reef crest and some fleshy types such as *Laurencia*.

Further from the seaward edge and down the reef slope, crustose corallines such as *Neogoniolithon* are the most abundant algae. There are few fleshy algae, with only the burgundy-coloured *Plocamium* and the brilliant green *Chlorodesmis* at all conspicuous. On the windward edge of these reefs are the intriguing spur and groove structures, which have been the focus of a lengthy debate over whether they were formed by erosion or construction. The spurs and grooves are characterised by luxuriant development of pink crustose corallines on the spurs whereas the grooves are devoid of algal growths.

The differentiation of algal functional types is a consequence of the interaction between a variety of physical and biological agencies. Of these the most notable are wave action and the intensity of fish grazing, which increases to seaward.

A complex web of intrigue

The macroscopic algae are seemingly benign and passive organisms. They provide the basis for the herbivore food chain, and also play a more variable role in the structuring of the coral reef.

Due to overgrowth and shading, the fleshy algae inhibit the growth and abundance of the crustose coralline algae. Similarly, the fleshy algae also inhibit coral growth and abundance by pre-empting substrate suitable for coral larval settlement. On the other hand, encrusting coralline algae make successful coral settlement easier, although this is not always the case. This inhibition of settlement and growth of many sedentary reef organisms can be improved by the removal of the fleshy algae by herbivores, a process that occurs constantly on many parts of the reef.

The continuous interaction between fleshy algae and corals causes an inverse relationship in the abundance of these two groups. This is especially obvious in the Capricorn-Bunker group in the southern section of the Great Barrier Reef. In those areas where fleshy algae predominate, the quantity of coral is reduced and coral colony sizes tend to be small. On the other hand, where fleshy algae are less common, both coral abundance and colony size are increased.

A balancing trio

Another interesting ecological grouping occurs on coral boulders on the reef flat and features a group of encrusting algae (the brown *Ralfsia expansa* and the pink coralline *Porolithon onkodes*), an air-breathing limpet, *Siphonaria australis*, and groups of fine turf algae (including *Jania*, *Phoysiphonia*, and *Gelidiella*). The limpet lives on the portion of the boulder exposed during low tide. This surface is also covered with both *Ralfsia* and *Porolithon*, whereas the turf algae occur only below the low-tide mark due to the grazing activity of the limpet. In the absence of grazing limpets the turf algae cover the entire boulder and exclude the encrusting algae.

What of the two encrusting algae themselves? Interestingly enough, if there are very few limpets on the boulder, *Ralfsia* tends to overgrow *Porolithon*, eventually excluding it altogether. Inevitably the turf algae, due to reduced grazing intensity, will then overgrow *Ralfsia*. A tenuous situation, whereby the identity of the dominant organism depends on the presence and density of the grazing limpet.

Though not obvious to the casual observer, there is another common and striking example of the herbivorous benefactor favouring one algal group over another. These herbivores are the territorial, pomacentrid fishes. Highly selective grazers, they will aggressively defend their territories against the intrusion of other, larger and less selective herbivorous fishes. This behaviour results in the development of a distinct algal group which is largely restricted to pomacentrid territories. These algal lawns would otherwise be considerably reduced outside those territories by the grazing of scarids and acanthurids.

The struggle for prominence

Consequently, three major components of the reef ecosystem (the algae, corals and herbivores) are involved in a complex web of interaction and a struggle for prominence.

Single-celled green alga, *Valonia ventricosa*

Historically, the contribution of algae to the dynamics of coral reefs was recognised well over a century ago. In 1842, Charles Darwin noted the role of the encrusting coralline algae (known in Darwin's day as *nullipores*) in cementing the reef substrate together and hence increasing reef resistance to wave erosion. Most reefs are built primarily from coral, but core samples from some 'coral' reefs show more calcium carbonate from plants. Algal spores cannot settle and grow on living corals, and therefore algae tend to settle and grow in areas of the reef that are unsuitable for corals.

The marine plants have had a long and illustrious geologic history as the principal contributors either directly or indirectly to the production of reef sediment, and as substrate stabilisers. Most importantly, they form the basis of the food chains that are essential to the maintenance of the coral reef ecosystem. □

'Seaweeds have been part of the ecological scene for a very long time – about two billion years.'

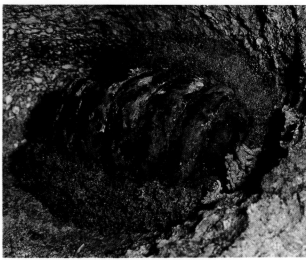

Green alga, *Enteromorpha clathrata*

△ *During winter and spring, flecks of this green alga can be found growing on beach rock though it is usually more abundant on the margin of the grazing chiton,* Acanthozostera gemmata. *Chitons, with their excavating feeding apparatus, are capable of removing all traces of developing algal growth and are responsible for the limited algal growth on the beach rock.*

△ ◁ *Algae include many bizarre and unusual forms. This single-celled green alga consists of a balloon-like vesicle and is mostly found underneath boulders, especially on the reef flat, where it is sometimes found encrusted with crustose coralline algae.*

Sponges: the ultimate survivors

The first multicelled animals

If we could go back 420 million years to the Devonian period and dive on a reef in 'Northern Australia', it would be possible to recognise some features found on modern reefs. Many of the sponges, for instance, would appear very similar to those we now see on the Great Barrier Reef. They are found in the fossil record as far back as the Precambrian (650 million years ago), where they were probably the first multicelled animals. The basic structure of the reefs on which they are found, however, has changed.

Unlike current reefs which have a base on stony corals cemented together by algae, the basic structure of many Devonian reefs consisted of sponges with solid skeletons of calcium carbonate, the stromatoporoids, along with the ancestors of modern corals. Many of these fossil reefs are now part of the continents and include the Ural Mountains in the Soviet Union and parts of the Great Dividing Range of Australia. These solid calcareous sponges have survived, although only as shadows of their former selves, and their major role in reef formation has now been supplanted by the reef-forming corals.

Destructive builders

The sponge's role in laying down new limestone for coral reef growth is now minor but sponges play an important part in the complex structural processes which form the solid structures we call coral reefs. The importance lies not in its 'constructive' abilities but rather in the powerful 'destructive', boring powers of only a relatively small proportion of its numbers.

The boring sponges chemically digest the limestone skeletons of corals during their search for living space and possibly for food. When they bore into the coral they dissolve about ten per cent of the skeleton as each cell cuts or more aptly scoops out a chip using a mechanism resembling an ice cream scoop. The tiny chips are expelled into the water and constitute a considerable proportion of the fine sediments which percolate into the holes of the reef structure or settle in the reef lagoons.

As the sponges bore into corals they weaken the skeletons, especially those of the fine branching corals, which eventually crumble during storms.

Boring sponge, *Cliona*

△ *Fine details of how sponges bore into corals are only seen through an electron microscope. These sponges seek a place to live away from predators and may extract some nutrient left in the coral skeleton. In doing so they remove very small chunks of the calcium carbonate which are shed into the water as fine sediment. The removal of these chunks creates the galleries and tunnels for the tissue to proliferate. The coral skeleton on the left is normal, compared with the heavily bored coral on the right, which has a characteristic scalloped surface.*

▷ *This sponge lives on the walls and ceilings of deep caves in the reefs towards the edge of the continental shelf where the water is generally very clear. Unlike most sponges, it has a solid limestone skeleton with a thin layer of living tissue over the surface. Sponges like this one are the tiny, living descendants of the massive stromatoporoid sponges which were dominant in the formation of reefs several hundred million years ago.*

'Living fossil' sponge, *Astrosclera willeyana*

The shattered skeletons are further broken down to rubble and eventually into coral sand which fills holes in the reef, adds to the lagoons or goes to make up reef islands. Through the long process of geological time these fine and coarse sediments are cemented together to form the reef rock which is the real base of the coral reefs. The fragile upward growth of corals towards the sunlight is slowed and the base consolidated against the rare but powerful forces of nature such as cyclones. The destructive actions of boring sponges result in a loss of only about ten per cent of the limestone from a reef; the rest is redistributed on the reef as the corals gradually grow upwards.

Living vacuum cleaners

Sponges are probably the most efficient 'vacuum cleaners' in the sea, cleaning the water by filtering out most of the tiny food particles such as bacteria, detritus and coral mucus. They can remove as much as 99 per cent of all bacteria. Other filter-feeding reef animals, however, such as giant clams, feather stars and even some of the corals themselves, consume larger particles of nutrient such as algae, fish larvae and crustaceans.

The ability of sponges to consume bacteria is one reason why they occur in great numbers at the entrances to harbours and rivers where currents carry large quantities of small food particles.

Food filters

To obtain sufficient nutrient from the clear waters of a coral reef, sponges have to filter large volumes of sea water almost non-stop throughout both night and day. Sponges will filter their own volume of water every four to 20 seconds, therefore in one day a teacup-sized sponge pumps about 5000 litres of water through its body. Most of this water is propelled through the sponge canals by the beating actions of millions of tiny whiplike cells, the choanocytes, which line all the feeding chambers. The continual beating assists in trapping the nutrient particles in the fine collars around the cells as well as creating a current which brings in the nutrient-rich sea water and carries away waste products.

Sponge chimneys

For many coral reef sponges, however, this incessant beating does not provide sufficient food to fuel these cells, and nutrient is also needed for growth and reproduction. To overcome this many sponges have 'learnt', through the long processes of evolution, to use the prevailing currents to drive water through

Fossilised sponge

◁ *This limestone pinnacle, consisting almost entirely of sponge skeletons, was part of a 420 million-year-old Devonian reef which was exposed by the rushing waters of the upper Burdekin River. This reef near Charters Towers is more than 100 kilometres from the coast near the central section of the Great Barrier Reef.*

the canals. Sponges use the same principle that is involved in the function of an efficient fireplace. Chimney-like structures are erected into the water where currents are stronger. The passage of water over the chimneys causes an 'updraft' that results in the passive flow of water into the myriads of tiny incurrent pores, the ostia, lower down the sponge body. The word 'ostia' is from the name of the Roman port city, Ostia, which was the entry point of food for the ancient city of Rome.

Throughout more than 600 million years of evolution sponges have developed highly efficient structures to increase water flow through the feeding chambers.

The skeletal structure

To most of us, a sponge is associated with bathroom use but the household sponge is just one type of skeleton of several sponge species among the

Yellow burrowing sponge

△ *Some sponges rely totally on chimneys for feeding while the bulk of the body is buried deep in the coral rock. Fine pores and canals at the base of the chimney convey water down to the sponge and the outcurrent water passes out through the top of the chimney.*

▷ *Some sponges use chimney-like structures to increase the flow of water through the canals. The canals that expel the water are raised up into the currents and act like a chimney to draw water in through many small pores, lower down the body. Among the many large erect chimneys of this sponge, which grows in back reef areas, nestles a similarly coloured feather star.*

Yellow-red vasiform sponge

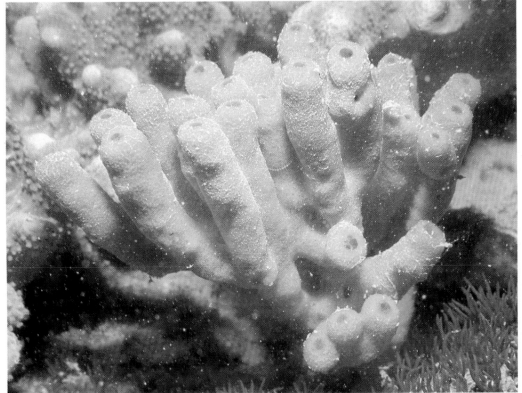

Tubular sponge, *Clathria*

'Sponges are the most efficient "vacuum cleaners" of the sea.'

◁ *The erect tubes of this sponge are not only useful as chimneys but allow it to feed above the fine sediments that would otherwise block its feeding canals when it is half buried in fine sand.*

▽ *The largest proportion of sponge species have a mixture of fibres and spicules in their skeletons. The fibres of this thick yellow fan are reinforced with spicules embedded inside. Other spicules support the canals and protrude through the outer skin.*

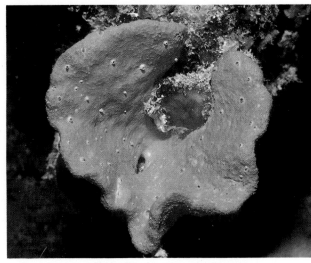

Thick yellow fan sponge, *Phakellia aruensis*

◁ *Most people know sponges by the fibrous skeletons that are the remains of only a small proportion of sponges after the cellular tissue has been removed. Sponges have a number of different skeleton types. The calcareous sponge has a skeleton consisting of millions of three-pointed and four-pointed stars (spicules) that are similar in composition to the calcium carbonate found in coral skeletons. These spicules, with the collagen fibres and cells that hold them together, support the sponge's canals and filter-feeding chambers.*

Calcareous sponge, *Pericharax heteroraphis*

'A teacup-sized sponge can pump 5000 litres of water through its body in one day.'

▷ *The brilliant pink sponge has a skeleton of long, needle-like spicules that are hooked at one end like an anchor and pointed at the other. They may be tens of millimetres long and radiate out from the centre.*

▽ *A sponge takes in sea water through incurrent pores called ostia, and then filters it through a series of canals until it enters the feeding chambers. There, flagellated cells beat the water through the canal system and circulate food particles until they are trapped in the choanocytes. The water then passes out through large outcurrent openings called oscules.*

Magnified cross section of a typical sponge

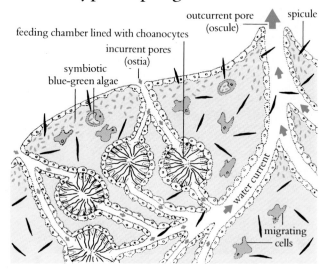

feeding chamber lined with choanocytes
outcurrent pore (oscule)
spicule
incurrent pores (ostia)
symbiotic blue-green algae
water current
migrating cells

Pink sponge, *Cinachyra*

thousands that live in the sea. Around these skeletons, making the sponge a living thing, are the simplest of the multicellular animals that trace their ancestry back to the unicellular animals, the protozoa.

The fibrous skeleton is one example of the different types found in sponges. Most sponges, however, contain spicules that strengthen the fibres of some and act as a skeleton in others. These spicules are composed of either glass-like silica or limestone, and come in an infinite variety of shapes and sizes, including multipointed stars and spirals. Most, however, are simple, pointed needles. These spicules are useful for identifying sponges, as they are the only parts that remain in the fossil record.

A typical sponge makes its living by filtering sea water and by being host to blue-green algae that provide additional nutrient. Water passes in through many fine incurrent pores, the ostia, and then percolates through a system of ever-decreasing

canals until it enters the feeding chambers. Here the frenetic, but co-ordinated, actions of the whiplike cells beat the water through the canal system and also circulate food particles around the chambers until they are trapped in the collars of these cells. Finally the water passes out through another series of canals to the large outcurrent openings, the oscules. All round this is a thickened fluid area in which all the other cells meander: skeleton-making cells, digestive cells, cells which hold the algae and other cells which nurse developing larvae. The mobility of cells is essential for circulating food and for repairing damaged tissue.

Sponges reproduce either sexually, through the production of swimming larvae that settle out and grow into adult sponges, or asexually. In this way the adult sponge will produce buds that break off and quickly form new adults. Sometimes, when sponges are torn apart by storms, the fragments will reattach and grow. This ability was utilised by ancient Greek sponge divers (and still is), who cut sponges into pieces and tied them to rocks or broken pottery where they grew into large bath sponges.

Symbiosis – a tropical trick

Sponges are efficient filter feeders and are able to use reef currents to assist their feeding mechanisms, but the clear blue waters around coral reefs contain insufficient nutrients to sustain large sponge

populations. They do, however, exist in large numbers because the majority use the same method of augmenting their food supply as other filter-feeding animals such as corals, giant clams and colonial ascidians. Algae grow within the animal tissues and their powerful photosynthetic abilities are used to provide nutrient in the form of glycerol, a sugar-like compound.

This symbiosis in sponges is a partnership with blue-green algae, but the host sponge gains most benefit. Energy-rich sugar compounds leak out of the algae that are imprisoned either inside sponge cells or in the fluid around the cells. Rather than eat the algae, the host sponge has developed a chemical mechanism to force the algae to leak as much as 80 per cent of their valuable products of photosynthesis directly into the sponge cells.

Many sponges on coral reefs, therefore, use the abundant sunlight in these clean water habitats to make up for the lack of other nutrients. To do this these coral reef sponges have evolved from spherical or tubular shapes into dish, cup, fan or encrusting forms that are more efficient for trapping sunlight.

The symbiosis works so well in some sponges that most of their nutrition is provided by the algae; the filter-feeding mechanism is used only as a supplement to provide essential minerals and possibly vitamins. The blue-green algae are able to photosynthesise efficiently at low light levels which may explain why these sponges occur predominantly in deeper water, around 15 to 20 metres depth, beyond the most prolific growth zone of the hard corals.

The bulk of sponges on the Great Barrier Reef rely on symbiotic algae for some or most of their energy nutrient in the same way as the reef-forming corals rely on their algae, the zooxanthellae. The differences between these two types of symbioses may explain why corals replaced sponges on the reefs hundreds of millions of years ago. The algae in coral not only provide nutrient but play a prominent role in the rapid formation of the coral's solid skeleton. The ancient calcareous sponges probably did not have any symbionts to aid skeleton formation and hence were probably outgrown by the corals which, since then, have become the dominant reef builders.

The reef's hotels

In the complex world of a coral reef, space to live is rare. The ways in which the reef animals solve this problem are varied but some have found that sponges are good places to live on or in. The numerous canals and tubes provide ideal living and hiding places for animals such as shrimps and crabs, polychaete worms and brittle stars. In addition many animals associate with sponges because, being either toxic or distasteful, they repel predators.

The sponges are not welcoming hosts to all these

Thin yellow fan sponge, *Ianthella basta*

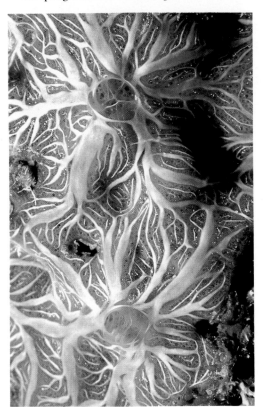

Red encrusting sponge

Cup-sponge, *Strepsichordaia lendenfeldi*; flattened sponge, *Pseudaxinyssa*

△ The thin yellow fan has no spicules, only thick, stiff fibres that hold the sponge erect across the prevailing current. In most fan-shaped sponges the pores that inhale the water face the direction of the main current flow, while the exhalant holes are on the down-current side.

◁ Sponges and corals use similar mechanisms to obtain additional nutrient in the clean waters of coral reefs. Inside the tissues there are symbiotic blue-green algae that give many of the sponges a distinct red-brown to purple colour; the colouring is due to a red pigment which masks the green chlorophyll pigments. In the dim light of deeper water the red pigment is enhanced. Sponges like the cup-shaped Strepsichordaia lendenfeldi, and the flattened Pseudaxinyssa with their symbiotic blue-green algae, tend to dominate regions where the coral populations are diminishing. A characteristic feature of many sponges inhabited by these algae is the evolution of flattened light-capturing shapes rather than spherical or tube shapes.

◁◁ A red sponge encrusting over coral rock can look like modern art. Sponges were long thought to be colonies of many filter-feeding units; however, the red encrusting sponge has interconnected feeding units. The pores that inhale the water are in the red tissue and, after the water is filtered, it is passed into the white canals to be expelled. The canals fuse until they join at the outcurrent holes, two of which are visible. The interconnecting canals permit a sponge to pump water through its body, and it functions even though some tissue may be damaged or blocked.

▷ *The sponge is losing ground to the more aggressive coral,* Montastrea magnistellata. *The effect, however, is not fatal for the sponge, which grows, apparently normally, away from the coral.*

▽ *Many animals use sponges as convenient places to hide or simply to get up into the currents where there are more nutrients. On top of this mauve vase sponge in a coral reef lagoon, three feather stars or crinoids extend their arms into the flowing sea water. As well as being a convenient place to sit, the sponge may also offer these crinoids some protection as a large number of sponges are either toxic or distasteful to predators.*

Mauve vase sponge, *Callyspongia*

Photosynthetic flattened sponge, *Phyllospongia lamellosa*

guests. The unwanted guests often are a considerable nuisance to the host as they tend to block up the canals which are the sponges' life-support systems bringing in food and oxygen and carrying away wastes. Some of the guests may also consume the host tissue or host food intake. Where possible, sponges will try to repel and lock out their guests. They also use their powerful chemical defences to deter the guests or use the ultimate defence and eat the invaders. The last method only works on the minute larval stages of invaders as sponges can consume only the smallest of particles.

Unappetising morsels
The larvae of sponges are eaten by all those animals that feed on plankton and more than 99.9 per cent of the larvae never grow. Once they become adult sponges, however, very few predators worry them because of either their toxins or their rough and

spiky skeletons which make a sponge meal very unappetising and tough.

Some fishes, turtles and molluscs do consume sponges but the most specific and bizarre predators are nudibranchs, the colourful sea slugs. They feed on a wide range of sponges including some of the most toxic ones and use sponge toxicity to their own advantage. The nudibranchs concentrate sponge toxins in their own tissue while feeding on the sponge, thereby making themselves toxic to potential predators. It has been shown recently that some nudibranchs will choose and then concentrate the most toxic out of a group of four or five compounds in a single sponge.

Toxic compounds
The pharmaceutical industry has shown considerable interest in sponges, focusing particularly on the search for new antibiotics and anti-cancer drugs.

Many interesting compounds have been found in sponges, but it is not known what role these compounds might play in the life of a sponge as bacteria-eating sponges are unlikely to need protection from bacterial infections. However, throughout their 600 million years of evolution, sponges have had the chance to experiment and produce new compounds as protection against all manner of competitors and predators.

There are apparently more toxic sponges in tropical regions than in cooler habitats. In the clear waters of a coral reef, packed with many potential predators and competitors, the sponges that succeed will be those that are toxic or distasteful and can keep away from or grow above the competitors. Cryptic and boring sponges have avoided predation by hiding in the holes of coral reefs and under ledges, but if they are exposed – such as when a coral rock is turned over – the predators rapidly remove them. □

'Sponges will try to repel and lock out their guests.'

Brown encrusting sponge, *Neofibularia irata*

◁ This encrusting sponge sometimes overgrows corals and eventually kills them. For many of the animals on coral reefs, space to grow in the light is of crucial importance because it is light that provides energy to many sponges and corals. This often results in a competition for survival.

▽ The synaptulid holothuroid is a common inhabitant on many sponges in the reef's lagoons. The holothuroid feeds on excreted mucus and the fine layer of detritus that collects on the sponge's inhalant surface by passing its feeding tentacles over the sponge's surface.

Tubular sponge, *Callyspongia*

◁ Victory in the competition for growing space does not always go to the sponge. Over a four-year period the result of a contest has not changed; the coral is still growing on its outer periphery, but the sponge has nowhere to grow but upwards. The zone between the two combatants is a 'no-man's-land' with evidence of damaged tissue in both the coral and the sponge.

◁ ◁ Being a host to a lot of other coral reef animals is often disadvantageous to sponges. Any animal that sits on the surface or inside canals disrupts the flow of water into the sponge and impedes feeding. Barring the method of entry is just one way a sponge tries to prevent animals coming into the canals. When the sponge projects one arm of its star-shaped spicules directly into the canal the flow of water is hardly impeded, but small predators and unwanted visitors cannot gain entry.

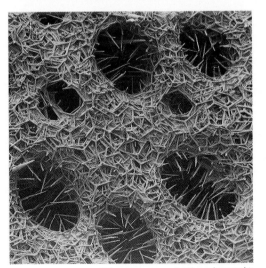

Calcareous sponge, *Pericharax heteroraphis*

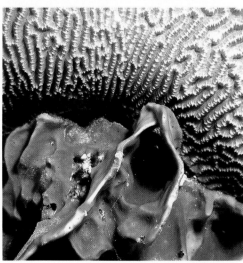

Brown encrusting sponge, *Neofibularia irata*

Marine worms: ubiquitous and cryptic

A vital part of the reef system

Brightly coloured, iridescent creatures with voracious jaws, well-developed eyes and amazing sets of sensory appendages ... such a description is far from the popular image of worms.

But such worms can be found. Some live in tubes, some swim gracefully through the water or glide effortlessly over the sand and coral, while others scurry rapidly back to their burrows when disturbed. Many occur on the Great Barrier Reef, but most are small and cryptic, and are therefore hidden from the casual visitor to the reef.

Borers and grinders

Worms are a vital part of the reef system. Their number and variety is best illustrated by a study conducted at Heron Island: a head of dead coral weighing over three kilograms was broken up and 1441 worms of 103 species – over two-thirds of the total fauna of this head of coral – were collected. These worms, together with the other animals found in the coral head, such as small crustaceans, form a closely knit community within the dead coral skeleton. Some of these animals bore into the coral skeleton either by chemically dissolving the skeleton or by mechanically grinding the coral, while others that cannot bore occupy the burrows made by the borers. Here, deeply embedded in the coral, the soft-bodied worms are relatively safe from the many reef predators.

Coral reefs are teeming with worms, for dead coral skeletons make up most of the reef – even a healthy reef. But all reef habitats are full of worms, including the sand and mud in lagoons or between the reefs. The worms range in size from microscopic to several centimetres in length and have a variety of life styles. Some live naked between the sand grains, moving freely through the sediments; others build tubes that they will drag for considerable distances; still others have far less permanent homes – a fine layer of slime through which they move. Finally, some live totally exposed on the surface of the sediment, relying on defensive mechanisms such as being unpleasant to eat, poisonous or mimicking poisonous species. This group includes the brightly coloured flatworms that are easily seen moving over the reef habitat.

Other types of worms are found in the plankton

Fan-worm, *Sabellid*

Christmas-tree worm, *Spirobranchus giganteus*

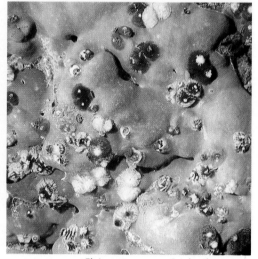

Christmas-tree worm, *Spirobranchus giganteus*

△ *The fan-worm, a sedentary species, grows to 50 or 60 millimetres, and builds muddy tubes that are wedged in coral or lie buried in sediment. Each of the filaments making up the worm's crown has many finely ciliated branches. The cilia create a water current that pushes the water through the interlocking mesh of the crown. Other cilia trap small particles in the water, wrap them up in sticky mucus and move them to the grooves that run along each filament. Another group of cilia transport these food parcels to the base of the crown where two pinnae, like paddle-shaped spoons, put the food in the mouth. The fan-worm has eyes or groups of pigment spots along its filaments, and it quickly contracts into its tube if the shadow of a predatory fish appears. If the worm does not contract rapidly enough, the fish bites off the crown. Until the crown regrows – usually within a few days – the worm cannot feed.*

△ *The Christmas-tree worm, which grows to a length of 50 or 60 millimetres, feeds in a similar way to the sabellids but differs in that one of the branchial filaments is modified to form a chalky plug or plate that seals the tube when the worm contracts into it. The Christmas-tree worm occurs in many colours – including blue, red, yellow, white, brown, purple and orange – and the reasons for this are not known. On a single head of coral a variety of colours can be seen. It seems that each worm can produce offspring of various colours, and there appears to be no reason for having all blue worms on one species of coral and all yellow on another.*

△ *The Christmas-tree worm can be found on several species of live coral. It does not bore into the coral, but the juvenile secretes a small chalky tube on the surface of the live coral, where a polyp has been damaged, for example, by a grazing parrotfish and therefore cannot sting and paralyse the worm. The coral grows around the worm tube and the worm tries to grow at the same rate as the coral, to make sure that the entrance to its tube – through which it feeds, breeds and excretes – is never sealed off by the coral. The Christmas-tree worm breeds in late December, and there are separate males and females. The gametes are spawned directly into the water, where fertilisation occurs and larvae are produced. After 10 to 14 days, depending on the water temperature, the worm settles and immediately secretes a miniature tube. Like all species that spawn in this way, however, few survive to settle in the coral. Most of the worms are either eaten or get washed out to sea at a great distance from any reef area: the only place where this species will settle.*

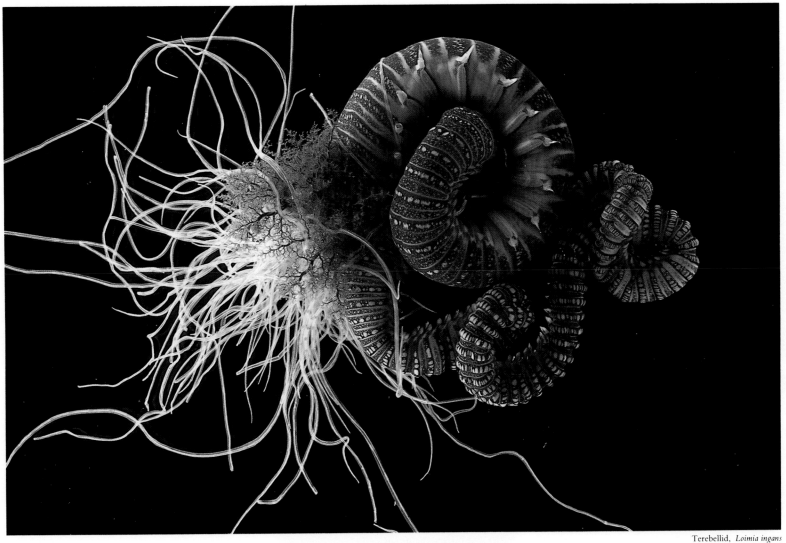

Terebellid, *Loimia ingans*

△ *Closely related to* Reteterebella queenslandica, *this terebellid has similar, visible branched gills. This species, which grows to 150 or 200 millimetres, builds a firm muddy tube, often strengthened by grains of sand or shell fragments, which is buried in the sediment next to the reefs (the photograph shows a worm with its tube peeled off). The banded feeding tentacles can often be seen stretched out over the sand. The head is modified into a series of glandular lips that sort sediment as it passes along the feeding tentacles. Fine sediment is ingested, medium-sized particles are used for tube building, and the largest particles are rejected. The worm can cough and throw the sediment away from the range of its tentacles, ensuring that it does not eat the same particles again.*

◁ *A piece of coral split open underwater shows various animals living inside it: polychaetes, sipunculans, hesionids, boring bivalves and sponges.*

'During their reproductive ritual, ripe worms leave the sediment or coral and swarm in the upper layers of the water, shedding their gametes.'

◁ Strings of white spaghetti-like strands, spread over the reef, are the feeding tentacles of Reteterebella queenslandica. Bundles of sediment can be seen moving along these strands, some a metre or more long, like a conveyor belt. If touched, the strands quickly retract into the sand and coral. Deep down in the substrate, the worm to which these strands are attached lives in a tube made of fine sediment (which has been peeled off in the photograph below) It obtains its food not from the sediment it swallows but from the micro-organisms and algae that live on the surface of the sediment. At the base of the feeding tentacles are three pairs of branched gills full of haemoglobin.

Reteterebella queenslandica

where some species spend all of their lives. These tend to be transparent, although they often have well-developed glands on each segment which may secrete a luminous substance that makes the worms glow at night. Some spend only their childhood in the plankton. Some other species inhabit the plankton for only their reproductive ritual when ripe, colourful worms leave the sediment or coral and swarm in the upper layers of the water, shedding their gametes.

A balance of growth and destruction

The roles of the many different types of worms in the reef system are probably as varied as the species themselves. But knowledge of the reef worms is limited; many are still to be named and described, and even in cases where this has been done their roles have often not been investigated fully.

Some of the worms that bore in the coral are important in the breakdown of coral, for the shape and form of reefs represents the balance between reef growth and reef destruction. Many of the characteristic parts of a reef, such as the sediment on the lagoon floor or the sediment that makes up sand cays, are produced from the breakdown of coral which begins as soon as the coral dies. Most live coral colonies overlay dead coral, and often only the top part of a coral colony is alive.

Many of the worms are important as food for other reef organisms. The gastropod *Conus* can suck

out worms living down in the coral by inserting its proboscis into the worm burrow, and many of the fishes that comb the lagoon sediments are looking for worms on which to feed. Because the worms are so numerous and breed rapidly – some every three or four weeks – their contribution to the food chain on the reef is high. Many of these worms exist independently, but there is also a group of parasitic worms that lives in or on fishes, birds, turtles and marine mammals.

Worms usually have well-developed eyes and respiratory, digestive and excretory systems. Most produce free-swimming larvae that spend some time in the reef plankton. However, within the group of animals known as worms there are several different phyla, or animal groups. Although superficially they all look like worms, they are not all related.

Marine worms can be divided into the simpler, unsegmented worms and the more complex segmented worms, although some of the

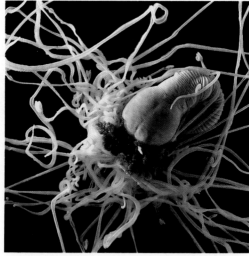

Reteterebella queenslandica

▷ Chloeia flava *grows up to 50 or 60 millimetres long. It is related to the fire worm, having similar bristles that break off easily when the worm is handled, and become lodged painfully in the hand. An active carnivore, the worm has a well-developed head with good eyes and sensory appendages that can detect light and dark, find food on sand grains and warn of approaching danger.*

Chloeia flava

Hesionid

Nematonereis unicornis

△ This active worm from the Hesionidae family is found among the coral. It is carnivorous and probably feeds by sucking out the contents of bryozoan or hydroid polyps with a muscular, pump-like pharynx. About 10 millimetres long, this worm has extremely well-developed sensory feelers on its front segments and moves by using each of its paddle-like legs to generate synchronised waves along the whole of its body.

▷ This elegant worm from the Phyllodocidae family is often iridescent, with distinctive pigmentation patterns. It has large, leaf-shaped feelers on each segment which lie across the back and almost meet in the middle. Many species of phyllodocids spawn over a short time and lay eggs in small capsules attached to the coral. All larval development occurs in these capsules, and miniature adults are produced. Phyllodocids, which range from three or four millimetres to 60 millimetres in length, have been observed in Moreton Bay in southern Queensland completely covering the surface of the mud at low tide just before spawning. At this time, the worms were apple-green, due to the colour of the hundreds of yolky eggs packed inside their bodies. Adult phyllodocids spawn only once and then die.

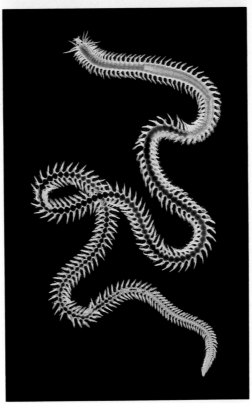

Phyllodocid

△ This is one of several species of polychaete worms that bores into the coral. How they actually bore is not yet clear; they may secrete an acid that dissolves the coral, they may grind the coral between their hard, horny teeth, or perhaps they use both techniques. Such animals are responsible for significant losses of calcium carbonate from the reef every year; this is called bio-erosion. But coral reefs maintain a balance between growth and destruction. This worm, which grows to 40 or 50 millimetres, is iridescent and has a visible dorsal blood vessel. Polychaetes lack distinct blood corpuscles; instead blood pigment, haemoglobin, is dissolved in the blood.

'If a segmented worm is punctured it loses its form, like a balloon, and cannot swim until the tear reseals.'

segmented worms, like leeches, have lost all external traces of segmentation and can be easily confused with the unsegmented types.

With and without segments

A segmented worm's body is built up of identical segments, bilaterally symmetrical and each with its own set of organs. On each side of a segmented worm are leg-like projections, sometimes equipped with bristles, and feathery appendages through which oxygen is absorbed. Within each side of the body wall there is a tube opening to the exterior from which waste is excreted. A gut, a large blood vessel and a nerve cord run from front to end through all the segments, linking and co-ordinating them; each segment is separated from the next by a vertical wall or septum. Segmented worms have a hydrostatic skeleton: a body cavity full of fluid that helps maintain the worm's shape and enables it to

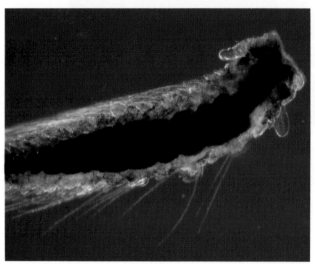

Spionid larva

Scale worm, *Lepidonotus*

swim. If a worm is punctured it loses its form, like a balloon, and cannot swim until the tear reseals.

As these segmented worms evolved, some parts of the body became specialised for particular functions, and often segments became fused. The several segments that made up the head often joined together, and sensory appendages like eyes – and various sorts of receptors such as those sensitive to taste, smell, feel and vibration – became concentrated in the head region.

Segmented worms are represented by the earthworms, bristle worms and leeches from the phylum Annelida, peanut worms from the phylum Sipunculoida, and echiuroids.

Unsegmented worms, although composed of three layers of cells like segmented worms, lack a true body cavity and serial sets of organs. Unsegmented worms from several phyla are found on the reef. Ribbon worms belong to the phylum

Nemertina, flatworms to the Platyhelminthes phylum and roundworms to the Nematoda phylum. Internal parasitic worms, including nematodes, trematodes and tapeworms – from the phylum Platyhelminthes – are also common in many reef animals. The trematodes may occur as external parasites on the gills of fishes, in the nasal respiratory passages of turtles, or as liver flukes in the guts of many vertebrates.

Elastic ribbon worms

Ribbon worms are often brightly coloured; they are very elastic and can stretch from several millimetres to 500 millimetres while moving along. They have unsegmented bilaterally symmetrical bodies that are soft and covered in sticky mucus. Some species have a flattened body and others are cylindrical. Ribbon worms are carnivorous and catch their prey, such as small crustaceans or worms,

△ *The scale worm is commonly found among coral rubble or under boulders. Many species occur on the reef and can reach 20 millimetres in length. These worms have scales attached to their backs by stalks, resembling a row of mushrooms. Some female scale worms incubate eggs under their scales. The worms are male or female and are often highly territorial. Normally, scale worms are carnivores or scavengers, and they use a muscular pharynx with horny jaws to catch prey.*

△ ◁ *Spionid larvae, about one millimetre long, are characterised by long, flowing setae that maintain buoyancy, and the beginnings of palps – long, fat tentacles like two ice-cream spoons, with which the animal feeds – at the front end. There is a rudimentary collar around the neck which will be used to build a tube; the worm will settle in this, shed its long setae and develop adult setae.*

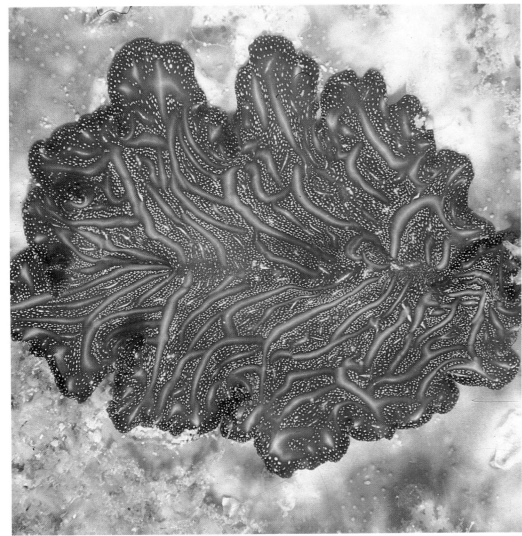

Flatworm, *Pseudoceros bedfordi*

Ribbon worm, *Pantinonemertes winsori*

with a flexible, muscular proboscis that can be shot out rapidly, rather like a sock being pulled off inside out. The prey is punctured by spikes on the lining of the proboscis, and poisonous fluid seems to be injected into the wounds made by the spikes. The stunned or partially paralysed prey is then pulled into the gut and eaten. In a few species, the spikes are not developed and the proboscis is used as a 'lasso' to catch the prey. These worms are usually hidden from view, living underneath coral boulders or among coral rubble, although some of the smaller, less colourful species can be seen in the sand. Ribbon worms may fragment when disturbed. The proboscis is often shed and then regrows easily, but when the body has fragmented only the anterior end is capable of surviving and growing a new tail.

Nemerteans have separate sexes and a simple reproductive system. At spawning time the males and females come together, or in some cases cohabit the same burrow for a short while before spawning. The mature gametes are shed and fertilisation occurs on the sand. The eggs are enclosed in gelatinous strings that attach themselves to the coral. Many species develop without a larval stage and miniature adult worms crawl out of these egg strings after several weeks. But in a few species, including some found in the reef, a free-swimming larva is produced, which spends some time in the plankton before developing into an adult.

Hermaphrodite flatworms

Flatworms, or turbellarians, belong to the phylum Platyhelminthes that also includes the parasitic tapeworms and liver flukes that infest many fishes, birds, reptiles and marine mammals. The colourful flatworms, a flattened leaf-shape up to 30 millimetres long, are very common on the reef and can be seen gliding over the coral layer or the sand. They secrete a mucus stream on which they ride, propelled by the fine bristles that cover their underbody. Some species swim by the movement of peristaltic contractions along the body.

◁ △ *This common species of segmented flatworm can both glide and swim. There are many different coloured flatworms found in reef waters. The species shown, which grows to about 20 millimetres, has branches of the gut and other vital organs dispersed throughout the body.*

◁ *This common ribbon worm is found in bark or cavities in rotten fallen mangrove timber at the upper tidal level. When fully extended, this worm reaches up to 100 or 150 millimetres in length. It creeps over the mud on a cushion of mucus and is a voracious carnivore. It is more active at night – hiding during the day – and is able to move about untouched by fishes and crabs.*

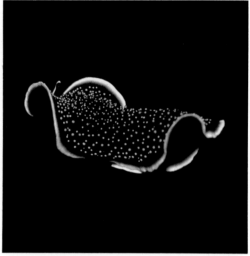

◁ Polynoid larvae, each about one millimetre long, can feed in the plankton and may distribute over hundreds of kilometres. The larva has a well-developed head, although it will develop more segments and replace its juvenile scales with adult ones.

▽ Peristaltic waves, generated along the flatworm's body, propel the worm forward. It is common in reef waters, and grows to a length of about 20 millimetres. This brightly coloured flatworm glides on a cushion of slimy mucus over a colony of compound ascidians. Species of flatworm are distinguished mainly by the arrangement of internal body organs rather than external colouring; within the one species many different colour patterns can occur. A few species living in the sediment are coloured by the single-celled plant that lives symbiotically with the worm. These species must sun themselves daily for the algae to grow and reproduce.

Free-living flatworms are carnivorous and, like ribbon worms, have a flexible muscular pharynx that is used to trap prey. Their highly coloured body patterns possibly act as a warning to predators that the worms are unpleasant to eat. Many flatworms have remarkable powers of regeneration, and some species can be cut in several pieces and each piece will grow a new head and tail. This ability to regenerate is also used by the worm as a method of asexual reproduction.

Most flatworms are hermaphrodites, but they are not self-fertile. At the time of breeding, two worms each insert their male reproductive organ into the female opening of the other. After copulation the worms separate and later each worm produces a string of yolky eggs that become attached to the coral. The shell of the egg hardens to protect and prevent the contents from dehydrating. In some species, juvenile worms hatch from the egg capsules but in others a free-swimming larva is produced which spends several weeks in the plankton before developing into an adult flatworm.

Iridescent roundworms

Roundworms are a large group that includes many parasitic and free-living species. The parasitic forms occur in many animals and plants and can often be seen in the muscle, gut or liver when gutting or cleaning a fish. Parasitic roundworms have a strongly iridescent skin, are unsegmented and have fairly rigid bodies that often grow to 10 or 20 millimetres. Many species, however, are free living and large numbers occur in all reef environments, especially in the sand and coral. They are hairlike but may reach up to 10 millimetres in length. Like the parasitic worms they are unsegmented and have iridescent skin.

Males and females are quite distinct, and many males have complicated sets of organs that are used to hold the female while mating. After copulation the eggs are fertilised inside the female body cavity, and subsequently a fertilised egg covered with a protective shell is released. Development occurs within the shell, and immature adults are released. Roundworms rapidly reach sexual maturity and a large population can form quickly.

Sea worms and earthworms

The phylum Annelida is made up of oligochaetes or earthworms, polychaetes or sea worms, and hirundinaetes or leeches, all of which are found on coral reefs. They are segmented worms, although in the case of leeches some of the segmentation has become indistinct.

Marine earthworms were thought to be rare in reef habitats until recently, when careful sieving of coral sands revealed large numbers of microscopic species. Marine earthworms closely resemble garden

earthworms and appear to play a similar role, turning over and aerating sediment. Marine leeches are commonly found on fishes and turtles and can be easily recognised by two suckers, one at each end. They may occur on the outside or inside of the gill chambers or respiratory passages.

Sea worms live almost exclusively in the sea or in estuaries. Their name 'polychaetes', from the Greek word *polukhaites* meaning 'having much hair', refers to the many bristles that stick out from each segment. They are a diverse group of worms and are represented by over 70 families. On the Great Barrier Reef there are hundreds of species, many still unidentified, ranging in length from a few millimetres to many centimetres. Polychaetes are often highly coloured, many are iridescent, and some are luminescent at night. In many species bright red blood can be seen being pumped through the blood vessels. But the most distinctive feature of polychaete worms is their variety of size, body shape, feeding methods, and reproductive methods, which enable them to live in many different habitats. Polychaetes have been found in large numbers in marine and estuarine habitats from shallow areas to the deepest ocean trenches. Some sea worms live among the coral rubble or sand; others bore into the coral and live permanently in these burrows; some secrete chalky tubes on the surface of the coral; others build sandy or muddy tubes attached to the coral, and a few live in the water above the reef as a permanent part of the plankton.

Most sea worms have either male or female reproductive organs, but some species are both male and female. The latter species cannot necessarily fertilise themselves. The most common method of reproduction is for all the males and females to develop their reproductive cells at the same time. In response to a particular cue – perhaps a phase of the moon – all the adults spawn their gametes into the overlying water where fertilisation then occurs. In some species, just before spawning, the worms undergo bodily changes such as the development of large swimming lobes, long bristles and enlarged eyes. The adult worms swarm in the surface water performing a nuptial dance and releasing their gametes. The worms then die and their spent bodies are eaten by fish and other predators. Meanwhile, the eggs are fertilised and produce free-swimming larvae that may spend several weeks in the plankton. As the polychaete larvae develop the family of polychaetes to which they belong can be determined.

Spawning on the reef
In Samoa, the inhabitants can establish the exact day on which the palolo worm will spawn on the reef. The ripe, swimming adults are considered a great delicacy by the locals who on the calculated day launch their boats and catch the worms as they swim up to the surface waters to spawn. Closely related species occur on the Great Barrier Reef and can sometimes be seen on very still nights at low tide. What appears to be a small burst of light on coral is, in fact, a sea of ragworms, or nereids, engaged in a strange, suicidal breeding ritual. One after the other, thousands of swollen bodies burst open, releasing a stream of eggs or sperm into the water, where fertilisation occurs. Many of the eggs and sperm, together with adults, however, are trapped and eaten by the carnivorous corals.

Similar events occur in temperate waters, and areas of Botany Bay, on the coast of New South Wales, can resemble a sea of writhing worms before the thousands of spent bodies are washed up, completely changing the colour of the beaches.

A worm within a worm
If one dives at night on the reef a long green tentacle, several centimetres long and forked at the end, can sometimes be seen stretched over the coral; when touched, the tentacle quickly contracts. This

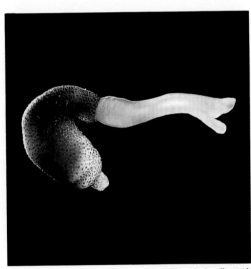

Echiuroid, *Bonellia viridis*

belongs to an echiuroid, *Bonellia viridis*, which lives in a crevice in the coral. The worm is a vivid green and appears to be closely related to the annelids, although all traces of external segmentation have disappeared. The large bulbous worm is the female; all that remains of the male is the reproductive system, living inside the female as a sort of parasite. The pygmy males enter the body of the female and live in her body cavity.

Bonellia viridis has an unusual method of sexual determination: any larvae that enter the female's body are induced by a female hormone to develop into dwarf males; larvae that do not come into contact with a female develop into females.

Echiuroids feed on small organic particles by extending their proboscis over the coral. Fine organic particles are swept into the groove on the underside of the extended proboscis by a current created by fine cilia lining the groove. The particles are then wrapped in sticky mucus and the food parcel is transported back along the proboscis to the mouth at its base.

Grinding the corals
Peanut worms range in size from a few millimetres to several centimetres and are rather drab coloured; their skin contains a variety of hooks and spines. One species, *Aspidosiphon*, resembles a pineapple with its complex set of spines and hooks at the front end. These spines help the worm to bore into coral and act as grinding plates once the coral has been softened with acid.

There are separate male and female peanut worms. The ripe gametes are shed from the body cavity through the kidneys and fertilisation takes place in the water column. Once the males have spawned the ripe sperm stimulates neighbouring ripe females to spawn, thus ensuring fertilisation.□

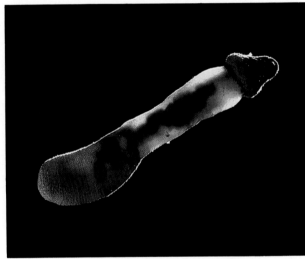

Peanut worm, Sipunculan

△ *Peanut worms, which grow rapidly to a length of 50 millimetres, bore deep into the dead coral substrate, keeping an opening to the outside through which food can be collected and waste products and gametes can be released. Most species bore deep into dead coral, probably by chemical secretion; and only at the larva stage. If an adult peanut worm is dislodged from its burrow, it cannot make another one.*

△ ◁ *Underwater, all that is visible of this echiuroid is its long green feeding tentacle; it can stretch up to a metre and contracts rapidly if touched. Buried deep in the coral, in a flask-shaped burrow, lives the soft-bodied female, about the size of a small hazelnut. All that remains of the male is its reproductive system; it exists merely as a sperm-producing organ inside the female.*

Molluscs: animals with shells, tentacles and brilliant colours

Voyagers and collectors

Anyone who has visited a beach will at some time have picked up a seashell, either to admire its beauty or just from idle curiosity. But few will have realised that seashells are the skeletons of animals which, with the garden snail, the octopus, oyster and giant clam, form one of the largest divisions of the animal kingdom, the molluscs, with over 100 000 different known kinds or species.

Although shells have been used since prehistoric times for adornment and as a sign of wealth, modern shell collecting began in early 18th century Europe. The voyages of James Cook to the South Seas and, in particular, to the Great Barrier Reef, revived European interest in shell collecting, for many of the sailors collected shells, which they took back to England and sold. The voyagers of the 17th and 18th centuries opened the eyes of Europe to the great variety of life on earth, and shells, because they were easily stored, could be brought back to Europe to illustrate this variety.

A class distinction

There are four major groups of molluscs and a few minor ones. The gastropods form the largest group, or 'class' as it is known scientifically. They include the sea snails, land snails and slugs, and the opisthobranchs, or sea slugs. Oysters, scallops and clams belong to the second largest class, the bivalves, which have two valves or parts to their shell.

The third largest class, the cephalopods, includes the octopus and the squid. These animals seem to have little in common with the humble garden snail, but their anatomy and fossil history show they are closely related. The fourth class includes the chitons. Often known as the coat-of-mail shells, chitons are the molluscan equivalent of the terrestrial armadillo.

Molluscs are soft-bodied animals that cover themselves with a hard shell of calcium carbonate into which they can retreat when in danger. The shell, which is usually big enough to contain the whole animal, is attached to it by special muscles. For some groups, such as the slugs, the shell is no longer important.

Molluscs have a unique flap of skin over their body called the mantle. The edge of the

Tubastrea; wentletrap snail, Epitonium

△ *Few animals or plants can live on the reef free from the attentions of others, for they all need food and shelter. This beautiful coral is no exception. Here only two of the flower-like polyp animals have survived the ravages of a hungry wentletrap snail, 12 millimetres long, which has moved on after laying strings of bright yellow eggs in each of the eaten-out coral skeletons.*

▷ *This is one of the few corals that extends its polyps during the day. The wentletrap snail, cunningly camouflaged in its egg mass, has eaten many of the polyps and is now laying its eggs on the remains of its meal.*

Tubastrea; wentletrap snail, Epitonium

Chiton, *Acanthopleura*

Tubastrea; nudibranch, *Phestilla melanobrachia*

Giant clam, *Tridacna maxima*

mantle, which sits alongside the edge of the shell, makes the shell by adding new layers of calcium carbonate along its edge. In snails, the shell grows by the addition of layers around the mouth of the shell; in bivalves, by the addition of layers along the two edges. It is usually easy to see how bivalve shells grow. At the pointed part of the shell, near the hinge that joins its two parts, the tiny shell the mollusc had as a juvenile can be seen. Between the hinge and the edge of the shell are curved ridges parallel to the outer edge; these growth lines show when the mantle has stopped secreting shell between periods of growth. In snail shells, the microscopic shell the snail had as an embryo or larva can often be seen at the pointed end. Usually it is smooth and uniformly coloured, although the rest of the shell may be sculptured, or rough, and have a distinctive colour pattern.

△ *What looks like the tentacles of a beautiful coral polyp is in fact a nudibranch sea slug, which feeds exclusively on* Tubastrea. *Unlike the wentletrap snail, which leaves part of the tissue intact, this nudibranch, over 30 millimetres long, eats all the tissue, leaving only the white coral skeleton behind.*

△ ▷ *Chitons are an ancient group of molluscs that have eight shell plates held together by an encircling leathery band. This species is commonly found on high tidal rocks, often uncovered for most of the tidal cycle, but usually it remains moist in some shady crevice. At night or early in the morning* Acanthopleura *crawls over the rock, grazing on microscopic algae.*

△ *Although not the largest of the giant clams, this is one of the most common and widespread species. It is usually found on the surface of the sand or reef or sometimes partly embedded in coral. The mantle is usually vividly coloured and visible from some distance; no two specimens are exactly the same colour. It grows up to 300 millimetres long.*

'Shells are to molluscs as skeletal bones are to fish.'

Red-mouthed stromb, *Strombus luhuanus*

Between the mantle and the back of the animal is a gap called the mantle cavity, in which the mollusc gills sit in safety.

One of the most beautiful and mechanically refined structures in the animal kingdom is the radula, an organ unique to the molluscs, but even most shell collectors have never seen one. The radula, the mollusc's feeding organ, is found in the mouth of all molluscs except the bivalves. It is a horny tooth-bearing strip on a flexible tongue, or radular ribbon, attached to the floor of the mouth. Chitons, and some snails that feed on minute weeds growing on rocks, scrape weeds off the rocks by thrusting the radular ribbon in and out of the mouth. The shape of the radula and the individual teeth vary widely among the molluscs; different tooth shapes have evolved for different types of feeding. Probably the most amazing modification is found in the poisonous cone shells, *Conus*; the teeth have become long, slender, barbed darts, like a whaler's harpoon, which can be filled with poison and shot out to paralyse and kill prey – in some species other snails, and in others fishes.

The secret of life

Because the anatomy of land vertebrates is easy to relate to our own, we take many aspects of, say, a lion's biology for granted. We can see, for example, how it breathes, sees, feels, smells, feeds, moves, breeds and grows, but what of a mollusc?

Breathing through gills

Most marine molluscs remove oxygen from sea water with the help of a gill, filled with blood pumped to and from the gills by a simple heart. The blood system in most molluscs is not as efficient as ours, and although some blood travels in vessels,

Cone shell, *Conus textile*

△ *The tip of a tooth of this venomous cone is remarkably like that of a whaler's harpoon. The shaft of the tooth has a groove along its side filled with poison to kill its prey. Human fatalities have occurred from the sting of various cone shells. (This photograph is magnified 400 times.)*

△△ *The regular rows of teeth found in the red-mouthed stromb show how most mollusc teeth are arranged on a horny tongue or ribbon. The teeth of this stromb scrape algae into the mouth of the snail. (This photograph is magnified 90 times.)*

▷ *These brightly coloured bubble shells, up to 10 millimetres long, are often quite common intertidally. They were first found in Hawaii over a century ago and are now known from all parts of the tropical Pacific and Indian oceans. These snails have a transparent, fragile shell and are primitive opisthobranchs or sea slugs. They are herbivores that graze on algae growing on the rocks.*

Bubble shell, *Haminoea cymbalum*

most of the blood is loose in the body cavity. Only a few molluscs, for example the common bivalve *Anadara*, the bloody cockle, have red blood with the efficient oxygen-carrying pigment haemoglobin. Most have colourless blood containing a less efficient oxygen-carrying pigment called 'haemocyanin'. Most molluscs are much smaller and less active than vertebrates, and their blood system does not need to be so efficient. In the squid, however, the blood system and gills have been greatly modified to supply sufficient oxygen to the muscles and brain of these very active and sometimes very large animals.

Seeing the light

Most of us are familiar with the eyes of a garden snail, a tiny black spot on the tip of each eye stalk, but the eyes of most molluscs can do little more than sense light; they can't see or form images. Most snails have a pair of eyes on the head, but in burrowing species the eyes are often buried deep in the skin. In chitons, the eyes are microscopic spots on the surface of the shells. One species is recorded to have about 12 000 of these tiny eyes. The bivalves no longer have a head, and they have usually lost these eyes, but many have evolved secondary eyes or light-sensitive regions on the mantle, at the edge of the shell. Again they can't see objects, but they can detect shadows and movement, and close their shells rapidly to protect them from danger.

The cephalopods are fast-moving hunters, and their eyes, unlike those of other molluscs, are as complex and well developed as most mammals. The eyes of the squid and cuttlefish enable them to see fishes or crustaceans, and their well-developed brains enable them to catch these elusive objects. The octopus, through sight and touch, is able to distinguish different shapes, textures and colours. It is their excellent vision that has enabled the cephalopods to become so successful.

Cuttlefish, *Sepia latimanus*

▷ ∆ *Few people realise that the cuttlebone we give to cage birds to keep their beaks in trim is the internal bone of a squid, the cuttlefish. This large species grows to more than half a metre in length and is common in reef waters. There are probably ten or more different species found in tropical Australia, and their bone is often found washed up in large numbers on the beach. The bone is made of very thin layers. The cuttlefish fills the gaps between the layers with gas and uses the bone both as a skeleton and a flotation chamber.*

▷ *The squid rival fishes as superb swimming carnivores. Many swim in large schools, and feed on crustaceans and fishes, caught with two very long tentacles, which are usually retracted into pockets near the mouth but can be shot out with great speed and accuracy when prey is sighted. The white spots in the photograph are specks of flashlight reflected off microscopic planktonic plants and animals that swarm in the reef's surface waters at night.*

Squid

Feeling the environment

Most snails have tentacles on their heads, and many also have long projections along the edge of their mantle or foot, which they use to touch things around them in order to give them some idea of their environment.

The bivalves have feelers all around the edge of the mantle, and when the valves of the shell are partly open these sensory tentacles extend out. They warn the bivalve of approaching animals – which could be about to eat them – so the bivalve can quickly shut its shell for protection. Their sensory tentacles are also used in feeding. Most bivalves feed by filtering tiny plants out of the sea water. The sensory tentacles can quickly tell if the water is becoming silty or dirty, so the shell can close up and avoid becoming clogged with mud.

Among the cephalopods only the octopus, which spends most of its time on the sea bottom, has a good sense of touch and its eight long tentacles are constantly moving and feeling. It is able to identify objects just from the way they feel.

Smelling with siphons

In animals living in water, 'smelling' is the ability to sense chemicals in the water. All molluscs can do this to some extent, but smelling is best developed in the marine snails, and particularly the carnivorous snails. They have a special organ, the osphradium, in the mantle cavity, which senses chemicals in the water flowing to the gills. Many carnivorous snails have evolved a long tube or siphon through which the water enters the mantle cavity, and by waving this around they can sense the direction a smell is coming from and so find their food. In nudibranch sea slugs, the shell, the mantle cavity and its associated organs are lost. On their heads are a pair of special tentacles, used to smell their food.

File shell, *Lima*

△ *The file shell, which is 40 millimetres long, can be a startling find under coral rocks and boulders for, unlike most bivalves, it can move very rapidly when disturbed, swimming off in a series of jerks by rapidly opening and shutting the valves of its shell to force out a jet of water. The mantle is bright red, and around the edge are long, sticky, retractile tentacles, which continuously wave around. When touched, the tentacles stick to whatever touches them, and they often break off. They are probably defensive, confusing fishes by sticking to their mouths and waving about, while the shell rapidly jerks away.*

'The octopus, like other cephalopods, swims by jet propulsion.'

Octopus

Blue-ringed octopus, *Hapalochlaena lunulata*

Getting about: sliding, walking and swimming

The land snail or slug looks as if it is crawling on its stomach, but zoologists call this its foot, although it certainly does not work in the same way as a human's. The sole of the snail's foot produces a thin mucus or slime, along which the snail or slug crawls or slides, either by waves of muscle contractions or by beating microscopic hairs or cilia. Chitons also move this way, but in bivalves which normally spend their life attached to a hard surface, such as rock oysters and mussels, or buried in sand or mud, such as pipis, the foot is no longer used for crawling. Bivalves that burrow in mud and sand now use the foot as a digging tool, which allows them to rebury themselves very quickly if they are washed out by waves or dug up by humans in search of food or bait.

Only the octopus can walk in a manner similar to humans. The eight tentacles, often called 'arms' or 'legs', have suckers which make them ideal for not only holding prey but also walking.

Cephalopods, including the octopus, are swimmers, and this is usually by jet propulsion. Water brought into the mantle cavity for the gills is re-used for a second purpose. By contracting mantle

◁ *Most species of octopus are experts in camouflage, and they are seldom seen except when disturbed. The secret of their success is the small elastic bags of colour pigment they have in their skin. By stretching the bags out to cover a large surface they become very dark, and by allowing the bags to shrink to tiny specks they can become almost white. As different bags can be stretching or contracting simultaneously in different parts of the body, an octopus can blend in well, even against such a difficult background as coral rubble.*

◁ *When disturbed, the brilliant display of this mollusc instantly identifies it as the blue-ringed octopus. Growing to 150 millimetres, it is found from northern Australia to southern Japan. Like the closely related* Hapalochlaena maculosa, *of temperate Australia, the northern species possesses a deadly venom capable of killing humans. Both species feed on crabs and molluscs, which they paralyse by injecting poison with their beak-like jaws.*

▷ *The ancient ancestors of the octopus, squid and cuttlefish had external shells, just like other molluscs do today. Five hundred million years ago, before fishes evolved, the nautiloid and ammonoid shelled ancestors of today's cephalopods were the major marine carnivores. Today, only a few shelled cephalopods survive, and the chambered nautilus is the best known. This species, which grows to 200 millimetres in diameter, is found throughout the tropical West Pacific. The shell is divided into chambers, and the animal can control its own buoyancy by changing the amount of gas and fluid in them.*

Chambered nautilus, *Nautilus pompilius*

Scallop

△ *A scallop's contact with the environment is solely through the edge of its mantle. It uses it to touch, see and smell. The long transparent tentacles are waved about and are highly sensitive to touch. Here, fully retracted tentacles can be seen as short fat stumps. In the groove in the centre – where the upper and lower lobes of the mantle touch – the shorter yellow, black and white tentacles of the inner mantle lobe form a coarse sieve that tests water entering the mantle cavity. In some other scallops, a series of small black eyes along the mantle are used to sense shadows and changes in light intensity, which may warn of approaching danger.*

muscles, a jet of water can be quickly squeezed out of the mantle cavity through a tube, or siphon, and, like the air of a jet engine or the exhaust of a rocket, propel the animal along, sometimes very quickly. By waving the tube around, the squid can steer in any direction.

Surprisingly, some bivalves can swim by jet propulsion as well. The best example is the scallop. It lies on the surface of the sand filtering its food from the water but, if attacked by a predatory starfish or snail, it can, by rapidly opening and shutting its shells, squeeze jets of water out of its mantle cavity and jump or swim away.

Ways of feeding

Molluscs eat a wide range of food. The chitons and many primitive snails scrape minute layers of algae off the rocks they live on. Some snails and bivalves

eat bacteria and algae found in silty and muddy areas. Many snails are carnivores and feed on sponges, coelenterates, worms, other molluscs and fishes, and some are scavengers, feeding on any dead or decaying material.

The cephalopods are specialised hunters, and while the octopus usually feeds on crabs and crustaceans, the squid and cuttlefish are efficient hunters of fishes.

Unlike other molluscs, the bivalves, although they still have a mouth, have lost their head and have no radula. They usually feed by filtering fine plankton out of the water they live in, and for a sieve or filter they have evolved huge gills, much larger than those needed for breathing. As the water passes through the gills, food is filtered out, and by a complicated system of sticky mucus and fine ciliary hairs, the plankton are tangled into food strings and moved to the mouth.

Vermetid snail, *Vermetidae*

▷ The worm-like tubes are made by snails appropriately known as vermetids, from the Latin word vermis meaning worm. The snails can no longer crawl about and so, like oysters and barnacles, they feed on microscopic plants and animals that float past them in the water. In some species the gill has become enlarged to sieve food out of the water, and in other species, such as Dendropoma maxima shown below, long, sticky, mucus threads are dangled in the water to entangle prey. At intervals each thread is pulled up by the snail and eaten. The two small eyes at the base of pointed tentacles clearly show that this mollusc is a snail. The large hole on each side allows water into the mantle cavity.

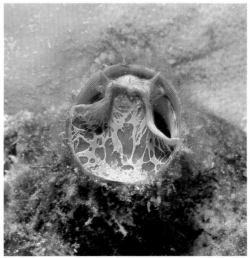

Vermetid snail, *Dendropoma maxima*

▷ Although not beautiful, clusters of this snail on intertidal beachrock are a spectacular sight. When the tide covers the rocks, the snails disperse to graze on algae, but as the tide recedes they return to a cluster. The snails, which are about 150 millimetres long, have a built-in rhythm, and even if they are kept in an aquarium with no tide, they will periodically form clusters and disperse in time with the tidal rhythm of the place they were caught. The great advantage of clustering for snails living on hot tropical intertidal rocks is that a film of water is retained by the cluster, so no snail dries out. A snail left by itself will easily die from desiccation before the tide returns.

Snail, *Cerithium moniliferum*

> In animals that cannot move, mating between males and females is impossible. Bivalves reproduce by releasing clouds of eggs and sperm into the sea water. To ensure that fertilisation occurs, spawning is usually synchronised so that spawn from many individuals is released over a very short period. Simultaneous spawning by large bivalves like the giant clam is a spectacular sight, as it clouds the surrounding water. The giant clam is unusual among bivalves in being able to produce both eggs and sperm, but these are usually not released together.

▽ Mollusc egg capsules often puzzle the visitor to the shore, because they are of intricate shape and give few clues to what they are. The egg capsules of cone shells are laid in aggregations under rocks or in crevices. Sometimes several females will lay their eggs together. Each capsule is a sealed bag, in which the eggs develop free from the dangers of predators and physical stresses.

Giant clam, *Tridacna maxima*

Cone shell egg capsules

Making more molluscs

Most molluscs have separate sexes, although sea slugs and land snails are hermaphrodite; that is, fully functional as both male and female at the same time. Some snails, the most well known being the slipper limpets, are remarkable in changing sex during their life, beginning as males and later becoming females.

In chitons, bivalves and primitive snails, the male has no penis, and fertilisation of the female's eggs usually occurs outside the body in the surrounding sea water. As this could lead to great wastage of eggs and sperm, many species have adjusted their spawning to avoid such wastage. Some limpets, for example, will only spawn when close to one of the other sex, and in some chitons, snails and bivalves, males spawn first and eggs are released by females only when there is sperm in the surrounding sea water. Others, especially bivalves, have epidemic

spawning, and a whole population will spawn within a few hours. Some change in temperature or salinity in the water triggers this spawning.

Eggs fertilised externally usually have little protective coating. They drift in the water, with each egg dividing and growing to form the characteristic shelled veliger larva of a mollusc, and feeding on planktonic algae. After drifting in the sea, in some species for 40 hours, in others, 40 days, the microscopic larvae settle on the bottom or the shore and begin to grow.

Animals with internal fertilisation can develop special shells and capsules to protect their fertilised eggs both from predators and from drying if they are laid intertidally. Some species lay eggs in long strings embedded in a jelly-like mucus; others produce a tough capsule, sometimes with many eggs, sometimes with just one inside. In most cases, the larvae hatch out of the capsule and swim off as

veligers to spend time in the plankton before settling. In other species, there is no free-swimming larval stage, and a crawling 'baby' snail hatches out of the egg capsule. Just as many eggs and sperm are wasted when they are released straight into the sea, many veliger larvae are lost before they are able to settle, and most molluscs with veligers can be identified by the enormous number of eggs they produce. Direct development, in which the young hatch from the egg at the crawling stage, is a much safer way of ensuring that the young will at least settle in a reasonably good place to live. For this reason, direct developers usually produce very few eggs, because many will survive.

The behaviour of cephalopods is much more highly organised, particularly in reproduction. Courtship and mating often follow elaborate rituals, reminiscent of bird displays, and in many cases parental care is strongly developed.

Cuttlefish eggs, *Sepia*

Where do molluscs live?

As in other shores, there is a distinct pattern of mollusc distribution on the Great Barrier Reef. Not all species live everywhere; most occupy a zone on the shore. Some occur high up the shore, where they are hardly ever covered by the sea; others are found low down, always covered by sea water and only seen alive if one visits their world by snorkelling or scuba diving. Between these two extremes are a vast variety of species, many well known to shell collectors throughout the world.

The mangrove swamps are an integral part of the reef ecosystem. Far from being just stinking mud and mosquitoes, they are home for a great variety of life. The molluscs found there, although they may not be pretty, are very numerous.

Found highest on the shore, and hardly marine at all, are the periwinkles, *Littorina*, which live on the

Cowry, *Cypraea caurica*

△ *Cuttlefish eggs are laid in characteristic capsules with a leathery protective skin. They are usually laid under rocks or in small caves or crevices, and in some species the mother protects the capsules until they hatch. Soon after being laid, the capsules are an opaque white, but, as the egg develops, the capsule begins to clear and the growing cuttlefish can be seen, one to each capsule.*

◁ *One common sight when a rock is turned over is the egg mass of the cowry. Often a female will be found on a complete or half complete egg mass with a second snail, perhaps the male, nearby. The egg mass has several hundred capsules cemented together, each containing up to 300 eggs. This species grows to an adult length of 50 millimetres.*

Dog whelk, *Nassarius dorsatus*

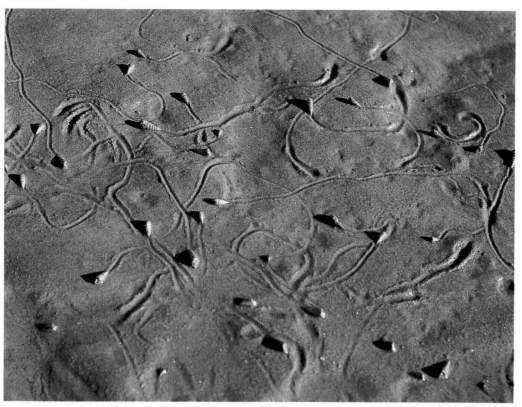

Cerithiid, *Rhinoclavis*

Periwinkle, *Littorina*

▵ *At first sight, mud flats and sand flats look devoid of life. But tracks, grooves, and little lumps betray the presence of many snails, crustaceans and sometimes fish. This cerithiid or creeper feeds on microscopic particles on the surface of fine sand and mud. It grows to a length of 60 millimetres.*

◁ ▵ *Dog whelks are the scavengers of sand and mud flats. As the tide recedes, they can be seen purposefully following a scent upshore, waving their long siphon from side to side to be sure of the direction to follow. They grow to a length of 250 millimetres.*

◁ *The periwinkles, or littorinids, are common inhabitants of the spray zone, the highest part of the shore, which is dampened only by the sea spray, and in tropical regions mangrove trees provide a perfect home for them. Some live on the leaves, others on the trunks, and different species prefer different species of tree and different parts of the trees, where they feed on microscopic plants. The periwinkle grows to a length of 25 millimetres.*

leaves and trunks of mangrove trees. There are probably several species of *Littorina* living around Australia, all occupying slightly different environments. Some species are variable in colour, with darker-shelled specimens living on the darker trunks, and light or yellowish-shelled specimens living on the leaves, each camouflaged against the birds that feed on periwinkles. Such high-tidal animals, which may never be immersed in sea water, can no longer lay eggs that hatch into veliger larvae, so they have evolved a special pouch in their mantle cavity where the eggs are brooded until they develop into young crawling snails, which are then released. In other species, the egg capsule is laid, and the free-swimming veliger stage is passed while the young is still in the capsule, and again young crawling snails are hatched.

Low on the trunks of mangrove trees, on aerial roots and sometimes on the mud, live species of *Onchidium*, an air-breathing slug that has lost its gill and has evolved a lung that enables it to live out of water. It can be immersed in sea water for short periods and needs to remain damp. Like littorinids, it feeds on a thin layer of microscopic plants that live on mangrove trees. Both littorinids and onchidiids are related to marine snails, but they have adapted to living mostly out of the water.

On the mud the most common snails are the mud whelks or creepers known as the potamidids. The snails *Terebralia* and *Telescopium*, which have large

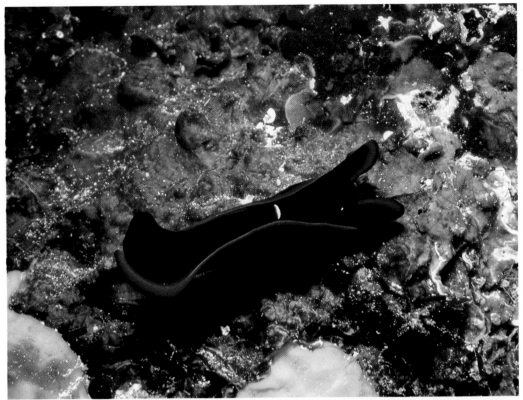

◁ *Although this sea slug is brightly coloured and has no external shell, it is not a nudibranch. It is a relative of the bubble shell Haminoea, and it has a little, fragile internal shell. With its brilliant blue borders, it is often seen crawling over the white coral sand of the lagoon, but it is also found on coral rocks. It grows to 70 millimetres and belongs to the tailed slugs of the family Aglajidae, a group of primitive sea slugs that feeds on worms and other bubble shells.*

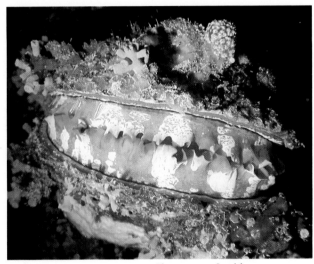

Thorny oyster, *Spondylus*

Δ *The thorny oyster is completely covered with algae and colonial animals. When the oyster is alarmed, the two shell valves are closed tight, but usually they sit apart, with the frilly yellow and white lobes of the mantle forming a curtain across the entrance to the mantle cavity and the gills. Oxygen and possibly food-laden water is sucked into the cavity through the mantle curtain. The long pointed spines on the shell help to anchor it, and also help marine growths to become attached and camouflage the shell, which can reach 70 millimetres in length.*

Tailed sea slug, *Philinopsis gardineri*

brown shells up to 120 millimetres long, and the smaller *Cerithidea* often form large aggregations. They feed on detritus and on the fallen leaves and fruit of the mangrove trees. The mangrove swamp harbours great numbers of animals, but they are of only a few different species.

On mud and sand

Mud and mangroves are few people's idea of an exciting holiday, so most visitors to the reef miss the home of a wide variety of tropical molluscs. In sheltered bays and shallow waters on the seaward side of the mangrove swamps, vast areas of muddy sand flats or sandy mud flats, often partly covered with sea grasses, are home for many herbivorous snails and bivalves. Often the only indication of what bivalves are present is the dead shells. The mud can also be dug up and carefully sieved to find out what molluscs live there. The bloody cockle, so called because of its red blood, usually lives on or just below the surface.

Another common bivalve of the flats is the horse mussel, *Pinna*, which can grow to 200 millimetres long. It is also known as the razor clam, because it sits completely buried, except for its thin, sharp and fragile upper edge, which is renowned for lacerating bare feet. One of the most beautiful bivalves, the thorny oyster, *Spondylus wrightianus*, also lives on mud flats. Few who have seen a cleaned specimen of this

beautiful shell would recognise it as the spiny, muddy lump, covered in marine growths, that is its natural state.

Snails of the soft shores

Most of the marine snails belong to families more at home in the cleaner waters of the reef. But the thorny oyster has its snail counterpart in the murex shells, many of which live on these sandy muddy shores, their spines covered in marine growths that help camouflage them from fish predators.

One common snail on mud and sand flats is the dog whelk, *Nassarius*. These busy little scavengers are often found clustered, like miniature vultures, around dead and decaying animals. As the dog whelk crawls along, it waves a long tube in front of its shell. This siphon sucks in water, which is 'tasted' or 'smelt' by the snail. By knowing in which direction the siphon is pointed when a 'good smell' is detected, the snail finds its way to its next meal.

Another snail common on these soft shores is the false trumpet shell, *Syrinx*. It is found only on mud flats in northern Australia, and it is probably the largest snail in the world, growing to 700 millimetres in length. But visitors to the coral areas of the reef will look in vain there for this giant among snails.

In clear water

The coral reef and regions with clearer water harbour the greatest variety of tropical marine

Cone shell, *Conus capitaneus*

Leaf oyster, *Lopha folium*

△ *The leaf oyster, which grows up to 50 millimetres long, is usually found attached to hydroids, Gorgonians or similar branching coral colonies. Like most hard surfaces on the reef, it is covered with marine growths; the red is a sponge, and the pink, a colonial ascidian.*

▷ *This abalone, which grows to 150 millimetres, is known as the ass's ear, although the resemblance is difficult to see in the living animal. This common intertidal reef snail may often be found under a dead coral slab; when disturbed it will rapidly crawl away from the sunlight. All abalones are herbivorous, and this species grazes on algae growing on the rocks. Abalones have a row of holes in their shell through which water is expelled from the mantle cavity after the gills have removed the oxygen. Sea water enters the mantle cavity through the gap below the shell that can be seen behind the head.*

animals. But not all molluscs live in all places. On beachrock and dead coral boulders high on the shore, only covered by sea water for a short time each high tide, are chitons, some cerithiid snails (related to the mangrove creepers), carnivorous muricid snails of genera such as *Thais*, *Drupa* and *Morula*, and some species of cone shell, such as the distinctive black-spotted *Conus ebraeus*.

Waders and burrowers

The soft, sandy bottom of lagoons has a different fauna, with burrowing bivalves and snails as well as surface dwellers. In shallow water cerithiid creepers and the red-mouthed stromb, *Strombus luhuanus*, often in large numbers, feed on microscopic algae on the surface of the sand. The bubble shells, primitive sea slugs that still have shells betraying their snail ancestry, burrow through the sand. Species of the worm-feeding genus *Pupa* and the herbivorous *Atys* are particularly common. Another group of bubble shells often represented are the aglajiid slugs, which have a fragile internal shell. One frequently seen species is *Philinopsis gardineri*, which is black with brilliant blue borders; it

◁ △ *This species, which grows to 75 millimetres, is a worm-feeding cone, and like many of the intertidal rock-dwelling species, the shell is covered by the hairy periostracum, which prevents algae and other encrustations from burrowing into and weakening the shell.*

probably feeds on worms. Many of the sand-dwelling molluscs live buried, especially at low tide, or they hide under rocks or live in deeper water, where they may only be seen by snorkelling or scuba diving.

Many of the carnivorous cones are sand-dwellers, and so are the terebrids, mitres, turrids, many muricids and most bivalves. Some species are abundant, but it takes many visits to the reef shores before one can get a full idea of the variety of molluscan life.

The reef flat, crest and outer slope provide a vast array of habitats, and we are only now beginning to comprehend the complexity of life there. Many molluscs appear to be able to live in a variety of habitats, others have very special requirements, so they are found only in association with a particular coral, sea urchin or other animal, or only with a particular alga. Some live on intertidal coral heads, others in places never uncovered by the tide.

Ubiquitous gastropods

The gastropod snails and slugs are the most numerous, most diverse and the most collected of the reef molluscs.

Many of the more primitive marine snails graze algae from rocks. The frilly, dark green mantle of the ass's ear shell, *Haliotis asinina*, is a common sight intertidally. It is an abalone, and if disturbed or

Ass's ear abalone, *Haliotis asinina*

◁ *This spider shell has been turned over to show its distinctive operculum, which is much smaller than the shell opening and is no longer able to serve as a door to protect the animal from predators. Such passive defence has been replaced by a more active method, with the operculum forming a sharp claw on the end of the muscular foot. It is used to deter predators and also to dig into sand, so the foot can flip the shell over if it is moved on to its back. The shell grows to 200 millimetres.*

▽ *The egg cowry, which grows to 120 millimetres, is common throughout the tropical Indo-West Pacific region. The egg cowries all feed on coelenterates, and each species specialises on one particular food. This species is commonly found on a colony of the fleshy soft coral* Sarcophyton. *The black mantle that usually envelops the shell sharply contrasts with the white of the shell.*

Egg cowry, *Ovula ovum*

Spider shell, *Lambis lambis*

exposed when a rock is turned over, it can crawl rapidly away, usually in search of another shady spot to hide.

Two large families of herbivorous molluscs are the top shells (Trochidae) and the turban shells (Turbinidae). Many top shells are heavy, conical, and often covered with weeds and other growths when alive. Some of the larger species, such as trochus, *Trochus niloticus*, grow to 150 millimetres in height. These once formed the basis of a large industry, as their shells were used in making mother-of-pearl buttons. Snails of the other large family of herbivorous molluscs, the Turbinidae, can be recognised by their hard, calcareous operculum, the snail's trapdoor, which allows it to hide in its shell to escape predators or harmful physical conditions, such as those that could lead to it drying out. In some species of Turbinidae, this is perfectly

circular, with one convex side mottled white and green giving it the appearance of a cat's eye, a name by which it is often known.

The fragile shells of the wentletraps family, Epitoniidae, contrast with the solid, heavy shells of the herbivorous top shells and turban shells. It is often difficult to recognise individual species among the wentletraps simply on the shape of the shell. All of the species that have been studied feed on sea anemones or other coelenterates, and apparently each species feeds on only one species. On the Great Barrier Reef, one species is often found on the underside of the solitary coral *Fungia*, and another with the coral *Tubastrea*.

Shells with peepholes

The family Strombidae, called strombs, scorpion shells, or spider shells by collectors, are synonymous with the tropics. They are recognised by a notch on

the lip of the shell, which is used as a peephole for the characteristic stalked right eye. They can also be recognised by the sharp, knife-like operculum, which is carried on the muscular 'tail' or posterior end of the foot. The operculum is not large enough to act as a trapdoor, as in the top shells, and it has evolved as a weapon of defence or as a lever to pull or push the animal along or turn it over when it has been rolled on its back. There are many species of stromb shells, ranging from about ten millimetres long to the large spider shell, *Lambis truncata*, which can grow to 350 millimetres. All species are herbivorous and feed on algae or detritus on sandy parts of the reef. The strombs are often difficult to see, as the shell is covered with growths of seaweed.

Glossy cowries

The cowries, of the family Cypraeidae, are probably the most collected and best known of tropical shells.

Mole cowry, *Cypraea talpa*

Many species are common, easily collected and have glossy shells, often with spectacular colour patterns. They have been used for decoration, and the money cowry, *Cypraea moneta*, got its name from its use as a sign of wealth and as a trading token in the Pacific. This large family illustrates how much there is still to learn about the biology of tropical animals, for apart from a few species, such as *Cypraea moneta* and *Cypraea tigris*, the tiger cowry, which are herbivorous, we know little of the feeding behaviour of the cowries, although it is suspected that some tropical species are sponge feeders.

The related egg cowries, of the family Ovulidae, and spindle cowries are typical of so many reef animals in having extremely specialised diets. The white egg-shaped egg cowry, *Ovula ovum*, is always found on the large, common, soft coral *Sarcophyton*, and each species of spindle cowry is associated with a different species of Gorgonian coral.

Moon snails at work

Often, dead shells, usually of bivalves, have a neat hole that looks as though it has been drilled for stringing the shell in a necklace or some other ornament. In most cases the hole was drilled by a moon snail, or naticid (Naticidae family), which feeds on other snails and bivalves by drilling a hole through the shell of its prey with its specially adapted radula. Moon snails live on sandy shores, and they can usually be found under small humps in the sand. Small tracks or grooves in the sand are also worth investigating, because they often betray the presence of burrowing animals.

Among the tropical snails there are many examples of strange and specialised feeders. The helmet shells, of the family Cassidae, feed on echinoderms and some even eat the sea urchin, *Diadema*, despite its long, brittle, needle-sharp spines. The related tun shells, of the family

Spindle cowry

'There are over 200 species of cowries, and most of them have brightly coloured, glossy shells.'

Eyed cowry, *Cypraea argus*

◁ Cowries are best known for their beautiful shells; each species has a characteristic colour pattern. The living animals can also be identified, for the colour and shape of the decoration on each mantle is distinctive. The mole cowry (far left) grows to 90 millimetres and the eyed cowry grows to 120 millimetres.

▽ Cowries are usually active at night, and when they are out crawling with the mantle covering the shell, it is difficult to recognise them. The long head tentacles with little black basal eyes clearly show that this is a snail.

Cypraea fimbriata

Spindle cowry

◁ In the same family as the egg cowries (Ovulidae) are the spindle cowries, so named because of the great elongation of the shell at each end. Spindle cowries are usually associated with Gorgonian corals, and it seems that each species lives and feeds on only one species of Gorgonian. Two species are shown here, one, far left, slightly more elongated than a normal cowry and the other greatly elongated, allowing it to hide very effectively along the branches of its Gorgonian host. This species is laying a string of translucent white eggs. The shell and the coloured mantle usually exactly match the colour of the Gorgonian, making spindle cowries nearly invisible to all but the most experienced eye.

'The spiny shell of the murex protects it from predators and provides camouflage when it becomes entangled with marine growths.'

▷ This carnivorous triton, with a shell growing to 450 millimetres, is one of the few animals known to feed on the crown-of-thorns starfish. It was at first thought that the taking of the triton by shell collectors had allowed the crown-of-thorns population to get out of hand, so collecting triton was banned on the reef. But the triton has never been common, and although it can eat Acanthaster, *it is now thought that it has little influence on the starfish population.*

Triton, *Charonia tritonis*; crown-of-thorns starfish, *Acanthaster planci*

Tun shell, *Tonna perdix*

Δ This tun shell, 140 millimetres long, looks as if it has outgrown its shell. Its head and body have been greatly distended by a large holothurian, or sea cucumber, that has just been eaten. Once the tun shell has engulfed the holothurian, it must gradually break the sea cucumber into bits inside its mouth. It will be many hours before the snail can retreat into its shell, and if it is in great danger it will regurgitate its food so that it can get back inside.

▷ The sharp spines of the spiny murex shell ensure that most predators leave it alone. This species, which grows to 110 millimetres, is found across northern Australia's coast and lives on soft sand or muddy bottoms. Here one eye can be seen as a tiny black speck halfway along the tentacle to the left. The brownish disc on the foot is the operculum, a horny plate that acts as a door and protects the foot when the snail withdraws into its shell.

Murex, *Murex acanthostephes*

Tonnidae, feed on holothurians, commonly known as sea cucumbers. After eating a holothurian longer than itself, the snail is unable to retract into its shell for many hours, until the sea cucumber is digested. Starfish, sea squirts and other molluscs are the food of different species of triton and trumpet shells, of the family Cymatiidae; the magnificent triton *Charonia tritonis* feeds on starfish, including the crown-of-thorns starfish, *Acanthaster planci*.

The murex shells, the Muricidae, form one of the largest families of carnivorous marine snails; there are about a thousand different species. They are all carnivorous, and many of them feed by drilling holes through the shells of their prey. The spiny murex shells, as their name suggests, have developed spines, often of bizarre design and shape, all over the shell. These beautiful snails usually live on muddy shores, and their spiny shells protect them from being eaten and also help to camouflage them by

◁ The shape of this shell shows how the cone shells got their name. There are over 500 species, most of which live in the tropical Indo-West Pacific Oceans. Each species has a distinctive colour pattern on its shell, but this is often obscured by the periostracum, a horny covering produced by the snail, or by marine growths. In this specimen, which grows to 75 millimetres, the pointed spire has pink encrustations of coralline algae and the brownish tinge of the shell is caused by the periostracum, which prevents encrustations burrowing into the shell.

▽ The mulberry whelk, which grows to a length of 30 millimetres, is a member of a big group of thaid snails often found in large numbers on intertidal rocky shores. They are all carnivores that feed on sessile animals – those that are stuck to one spot and can't move about, such as barnacles and bivalves. This species is found in Queensland and New South Wales. Here it feeds on barnacles, but it is also a pest of oyster farms.

Cone shell, *Conus mustellinus*

Mulberry whelk, *Morula marginalba*

Nudibranch, *Phyllodesmium longicirra*

◁ This truly solar-powered nudibranch feeds on the soft coral Sarcophyton and removes symbiotic zooxanthellae (one-celled plants) from the coral and farms them in its own tissues. The cerata, instead of being tubular like those of other aeolids, have become large, flattened solar paddles, and the brown rings on them are little gardens of algae that are living in the aeolid. Most of the food the plants make, by photosynthesising in sunlight, is taken by the nudibranch for its own use. Although quite commonly seen crawling on sandy lagoon bottoms, it has only once been seen feeding on soft coral, so it probably only has to recharge its solar batteries occasionally by getting a supply of zooxanthellae from the soft corals. It can grow up to 100 millimetres long.

allowing weeds and other marine growths to become entangled in the spines. Another group of murex shells, the thaids and drupes, usually have heavy shells without spines. They live on rocks and coral blocks at various levels on the shore and feed on a wide variety of animals, such as snails, barnacles and worms.

The spiral shell

No description of the molluscs of the Great Barrier Reef could ignore the volutes, for although they are found throughout the world, almost half the known species live in Australia. Over the course of thousands of years many of the molluscs now found on the Great Barrier Reef have become distributed throughout the tropical Indian and west Pacific Oceans because their veliger larvae have drifted there on favourable currents. The volutes do not, however, have a free-swimming larval stage, and the young hatches from the egg capsule as a small crawling snail, and it is for this reason that most species of volute are restricted to small geographic areas. One species, the Heron Island volute, *Cymbiolacca pulchra*, is found along much of the central and southern Queensland coast. Because individuals cannot move far, on each island or reef a distinctive colour pattern has developed and experienced conchologists, those who study and collect shells, can say which reef a specimen has come from by just looking at the shell. The carnivorous volutes suffocate their prey by wrapping their large foot around it.

Beautiful but venomous

Cone shells are well known among shell collectors, for like the cowries, the shells are often beautifully coloured, and there are many relatively common species among the 500 that have been named. Behind their beauty, however, lurks one of the most venomous of marine animals: at least 20 people are

▷△ *This volute, which grows to 80 millimetres, is found intertidally and in shallow waters of the Great Barrier Reef. About 70 species of volute are known from Australia, where the family has been spectacularly successful, with almost half of all the world's living species being found only in Australian waters. Most species have brightly coloured animals, as well as brightly coloured shells. They live in sand and are carnivorous hunters that feed on other snails and invertebrates.*

▷ *The Heron Island volute, like more than a third of the world's volutes, is found only in Australia. This species is found on central and southern Queensland coasts, and on every island or cay in the region a local population with a distinctive colour pattern occurs. As most volutes do not have a free-swimming veliger larval stage, local populations with distinctive variations have been able to evolve in isolation. The volute grows to a length of about 85 millimetres.*

Volute, *Amoria maculata*

Heron Island volute, *Cymbiolacca pulchra*

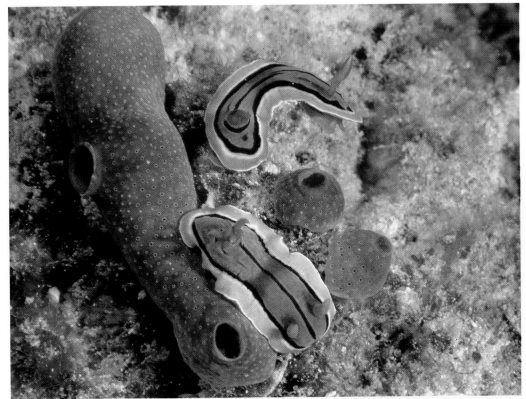

Nudibranch, *Chromodoris elisabethina*

◁ There are probably more than 400 species of the brightly coloured chromodorid nudibranchs in the tropical Indian and Pacific Oceans. Each species can be identified by its distinctive colour pattern.

▽ The baler is the largest of volutes; the shell is reported to grow to 560 millimetres in length. It is found only in northern Australia and, like other volutes, feeds on other sand-dwelling molluscs. The shell is commonly known as the baler shell, a misspelling of 'bailer' which is what the early Europeans saw the Aborigines using them for. Today, when cleaned of external growths, the beautiful shell is prized by shell collectors. The large grey tube in front of the shell is the siphon, which helps to test the water for the scent of potential food.

Baler shell, *Melo amphora*

◁ The resemblance of the shell's colour pattern to a piece of woven cloth makes the name of this cone shell particularly appropriate. This relatively common species, found on sandy patches on the reef, feeds on other molluscs, which it kills by stinging them with a harpoon-shaped tooth filled with poison. At least two people have been killed by stings from this mollusc, and all cones should be handled with great care, if at all. The shell of this species can grow to 130 millimetres.

'The volutes and cones are carnivorous hunters that often feed on other species of molluscs.'

Cone shell, *Conus textile*

known to have died from cone shell stings and others have been severely affected by the venom. Cone shells are hunters; most of them feed on worms, but some species specialise in other snails and a few on fishes. The radular teeth of cone shells have become hollow tubes, with pointed barbs at the tip. These 'harpoons' are filled with a deadly poison before they are thrust into the prey. The poison is extremely powerful and acts almost instantaneously on the victim. The poison has to act quickly to be effective, for there would be no point in the cone shell poisoning its prey merely to watch it swim or crawl away to die out of reach.

Two other families, the terebrids and turrids, are closely related to the cone shells and many of these feed on worms by poisoning them. They usually burrow in sand, and the turrids, with thousands of different species, make up probably the largest family of marine snails.

Colourful sea slugs

Few animals can rival the beauty and range of shape found in the nudibranchs. It is unfortunate that these shell-less snails should bear such an ugly name as sea slugs. Whereas most mollusc evolution has revolved around changing the shape and the colour of the shell, the nudibranchs have discarded this important protective case and have experimented instead with all manner of shapes and colours. We are only just beginning to learn a little about nudibranch biology and the importance of these brilliant colours. Many species have poisonous or bad-tasting glands in their skins and it is thought that the colours warn possible predators that the nudibranch tastes terrible.

Nudibranchs feed on a huge variety of animals, but most species have quite specific diets. Two major groups of nudibranchs are the dorids and the aeolids. Many of the dorids feed on sponges, but each species will only feed on a few types of sponge. Other dorids feed on ascidians (sea squirts) or bryozoans, and the gymnodorids hunt down other nudibranchs. The aeolids, on the other hand, feed on coelenterates, corals, sea anemones, soft corals and hydroids. One characteristic of coelenterates is that they have special stinging cells, nematocysts, for both defence and catching their prey. Aeolids can be recognised by the long tubular projections on their back, called cerata. At the tip of each of these cerata

◁ *The aeolids are one of the major groups of the nudibranchs. This species is crawling on a hydroid, which is a colony of polyps, like coral, on which most of the genus feed. Aeolids have many cylindrical projections called cerata on their backs.*

▷ *The chromodorid nudibranchs are specialist feeders, each species feeding on a particular sponge. This species, although it is common on the Great Barrier Reef, has only recently been given a species name.*

Aeolid nudibranch, *Cuthona*

Chromodorid nudibranch, *Ardeadoris egretta*

'The nudibranchs have discarded the mollusc's protective shell and experimented instead with all kinds of shapes and colours.'

▷▷ *The nembrothid nudibranchs feed on ascidians or sea squirts. Each species has a distinctive colour pattern.*

▷ *Anyone who has seen this beautiful mollusc with its swirling skirt, will understand why it is known as the Spanish dancer. The dorid nudibranch, which grows to 300 millimetres in length, usually crawls over the sea bottom like other nudibranchs, but when disturbed it is able to swim by vigorously undulating its body. This nudibranch was first discovered in the Red Sea 150 years ago, and it has since been found throughout the tropical Indian and west Pacific oceans.*

▽ *Although nudibranchs no longer have a shell to protect them from predators, many, like this one, have glands in their skin which secrete toxic chemicals when they are disturbed. These glands can be seen as white patches on the large rounded bumps. The bright colours are probably used to remind and warn predators that this particular specimen is not very nice to eat.*

Spanish dancer, *Hexabranchus sanguineus*

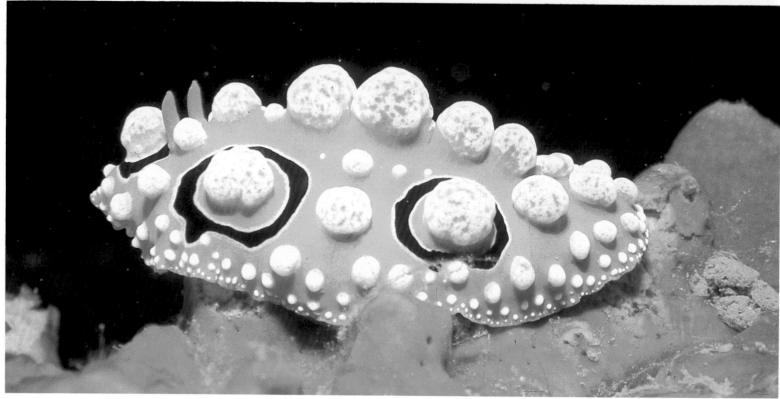

Nudibranch, *Phyllidia ocellata*

Red-striped nudibranch, *Nembrotha rutilans*

is a little sac called the cnidosac in which the aeolid stores a supply of the stinging cells that it has obtained by eating the coelenterate. When it is attacked, the aeolid can fire off these stolen weapons in its own defence.

Another trick of some aeolids is to remove the symbiotic zooxanthellae from the coelenterates they feed on and farm them in their own tissues. The zooxanthellae have an important role in reef-building, and these same plant-like cells are stolen by the nudibranchs, which use them to produce a major source of food.

Conservative bivalves

Most of the many species of bivalves have a very conservative life style. Most species bury in sand or mud, or attach themselves to something hard and spend their lives filtering microscopic plants from the water with their greatly enlarged gills. On soft shores, they are an important source of food for snails and fishes. Some families, such as the tellinids, have evolved in such a way that they feed on detritus and organic material that lies on the surface of the sand. On sandy tropical shores the butterfly shell, *Donax cureata*, can occur in large numbers. It is a remarkable sight to watch thousands upon thousands of *Donax* pop out of the sand and be rolled gently up or down the shore, depending on the tide, and then rapidly bury themselves again. In this way they migrate up and down the shore on each tide, but they stay in the zone of turbulent water, where the water is full of the suspended organic particles on which they feed.

The building of a coral reef is balanced by the many physical and biological forces that destroy it. Some bivalves, passive filter feeders though they may be, are one of the forces of destruction. In tropical waters some species of the mussel family, Mytilidae, burrow into coral skeletons; they have been given the appropriate name *Lithophaga*, 'rock eater'. Some species bore into living corals and others into dead corals. Bivalves of other families are known as coral 'nestlers', because they live in existing holes, burrows or cracks in the coral.

Such burrows and holes in the coral weaken the coral skeleton and allow other burrowing organisms in. This continual undermining of the skeleton will eventually result in its collapse.

A fabled mollusc

No description of a coral reef could possibly be complete without mention of the giant clam, which is supposed to sit with mouth agape waiting to catch the foot of the intrepid cartoon hero. By any scale, a fully grown giant clam, *Tridacna gigas*, of over one metre in length is a large animal, but it is unlikely that the shell valves open wide enough to allow a

'The mussels that burrow into coral skeletons are called *Lithophaga*, which means "rock eater".'

▽ *Reef building is in a constant state of growth and destruction, and boring organisms are an important agent in breaking down the massive coral colonies. Curious holes in the coral are usually a sign that some animal has a burrow within the coral skeleton. In some cases the coral grows around the mollusc or crustacean boarder, and in other cases, such as this one, the burrow of the rock-boring mussel is enlarged by both the growth of the coral and the boring activity of the bivalve, which is approximately 70 millimetres long. The holes in the brain coral colony are the openings of lithophagid burrows.*

Sacoglossan sea slug, *Cyerce nigricans*

△ *A common sight on reef walks is this Sacoglossan sea slug that is often mistakenly called a nudibranch because it has no shell and is brightly coloured. The Sacoglossans all feed on algae. The leaf-like projections on the slug's back contain branches of the gut but, more importantly, they contain glands that exude noxious secretions when the animal is attacked. It can grow to 40 millimetres.*

▷ *The magilids, or coral shells, are a small family of snails that live in close association with corals or other coelenterates. This species, which grows to 25 millimetres, is always found on colonies of the coral Porites. The biology of these snails is still a mystery. They do not move far and form a homing scar on the coral colony at the spot where they normally sit. One scar can be seen on the left, where a snail has been removed. Most puzzling is how they feed. No feeding damage has been found on the coral colonies they inhabit, so perhaps they feed on the mucus exuded by the coral colony when it cleans itself.*

Coral shell, *Coralliophila violacea*

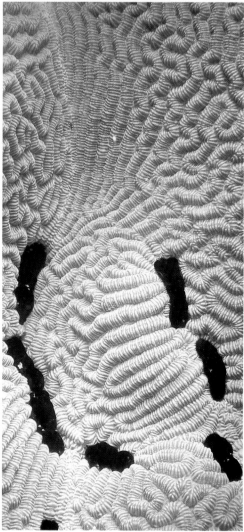

Boring mussels, *Lithophaga*

foot to enter. There are a number of species of giant clam, all of the family Tridacnidae. The largest, *Tridacna gigas*, lies loose on sand or in sandy pockets on the reef, but it is found only in the northern half of the reef. The most common giant clam of the reef is *Tridacna maxima*, which grows to about 300 millimetres in length. It is a reef-top species that lives on the surface of the reef or sand, usually with its vividly coloured mantle exposed, making it visible from some distance. Another common reef species, and the smallest, is *Tridacna crocea*. It is sometimes called the boring clam, because it is usually imprisoned in a coral block, the hole through which it can be seen being much smaller than the clam shell.

Living with the giant clam

The size to which some giant clams grow and the unusual shape of their shell and their mantle are related to a remarkable association between the mollusc and microscopic dinoflagellates, the zooxanthellae. We are still only beginning to understand the relationship between zooxanthellae and their animal hosts, but it is apparent that the clam farms the single-celled plants in its greatly enlarged mantle folds and obtains nutrients from them. In return, the zooxanthellae have a living greenhouse in which they can grow and reproduce.

A brief account such as this can do no more than describe some of the diversity of molluscan life found on the reef. The cephalopods and chitons have been mentioned only in passing; there are also the tusk shells, or scaphopods, which burrow with an extensible lobed foot. Molluscs abound on the Great Barrier Reef; their beautiful shells are visible signs of a rich and diverse group of animals whose lives are intertwined with all the other life forms on the reef.□

'The large, fleshy mantle of the giant clam is specially adapted for farming microscopic, one-celled algae, the zooxanthellae.'

▽ *In the giant clams, the mantle on each side fuses so that the mantle cavity within the shell is completely enclosed except for two holes or siphons. The one at the right is the inhalant siphon, that lets water into the shell. It is surrounded by a frill of sensory tentacles that check how clear the water is. The large tube-like siphon in the centre is the exhalant siphon through which water leaves. The giant clam, by rapidly closing its shell, can squirt a powerful jet of water out by the exhalant siphon.*

Giant clam, *Tridacna maxima*

◁ *The bright splashes of colour on an otherwise bare limestone rock are colourful evidence of the presence of a close relative of the giant clam. The boring clam lives completely imprisoned in coral pockets and can only be removed by smashing the limestone rock. All that can be seen is the colourful fleshy edge of their mantle which, when fully expanded, fills the opening of the clam's prison. If disturbed, the mantle will partly withdraw and the wavy edge of the shell will be seen. This clam grows to about 140 millimetres.*

Boring clam, *Tridacna crocea*

Crustaceans: diverse and adaptable

Night feeders

Coral reefs abound with brilliantly coloured crustaceans, one of the most diverse groups of animals. Some are very large, others so small that their beauty is revealed only through a microscope. No one has yet attempted to count the number of species on even a small reef.

Many crustaceans live in hiding, as they are a succulent food for predators. Only a few, such as the larger spiny lobsters whose size makes them relatively immune from attack, expose themselves to view. But even these are usually careful to secure a safe retreat by day and are mainly active at night, when many of the smaller crustaceans also leave their hiding places and forage for food.

The reef crustaceans have a strong protective covering, the exoskeleton, which protects their internal organs and muscles. These operate in such a way that the limbs are able to move in almost every direction. Anyone who tries to tie up a large mud crab soon learns how manoeuvrable the crab's large nippers can be.

The most conspicuous parts of crustaceans are their legs, the small paired appendages under the abdomen called swimmerets, and the tail fan. The antennae and eyes are also specialised; the eyes are generally small, but often well developed, particularly those of land-based species such as ghost crabs and fiddler crabs.

All crustaceans grow very rapidly in short bursts because they can only increase in size when they have cast off their hard, calcified skins. The old skin splits, and the soft new skin is expanded rapidly before it too calcifies and hardens for protection. As in most other reef animals, male and female crustaceans are distinct. After mating, the female lays eggs, which usually remain attached to her while they develop. On hatching, a larval stage is released into the water currents, during which further development takes place. Ultimately, and probably a long way from its parents, the last larval stage moults and changes into a miniature adult that settles, if it has found a suitable habitat.

Many crustaceans lay vast numbers of eggs, only a few of which develop into adults, but not all reef crustaceans have planktonic larval stages. Some incubate their eggs in brood chambers until they hatch out as miniature adults.

Banded coral shrimp, *Stenopus hispidus*

Palaemonid shrimp, *Leandrites cyrtorhynchus*

Pontoniine shrimp, *Periclimenes psamathe*

Crustacean symbiosis

Little is known about the food, feeding methods or behaviour of reef crustaceans. Their habits are probably the same as crustaceans found in temperate or colder waters, except for the use of symbiosis, the specialised association of some animals with others. Symbiosis occurs in many coral reef crustaceans, but it is not obvious in temperate waters and is virtually absent from cold shallow seas.

Many reef crustaceans live in permanent symbiotic relationships with a wide variety of animals – sponges, corals, anemones, Gorgonians and other coelenterates, molluscs, echinoderms and sea squirts. These associations are a major factor in the enormous diversity of crustacean species found in coral reef habitats because they enable many species to live close together in small areas.

The nature of these relationships is still not fully understood. The smaller partner could be a predator, parasite or scavenger feeding on the dead tissue of the host, or it could feed independently of the host on plankton or other animals sharing the same host habitat. Some relationships probably only involve shelter and protection from predators. Alpheid shrimps, for instance, live with sea urchins, although they appear to rummage for food on the reef surface under the shelter of the sea urchin. In general, the hosts are large animals attached to the substrate, and often secrete a lot of mucus, now known to contain nutritious waxes.

Some crustaceans are cleverly modified to suit their environment. *Caphyra rotundifrons*, which is found in tufts of green alga, is the same colour as its host; *Caphyra laevis* is found on soft corals of the genus *Xenia*, and is white like its host; and the conspicuous black and white crab, *Lissocarcinus orbicularis*, lives on sea cucumbers.

Kicking in food

Barnacles were only discovered to be crustaceans when it was found that their larvae were of the crustacean type. After the larva's planktonic period, it settles on a solid surface to develop into an adult barnacle, surrounded by a strongly calcified shell, and feeds by filtering the plankton-bearing currents through a basket of slender tentacles called cirri.

The settling larva attaches itself headfirst to the reef surface where it can move around by using its first antennae as limbs. On finding a suitable site, it then becomes permanently attached, using a cement from a special adhesive gland. In this inverted position, the barnacle changes into an adult and spends the rest of its life upside down, kicking food into its mouth.

Any exposed hard surface on the reef can be colonised by settling barnacles. They will attach themselves to exposed rock and dead coral as well as the shells of crabs, lobsters and turtles. Various reef species settle in different habitats, from protected rock crevices to shallow water exposed to the waves.

△ *This shrimp is found on Gorgonian corals and is a beautiful, slenderly built creature, with one of its two claws greatly elongated. The shrimp's body reaches a length of about 20 millimetres and is almost transparent. Often large numbers are found on a host Gorgonian coral.*

◁ *The night diver is often rewarded by the sight of this distinctive banded coral shrimp. It feeds on small animals on the reef bed and also acts as a fish cleaner.*

△△ *This shrimp is common through most of the reef. It has been observed 'cleaning' fishes, although it may be feeding on mucus secreted by the fishes. Like other 'cleaner' shrimps, this species often rolls or sways its body as it moves, which may – along with the bright colour pattern – inhibit predators.*

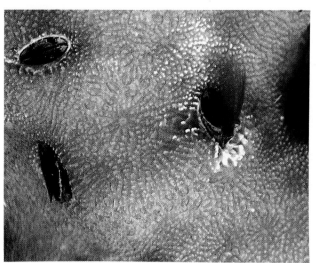

Barnacle, *Berndtia purpurescens*

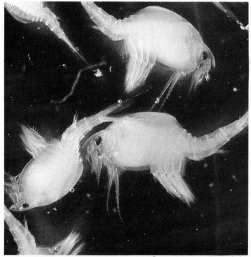

Leptostracans, *Paranebalia*

◁ *This small group of crustaceans has many fossil relatives. Little is known about their ecology in the tropics but they are probably detritus feeders or scavengers, as they will enter small baited traps. These specimens are about ten millimetres long and are found under dead coral blocks.*

◁◁ *Barnacles are common but inconspicuous on most coral reefs. Many species are found embedded in coral colonies and most are concealed by an overgrowth of coral tissues. The exception is this small barnacle with bright purple exposed valves, through which a reddish cirral net extracts food from the water.*

Many barnacles are small, less than ten millimetres long, but others, such as *Balanus (Megabalanus) stultus* may reach about 100 millimetres.

Most reef barnacles belong to the order Thoracica and do not settle on rock or carapaces, preferring to live in symbiotic associations with other marine animals such as sponges or corals. Some barnacle species seem capable of settling on a wide variety of corals, others have a more restricted choice of host. The small black goose barnacle, *Microlepas*, is attached to the tips of the long-spined sea urchin, *Diadema*, with which it blends, becoming almost indistinguishable from its host.

Some barnacles have evolved a fully parasitic way of life and live inside other crustaceans. Species of *Sacculina* infect a wide variety of crabs and can be identified by the development of a single, large sac-like reproductive body, usually olive-brown or green, which lies beneath the host's abdomen. The vital organs of the parasite are all deep inside the host's body, and the parasite's digestive system branches throughout the host's internal tissues.

Marine insects

Members of the class Copepoda, 'the insects of the sea', are abundant throughout the reef. However, because of their microscopic size they are rarely visible to the naked eye.

Many species of copepods are planktonic and free swimming, particularly those of the order Calanoida. They are present in large numbers in the ocean currents that bathe the coral reefs, although many are not particularly associated with the reef environment. Minute crawling species of the order Harpacticoida are frequently found wriggling through the tiny spaces between grains of sand or coral rubble. Other crustaceans living in the sediments between reefs, rather than on the reefs themselves, are the Ostracods. They can be found in almost any handful of sand picked up from between

Copepod, *Peltidium*

Δ *The small and abundant copepods are present in every conceivable niche of the reef. About one millimetre in length, this prettily marked species is commonly found among algae or algal detritus in reef flat pools.*

'Mantis shrimps prey on fishes, worms, crabs or molluscs, smashing the shells easily with their ferocious claws. Even in the larval stage, these claws are impressive.'

Possum shrimps, *Heteromysis harpaxoides*

Δ *The red and white possum shrimp is about ten millimetres long and lives inside the coils of gastropod shells that are occupied by large hermit crabs. Numerous specimens are frequently present in one shell, often consisting of an adult male and female and a brood of their young. They may be faecal feeders, helping to keep the shell interior clean.*

▷ *This colourful mantis shrimp is an active mollusc predator, and its powerful claws are capable of smashing the protective shells of their prey so that the smaller limbs can extract the contents. Normally carried carefully folded beneath the front of the body, these appendages can be rapidly extended with considerable force.*

corals. Their fossil relatives have attracted much attention from geologists and palaeontologists and are of fundamental importance in identifying sedimentary rock sequences.

In complete contrast are the mantis shrimps, the Stomatopoda. Although some adult species are only 30 millimetres long, many others grow up to about 300 millimetres. Stomatopods are specialised and highly predatory carnivores.

Most of the larger species – particularly those of the genus *Lysiosquilla* that are often found in vertical burrows on the reef flats – are fish predators, but others prey on worms, crabs or molluscs. Their strong claws, which resemble those of a praying mantis, can smash the shells of their prey. These claws are normally carried folded up beneath the shrimp's head and thorax but can be extended and retracted with extraordinary speed, rather like a double-jointed penknife being folded. Mantis

shrimps of the genus *Lysiosquilla* have broad yellow and black bands across their bodies. Other species are of various colours and frequently have bright eyespots that may enable members of a species to recognise each other.

The smaller species common on the reef, such as *Gonodactylus* which grows to a length of about 100 millimetres, are often found curled up in small cavities in dead coral. There they look after their batches of developing eggs, sometimes carrying them with their front limbs. The mantis shrimps have a series of planktonic larval stages that often show little resemblance to their parents, except for the healthy development of a ferocious claw.

The prevalent peracarids
The tiny members of the vast Peracarida order include Mysidacea, Amphipoda, Isopoda, Tanaidacea and Cumacea. They are all distributed

widely on the reef, although they have no planktonic larval stage; their eggs hatch, after a period of development in a pouch, into miniatures of the adult form.

Possum shrimps can often be seen hovering in small, dense clouds in depressions or sheltered nooks and crannies between corals on the reef flat or slope. They are generally shrimp-like in appearance but may be either slender and elongated or short and dumpy; highly transparent or deeply pigmented; living independently or in symbiotic relationships.

One of the most brightly coloured species, the red and white possum shrimp, *Heteromysis harpaxoides*, is found mainly in gastropod shells occupied by large spotted hermit crabs of the genus *Dardanus*. The shrimps may clean the shells by feeding on the host's faeces. Other species have been found with sponges, anemones, corals and basket stars. Most possum shrimps filter plankton from the water or

Mantis shrimp, *Odontodactylus scyllarus*

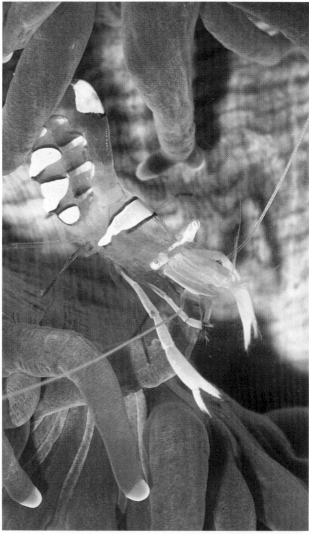

Commensal shrimp, *Periclimenes magnificus*

△ *One of the most beautiful shrimps, this species was first discovered off Heron Island on the southern Great Barrier Reef, living in association with the coral* Catalaphyllia plicata. *It is about 30 millimetres long.*

▷ *This isopod lives as a parasite on some other crustaceans. It causes a large swelling of the gill chamber of its host, a hippolytid shrimp. The female parasite causes the swelling as it produces a vast number of eggs, but a minute male is also present in the chamber with its partner.*

feed on fine food particles on the surface of the reef. Some species, such as those of the genus *Siriella*, may be scavengers or predators.

Scuttling and swimming

Amphipods are small crustaceans, measuring from two to ten millimetres and flattened from side to side. The diversity of the amphipods is enormous – about 4500 species have already been identified from temperate waters. They are well known as sand hoppers on beaches, but are far more abundant and varied at lower tidal levels. In rock pools many live symbiotically with algae and many burrow in detritus-filled depressions or among the roots of sea grasses. If dead corals are overturned, amphipods can be seen scuttling away on their sides, rather than swimming upright.

The isopods are almost as numerous as the amphipods, but unlike them, several groups have specialised in a truly parasitic way of life. At present nearly 200 species are known from the Great Barrier Reef. Most are active swimmers, flattened from top to bottom, and can be two to fifteen millimetres long. Among the best-known isopods are the cirolanids, often referred to as 'sea lice', because of their ability to scratch the skin and suck blood from swimmers. Usually buried in sand, they scavenge on a wide range of prey. Some sea lice are found in gastropod shells occupied by hermit crabs, and some are associated with feather stars.

Also common on the reefs are the sphaeromatid isopods. These are a stoutly built, heavily calcified species, herbivorous and usually free living, although some live on Gorgonians and are coloured to mimic the host's branches and polyps.

One interesting but little-studied group are the bopyrids, which are parasites mostly of shrimps and crabs. They occur as male-female pairs in the gill chambers of their hosts, which they distort by forming a conspicuous swelling.

The Tanaidacea are another group of small, cryptic crustaceans ranging from about one to ten millimetres in length, commonly found in reef sediments, often occupying minute, tube-like burrows. Two main groups are the filter-feeding Apseudomorpha and the particle-feeding Tanaidomorpha.

The small cumaceans burrow in coral-covered areas, in lagoons or sea-grass beds and many can be found among the plankton at night. They are tadpole-like, with a bulging shell and a long, thin abdomen. Cumaceans feed on algae, bacteria and detritus on the sand.

The dominant decapods

The reef's most conspicuous crustaceans are shrimps, prawns, lobsters and crabs – the decapods. They are characterised by five pairs of legs, the front pairs often having nippers or large, pincer-like claws called chelae. They cover a wide range of sizes from

Isopod, *Bopyrella*

Pontoniine shrimp, *Periclimenes kororensis*

△ *The mushroom coral,* Heliofungia actiniformis, *is just one of the numerous habitats of Pontoniine shrimps. The shrimps usually favour coral with polyps expanded by day, perhaps because they provide better protection.*

◁ *This elongated shrimp, about 100 millimetres long, lives on a Gorgonian coral host. Other hippolytid shrimps live independently or symbiotically with other animals such as soft corals, anemones, scleractinian corals, hydroids and sponges.*

Hippolytid shrimp, *Tozeuma armatum*

'Decapods occur in a wide range of sizes, from minute shrimps to large mud crabs and spiny lobsters.'

▷ *Banded coral shrimps are some of the best known of the 'cleaner' shrimps. They are nearly always found in pairs when adult, although juveniles are usually solitary. The males are smaller than the females, sometimes almost dwarfs, and they will sometimes hitch a ride on the larger female.*

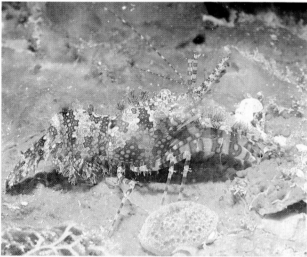

Hippolytid shrimp, *Saron marmoratus*

△ *This large shrimp is common on reef flats. It is brightly coloured but its colour merges with that of its natural habitat, making it quite inconspicuous. It has several distinct colour patterns, even in one locality, but it is possible that the different coloured shrimps may belong to closely related species.*

Banded coral shrimp, *Stenopus hispidus*

Hinge-beak shrimp, *Rhynchocinetes hiatti*

minute shrimps and crabs to large spiny lobsters. Like the rest of the reef crustaceans, most decapods remain out of sight of the casual reef walker and scuba diver, or the passing predatory fishes.

Prawns are the basis of extensive commercial fisheries in the shallow waters of the tropics but are in general poorly represented on coral reefs. A few species of the genus *Metapenaeopsis*, often called coral prawns, occur in the sandy areas between patch reefs, and the young of many of the larger species may be found on reef flats and sea-grass beds. All are active by night and remain buried by day, to avoid being preyed upon by fishes.

Shrimps and symbiosis

Coral reef shrimps are a diverse part of the reef fauna, with even a small reef like Heron Island supporting over 250 different species. The dominant pontoniine shrimps; snapper shrimps, Alpheidae;

and grass shrimps, Hippolytidae, often live symbiotically with other marine animals.

The pontoniine shrimp also plays the role of fish cleaner. Although most reef symbiotic relationships are long term or often permanent, fish-cleaning indulged in by the colourful shrimps of the Stenopodidae, Palemonidae and Hippolytidae families is a transient relationship. These shrimps form pairs or group in larger numbers and take up conspicuous positions where they are visited by a succession of fishes. The cleaning process takes the form of the shrimps nibbling all over the body of the fish. Once considered to be removing parasites from the fish, it now seems that the shrimps are feeding on the host's mucus, although the cleaners may also remove any external parasites they find. When approached by a small fish, however, some larger shrimps exhibit what looks more like aggressive or predatory behaviour.

Another style of crustacean-fish symbiosis has been evolved between several species of snapper shrimp belonging to the genus *Alpheus* and a variety of tropical gobies. The shrimps, which are normally found in male-female pairs, excavate complex burrows that are used by the gobies as a refuge. The warning system provided by the fish has distinct advantages for the shrimps, which are difficult to catch and identify as a result.

The small shrimp *Periclimenes soror* is often found between the spines of the crown-of-thorns starfish. This small pink and white banded shrimp blends well with its host's colours, making it relatively inconspicuous. In contrast, the pink, white and blue colouring of *Hymenocera picta* makes it very noticeable as it moves around slowly in male-female pairs. However, these colours may inhibit attacks by feeding fishes as the shrimps appear to be rarely molested. They prey on reef starfish, including the

Pontoniine shrimp, *Dasycaris zanzibarica*

Snapping shrimp, *Alpheus*

Gnathopyllid shrimp, *Hymenocera picta*

◬ *This shrimp is found only on whip corals of the genus* Cirripathes, *where this species lives in male-female pairs. It has a translucent body, strongly banded with yellow of the same tint as the host's polyps, so that it is scarcely visible when these are expanded. These stout shrimps are rather sluggish in their movements and they never leave their hosts voluntarily.*

◁ *Hinge-beaked shrimps have bright, conspicuous colour patterns, which vary between species, and a rostrum that is capable of being moved up or down. Some species live in the protection of the long spines of sea urchins but most live independently, gathering in dark coral caves by day and becoming active at night.*

◬ *A number of alpheid shrimps live together with a goby,* Amblyeleotris periophthalmus – *each deriving benefit from the association. The shrimp, with its heavy claws, digs a deep burrow, and a pair of gobies usually joins it. The gobies sit in the entrance, moving aside as the shrimp bulldozes out a pile of dirt. But if there is danger the gobies retreat into the hole, their tails warning the shrimp of danger. Other alpheid shrimps occupy a wide variety of habitats and may live in sponges, or with corals, anemones or feather stars.*

◬ *This gaily coloured shrimp is a predator of the crown-of-thorns starfish. As a rule it is far too sparsely represented on the reefs to make much impact on a starfish plague. These shrimps make little attempt to conceal themselves by day.*

Painted reef lobster, *Panulirus longipes*

crown-of-thorns, but are probably not sufficiently plentiful to affect its numbers. The small yellow and black banded shrimp, *Gnathophyllum americanum* is a more noticeable echinoderm predator. It may have a greater effect on echinoderm populations because it feeds on juvenile starfish rather than the adults.

Hinge-beak shrimps, Rhynchocinetidae, are found either in small groups that gather in caves, where their bright colour patterns are concealed from view, or living in symbiotic association with sea urchins. As their name implies, these shrimps have an unusual, moveable, beak-like protuberance.

The elusive lobster

One of the prettiest coral reef decapods is the lobster-like axiid, *Enometoplus occidentalis*. Like the larger, cold water true lobsters, it has well-developed nippers. It is a small but beautifully coloured species, rarely seen because of its nocturnal

habits and preference for settling on exposed seaward reefs.

Several species of spiny lobsters, with long slender antennae and small nippers, occur on coral reefs. The most common are the large ornate and painted crays, *Panulirus longipes* and *Panulirus versicolor*, both of which are very tasty. The attractively coloured Spanish or slipper lobsters – with short, flat, plate-like antennae – are difficult to see on the reef because they are nocturnal feeders, sometimes preying on giant clams. Slipper lobsters may reach a length of 250 millimetres, while species of the related genus, *Scyllarus*, found on sand between reefs, grow to a length of only 30 millimetres.

Finding a home

Hermit crabs are common on the reef among the corals, on the reef flat and on sea-grass beds. Most use empty gastropod shells as protection for their

Spanish or slipper lobster, *Parribacus antarcticus*

Sponge crab, *Dromiopsis edwardsi*

Porcelain crab, *Neopetrolisthes maculatus*

Δ *The slow-moving, nocturnal Spanish or slipper lobster is inappropriately named scientifically, as it has never been found in the Antarctic. It is a large lobster and may reach a length of 250 millimetres.*

Δ Δ *The panulirid lobsters are the largest crustaceans found on the coral reefs. Several species are known, and some are brightly and decoratively coloured. They are much sought after for their tasty tail meat. Their popularity has given rise to a confusing variety of names, all in current use – crayfish, cray, lobster, rock-lobster and spiny lobster. By day they usually occupy holes or caves on the reef and search for food at night.*

Δ *This crab carries around a protective covering of sponge, held in place by the last two pairs of walking legs, which are small and provided with special claws. Most sponges are considered to be distasteful to marine predators and this may be why they provide good protective value. Some related crabs carry over themselves an envelope of sea squirts that probably protect them in the same way.*

Δ *Porcelain crabs are found in a wide variety of situations on the Great Barrier Reef. Many are commensal, many are independent, and for quite a few, the style of living is not yet clearly defined. Some are flattened and are common under rock slabs at the upper beach levels. Others, such as this species, are found on giant anemones. A similar, closely related species, Neopetrolisthes ohshimae, also occurs on the anemones of the Great Barrier Reef and can be identified by its colour pattern, often the easiest way to distinguish some related species.*

soft abdomens. Members of the genus *Coenobita* have become land dwellers and are usually found along the upper levels of the shore, but more typical hermit crabs are the species *Calcinus* and *Clibanarius* that live in reef pools. Large spotted hermit crabs, including a conspicuous bright red crab, *Dardanus megistos*, are also found in pools. Some hermit crabs carry the additional load of an anemone, *Calliactis parasitica*, which sits attached to the shell house and takes part of the hermit crab's food.

Many of these hermits have colour patterns that easily distinguish the different species. Among the most unusual are the small crabs that belong to the species *Paguritta*. These are usually bright yellow with reddish antennae, and they live in burrows in massive corals, feeding by filtering water. A male and female crab occupy tubes close to one another and at a distance from others in the same host coral.

Squat lobsters, Galatheidae, and porcelain crabs, Porcellanidae, are small creatures with back legs so tiny that the lobsters appear to have only four pairs of legs, not five. Squat lobsters and porcelain crabs can often be seen under reef flat boulders, although many live symbiotically with other marine animals. The squat lobster, *Allogalathea elegans*, for instance, can be found with feather stars. Other related forms can be discovered on corals, or among the tentacles of anemones.

The ghost shrimps, Thalassinidea, and their related forms usually live in heterosexual pairs beneath dead coral boulders or in burrows in sand or coral rubble. The burrows are often extensive, with numerous branches and chambers.

Crab-like crustaceans

The sponge crabs, members of the family Dromiidae, are among the most interesting of the crab-like crustaceans. The back pairs of the crab's legs are small with hook-like claws that are used to hold a cup-shaped sponge or sea squirt on the back; the crab is almost completely enveloped by this covering layer. Sponge crabs are nearly globular in form and rather sluggish. They are small but can be up to 200 millimetres wide.

Spanner crabs, members of the family Raninidae, are burrowers with wrench-like claws. They are usually found in sand between reefs rather than on hard surfaces. Box crabs, Calappidae, also have distinctive claws that are used for destroying the shells of the molluscs on which they feed. Some species are about 200 millimetres long, but most of those found in the pools and sand-filled depressions of coral reefs are much smaller. They are short and broad, and hold their expanded claws crossways in front of the mouth.

Pebble crabs, Leucosiidae, are a more usual shape and occur on the reef wherever they can burrow

Hermit crab, *Trizopagurus strigatus*

Δ *This small hermit crab has a strongly flattened body that enables it to use an empty cone shell as protection for its soft fleshy abdomen. These shells are used by all members of this species. The hermit crabs are usually found under blocks of dead coral on the reef flat, and are identified by their bright orange and strongly ridged legs.*

◁ *Hermit crabs are usually found living in the empty shells of some gastropod molluscs, but a few specialised forms live in other situations. Both species known from the genus* Paguritta *live in tubes about 100 millimetres long. They penetrate a massive coral such as* Cyphastrea *and feed by filtering material from the passing plankton with specially modified feathery antennae. They are usually found in pairs, with a male and a female in adjacent tubes.*

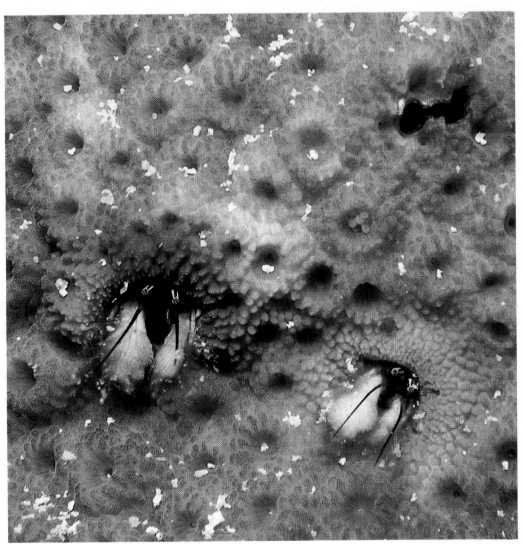

Hermit crab, *Paguritta*

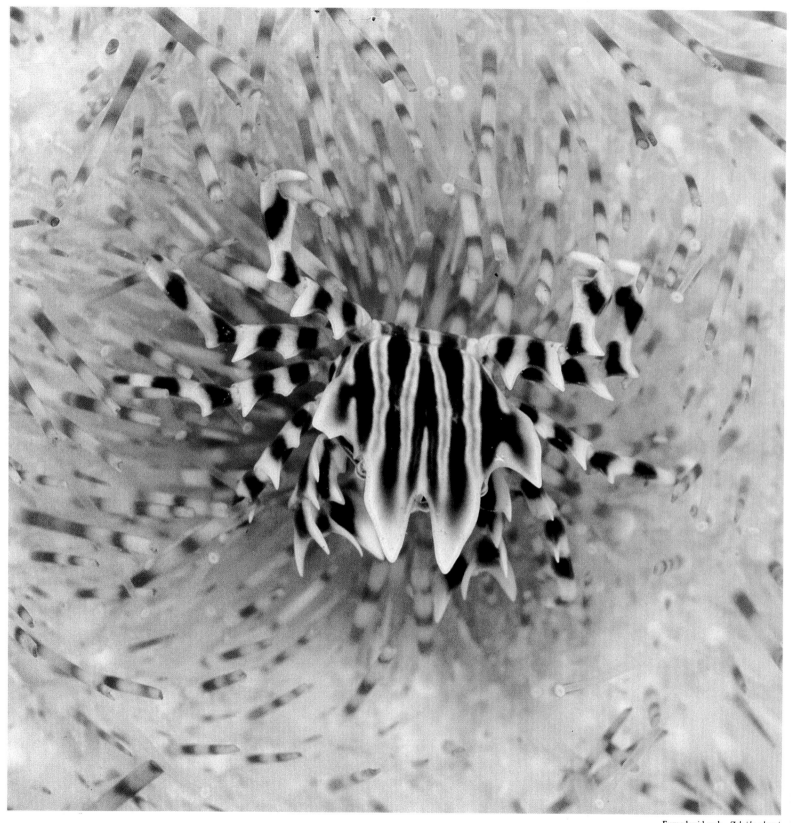

Eumedonid crab, *Zebrida adamsi*

under soft sediment. These crabs are small with attractively marked bodies, often of a porcelain-like sheen. Their claws are not well developed.

Spider crabs, Majidae, are plentiful and can be recognised by their long slender legs, although they are usually inconspicuous and adopt various forms of camouflage or mimicry. They tend to be slow moving, and many species, such as *Camposcia retusa*, cover themselves with fragments of other animals in the surrounding habitat. One spider crab, *Oncinopus araneus*, is often found with its back legs wrapped around hydroids. Another, *Xenocarcinus*, has an elongated body and short legs and is well camouflaged to merge with Gorgonian coral.

Some of the larger species of spider crabs, such as *Daldorffia horrida*, are covered with pockmarks. This crab has lumps and irregularities all over its body so that it closely resembles a piece of coral rubble; by day it rests half buried in the gravel.

Calthrop crabs of the subfamily Eumedoninae live on sea urchins and feather stars and have striking colour patterns that make them almost invisible against the background of their host animals. Most live wholly externally, but some species, such as *Echinoecus pentagonus*, will also enter their host's intestinal canal.

The most numerous and diverse family of crabs on the reef are the swimming crabs, Portunidae, and the rock crabs, Xanthidae. The swimming crabs include the Queensland mud crab, *Scylla serrata*, which inhabits mangrove areas.

Found under boulders

The dark-fingered crab from the family Xanthidae represents a range of life styles from specialised predator to herbivore; it also lives in symbiotic associations with sponges and coelenterates. This crab is found under dead coral blocks on the reef

flats and slopes, and if not disturbed it can be seen moving among live corals, even leaving the water at times in the daylight search for food.

The most common xanthid crab, *Leptodius exaratus*, is usually found under boulders. It is dark grey, almost black and about 30 to 50 millimetres wide. Another xanthid often active by day is *Eriphia sebana*, which has conspicuous red eyes. It is found among beach rock and under stones. The numerous species of *Pilumnus*, covered with shaggy coats of long woolly bristles, are more cryptic creatures, usually found under rocks in pools.

The small, brightly coloured crabs of the genus *Lybia* hold minute anemones between the fingers of their chelae. One of the more unusual associations is between *Actunmus antelmi* and scleractinian coral, where the crab lives in a hollowed nodule of the coral and, while walking around, holds it in place by its back legs. The crab is almost completely

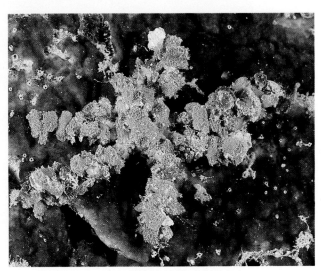

Spider crab, *Xenocarcinus*

Decorator crab, *Camposcia retusa*

△ *Spider crabs have a wide range of anatomical variations and are generally slow moving, cryptic animals, often using material from their habitat as camouflage. Others mimic their backgrounds without the use of additional material, such as this species, which closely resembles the colour of the sea fans on which it is found.*

◁ *This conspicuously coloured crab lives in pairs on a variety of sea urchins. Situated on its host, however, the crab's colours allow it to blend into the background of its host's spines.*

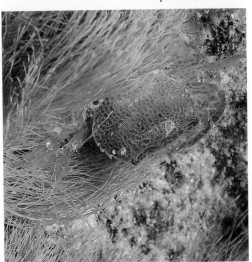

Turtle weed crab, *Caphyra rotundifrons*

△ *Decorator crabs are so-called because they dress themselves with assorted items of debris or other animals, such as sponges or bryozoans, to mask their outlines and make them almost invisible in their chosen habitat. If the camouflage material becomes inappropriate through a change of locality, it is removed and replaced by a selection of fresh material that is held in place by masses of minute hooked setae.*

◁ *Unlike most swimming crabs, the turtle weed crab is not an active swimmer, but remains almost permanently ensconced in pairs in a tuft of turtle weed, a bright green alga which it closely resembles in colour. Although associations between crustaceans and other marine animals are common in tropical waters, similar associations with plants appear to be infrequent.*

◁ *Numerous species of xanthid crabs are found on coral reefs. It is difficult to pick up a branching coral without finding some of these small, brightly coloured crabs at the base of the branches. Even small corals of about 30 millimetres wide usually have a male-female pair, and large colonies have many individuals, sometimes of more than one species. It has been suggested that these crabs may help to protect their host corals from attack by the crown-of-thorns starfish,* Acanthaster planci, *by nipping its tube feet and therefore causing it to withdraw.*

▷ *Ghost crabs are common on tropical sandy beaches, where they can often be seen running along until they disappear down their sand burrows. The ghost crab can be recognised by horn-like growths on its eyestalks. It digs deep burrows and scavenges food washed up by the incoming tides and winds, and preys on newly hatched turtles.*

Crown-of-thorns starfish, *Acanthaster planci*; xanthid crab, *Trapezia*

Coral gall crab, *Hapalocarcinus marsupialis*

▷ *Most species of pea crab are pea-shaped and sized. This species is about 20 millimetres across the carapace, on which ridges are formed. It lives inside the mantle cavity of the giant clam,* Tridacna gigas, *where it must be relatively well protected from potential predators. The unusual size and shape of the crab are presumably associated with the increased living space available inside the clam's protective cavities. Only one male and one female are found inside each clam, although there would appear to be enough space for several pairs. Once a pair have established themselves they probably prevent the settlement of any further post larvae of the same species, possibly by cannibalism.*

△ *Female coral gall crabs are found in readily visible galls on the branches of Pocilloporid corals. The males, which are rarely seen, are very small in order to be able to enter the tiny apertures in the galls.*

concealed, and the coral colony appears to be moving along by itself.

On the reef flat, exposed at low water, and adjacent areas of beach are several crabs of the Grapsidae family. The larger species, like *Grapsus strigosus*, have a flattened shape, but they are agile, fast runners, often active by day but disappearing into rock crevices when approached.

Families that are represented by a smaller variety of species are the soldier crabs, Mictyridae, which march in dense packs across exposed sand flats, and the pea crabs, Pinnotheridae, which are the size and shape of peas and live in pairs in molluscs. More

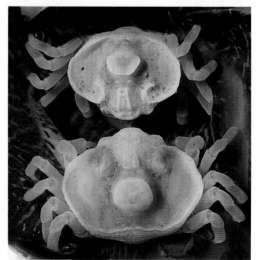

Pea crab, *Xanthasia murigera*

Ghost or sand crab, *Ocypode ceratophthalma*

conspicuous than most is *Xanthasia murigera* which lives in pairs in the mantle cavity of the giant clam, *Tridacna gigas*.

Ghost or sand crabs, *Ocypode*, and fiddler crabs, *Uca*, which inhabit muddy areas, belong to the Ocypodidae family. Sand crabs are runners and burrowers and live on sandy beaches where they feed by scavenging. Fiddler crabs feed in softer areas of the shore than beaches. The male fiddler has one enlarged and brightly coloured nipper. Stalk-eyed crabs, *Macrophthalmus*, are found on still softer substrates, where they appear to be constantly idling about.

A coral home
Some of the most interesting coral reef crabs are the small members of the Hapalocarcinidae family, which live on scleractinian corals. The best-known is the coral gall crab, *Hapalocarcinus marsupialis*, which settles in its post-larval stage on the coral of its choice, and causes the coral's growth pattern to alter so that it becomes enveloped by a chamber with only a few minute apertures. These outgrowths are situated near the ends of the host coral's branches and are easily seen, being 10 to 15 millimetres wide. Related crabs live in tubular cavities in massive corals. In these interesting tube-dwelling species the front shell and claws are shaped so that they block the entrance to the tube and therefore protect the occupant from attack.

The not-so-silent underwater world
A number of crustaceans contribute to the underwater sounds of coral reefs and some even to the noise on land. With an ear to the sand of a tropical beach it is often possible to hear the ghost crabs rubbing their legs together and making sounds like crickets. The function of these sounds is not clear but they may act, like bird song, to establish a presence in the territory.

Underwater, over a reef, a diver is usually conscious of a continuous background clicking noise. These sharp sounds are produced deliberately by stomatopod and alpheid crustaceans. The noise produced by mantis shrimps may just be incidental to their striking out at prey or attackers with their powerful claw. The snapping shrimps have only one chela, modified for sound production by means of a 'pit and hammer' system on the fingers. The loud snap produced is probably the shrimp's main means of defending itself against intruders wishing to enter its burrow. Some pontoniine shrimps use their enlarged claws alternately to produce a rapid series of loud staccato clicks. Other underwater sounds made by crustaceans are the creaking noises caused by the movements of alarmed spiny lobsters' antennae and the rasping noises of crabs. □

Bryozoans: coloured mats of the sea

The first settlers

In the hidden places of the Great Barrier Reef, under its coral masses, or in its caves, are surfaces encrusted with moss-like bryozoans. These minute animals, living together in colonies, forming coloured mats over rocks or plants, are often the dominant form of life in an area of the reef.

Bryozoan colonies differ in their structure and habitat. Some grow on rigid surfaces, others attach themselves to moving things while others move around freely in the water. They may grow rapidly or slowly. Within such basic groupings there may be more than ten different forms of colony. In some colonies individual animals are hard and bony from the presence of calcium, while in others, where there is little calcium, the individual is protected by layers of tissue. It is even possible for the same species of bryozoan to vary its colours and forms depending on where it grows.

Some species of bryozoans on the Great Barrier Reef grow quickly and can be as much as 40 millimetres in diameter after less than three months. Such large colonies, as well as those composed of only a few individuals, contain fertile reproductive chambers in early stages of growth. When a panel is placed in the reef environment in order to research the forms of life that might attach themselves to it, bryozoans are the first organisms to settle. They will appear in light or shaded areas, but are far more numerous in shade, with more than 100 colonies often being found on the undersurface of a panel 140 millimetres square. Such an accumulation can occur in less than three months in a north Queensland winter. Such experimental panels must of course be protected with wire from foraging fishes.

Variations in form, growth and place

Because the individual animals are so small it is difficult to study bryozoans, and often a very powerful electron microscope is needed to identify them. The appearance of individuals in different parts of a colony may vary because of the physiological make-up of the colony or because of small changes in the environment. The appearance of a whole colony may also alter. Many encrusting colonies, for instance, have the ability to grow erect and firm at some stage of their development. This enables them to live in places where there are

Bryozoan

△ *Many bryozoans have this erect and flexible growth form. They can live in areas of current action and the connections between the branches give the colonies added support in a more rigorous environment.*

▷ *Small individuals are separated from one another throughout the complete colony by nodes of fibrous collagen. Between the nodes may be two individuals, a mother and its asexually budded offspring, and here branching takes place. From a very small initial individual, colonies of up to 300 millimetres in diameter can be formed. The branching pattern is constant through the colony and is affected only by reproduction. Colonies are anchored to the substrate by a series of rootlets which develop from many individuals. Each rootlet is less than one millimetre in diameter but the accumulation at the base of a large colony may be up to 10 millimetres wide.*

Catenicelliform bryozoan, *Scuticella*

Bryozoan, *Iodictyum*

△ *These erect, rigid colonies of lace coral vary greatly in shape depending on the amount of sedimentation in the environment. In areas of much sedimentation they tend to form a large funnel to keep the growing edge of the colony above the sediment–water interface, and in areas of little sedimentation they tend to form many funnels. In these large bryozoan colonies the base of the colony may be dead but the top of the colony is still alive and reproducing sexually and asexually.*

deposits of sediment in which they would not normally be able to grow, since the growing edge of the colony can keep above the sediment. In the same way, colonies can live among thread-like algae because they can grow above the chains of cells.

A study of reef bryozoans has not been attempted, but it might include more than 300 species if it were, some of which would be new. □

Bryozoan

'These minute animals living together in colonies, forming coloured mats over rocks and plants, are often first to settle and become the dominant form of life in an area of the reef.'

◁ *This colony of bryozoans, hard with a high calcium content, forms a crust on a firm surface. The growing edge is marked by a white semicircle, and each individual is about one millimetre across.*

Bryozoan, *Parmularia*

△ *This colony exists in sandy areas. It is about 30 millimetres across the base and it is anchored to the substrate by a rootlet about 3 millimetres in diameter. The growing edge of the colony around the circumference can be seen and the raised areas on the surface of the colony are reproductive chambers. When larvae are released from these chambers they fall to the substrate and then burrow into it before beginning their development. When growing, living chambers develop and the rootlet, which may be three times the diameter of the colony in length, is produced.*

◁ *A colony can increase in size by its tissue ballooning upwards, forming a new layer of individuals and killing the layer below. The colony expands upwards and outwards, and some colonies may form large spherical masses about 200 millimetres in diameter.*

Bryozoan

Feather star, *Himerometra robustipinna*

Echinoderms: a zoological puzzle

Separate but similar

Five different kinds of closely related strange animals are, after fishes and corals, the most conspicuous creatures on the Great Barrier Reef...

Bright, cobalt blue sea stars with five long, radiating arms lie draped over rubble in very shallow water. Under a nearby algae-covered piece of debris, a mass of thin, coiling arms resolves itself into an animal with a small, rounded body and five long, spiny arms – a brittle star – which proceeds to row jerkily away under the rubble.

In a deeper pool, dark green, sausage-shaped sea cucumbers lie quite still on the bottom. Others are black, with a light sprinkling of sand grains over their surface. The edge of the pool bristles with long black spines, waving menacingly; bright spots of red, iridescent blue and white reveal several sea urchins clustered there, each with a spherical body bearing numerous radiating spines.

Further out, attached to the top of a coral colony right on the reef's edge, the delicate arms of clusters of flower-like feather stars flutter in the gentle swell.

All five creatures – sea star, brittle star, sea cucumber, sea urchin and feather star – are echinoderms, and they respectively represent the five classes into which the phylum Echinodermata is usually divided: Asteroidea, Ophiuroidea, Holothurioidea, Echinoidea and Crinoidea.

Worldwide, these five classes include around 6000 species, 350 of which have so far been discovered living along the coast of Queensland and on the Great Barrier Reef itself.

Echinoderms are an ancient group of animals; their fossil ancestors are recognisable in rocks over 500 million years old, and today's living representatives are a mere remnant of the numbers known to have existed during their long history. Exclusively marine and almost all bottom-dwelling, they occur from between the tides to the deepest parts of the ocean. They are found both on hard, rocky substrates and in soft sediment; and while almost all are capable of some movement, many are sedentary.

Stars of the sea

Asteroids are the familiar sea stars, or starfish, and while most are basically 'star-shaped' with five fairly smooth arms radiating from a small central body,

◁ *More like some exotic crimson plant growing from the surface of the reef, it is hard to think of this as an animal at all, let alone an echinoderm. However, this beautiful animal with its many feather-like arms waving in the current is a common species of feather star, often forming clusters in the top few metres of water near the reef crest or festooning prominences on the sides of coral bommies.*

▷ *This beautiful urchin, while quite rare on the reef, is one of the most easily recognised. It has ten broad, naked areas on its body, and finely banded spines of equal length. Not growing large – adults are only 40 millimetres across – it is usually found under rubble. It grazes by night on hard surface areas.*

▷▷ *Most reef sea cucumbers feed on the soft sandy sediments of the lagoon floor. This animal, however, clambers over the hard substrate of the reef itself, unworried by sharp corals and the stinging cells lining their tentacles. Fully exposed by day but well camouflaged by its speckled brown colours, this species is a frequent sight on the reef slopes or sides of bommies.*

▷ *A common inhabitant of the shallow waters of the lagoonal patch reefs, the blue sea star is one of relatively few asteroids exposed by day. Perhaps its bright colour warns potential predators of the toxic substances within, thus making a nocturnal existence unnecessary.*

▷▷ *Much more active than the sea star, the brittle star crawls quickly using a rowing motion with its arms rather than its tube feet, which are used more for feeding. This species belongs to a group of predatory brittle stars that capture their prey by looping a lightning-fast arm coil around it then transferring it to the mouth.*

Sea urchin, *Mespilia globulus*

Sea cucumber, *Bohadschia graeffei*

Blue sea star, *Linckia laevigata*; brown sea star, *Nardoa novaecaledoniae*

Brittle star, *Ophiarachnella gorgonia*

Outside and inside echinoderms

The Echinodermata of the reef come in five basically different shapes; the usually five-armed sea stars (Asteroidea); the five-armed or many branched brittle and basket stars (Ophiuroidea); the globular sea urchins (Echinoidea); the feather stars (Crinoidea) and the elongate sea cucumbers (Holothurioidea). These animals look quite different on the outside but they have three basic structures in common linking them together as echinoderms. These features are: the five-fold symmetry of their body plan, a skeleton of reticulate calcite plates (microscopic in holothurians) and a unique water vascular system filled with liquid which operates the tube feet by hydraulic pressure. The exploded colour-coded diagram shows these features, together with the gut and gonads, in a sea star. This basic arrangement is found in each of the five echinoderm types but is differently arranged to fit into the different-shaped bodies.

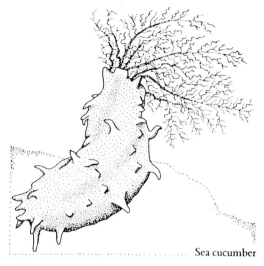

Sea cucumber

the number of arms, extent of ornamentation and overall shape may vary greatly. The crown-of-thorns starfish, *Acanthaster planci*, may have up to 23 arms, although 15 or 16 are more common. It has a large disc, short arms and is covered with long, very sharp spines. The pincushion star, *Culcita novaeguineae*, has a very swollen body, almost no arms, and is covered in rough granules. The sea star's mouth is in the middle of the underside, and the anus is on the upper surface of the disc.

The arms of regular sea stars, such as the blue sea star, *Linckia laevigata*, contain identical sets of respiratory, digestive, locomotory, sensory and reproductive organs. Running along the underside of each arm is a groove edged with protective spines from which protrude a series of tiny, hydraulic suckered appendages called tube feet. These are responsible for the slow, creeping movement of the sea star across the ocean floor.

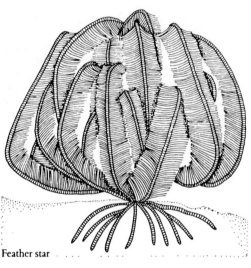

Feather star

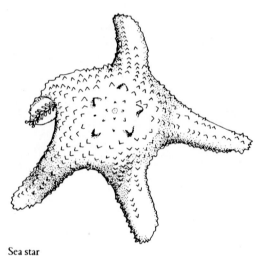

Sea star

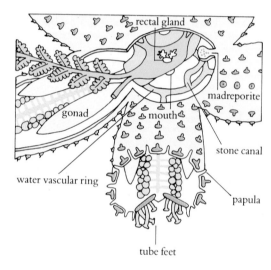

rectal gland

madreporite

gonad

mouth

stone canal

water vascular ring

papula

tube feet

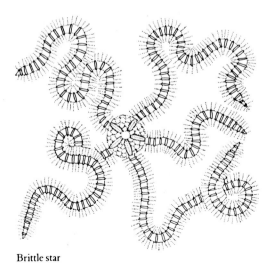

Brittle star

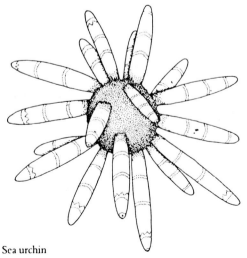

Sea urchin

Fragile arms

Most ophiuroids are brittle stars with five long, thin arms sharply differentiated from a small, rounded central body. Smaller and more delicately constructed than sea stars, their major systems – such as stomach, digestive glands, respiratory and reproductive organs – lie within the soft central disc. Unlike the sea star, the brittle star's arms are not hollow but are made of a series of solid little segments of skeleton, joined by muscles and ligaments, rather like the vertebrae in a backbone. They are not strong, however, and brittle stars are aptly named, for any shock or rough handling causes their arms to break off.

Brittle stars, like nearly all echinoderms, have no sort of 'head' and can move in any direction. The arms are edged with small spines for their whole length, the mouth is in the middle of the underside and there is no anus. A small group with extremely

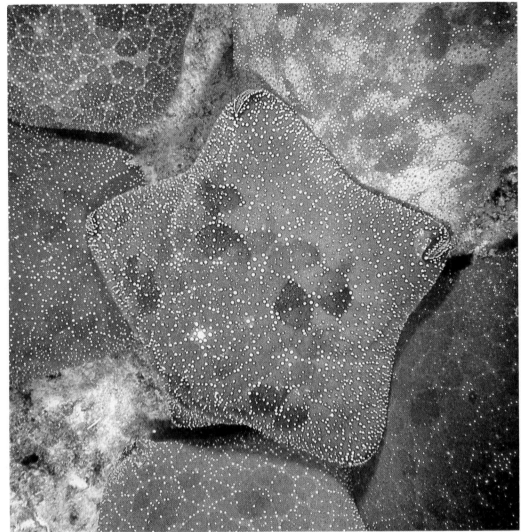

Pincushion sea star, *Culcita novaeguineae*

◁ Some of the largest and most colourful sea stars of tropical waters belong to the family Oreasteridae and are common in protected sandy areas and sea-grass beds. The pincushion sea star is an extreme variation of the typical asteroid plan; it is the size and approximate shape of a slightly deflated soccer ball. The massive body is swollen, leaving it almost without arms, but it has five furrows with numerous tube feet radiating from a central mouth.

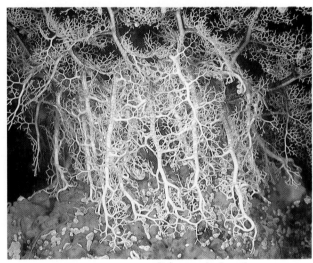

Basket star, *Astroboa nuda*

△ Soon after dusk, along the channels and edges of the reef where good currents flow, the massive fans of basket stars, up to a metre or more across, are used to trap unwary plankton. Unlike the rest of the ophiuroids, the arms of these animals fork repeatedly to create great fishing nets. This basket star can trap prey of 10 to 30 millimetres – including a wide range of fish and crustacean larvae, shrimps and worms. When an animal strikes the net the arm tip bends and encircles the prey that is impaled on numerous tiny hooks on the underside of the arms.

◁ Serpent stars have extremely long arms covered by soft, thick skin. They come in a variety of colours but two predominate – reddish brown and creamy yellow. Pale specimens frequently have a longitudinal dark line down the middle of the upper side of the arms, and the dark variety may have two dark lines within a pale line.

Serpent star, *Astrobrachion*

Sea cucumber, *Pseudocolochirus axiologus*

△ *This beautiful sea cucumber, usually found only at the base of reefs, is a member of the Dendrochirotida family. These are almost exclusively suspension feeders and have enlarged tentacles with branching dendritic ends. They are not common on the reefs but are dominant on the vast areas of soft muddy-sand substrate in between the reefs. The rows of crimson tube feet of this species can clearly be seen against the smooth blue body wall. A feeding tentacle is just being withdrawn from the mouth – the captured particles, mainly diatoms, have been wiped off, and the tentacle has probably been recoated with mucus.*

long, skin-covered arms are the serpent or snake stars, such as *Astrobrachion adhaerens*. Another group, the basket stars, such as *Astroboa*, have branching arms and grow to a metre or more across.

Crawling cucumbers

Holothurians, or sea cucumbers, are elongate, sausage-shaped animals with a mouth at one end, surrounded by feeding tentacles, and an anus at the other. The majority of reef holothurians are large, with leathery, flexible bodies, and feed from the sand across which they crawl. They belong to a particular group called the aspidochirote holothurians. Certain species within this group are commercially fished and are known as bêche-de-mer or trepang.

A second major group are the dendrochirote holothurians. More sedentary, they have finely branching (dendritic) feeding tentacles that are held

upwards in the water to catch plankton. Often brightly coloured, they are less common on the reefs themselves but are the most abundant sea cucumbers on the soft, muddy sand areas of the continental shelf between the reefs.

The third major group on the reef are the apodous holothurians. They are extremely sticky to touch, have thin, sometimes almost translucent body walls and move by waves of peristaltic contractions of the body. While some are tiny, such as *Synaptula lamperti*, others such as *Euapta godeffroyi* are about a metre, while *Synapta maculata*, a huge snake-like sea cucumber, has been recorded at five metres.

Prickly urchins

Echinoids or sea urchins are the animals which gave the phylum its name – Echinodermata being derived from the Greek words for 'spiny' and 'skin'. Most have numerous projecting spines covering a

'Some sea cucumbers have thousands of tube feet – others move by peristaltic contractions of the body.'

Sea cucumber, *Synaptula lamperti*

◁ *This little striped synaptid, about 30 millimetres long, is often found entwined in hundreds over the surface of certain sponges. Recent research indicates that substances given off by the sponge are being taken in as well as some detrital material in a more normal feeding mode.*

Sea urchin, *Tripneustes gratilla*

△ *This sea urchin is a regular echinoid with a large rounded body and fairly short spines with no great difference in length between primary and secondary spines. Its hundreds of long white tube feet can be seen waving in the current beyond the protection of its sharp white spines. Contractions of fluid-filled sacs, lined with muscles and located on the inside end of each tube foot, control their long extension. Their important role as a kind of long adhesive 'grapnel' for hauling the urchin around the sea floor, is aided by the spines on the oral side, which act as dozens of little levers to help propel the animal.*

◁ *This sea cucumber has a thin, almost translucent body wall and lives hidden under coral rubble. It has thin papillae bearing tube feet necessary for secure attachment and locomotion in high energy areas near the reef edge where it lives.*

Sea cucumber, *Labidodemas semperianum*

Feather stars

rigid, spherical body with the mouth below and the anus in the middle of the upper side. These 'regular' echinoids make up the majority of the urchins on the reef. Cidaroid urchins, such as *Phyllacanthus imperialis*, are primitive members of this group; they have massive primary spines surrounded by a ring of small flattened ones.

The second major division of echinoids are the 'irregular' echinoids – the sand dollars and heart urchins. Both of these groups live in or on soft sediment, in contrast with the hard substrate favoured by most regular urchins. They retain the rigid body of other echinoids but have smaller spines. The sand dollar's body is a flattened disc, and while the mouth is still in the middle of the underside, the anus is usually located near one edge of it. The heart-shaped body of the heart urchin is even more changed from the basic urchin, with the anus positioned at the rear end and the mouth sited further forward on the underside. The spines are often curved back over the body.

Lilies of the deep

The most ancient and primitive of the echinoderms are the crinoids. Over 300 million years ago, crinoids dominated the seas, but subsequently all known kinds became extinct. Others survived, for a few close relatives are alive today – the stalked crinoids or sea lilies. These animals, attached to the sea floor, only live now in depths greater than 100 metres; those seen on the reef are comatulid crinoids or feather stars.

Although they pass through a short attached phase as juveniles, the adults are free to crawl and in some cases to swim. Usually, however, they attach themselves to the reef with grasping organs called cirri. Their arms have numerous fine side branches called pinnules that give each arm its feathery appearance.

The number of arms on a crinoid varies considerably. A tiny, secretive, grey-brown feather star, *Eudiocrinus tenuissimus*, living in crevices in the vertical walls of the deep passages between northern reefs, is the only five-armed species known from the Great Barrier Reef. *Oligometra serripinna* is one of the many species with ten arms while some, such as *Comanthina nobilis*, may have up to 200.

The position of a feather star's mouth and anus differ from other echinoderms in that both are on the same side facing upwards, away from the substrate. This is thought to be the original way in which echinoderms were orientated and is associated with the feeding habit of the crinoid. Their multiple arms with numerous side branches have evolved as a high surface area net for catching food-plankton wafting by in the water.

Radial symmetry

Echinoderms are an extremely diverse group, however they share several features that separate them totally from all other known creatures.

Feather star, *Comanthus mirabilis*

Pre-eminent among these features are their symmetry, their skeleton and a system of fluid-filled canals and tentacles – their water-vascular system.

Radial symmetry is found in many primitive, attached organisms. Like a coral polyp or sea anemone, echinoderms are similar all the way around. Each echinoderm is divided into five identical areas. The tiny gelatinous larval stage – through which most tropical species pass during early development – is, however, organised differently, with a head and left and right sides. They are the only known example of a group having a bilaterally symmetrical larva that changes into a radially symmetrical adult. The reverse situation is quite common among invertebrates.

Some adult sea cucumbers, sand dollars and heart urchins have a two-sided symmetry superimposed on their five-fold symmetry. Perhaps their active burrowing habit – associated in most cases with the processing of large quantities of sediment through their guts – has brought about this evolutionary change.

Light but strong skeletons

The echinoderm skeleton is a miracle of biological engineering. In contrast with the skeletons of many invertebrates, such as the carapace of a crab or shell of a snail, it is internal and every element is covered by a layer of living tissue. Indeed, the relationship between the crystalline part of the skeleton, made of

△ *This conical structure is the central body area of a recently described feather star. The anus is at the top of the cone so that the faeces are carried away by the current. The mouth, with its converging food grooves, is at the margin. It is surrounded by numerous elongate segmented structures – oral pinnules that are modified versions of those lining the arms. Some species have heavy spike-like oral pinnules which appear to protect the vulnerable body. This animal is a member of the family Comasteridae which has come to dominate the shallow water of the reef. They typically have tiny combs on the tips of their oral pinnules. These have recently been found to be extremely good taxonomic features for separating one genus from another. However, whether their primary role is in feeding, defence or cleaning is unclear.*

◁ *The glorious, glowing colours and varied shapes of at least six different kinds of feather star crowd together around this one soft coral. Dense masses of numerous crinoids of many different species are common on the reef. In some places there may be over 20 species packed into an area of just a few square metres. Certain sites, particularly mid-shelf reefs, have revealed over 50 different species. It is not known how they survive together, apparently using the same basic resource of water-borne food, or how they have all evolved.*

▷ Some feather stars, disliking strong currents, seek out quiet waters but they still require slight currents to bring their food. Comanthina nobilis lives in areas of medium strength current – it has no cirri but uses several of its arms with their spiny pinnules to anchor it to the reef.

▽ At first glance, the shape of a feather star shows little obvious similarity to its relatives the sea stars and brittle stars. Their orientation is different – both mouth and anus are located on the upper side of their small rounded body, which is set in a cup of interlocking calcareous plates.

Feather star, *Comanthina nobilis*

Feather stars, *Oxycomanthus bennetti*

▷ Crinoids can be very numerous in the areas of a reef where good currents flow. Such locations as along the ridges of a spur and groove system on the front slope, down the vertical walls of a deep channel between two reefs or on the sides of a back reef bombie may be dominated by hundreds of large feather stars, their bewildering array of patterns providing a riot of colour. Often prominently located, like these three feather stars, they are the most conspicuous echinoderms of the reef, rivalled only by the large sea cucumbers of the lagoon.

Feather star, *Oxycomanthus bennetti*

Feather star, *Himerometra bartschi*

Suspension feeders

'Feather stars may have anything from five to over 200 arms, all of which radiate from five regions near the base; these arms are held in the current, trapping plankton.'

Feather star, *Comanthina nobilis*

△ Once a favoured position has been found by climbing or swimming, many feather stars that stay exposed by day will remain there permanently. Often their grasping cirri become overgrown with algae and other encrusting organisms. A tightly held sea whip or Gorgonian may die around the area grasped by the feather star. The immobility of feather stars has encouraged the mistaken concept that they are not animals but plants.

◁ Large feather stars with many arms adopt a hemispherical feeding posture. They are usually the species that grasp the substrate with their arms rather than using cirri. This brilliant yellow feather star has formed just such a bushy, multi-layered filtering device. It is also useful if the current direction is highly variable.

'A series of tiny, hydraulic, suckered appendages called tube feet enables the sea star to crawl about slowly on the ocean floor.'

▷ *This delightfully marked little biscuit sea star is a splash of colour amid the drab rubble of many areas of the reef. Usually only 50 millimetres across, it is a grazer on encrusting organisms. The family Goniasteridae, to which it belongs, has particularly large skeletal plates along the edge of the arms. In this species, small yellow granules define the edge of large red plates. The interlocking plates, embedded in the body wall, provide a light but strong framework surrounding the fluid-filled body cavity in which the organs lie.*

Biscuit sea star, *Tosia queenslandensis*

Sea star, *Echinaster callosus*

△ *In some cases the sea star's skeleton is much more open and less massive, leaving larger areas of soft tissue between each plate.*

▷ *The ornamentation on the plates of a sea star can vary from just skin through small granules to massive tubercles or long, dangerous spines. The rhinoceros or horned sea star is a typically massive member of the family Oreasteridae, growing to a diameter of almost 400 millimetres. Common in sea-grass beds in shallow water, it feeds on the film of detritus and micro-organisms. This sea star is protected by large, sharply conical tubercles which give it its most appropriate name.*

Horned sea star, *Protoreaster nodosus*

calcium carbonate, and the living cells that create it, is very intimate. The skeleton is a fine honeycomb with living tissue interwoven through so that each piece of skeleton is light but strong and can be reabsorbed or grow out in any direction.

This is vital for a growing sea urchin with a skeleton made up of a hollow, rigid sphere of plates. Being internal, it cannot be shed as would a crab's; instead it must change steadily as the urchin grows. The many separate plates of the sea urchin are rigidly attached to each other. When alive, apart from the digestive tract, the inside is largely fluid filled, a receptacle awaiting the great expansion of the reproductive organs in the breeding season.

The outside of the skeleton or 'test' shows five double rows of plates with numerous pores through which the tube feet protrude. The test is further ornamented with small, round nodules or tubercles

Sea star, *Fromia monilis*

△ *The extensive system of thin-walled canals and numerous tube feet that constitutes the echinoderm water-vascular system is always leaking, and not only from direct damage. To operate under pressure it must be topped up, and on the surface of most echinoderms there is a special sieve plate through which sea water can be pumped into the water-vascular system. It is frequently the only structure that mars the otherwise perfect radial symmetry of an echinoderm. The sieve-plate or madreporite of this sea star is easily visible as a crimson patch on the disc between two arms.*

on which the spines are mounted. Operated by a cone of muscles around their base they are highly manoeuvrable. Amazingly, every element of the echinoderm skeleton – every plate and every spine – appears to be a single crystal.

The calcareous plates or ossicles of the sea star skeleton are embedded in the body wall and joined by connective tissue and muscles. While a fluid-filled cavity is enclosed within the disc and arms, as within an urchin, the skeleton is a much more flexible structure, allowing the sea star to bend easily. The plates may bear granules, massive tubercles or sharp spines, as in the urchin.

The skeletons of the brittle star and feather star are similar, with each arm consisting of a line of solid articulating vertebrae joined by muscles and ligaments. Each arm segment of a brittle star typically has an external covering plate above, below and on each side, all embedded within the

skin. The side plates support rows of arm spines. The arms converge at the mouth and become part of the jaws. Complex sets of tiny teeth identify separate groups of brittle stars.

Each segment of the crinoid arm has a side branch or pinnule, composed of a string of small, linked ossicles, like the arms. Powerful ligaments extend the arms, and muscles linking their upper sides may fold them. Many of the small skeletal segments – especially those of the grasping cirri and towards the pinnule tips – are extremely hooked and thorny. This ornamentation helps the crinoids attach themselves to the reef. They have no true spines.

The holothurian skeleton is very strange. Situated within the leathery body wall, it has become reduced to microscopic spicules of calcite only hundredths of a millimetre in length. There may be millions of these in the skin of a normal sea cucumber. The apodous holothurians make great use of them – they lack the suckered tube feet of typical sea cucumbers and their ossicles are larger and shaped like anchors. The flukes penetrating the body wall serve as friction points on which the muscular contractions can act.

Canal networks

A unique water-vascular system is perhaps the main feature of echinoderms. It differs in structure and function among the five classes, but a basic plan is common to all. Internal fluid-filled distribution canals supply numerous tubular extensions called tube feet that pass to the outside of the animal. These are hydraulically operated and extend by the contraction of muscular sacs called ampullae.

In sea stars, a circular ring in the disc supplies a radial canal running up each arm. Side branches supply the numerous tube feet, which are protected in the ambulacral groove on the underside. Powerful muscular sacs extend each tube foot, which usually has a sucker at the end. Employing both suction and adhesive mucus for attachment, the tube feet of a sea star are used primarily for movement although they are sometimes important in digging for prey and pulling apart clam shells.

Various fluid reservoirs open off the ring canal in the disc. A single external opening, a sieve-like plate called a madreporite, is located on the disc's upper surface and is connected to the ring canal by a powerful pumping organ, the stone canal. Any fluid lost from the tube feet through accident or leakage can be made up by intake via the madreporite.

Food traps

The brittle star system is similar, but the tube feet have no suckers and are generously endowed with mucus-secreting papillae. Their role in movement is limited, this being accomplished mainly by a rowing action of the arms. The tube feet are primarily used to trap plankton, detritus and fine particles of food. The madreporite is located on a modified plate near the mouth.

▷ *This little urchin, the size of a child's fist, is probably the most numerous and widely distributed species occurring in the shallower parts of reefs. With its unusual ovoid body,* Echinometra mathaei *is a member of a quite advanced group of regular echinoids. The spines are usually white tipped but the main colour is highly variable, with pink, purple and brown varieties, as well as this olive green form.*

▽ *The brightly coloured candy sea cucumber has mottled, finely branched feeding tentacles spread for suspension feeding. A sedentary animal, it may never change position once it has found an ideal location, usually the highest spot to spread its tentacles in the current.*

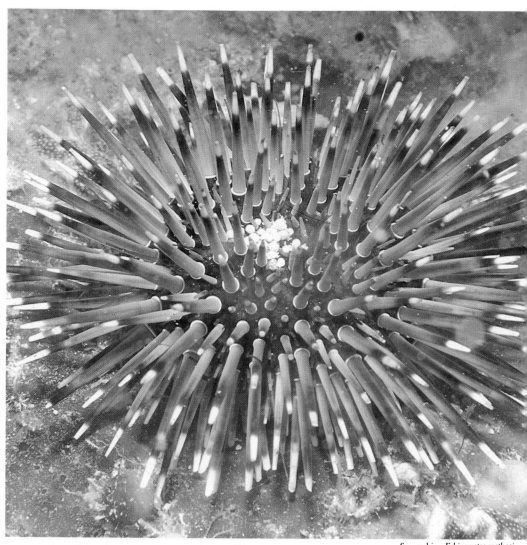

Sea urchin, *Echinometra mathaei*

Candy sea cucumber, *Colochirus anceps*

▷ *Normally covered by a thin layer of sand, this very large sand dollar is nearly the size of a man's hand. It is common in the deeper water between the reefs but is sometimes found in the sand around a cay or in the lagoon. Covered with thousands of tiny spines and tube feet, sand dollars are basically a very flattened version of a regular echinoid. The mouth is still in the centre of the underside, but the anus is in a spot near the trailing edge instead of the centre of the upper side. The characteristic five-rayed petal on the upper side is the site of a series of extraordinarily modified tube feet. No longer used for movement they are thin-walled hollow extensions of the body, stacked in neat rows around the petal – these are the animal's gills, constantly exchanging gases with the surrounding water.*

Sand dollar, *Clypeaster telurus*

The water-vascular system of the feather star has similar radial canals along each arm and pinnule, but on the upper oral side, lying just below the food groove. Lining the sides of these gutters are the simple tube feet or tentacles. Extended, they form a fringe to every pinnule, increasing the area and efficiency of the food-catching net. Arranged in bunches of three, and often producing copious amounts of mucus, the tube feet are in constant erratic motion when feeding, grasping small particles and flicking them into the food groove. Wiped off the tiniest of the trio of tentacles and trapped in strings of mucus, the food sails off down the gutter on its long journey to the mouth, propelled by the beating of millions of tiny hairs lining the floor of the groove. The total catching area of this superb feeding apparatus is astounding. A large, multi-armed feather star may have a total food groove length of around 100 metres.

Heart urchin, *Lovenia elongata*

◁ *The heart urchin, with its oval body and long recurved spines, is normally hidden in a shallow burrow in soft sand. Even further modified away from the basic urchin plan, the mouth has migrated forward in these animals and the Aristotle's lantern has been lost. Specially modified tube feet looking like sticky daisies pluck food from the walls of the burrow while others equipped with calcareous blades are used for digging.*

▽ ◁ *The tips of five strong white teeth protrude from the mouth on the underside of the slate-pencil sea urchin. Surrounded by short blunt spines, these teeth are all that can be seen of the jaw apparatus, an extraordinary structure called the Aristotle's lantern. Found in all echinoids except the burrowing heart urchins, the lantern consists of 40 separate calcareous pieces, articulated by a complicated set of muscles and ligaments.* '

three) may be distinct, or they may simply be distributed over a flattened 'sole' on which the sea cucumber slowly crawls.

Within the echinoids the water-vascular system of the echinoderms reaches its zenith. The diversity of both form and function is extraordinary, with tube feet becoming involved not just in feeding and movement but respiration, excretion, touch and chemical sensing and the digging and maintenance of the animals' burrows.

The basic arrangement is similar to that of the sea star but the tube feet tend to be much longer. The ambulacral plates through which they protrude are arranged in ten vertical series consisting of five pairs. Each plate may bear several tube feet. They help in movement by attaching and hauling the animal forward, but much is actually done by the spines,

Slate-pencil sea urchin, *Heterocentrotus mammillatus*

Prickly red fish sea cucumber, *Thelenota ananas*

Prickly red fish sea cucumber, *Thelenota ananas*

Sticky tentacles

The water-vascular system of ancient echinoderms is thought to have had feeding as its primary role, as in the crinoid. Its role in movement evolved later as echinoderms ceased to be permanently attached to the substrate. The water-vascular system of the sea cucumber has many functions. Several tube feet at the front end are greatly enlarged and substantially modified for their role as feeding tentacles. Tipped with both sticky mucus and a maze of tiny crevices that mechanically trap particles, the tentacles are used to gather food. Aspidochirote holothurians have flattened, rounded tips that gather sediment particles, while the tentacles of dendrochirote holothurians have greatly expanded, finely branching ends used for trapping plankton and detritus suspended in the water. The fine surface detritus that forms the food of many apodous holothurians is gathered by highly active elongate

tentacles shaped like feathers – pinnate tentacles. Having collected sufficient material, the tentacles are inserted into the mouth where they are wiped clean and, in many cases, recoated with mucus.

Dendrochirote holothurians are sedentary – having found a good current in which to place their tentacles they attach themselves with their tube feet and remain. Aspidochirotes, on the other hand, use their rows of tube feet for locomotion. A large sea cucumber, such as *Thelenota ananas*, has thousands of tube feet with suckers like those of the sea stars and sea urchins. They are arranged in five rows running down the length of the body. In a few holothurians the tube feet are equally spaced around their circumference but usually they are modified. The rows (usually two) on the upper side, no longer used in movement, have become largely sensory in function, and frequently spread out to cover the upper surface more evenly. The lower rows (usually

△ *The distinctive pointed protuberances of the prickly red fish sea cucumber are extensions of the body wall. These papillae give shelter to a variety of small brittle stars, shrimps and scale worms. A scale worm lies among the papillae ,above centre, of a prickly red fish sea cucumber. The smaller protuberances, on the animal's underside, are tube feet.*

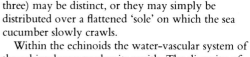

'Echinoids or sea urchins are the animals which originally gave the Echinoderm phylum its name; Echinodermata being derived from the Greek words for "spiny" and "skin".'

▷ From the safety of its hole in the coral this species of suspension-feeding brittle star has long, thin arms spread in the current. It probably traps its food solely by means of its long tube feet.

▽ This delicate but highly spiny animal is identified by the purple line down the middle of its arms. Probably another suspension feeder, it is often found on soft corals, sponges and Gorgonians. It is more openly exposed during the day than most brittle stars – possibly the needle-like spines on disc and arms, below right, deter predators.

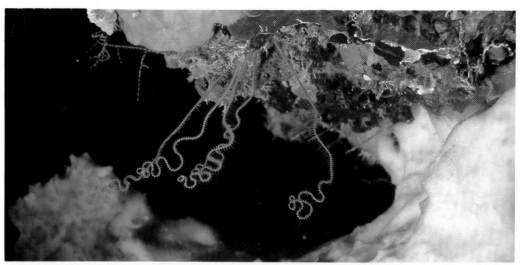

Brittle star

Brittle star, *Ophiothrix (Acanthophiothrix) purpurea*

Brittle star, *Ophiothrix (Acanthophiothrix) purpurea*

acting as levers to propel the urchin. The tube feet are frequently employed to transfer food to the mouth and are particularly important in those urchins that rely entirely on trapping drifting food for their survival.

The importance of tube feet

The tunnel-building feats of the heart urchins are due primarily to their tube feet. Some bear large sickle-shaped spicules that are used to scrape away sand. These calcareous blades work in conjunction with other tube feet that produce and apply mucus to the burrow walls to prevent collapse. Frequently, a sanitary drain is maintained behind and a respiratory funnel is kept open to the surface. Specialised feeding tube feet, with radiating terminal fingers supported by a tiny spicule and producing mucus, collect sediment particles that are then passed to the mouth and ingested.

The tube feet and tentacles of all echinoderms play a major role in respiration. The irregular urchins have tube feet modified especially; the petal-shaped marking on the upper side of a sand dollar is where these soft, greatly expanded flap-like structures emerge. Respiration is assisted by fields of beating cilia, on both the inside and outside of the tube foot. They beat in opposite directions to produce a 'counter current' – a highly efficient respiratory mechanism.

The regular urchins augment respiration via their tube feet by means of small gills, fleshy outgrowths of the body wall near the mouth.

The upper surface of a sea star is pitted with tiny holes through which emerge thin-walled finger-like extensions of the central body cavity; the sea star uses these in addition to its tube feet for respiration.

Feather stars, having such a high surface area, rely on their feeding tentacles and body surface for

respiration. Brittle stars also benefit from their tube feet. However, possibly because of their active mode of life, they require more oxygen and have special structures. On either side of the base of each arm are slits which open into ten cavities around the margin of the central disc. These respiratory sacs are irrigated with sea water by the rhythmic pumping action of muscles which expand and contract the entire soft body of the animal.

Some holothurians, such as the snake-like synaptids, handle their respiratory needs through the body wall itself. They are often extremely long which maximises their surface area to volume ratio, and the body wall is very thin, facilitating diffusion. Most sea cucumbers, however, have a pair of special internal structures called respiratory trees that open off the hind end of the gut and lie in the body cavity. They respire by a technique called 'anal breathing'. When not actually passing faeces,

Brittle star, *Ophiarachnella gorgonia*

◁ *These large brittle stars have stout arms, well fused with the edge of the disc, and small arm spines pressed to the sides of the arms. They are strong and active crawlers, usually found under coral rubble. While a wide variety of food is often taken, they are mostly carnivorous. Prey capture is usually by means of a loop of arm thrown around the victim. Some may move on top of the prey, engulfing it, or the powerful jaws and tube feet around the mouth may tear the victim to pieces.*

Sea cucumber, *Bohadschia graeffei*

△ *A highly active surface feeder, the oral hood of this sea cucumber is held some way off the substrate, allowing a close-up view of the food-collecting process. The huge black feeding tentacles with their white expanded tips are constantly in motion – either being extended slowly forward and pressed deliberately onto the substrate in order to pick up the thin food film, or retracted back to the central mouth into which they are carefully inserted and wiped clean by the buccal sphincter. The particles appear to be picked up by a combination of mechanical ensnarement in crevices on the tentacle tip as well as areas coated with sticky mucus.*

powerful muscles repeatedly distend the cloaca, filling it with fresh sea water and then pumping it into the finely branching respiratory trees where the gases are exchanged.

Feeding methods

Echinoderms have many feeding methods – they may be carnivorous, algal, suspension or detritus feeders or scavengers.

All feather stars, most dendrochirote holothurians, some brittle stars, the basket stars and a handful of sea urchins, are suspension feeders. Seeking an appropriate water current, they spread their highly varied food-capturing equipment into the flow and passively await the arrival of their sustenance. Their method of capture and retention may be quite active. The lashing, mucus-laden tentacles of a feather star; the lightning-fast arm coil of a brittle star flung around its passing prey;

the almost instantaneous folding of a basket star arm tip, enveloping a luckless worm and impaling it on numerous cruel hooks; or the soundless clash of spines around a piece of drifting algae – these are all finely co-ordinated operations of quite complicated structures.

The rich layer of organic material that seems to coat almost every underwater surface is much in demand. It is a breeding ground for bacteria that both help to break it down and themselves provide nutrients. Many sea stars use this food resource by turning their stomachs inside out through their mouths and draping them over the bottom on which they lie.

This rich organic layer may become concentrated in small pockets due to tidal currents or simply because of the topography of the reef surface. It is then a much-favoured food resource for the probing feeding tentacles of apodous holothurians, which can rake it up. It is also the primary food source of

Crown-of-thorns starfish, *Acanthaster planci*

△ Like most sea stars, crown-of-thorns have separate sexes. They breed once each year in midsummer, when eggs and sperm are released into the water. Group spawning appears to increase the normally rather low chance of fertilisation. A large female crown-of-thorns may produce up to 60 million eggs each year, so when crown-of-thorns do occur in high numbers their reproductive potential is enormous.

'When the numbers of crown-of-thorns starfish build to thousands on a reef, the immediate result can be catastrophic, with up to 90 per cent of the coral being killed in some areas.'

Crown-of-thorns starfish, *Acanthaster planci*

◁ The spiny embrace of a crown-of-thorns starfish means the end for at least part of this coral colony. Adult starfish emerge at night to feed, spreading their stomachs over a coral colony and usually digesting a patch about half their own size; an individual eats over five square metres of coral each year. They do not necessarily feed on the most abundant or fast-growing corals, although Acropora is often preferred, and coral species with large stinging cells are usually avoided. Crown-of-thorns are attracted by the presence of juices from other sea stars feeding nearby and gather in large groups.

most of the remaining non-carnivorous brittle stars including *Macrophiothrix* species whose long arms languidly brush the layer of the sediment while their tube feet gather the detrital layer.

This food source also occurs in the sediment itself, although in a more finely distributed form. Each grain of sand is coated with a thin layer of potential food and the water trapped between the grains is often rich in nutrients and bacteria as well as tiny specialised sand-dwelling organisms.

The irregular urchins are also deposit-feeders. Sand dollars concentrate on the surface layer of sediment and lie just on or under the surface. In the soft, muddy sand areas between the reefs and especially inshore where fast-flowing rivers bring extra supplies of nutrients, sand dollars abound. The heart urchin, usually deeper in the sediment, inches slowly forward, almost as if eating its way through the sediment. It is not very selective about the size of grains it chooses – indeed, few deposit-feeding echinoderms appear to select particular grain sizes as they feed. Perhaps time is short and the necessary quantities so large that they cannot afford to reject any particles. Most deposit feeders, however, are fairly selective about the type of sediment in which they live, and so different species tend to become separated through their choice of habitat.

Algal grazers
Coral reefs are richly supplied with encrusting animals and plants growing on the hard substratum. Most of the surface of a reef is not live coral but dead – often encrusted with coralline algae. This sort of surface is ideal for colonial animals such as sponges, bryozoans and sea squirts to attach themselves to, as well as for the growth of a short algal turf. The addition of a whole range of tiny animals such as worms and crustaceans makes this a marvellous layer on which to graze. The extraordinary jaws of sea urchins such as *Heterocentrotus mammillatus* are called an Aristotle's lantern and are particularly well adapted to grazing.

It is difficult to define categories within this broad group of echinoderm browsers – the primitive cidaroid urchins tend to be more carnivorous, seeking out encrusting animals to tear apart with their powerful teeth, while the majority of echinoids are vegetarian. When feeding on the reef's soft calcareous surface, both groups may grind off large amounts of calcium carbonate – an example of bioerosion. The Great Barrier Reef appears to support a much reduced echinoid fauna, both in terms of abundance and diversity. While the reasons for this are unknown, it is possible that the algal grazing role has been more exclusively filled by the herbivorous fishes that abound on the reef.

Extra-oral feeders
Many species of sea star feed on encrusting organisms, some using their elaborately toothed jaws for rasping while others use extra-oral techniques. The crown-of-thorns starfish is a specialised extra-oral feeder on the tissue of hard corals. On most reefs it is not noticeably common, hiding by day and emerging at night to find a suitable coral colony over which to spread its stomach. Some hours later, when digestive enzymes have dissolved the coral tissues, the stomach is withdrawn, leaving behind the bleached, white coral skeleton. This starfish kills an area about half its own diameter. While it can grow to over 600 millimetres in diameter, the average size is about 300 millimetres, which means a single individual kills over five square metres of coral each year.

The crown-of-thorns has definite preferences about the species of coral it likes to eat, although factors such as colony shape, the defensive capabilities of the coral (stinging cells and extruded digestive filaments) and even nips from the claws of resident crabs and shrimps may deter it. Huge

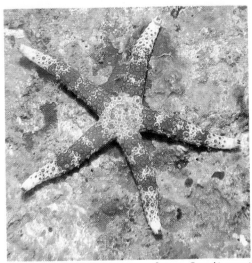

Sea star, *Gomophia watsoni*

outbreaks in its populations have been recorded over the past 20 years, both on the Great Barrier Reef and other parts of the Indian and Pacific oceans, and in some areas they have killed over 90 per cent of the living coral cover.

Brittle stars are more active echinoderm predators, and some will grapple fiercely with their prey. Usually, a coiled arm is flung around the victim, and a loop containing the prey then passes up the arm in a wave until it is pressed to the mouth below the upraised disc. Some brittle stars are able to simply engulf their prey.

Carnivorous sea stars feed either by engulfing their prey, like brittle stars, or by the extra-oral method of stomach eversion. The first is found particularly in the primitive sea stars *Luidia* and *Astropecten*, which have arms edged with spines and tube feet without suckers. They are adapted for digging and have large, double-headed muscular

ampullae that give a powerful thrust to their tube feet. *Astropecten* digs for its prey, mainly animals such as clams, snails and small crustaceans, which it takes in whole. A tell-tale bulge in the disc usually indicates a recent meal. *Luidia* feeds on a range of prey, which also includes quite large clams and snails. It is as a voracious predator of other echinoderms, however, that it is justly famous. This genus has been recorded feeding on many species of echinoderms, from all classes except feather stars.

Defence systems
With bodies largely composed of chunks of indigestible crystalline, calcium carbonate and often covered in spines or tubercles, most echinoderms would not appear to make a delectable meal. Many animals, however, are prepared to try – and as a result echinoderms have evolved a wide range of behavioural, chemical and mechanical defences.

Pincushion sea star, *Culcita novaeguineae*

△ *The pincushion sea star is also a predator of coral. It feeds on the detritus and micro-organism film on the seabed, often being found with its stomach everted over rather indeterminate matter. However, like the crown-of-thorns it can turn its stomach out through its mouth to externally digest the living tissue of a coral colony. It has not been observed in very large groups, but several are capable of killing a reasonable amount of coral.*

△ ◁ *The exact diet of this sea star is unknown but its method of feeding is common to most of the Ophidiasterids. It turns its stomach out through its mouth and externally digests the film of detritus and microscopic organisms that lies on the surface of dead coral and coralline algae. Usually emerging to feed only at night, this sea star is protected by its habits, camouflaged colour pattern and pointed tubercles.*

Some species, particularly of brittle stars, remain hidden deep among the branches of coral colonies or under rubble. Others, such as most irregular urchins, burrow deep into the sand. Many crinoids emerge only at night, when fewer potential predators are around. These kinds of behaviour are often augmented by a camouflage of dull colour.

Many echinoderms rely on chemicals within their tissues to make themselves either highly distasteful or actually poisonous, allowing them to lie out in the open during the day, safe from the myriad of predators that abound on every coral reef. Most tropical species of sea cucumbers secrete toxins, called 'holothurins'. These may be in the body wall, in the guts or in special defensive devices called Cuvierian organs.

When sufficiently disturbed, the animal may point its rear end at an intruder and discharge the long white Cuvierian tubules from the anus. Pumped up and stretching as they are extruded, the cells on the outer surface of the tubules split, releasing their strongly adhesive (and frequently poisonous) contents. These will readily immobilise a crab or small fish and can temporarily bind together the fingers of an inquisitive diver! The toxic properties of sea cucumbers have long been known to various Pacific islanders, who use them for catching fishes by poisoning reef flat pools.

Protective ornamentation

The skeletal plates of many echinoderms bear some kind of protective surface ornamentation. This ranges from granules through tubercles to the spines that give the phylum its name. These are found in three classes: asteroids, ophiuroids and echinoids. Spines have a wide variety of functions, being used in walking, digging, food collection and protection against waves, but one of their primary roles is in defence against predators.

Many brittle stars bear sharp needle-like spines, particularly for protecting their central disc. However, the greatest array of spiny protection is undoubtedly shown by sea urchins. Many, particularly within the family Diadematidae, have long, thin serrated spines that contain an irritant toxin. The small but extremely sharp secondary spines of *Echinothrix calamaris* are made more unpleasant by being backwardly barbed, making

▷ *Certain sea cucumbers, including the 'leopard' or 'spotted' fish, will eject a mass of sticky white threads from their anus when touched too roughly. The hind end of the body is directed at the stimulus, and as the threads are ejected they expand and swell up. Small organisms such as crabs or fishes become totally immobilised by the threads. The wall of the cloaca is ruptured during the discharge and the ejection is irreversible. The damaged organs are subsequently regenerated.*

Leopard fish sea cucumber, *Bohadschia argus*

Sea urchin, *Echinothrix diadema*

Sea urchin, *Diadema savignyi*

Sea urchin, *Echinothrix calamaris*

withdrawal almost impossible. Those of *Diadema* may be nearly 600 millimetres long and can be rapidly swung across and focused in a group on an intruder who has triggered the light-sensitive organs of the animal.

Some sea urchins have spines tipped with a poison sac. The flexible-bodied urchins of the family Echinothuridae have secondary spines of this sort, and penetration by the sharp spine creates pressure on the bulbous poison sac which causes immediate and painful irrigation of the wound by the toxin.

Many sea stars have a protective fringe of spines along the arms, while others, like the horned sea star, *Protoreaster nodosus*, are protected by massive pointed tubercles. The entire surface of the crown-of-thorns is covered by stout, reddish orange spines with sharp tips. The skin overlying the spine contains toxic material that can produce severe reactions in humans. It has been suggested that the crown-of-thorns is a fairly recently evolved species that came from stock more like its sand-dwelling relative, *Acanthaster brevispinus*.

Adopting a purely coral diet and inhabiting reefs with their many predatory fishes, the crown-of-thorns needed more protection and so evolved a more spiny and poisonous covering – but not a deterrent to all. Some species of triggerfish, family Balistidae, delicately take hold of an arm tip, flip the crown-of-thorns onto its back and chew in from the underside, where the spines are shorter and blunter. Several other species of fishes feed on adult crown-of-thorns, as do various shrimps and the giant triton, *Charonia tritonis*.

Sensitive jaws

Asteroids and echinoids possess calcareous appendages – tiny pincer-like organs with moveable grasping jaws – called pedicellariae. There are a

▷ *While many species of sea star aggregate to spawn, one species has gone a step further in increasing its chance of fertilisation. Archaster typicus is often common in sandy areas of the reef but at certain times of the year it is found in pairs with the male draped limply across the body of a female, arms entwined. They are indulging in a unique phenomenon referred to as 'pseudo-copulation' and lie clasped together until spawning has been effected.*

▽ *The underside of a crown-of-thorns starfish contains shorter and blunter spines – a fact known to some fishes that flip them over on their backs before starting to chew. The underside also reveals rows of thin-walled, suckered tube feet lining the grooves underneath each arm. These hydraulic structures, found in all echinoderms, are operated by complicated sets of tubes, valves, muscular sacs and storage reservoirs – the water-vascular system.*

Crown-of-thorns starfish, *Acanthaster planci*

Crown-of-thorns starfish, *Acanthaster planci*

Sea urchin, *Tripneustes gratilla*

△ ▷ *The muscular foot of the giant triton, Charonia tritonis, drags its heavy shell behind it as it approaches its prey – the crown-of-thorns starfish. Small prey may be swallowed whole, but large starfish are held, slit open with a radula – a cutting organ rather like a band-saw – and the proboscis inserted to suck on the soft tissues. Few sea stars escape once a triton has really latched on. It was originally suggested that the extremely heavy collecting of tritons for the tourist trade since World War II was the major cause of the high numbers of crown-of-thorns seen on many reefs in the past 20 years, but this now seems too simple an explanation. As well as being naturally rare, experiments have shown that tritons prefer other asteroids such as Linckia laevigata, Culcita novaeguineae and Nardoa species and eat few crown-of-thorns.*

number of different types and while their roles are incompletely understood, defence is clearly a function of some. They are often very sensitive and may respond to touch, chemicals and light. The closing of the jaws may be very rapid, particularly those on sea urchins. Sea star pedicellariae are simple, usually with only two opposing jaws. Those of urchins are stalked, have three jaws and may be used in grooming, feeding or defence. The latter may be highly poisonous.

Growing back

Echinoderms have highly developed powers of regeneration, which is of considerable importance both in avoiding and recovering from attempts at predation. Their general lack of any 'head' to bite off and their radial symmetry, leading to replication of their organ systems, enhances their chances of surviving an attack. A unique skeleton also allows

△ *A spawning sea urchin releases clouds of gametes from the five genital pores surrounding the anus in the middle of the upper side. The globular body of an urchin is largely empty apart from fluid. As the breeding season approaches, however, the space fills up with swollen gonads. There are separate sexes – as with all echinoids – and if the external fertilisation is successful, tiny gelatinous larvae will live and grow in the plankton for several weeks before being ready to settle on new reefs.*

excellent regrowth. A brittle star will readily lose an imprisoned arm, allowing it to escape, and crinoids have special articulations between particular arm segments which facilitate a clean break. Many feather stars can survive and regrow even after their arms have been grazed down to a few stumps devoid of pinnules. A large sea star such as the crown-of-thorns, if cut in half, has such an open body cavity that it rarely survives. By comparison, some sea cucumbers will regenerate into two complete animals after being cut in half.

Sexual and asexual reproduction

The amazing regenerative powers of echinoderms have been further exploited as a reproductive strategy. Many species reproduce asexually, splitting in half to create two 'new' individuals.

The sea star *Linckia multifora* divides by an extraordinary process – one arm just walks away from the others, which hold their ground, and the body wall eventually tears. The ends are resealed and regeneration begins. One frequently sees 'comet forms' with a large piece of arm regenerating four or five tiny ones and a central disc, complete with mouth. Sea cucumbers, too, may use this method. Often most of a population of the common black reef flat sea cucumber, *Holothuria atra*, may be in the process of regrowing 'head' or 'tail' ends.

Crinoids and echinoids are not known to reproduce asexually, preferring to rely entirely on sexual reproduction which is also the most usual method for the other three classes. Most species of echinoderms have separate sexes, except for the odd mistake. This appears to be the rule for the feather stars and sea urchins; however some asteroids, ophiuroids and holothurians are hermaphrodites, and in most cases protandric hermaphrodites, starting out life as males, becoming females later.

The breeding season

Sea stars, sea urchins and sea cucumbers all have substantial fluid-filled body cavities, which for most of the year seem to contain little except gut and digestive glands. As the breeding season approaches, however, they provide a space within which the gonads can safely grow. Often the digestive glands that have been built up shrink, as much of their stored nutrient is used up in the development of gonads. While asteroids and echinoids usually have five paired gonads, each releasing gametes through separate gonopores, sea cucumbers are unique in normally having a single gonad, releasing through a single gonopore in the top of the 'head'.

Brittle stars and feather stars, with their arms consisting mainly of solid calcium carbonate and possessing no substantial body cavity within which to expand their gonads, have a problem. The brittle stars have solved this by inflating their soft discs. Crinoids have their gonads either in a thin strand running along the arms or in special pinnules near the arm base, which lack a food groove and are remarkably expandable. The soft wall of these genital pinnules eventually ruptures to release the eggs or sperm.

Most echinoderms breed annually, although many have an extended breeding season with additional peaks. They spawn freely into the water, making fertilisation an external and rather chancy business. The fertilised eggs swiftly turn into tiny gelatinous larvae, which are quite distinct for each class. Some species, however, undergo direct development to a tiny version of the adult.

In many, supporting struts of calcite are laid down in the larval arms. They are characteristically ciliated, bearing bands of tiny hairs that are used for locomotion and catching food – usually phytoplankton. Most reef echinoderms produce many tiny larvae which live for several weeks in the plankton where they have to feed. Some produce just a few large larvae endowed with a good supply of stored food which may quickly develop. A few actually brood their young. This latter strategy is more common in cold-water echinoderms.

Most larvae undergo a radical metamorphosis or change in order to take on the adult form, their small multi-armed gelatinous design being suited primarily to their drifting life in the plankton. The change is very marked at metamorphosis:

Sea star, *Linckia multifora*

echinoderms are the only group in which a bilaterally symmetrical larva changes into a radially symmetrical adult.

Many reef echinoderms produce extraordinary quantities of eggs or sperm. A female crown-of-thorns may produce 60 million eggs in a year. This is the normal situation in animals where almost all the young may be lost and where many eggs may never get fertilised.

Sexual punctuality

Various techniques have evolved to increase the chances of fertilisation. Animals often gather before spawning, one sex may induce the spawning of the other and the whole procedure may be highly synchronised. In a species of Japanese feather star, *Comanthus japonicus*, the entire population spawns on the same day once a year – in the first half of October, when the moon is in its first or last quarter. Almost all the animals manage it between three and five in the afternoon! This degree of sexual punctuality ensures high rates of fertilisation.

Their behaviour is often modified during spawning, presumably to ensure a good release and distribution of gametes. Mud-dwelling brittle stars may emerge from the sediment and arch their bodies high above the substrate. An arched body, with only arm tips touching the ground, is also seen in sea stars – that often climb to the top of a suitable coral bommie before disporting themselves.

Perhaps the most seemingly excited by it all are the sea cucumbers, rising high above the substrate, balanced on their extreme tail ends as they spurt a stream of gametes from the top of their heads. Then bowing low they draw themselves up again to repeat the process.

The eggs and sperm drift off along the reef face and bathe others of the species.

Sea star, *Linckia multifora*

Δ *Many species of sea star, as well as brittle stars and sea cucumbers, can reproduce asexually by splitting and subsequently regenerating the lost parts. Some sea stars are particularly good at regenerating. While most sea stars require part of the disc and sometimes the madreporite for successful regrowth, some species can grow an entire animal from just part of an arm. Comet-shaped individuals in the process of regeneration, above left, are not uncommon around a reef. Regrowth can be rapid, taking weeks rather than months.*

Red sea star, *Fromia elegans*

Feather star, *Capillaster multiradiatus*; feather star, *Comanthus*

Perhaps one of the most extraordinary behavioural mechanisms is that of the sea star *Archaster typicus*, in which the male lies astride the female, their arms alternating. This posture is kept for several days and is followed by synchronous spawning and a high level of fertilisation.

Echinoderms produce many young. Only a few survive their long larval life, however it does serve to widely disperse the species. This may result in periodic lack of recruitment to an area, sometimes followed by a good year.

Living on a star
Many animals live in or on echinoderms, but symbiotic relationships are most common in the feather stars. A single animal may support two or three species of shrimp, a crab, a pair of squat lobsters, small fishes, several parasitic snails and scores of bristle worms. The complex form of the feather star gives shelter, but more importantly, the collected food of the host animal is carried along in open grooves to the mouth, providing a conveyor belt of sustenance to many of its associated animals. Their relationships may vary from being mutually beneficial, one-sided but harmless, or fully parasitic.

Confusing characters
The biology of echinoderms is little known and often poorly understood. A confusing and unlikely mixture of primitive and advanced characters, the phylum Echinodermata remains 'a noble group, especially designed to puzzle the zoologist'. Many of these same features, however, have enabled the echinoderms to colonise all areas of the sea bottom, utilising every habitat and living from the shoreline to the ocean deeps. Nowhere do they show such amazing diversity as in coral reef areas such as the Great Barrier Reef.□

△ *Deep in a crevice within the frame of the reef, white bryozoans grow out along the skeleton of a long-dead wire coral. Sheltered against the encrusted wall of a cave, the crimson arms of a shy* Comanthus *filter the gently moving water. Further out, waving in the stronger flow, clings a* Capillaster multiradiatus. *Its robust, pinkish arms and dark pinnules frosted with silver are held ready to gather food from the passing current.*

◁ Fromia *is an ophidiasterid genus in which the outline is even more defined by a series of slightly flattened plates delineating the edge of the arm. Several small species occur on the reef, rarely if ever growing greater than 100 millimetres across. They normally display the typical five-armed symmetry. However, this six-armed specimen is the result of an accident – incorrect regeneration following damage, or a mistake much earlier in its development.*

Ascidians: filtering water bags

Many colours, many shapes

Ascidians abound in all the oceans of the world, on the edge of the sea between tides, and on the sea floor from the low tide mark to the great depths of oceanic trenches. On coral reefs, vast populations of these animals, of many colours and various sizes and shapes, cover the undersurfaces of rocks on the reef flat and line the roofs and walls of caves on the reef slope. They are tucked into holes and crevices in the reefs, spaces around dead coral skeletons and the bases of living coral colonies. Ascidians also live among the rubble deposited in depressions around the reef rim and help to consolidate it.

The best-known ascidians are the sea squirts, found in large groups on rocky coasts. They seem to be merely a leathery bag of water (hence their name from the Greek *askos*, meaning a leather wine flask). There are other more delicate and intricate ascidians, however, that do not look at all like leather wine flasks, and though they may squirt water, they are too small for it to be noticed.

Ascidians are really invertebrates with a few features of the backboned animals, although they have many unique characteristics. In the coral reef community they fulfil two important roles. Firstly, they filter the water around the reef and help to keep it clear; and secondly, as they strain the minute dispersed plants and other organisms from the water for their own nutrition they are concentrating it into a form that makes it available to other animals. A small ascidian only 30 millimetres long can filter water at the rate of approximately one litre an hour.

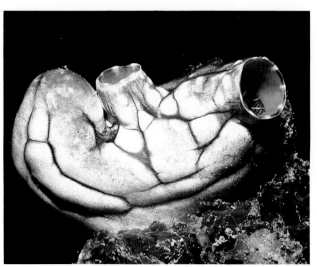

Common solitary ascidian, *Polycarpa aurata*

△ *A tough leathery test protects this ascidian. Its mouth, wide open in the feeding position, is curved over to the side so that sediments do not fall into it. Tentacles and a small part of the perforated pharynx are just visible inside the opening. The smaller excurrent opening is directed up and away from the animal and away from the mouth so that expended water, waste and reproductive products are not mixed with the incoming stream of water.*

△ ▷ *The yellow pigment of this ascidian is in blood vessels that branch in the translucent, gelatinous test and terminate in small rounded chromatophores (pigment reservoirs) just beneath the surface. Larger patches of yellow around each open aperture are light sensitive.*

Solitary ascidian, *Phallusia julinea*

Form and function

Ascidians do not have many external features to indicate that they are animals. They sometimes spontaneously close one or the other or both of their two funnel-like external openings, and they will always do so if disturbed. However, usually they are absolutely still, with both apertures wide open and the stream of water that they filter passing continuously through their bodies. They are fixed firmly and usually permanently to the substrate of rock, shell or sand or other ascidians by an adhesive, outer protective coat – the test. This coat is made of a substance known as tunicin, which has a molecular structure similar to the cellulose of plant cell walls. The ascidian lies inside the test, connected to it around the openings and also where it is penetrated by blood vessels from the body wall. Many ascidians, notably the colonial family Didemnidae, secrete minute, star-shaped calcareous spicules that

strengthen the test. These are the closest thing to a skeleton known in this group of animals.

An ascidian has two openings to the exterior: one incurrent and the other excurrent. The incurrent aperture, or mouth, opens into a large sieve-like pharynx perforated by many openings (stigmata) that are lined with minute hairs (cilia). The cilia beat regularly and set up the water current that is drawn into the ascidian's mouth, through the stigmata to the atrial cavity (a large pocket in the body wall that surrounds the pharynx) and back out by way of the excurrent opening. As the water passes through the stigmata, fine particles are strained into a sheet of mucus that passes up each side of the pharynx.

The muscles in the body wall can be used to close the external apertures, and they can also contract the body wall to force water out of the pharynx and atrial cavity before the apertures are closed.

Fixed, stationary animals

Only a limited range of movements can be performed by an ascidian. It cannot move away from predators or unpleasant substances in the water; nor can it move to richer waters or find itself a mate.

Everything that an adult ascidian does depends on

Blue ascidian, *Rhopalaea crassa*

Blue-pod ascidian, *Pycnoclavella diminuta*

◁ *Only the thorax is contained in the top, rounded part of each zooid in this colonial ascidian. The gut and gonads are in the relatively thick stalk. New zooids are added to the colony by buds that develop in the protective coating that connects the zooids to one another at the base of the stalks.*

▽ *This solitary species stands on its head. Water movements make it sway slightly on its flexible stalk, and the opening of its downwardly directed mouth faces the flow of water. The excurrent opening points in the opposite direction.*

Colonial ascidian, *Didemnum molle*

Ascidian, *Polycarpa clavata*

△ *White spicules and brown pigment protect the plant cells in the centre of these colonial ascidians from direct light. Some of the colonies are dividing and moving away.*

◁ *The huge pharynx of this young specimen is visible through the diaphanous protective coating. The abdomen, containing the gut and gonads, is embedded in the substrate behind the thorax.*

its ability to interact with the environment through its two apertures. It is like a man in a house without doors who conducts all his business through either the front or back window with whoever chances to walk past. The positioning of the apertures is of critical importance, and each ascidian must achieve the utmost advantage from water currents that pass by. The apertures are usually turned in different directions in order that the incurrent and excurrent streams do not mix and contaminate one another. The mouth is often turned downwards to avoid sediment falling into it, whereas the excurrent opening is usually turned up and to one side, away from the prevailing on-coming currents, so that its waste materials and reproductive products are carried away from the animal. The excurrent opening is smaller than the mouth, so that water leaving the animal is projected away from it under a lot of pressure.

Growth and habit

Solitary ascidians grow quite large, some up to 20 centimetres. Their tests are often tough and camouflaged with weeds, or other fixed animals, and sometimes have embedded or adherent sand grains and shell particles that strengthen as well as camouflage the ascidian. Many species are often too tough for all but the strongest predators, and

ascidians with a covering of sand and weed growing on them are almost invisible when their apertures are tightly closed.

Many ascidians subdivide or clone within the test to replicate themselves and form large colonies instead of the individuals themselves growing large. Some colonies reach a diameter of about 10 centimetres and contain hundreds of small individuals (zooids), often less than one millimetre and seldom more than 10 or 20 millimetres long. Calcareous spicules strengthen the protective coating of most species of the family Didemnidae and a few genera from other families. There are other species in which the test is strengthened with sand and shell particles.

Unlike solitary species, foreign organisms do not usually grow on colonial ascidians. There are two probable reasons for this. Firstly, the surface of a colonial ascidian is often crowded with the openings of all its zooids, and small larvae or algal spores that try to settle on a colonial ascidian are probably eaten. Secondly, there are large cells in the surface test of many colonies that generate acid when their cell walls are broken. The acid is immediately neutralised by sea water and any calcium carbonate particles, but it may persist for a sufficient time to stop small organisms from fixing themselves to the surface.

Colonial organisation

There are different levels of organisation in ascidian colonies. In some, the individuals are merely embedded in, or connected to one another by, the protective outer coating and each individual has its two openings to the exterior. In others, the individuals are organised into systems in which the zooids have independent mouth openings to the external environment, but their excurrent apertures open into a space or a system of branching canals, the common cloaca, deep in the test. The excurrent water from each single zooid in the system combines in the cloacal cavity (which may be an open space or a system of canals), and passes from the colony to the exterior by a single cloacal aperture. Individuals in colonial systems, having lost their own excurrent openings to the exterior, are well insulated from the surrounding water in their own micro-environment within the common test.

Colonies with more than a single system, or with branching cloacal canals, usually have an irregular shape and can adapt themselves to a wide variety of conditions and substrates. They are often flat and sheet-like, forming a thin layer over the substrate that is not dislodged by strong wave movement. Colonies with single systems tend to have a finite size and a definite, often upright, shape that results from the necessity for zooids to cluster around a single cloacal cavity. Such colonies are circular, dome-shaped, cylindrical, flask-shaped and spherical. These colonies are not so well adapted to turbulent conditions unless they are safely tucked into crevices

▷ *The prostrate zooids of this colonial ascidian are crowded together to form a mat-like colony that spreads over the substrate.*

▷▷ *The small, transparent, stalked zooids of this colonial ascidian have the thorax tipped on its side so that the mouth is directed downwards and the excurrent aperture is at the top. The bright arc curving around the lower part of the thorax is the endostyle, which secretes the mucus sheet that enmeshes food particles as it moves up over the pharynx.*

▽ *The row of blue pigment patches between the openings of each zooid are conspicuous on the otherwise almost transparent coating of this colonial ascidian. The transverse vessels between the rows of stigmata perforating the pharynx are clearly visible.*

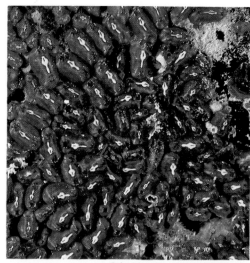

Colonial ascidian, *Eusynstyela latericius*

Colonial ascidian, *Pycnoclavella detorta*

Colonial ascidian, *Podoclavella moluccensis*

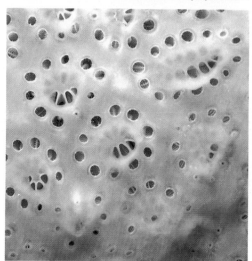

Colonial ascidian, *Eudistoma amplum*

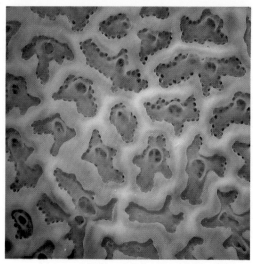

Cushion-shaped ascidian, *Aplidium cratiferum*

in the reef. Growth of such colonies results in a simple increase in size or subdivision of the colony.

Subdivision is associated in some species with the unusual ability to move, albeit slowly, at a rate of about 15 millimetres per day. Colonies can move away from one another and space themselves, and they can move towards or away from light.

Colonial ascidians appear to enjoy certain advantages in coral reef waters, where they are more numerous than solitary species. Colonies with a rapid rate of replication can grow out over the substrate and occupy space more rapidly than solitary species or those with a less prolific method of cloning.

The variation in shape that is possible for some colonies is probably also an advantage in reef waters. The fast growth rate of colonies may also be their best means of defence for, while molluscs, echinoderms and fishes prey on ascidians, the

colonies regenerate fast and recover quickly.

Further, all the individuals in the colony contribute to its maintenance, growth and sexual maturity; and embryos, protected within the colony, are released as well-developed, free-swimming larvae, vulnerable to loss through predation and dispersal for only a short time.

Reproduction and settlement

All ascidians are hermaphrodite. Occasionally they are self-fertile – each individual being both male and female parent. This is usually avoided by having one or other set of gonads mature at one time.

The first necessity for sexual reproduction in ascidians is sufficiently crowded populations to ensure an adequate concentration of gametes in the water. In externally fertilised species both male and female gametes are needed. Internally fertilised species (usually colonial) release only male gametes,

△ *These colonial ascidians have numerous systems, each with a single large common opening in the centre. The mouth openings of the zooids are inconspicuous in the circular depressed areas on the surface, each surrounded by high ridges that separate each system.*

△ ◁ *The openings of zooids of this colonial ascidian show how systems gradually evolve. The outer ring of incurrent openings and inner circle of excurrent openings result from the arrangement of zooids in circles.*

but in sufficient numbers for at least some to find their way through the pharynx of another individual of the same species. Following fertilisation the developing embryo either floats about in the sea or, if internally fertilised, is incubated in the ascidian. It develops into a larva.

After a brief period when a larva is free

△ *These colonies each consist of a single system. The incurrent openings of the zooids are around the outside of the colony. The excurrent apertures are inside the colony opening into the large central common cavity.*

▷ *The small yellow bubble-like zooids of this colonial ascidian are connected to one another and to the substrate by fine blood vessels covered with protective coating.*

Yellow bubble ascidian, *Perophora modificata*

coral reefs, sometimes whole reefs being almost surrounded by great sheets of algae-bearing didemnids. Unlike most ascidians they are also common on open reef flats, carpeting the sand with a mosaic of small colonies.

Some of the ascidian–*Prochloron* associations are so close that one cannot live without the other. The *Prochloron* transfers some of the products of its photosynthesis to the ascidian, which probably gains some of its nourishment that way (as do some corals from their contained zooxanthellae).

Some ascidians appear to have lived with *Prochloron* for many generations; the ascidian larvae have had time to evolve special hairs on the test and, sometimes, organs that sweep up plant cells as the larvae leave the parent colony. The plant cells stay attached to the larvae and are incorporated into the new generation colonies that develop from each larva. Adults also have evolved devices to suit their plant cell symbionts. For instance, in some species, the colonies that grow on the open reef flat exposed to bright light have calcareous spicules crowded in the surface test to protect the plant cells in the colony from the direct sunlight. However, if the colonies are growing in shade the spicules become less crowded in the surface test and no longer shade the plant cells.

Many of the ascidian-*Prochloron* relationships are not quite so well developed. Some ascidians, including members of families other than the Didemnidae, and even some in different sub-orders from the Didemnidae (but all colonial) have *Prochloron* spread so lightly on parts of the surface of some of their colonies, that they can be easily brushed off. It may be that these are species in which the relationship is just starting to evolve. If so, where do the *Prochloron* cells come from? No one knows. They do not appear to have been found anywhere else. □

swimming and at the mercy of prevailing water currents that distance it from its parents, it usually swims down, away from the light and into shadow. There it settles, attaching itself to the substrate, losing its tail and metamorphosing into a juvenile ascidian. Ascidian adults are completely dependent on their free-swimming larva to find them suitable places to live, and larval behaviour is always adapted to the needs of the adult. An example of this is the larvae from *Didemnum molle* near Lizard Island. These are released when the sun is at its highest. After less than ten minutes, the larvae seek a shaded place to settle. The time of larval release is undoubtedly a device to ensure that the juvenile colony is shaded from strong sunlight on succeeding days. The small colonies that do happen to be in exposed sites perish.

Communication and cohabitation

Little is known about the behaviour of most ascidian larvae. How is it that populations do not become isolated from one another and evolve independently into different species? The answer could be that some larvae do not settle as soon as others, but instead get swept out to sea where the normal stimulus for metamorphosis just does not occur. Soon, if ascidian larvae are washed near a neighbouring island or reef, they will be recruited into the populations of their own species that live there. In this way, a chain of recruitment from reef to reef, island to island, along the shores of continents and across the vast Indo-West Pacific coralline region, probably maintains the exchange of genetic material between the populations. Perhaps ascidian larvae have two strategies: one to maintain their population at home, the other to communicate genetic information to adjacent populations and maintain the species over wide geographic areas.

Many animals and plants live with ascidians. Plants, hydroids, and even barnacles live on the outer protective coating, and molluscs and filamentous algae bore into it and live there. Amphipods, copepods and small shrimps live in the pharynx and the atrial cavity.

Species of the single-celled, blue-green alga genus *Prochloron* are known to live in association with about 40 ascidian species that occur along the length and breadth of the Great Barrier Reef. These ascidian species are especially common on Pacific

Yellow-faced angelfish, *Pomacanthus xanthometopon*

Fishes: brilliant, abundant and diverse

A confusion of species

There are more species of fishes on a coral reef than in any other place in the sea, and there is no land habitat, even a rainforest, that has a greater variety of vertebrates (amphibians, reptiles, birds, fishes and mammals). As the reef fishes glide over and about their coral caves and turreted coral castles they are closer to the birds of the air than any other animal, but they far surpass even the most exotic tropical birds in number, variety of colour, shape, and behaviour patterns. A small coral reef of less than a hectare may contain about 200 species. The whole Great Barrier Reef may have a remarkable 2000.

Every conceivable form of body shape and way of life have been adopted by this adaptable group of animals. The scientist has no satisfactory explanation for the questions of why so many species evolved and how they co-exist. The first question will always be speculative. The second can be observed, studied and tested, and yet remains a puzzle.

Many fishes have evolved with the corals, other invertebrates and their fellow fish species on the reefs to form an extremely integrated system. Close links between species show that evolution of one species is paralleled by the evolution of the other, an example of which is a relationship between a burrow-making shrimp and its 'look out' goby that depend on each other for survival. While there are many fishes that are obviously reef fishes, others found on the coral reef may also be found near the shore in rocky areas, or outside the coral reef zone. A precise definition of a 'coral reef fish' is difficult.

Sizing up the species

The smallest species on the reef are the tiny gobies, some of them so small that they sit, almost invisible, on the stalk of a sea whip, their two ventral fins fused to make a delicate sucker that grips the thin

◁ ◁ *Masks are popular among angelfish, and the yellow-faced angel has an elaborate one, with golden eye bar and blue mesh on its cheeks.*

▽ *The blue tuskfish is one of the larger wrasses, growing to one metre in length and with powerful crushing teeth. Adults will lift rocks aside with their mouths to get at crabs beneath them. This one is being groomed by a small wrasse, and is having its head picked clean of parasites.*

Blue tuskfish, *Choerodon schoenleinii*; wrasse, *Labroides dimidiatus*

◁ *A gracefully shaped shrub coral,* Acropora, *stands above the rest of the living reef in shallow water, its different sections inhabited by different species of fishes. Well above the coral a school of fusiliers feeds on plankton floating in the water. Below them, also feeding on plankton, are various damsels, but they remain close to the corals, relying on them for shelter. Other species will feed on the algae growing on the dead faces of the coral, and still further species will feed on small animals living on the sea bed. Fishes are found in many places on a coral reef. One fish species may be found only in deep caverns, another only in the lagoon, and another only in deeper water. There is still little understanding of how this great species mix is retained without some species out-competing others and driving them to extinction. But it is known that there are very subtle differences in the foods that are eaten, and in the choices of places to live.*

Fusiliers, *Caesio*; damsels, *Pomacentridae*

'A tiny goby weighing less than a gram
has the same basic structure and body
organs as the tiger shark, a million
times its weight.'

▷ *Many of the smaller fishes on the reef have very
delicate colours and lovely patterns. Cardinal fish, also
unfortunately called gobbleguts, shun the bright light of
the day, and school in the shelter of caverns, or under
overhangs. Some, however, swim in the brighter light of
the staghorn thickets. They tend to have delicate colours
and patterns of red, silver and gold.*

Cardinal fish, *Apogonidae*

Mandarin fish, *Synchiropus picturatus*

Δ *The mandarin fish is a little 100-millimetre species of
the dragonet, Callionymidae, family and is found in
shallow water. Little is known about this beautiful fish.*

▷ *The size of the coral polyps shows that this tiny goby
is only about 20 millimetres long. Gobies are the smallest
living animals with backbones.*

▷▷ *Trevallies or jack mackerels work along the reef
edges for food, taking any unwary fishes, such as a plump
fusilier that does not race away fast enough. Over 40
species are known in the Pacific Ocean, most of which are
found on the reef. They are good angling fishes, usually
taken with lures or fish bait, and many make good eating.
The large turrum, growing to over 20 kilograms, is a
member of this family.*

Goby, *Tenacigobius*

Trevallies, *Carangidae*

Potato cod, *Epinephelus tukula*

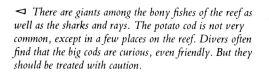

◁ There are giants among the bony fishes of the reef as well as the sharks and rays. The potato cod is not very common, except in a few places on the reef. Divers often find that the big cods are curious, even friendly. But they should be treated with caution.

◁ ▽ Manta rays are common in reef waters, and they are often seen leaping and falling back on the water surface with a resounding splash. This is said to be to remove parasites, but perhaps it is a display of territorial rights. A giant manta is harmless but it is an awesome sight underwater: two tonnes of large animal swimming by with strong and steady sweeps of its enormous wings.

Manta ray, *Manta alfredi*

Tiger shark, *Galeocerdo cuvieri*

Whale shark, *Rhincodon typus*

stalk. Some are only ten millimetres long, and are probably the smallest animals with backbones that exist on earth. They weigh less than a gram, yet have the same basic structure and body organs – heart and blood system, kidney tissue, gonads, liver, brain, eyes, gills – that their huge relatives on the reefs do. One of the largest of these, the tiger shark, may grow to over 1000 kilograms, and therefore be a million times the size of its fellow reef dweller. There are fishes of every size between, and on any reef the majority of fishes are small. Damselfish weighing a few grams are common in swarms above the coral and there are many species of fishes under half a kilogram – small wrasses, goatfish, butterfly fish, a number of small rock cod species and fusiliers. Fishes of about one to two kilograms are fewer but include parrotfish, sweetlips and wrasses, as well as many of the medium-sized fish predators, such as cod, hussars, emperors, and

trevallies. Above this size, reaching 30 kilograms and more, are the large predators that roam the reef edges – Queensland mackerel, tuna, large trevallies like the turrum, and large barracuda. The final group are the giant sharks and rays, the marlins and their relatives, and the large rock cods.

The numbers of species and individuals go down rapidly as the size of the fish increases. There are thousands of small fishes on the reef, hundreds of medium-sized ones, tens of large ones, and the giants are very rare. In general the grazers are small and medium sized; the plankton feeders and those who feed on minute crustaceans are tiny; those feeding on most molluscs, crabs and shrimps are medium sized, and fish predators range from medium to enormous in size, depending on the size of their prey fishes. There are exceptions, however, such as the huge plankton-eating whale sharks and sleek manta rays.

∆ The whale shark is the largest fish in the sea, reaching over 15 metres and weighing over 15 tonnes. It is found off the ribbon reefs of the outer barrier. This 'little' whale shark of four metres lazes just under the surface of the blue reef waters. In spite of their great size whale sharks are harmless to humans, and feed on minute planktonic crustaceans and small fishes.

∆ ◁ The tiger shark is a large animal that has a bad and thoroughly deserved reputation, for it is a scavenger that will take anything, large or small. It reaches over a tonne in weight, and close to five metres in length. Divers on the reef have little to fear from most sharks, but if a tiger shark is seen it is wise to leave the water! The slanted teeth are razor sharp. Male tigers, like many sharks, have a pair of grooved claspers for transmitting sperm, and insert one or both into the female at mating. A large number of vigorous young are born, fully toothed and capable of looking after themselves at birth.

'Many fishes from small parrotfish to large moray eels, visit the cleaning station to be serviced.'

▽ *The puffers and porcupine fish have strong parrot-like beaks, but unlike the vegetarian parrots they feed on hard-shelled animals such as sea urchins, molluscs and crabs, although small amounts of seaweed are also found in their stomachs. This little puffer has small but sharp bristles which become obvious when it is annoyed and inflates itself to twice its size – a good way to scare off a potential predator. It has spots above, and stripes along the belly, but it can grow large (to nearly 500 millimetres) and then these stripes disappear. The puffers have a very dangerous poison concentrated in the gonads and liver.*

Slingjaw wrasse, *Epibulus insidiator*

Puffer, *Arothron hispidus*

Slingjaw wrasse, *Epibulus insidiator*

Giants of the reef

Fishes have either bony skeletons or skeletons composed of tough elastic cartilage. Among the bony fishes, that form the bulk of the reef fishes, the giants are the huge marlins that are eagerly sought after by the big game anglers. Some bony fishes, like the black marlin, *Makaira indica*, become very large, and this species may reach one tonne. These graceful, sleek, but extremely powerful creatures can swim at great speed and yet are agile enough to spear tuna. Very occasionally they strike a boat, and their hard bony spear can easily penetrate solid oak. Although not true reef fishes, these ocean wanderers are commonly found in the Cairns waters both off the ribbon reefs and inside the outer barrier.

Some of the rock cods are also very large, and the great Queensland grouper, *Promicrops lanceolatus*, grows to nearly two metres, and over 200 kilograms. It may be physically capable of grabbing

△ *The slingjaw, top, is a wrasse with a remarkable specialisation, for although many fishes can achieve some extension of the mouth, the whole jaw system of the slingjaw is altered to give a forward movement when the mouth is opened, above. It can creep up to some unsuspecting fish or shrimp, and unsportingly fire its whole jaw forward, making a catch at a longer distance than its competitors.*

▷ *The cleaner wrasse has evolved a habit of feeding on the skin of other fishes, taking small animals, primarily crustaceans, that are parasites on the skin surface. Large fishes, quite capable of eating the cleaner wrasse, will suspend all predatory impulses during the grooming session, and hang in the water, mouths and gills open, while the cleaner picks over skin, teeth and gills. Here, two cleaners groom a big sweetlips, one of them working right inside its mouth.*

Blue-streaked cleaner wrasse, *Labroides dimidiatus*; sweetlips, *Plectorhynchus chaetodontoides*

Half beak, *Hemirhamphidae*

◁ *The reef fishes have adapted to many specialised living areas: most of the fishes on the deep outer reef are quite unlike those in the rich coral or the upper coral slopes; and the fishes in the lagoon differ from those on the more exposed reefs. Some fishes, like this half beak, use the area just under the surface, catching small animals that lie under the surface film. To do this the upper jaw is short, while the lower is long and tapering.*

Two of the largest sharks on the reef are the tiger shark, *Galeocerdo cuvieri*, and the hammerhead shark, *Sphyrna zygaena*, but the largest living shark of all, the whale shark, *Rhincodon typus*, may also occasionally be seen. The whale shark reaches 18 metres in length and a weight of over 15 tonnes. Both the tiger and the hammerhead sharks have razor-sharp teeth, and are known to have attacked divers, but the whale shark is a plankton feeder, and quite harmless in spite of its huge bulk.

Specialisations and professions

Competition for food and space on a coral reef is strong and fishes have variously adapted themselves in shape and behaviour to get the most that they can from the crowded reef. The delicate long-snouted butterfly fish, *Forcipiger*, has specialised by having a snout like a long tube with a tiny mouth at its end, ideal for poking into crannies for the shrimps that it eats, and which its less specialised relatives cannot do. The slingjaw wrasse, *Epibulus insidiator*, achieves the same result by having a jaw that pokes forward as it opens, extending into a long tube, ideal for sucking in small animals that come within a distance that would be safe from the pounce of a normal fish, but not from the remarkable slingjaw.

Teeth are greatly specialised. The parrotfish has teeth that are fused into a hard sharp beak, perfect for scraping the surface of coral to obtain the soft polyps, or for scraping rocks for their cover of algae. Some of the wrasses have such strong jaws that they can break hard cone shells. Among the fish predators teeth may be sharp for gripping other fishes, such as those of the red bass, *Lutianus bohar*, many other snappers and rock cods, or they may have a single row of sharp, close-set teeth that can take great bites out of other fishes, or sever them in half, such as those of the wahoo, *Acanthocybium solandri*, and its close relative the Queensland mackerel, *Scomberomorus commerson*.

Fishes may also specialise by developing different patterns of living from other fishes in an area. An unusual example is the cleaner wrasse, *Labroides dimidiatus*, that feeds on the parasites living on the surface of other fishes, sometimes even entering the mouth and picking at teeth, or the gill cover and picking over the gills. As large fishes find this helpful, they seek out 'cleaning stations' – as the feeding places of the cleaner wrasse are called – and the cleaner makes a bobbing dance to show that it is ready for business. Still more bizarre is the wrasse,

Sand divers, *Trichonotus setigerus*

Garden eel, *Congridae*

△ *The delicate sand divers hover above the bottom, and dive head first into the sand when frightened. These are a pair of males, recognisable by their dorsal spines that have been transformed into elongated filaments, probably displaying over a territorial dispute.*

△▷ *Even more linked to the bottom are the garden eels that remain safely in their tubes, with only half their bodies out to feed on the plankton. It is a strange sight to come across a garden of eels on a sandy lagoon floor, each protruding 50 to 100 millimetres, waving gently in the current. As they are approached they draw back into their tubes until only small heads and eyes are visible.*

and drowning a man, or swallowing a child whole. But this species is probably much maligned, and divers usually find them friendly and harmless. A good rapport often develops between divers working for a long time on an underwater project and the large groupers living in the area.

The largest inhabitants of the Great Barrier Reef are the cartilaginous fishes – the manta rays and larger sharks – that considerably outweigh the marlins and rock cods. The experience of swimming under a boat in deep water, and seeing a one-tonne giant manta sail by with its wings beating their steady, strong rhythm is frightening until one remembers that this vast body is nourished on plankton and tiny fishes. Mantas, usually of smaller size, are common about the reefs, and sometimes leap clear of the water, falling back with a huge splash and a loud noise. It is not known why they do this, but it is assumed that they are getting rid of parasites.

Banana fish, *Caesio pisang*

Yellowfin damselfish, *Glyphidodontops flavipinnus*

Blue devil, *Glyphidodontops cyaneus*

△ The damselfish are perhaps the most obvious and abundant small fishes on the reef, often swimming in small schools of half a dozen, sometimes in scores, and sometimes in hundreds. Many, like this little blue and yellow beauty, hover over or between corals. It is unfortunately named the blue devil but there is nothing devilish about this fish – a harmless, pretty blue damsel.

△△ The banana fish is a sleek swimmer. This is more to escape from its predators in midwater than to chase the slow-swimming or drifting planktonic animals on which it feeds.

▷△ There are 200 forms of damselfish and over 50 have been found on the Great Barrier Reef. The yellowfin damsel was not known until 1974, and was first collected and named on the reef.

Blue tang, *Paracanthurus hepatus*

Black-lined Maori wrasse, *Cheilinus diagrammus*

Red emperor, *Lutjanus sebae*

False cleaner, *Plageotremus rhinorhynchos*

Spotted sweetlips, *Plectorhynchus chaetodontoides*

◁ *Surgeonfish got their name from the sharp 'scalpel' that they have at the base of the tail. They have small teeth, sometimes more like bristles, and are algal feeders scraping the surface of the dead coral rock. There are probably two dozen or more species on the reef, from fish with sail-like dorsals, Zebrasoma; unicorn fish with their sharp pointed spike or large blunt bulb, Naso; to many typical surgeons or tangs. One of the most colourful is the blue tang, whose lovely colour, dark blue pattern and yellow tail make it a bright sight against the coral. The scalpel is sheathed, and is not visible in this fish.*

A myriad variety

'In a brief swim along the reef a hundred or so species of fishes, of all shapes, sizes and colours, can be seen.'

Δ *Some small blennies mimic the cleaner wrasse. They do this by looking much the same, and performing a similar dance. Fishes go to them expecting the comfortable grooming of their usual cleaner – instead the false cleaner rushes at them and takes a solid bite of fin or skin. Some species, such as the false cleaner, Aspidontis, have huge lower canine teeth. This false cleaner lacks the huge canines, but still manages to exact its pound of flesh. It has also been known to bite swimmers.*

ΔΔ *One of the most abundant groups on the reef are the wrasses and tuskfish of the Labridae family. They are usually predators, and may be small or large. The black-lined Maori wrasse is a common and typical wrasse but larger than many, reaching one metre in length. Its relative, the giant Maori wrasse, Cheilinus undulatus, grows to over two metres in length.*

Δ *The spotted sweetlips is plain in colour with hexagonal spots as an adult, but the juvenile is a gay creature, with large fins and a strong pattern breaking up the normal fish shape. The adults are large and slow-moving.*

ΔΔ *The small red emperor has an alternative name 'government bream' – an allusion to the red arrows on prison garb. As an adult this pattern is absent or faint. The family of the true snappers, to which the red emperor belongs, has many fish species that are sought for food – the red emperor being one of the most popular. The young may be found in mangrove channels but the adult is a fish of the reef and is commonly seen by divers.*

⊳ The small, orange-tailed damselfish is beautiful with a striking band on the tail fin. This species is rare, and is not often encountered by divers.

▽ The needle-like snout of the long-snouted butterfly fish allows it to get in cracks and holes that other fishes cannot reach. Individuals or pairs of this pretty little fish are common, particularly on the outer reefs. It probably feeds on crustaceans, worms and molluscs, but they must be exceedingly small for the mouth at the end of this long snout is minute.

Orange-tailed damselfish, *Chrysiptera cyanea*

Long-snouted butterfly fish, *Forcipiger longirostris*

Bearded triggerfish, *Xanthichthys auromarginatus*

Plagiotremus tapeinosoma, that copies the cleaner. This fish looks very similar in colour and even dances the same dance, but it takes a bite out of the skin or fins of any fish that approaches. It has two large lower canine teeth and sometimes takes a painful nip at a swimmer lazing over the reef.

Adapting to an area

Coral reefs are able to hold so many species because the reef is finely partitioned into many different habitats, with different species living in each. Coral reefs are not homogeneous – some areas experience strong wave action, others are sheltered. Algae grow well in shallow water with high light intensities and vigorous water movement and less well in deep or quiet waters. Corals grow in different shapes on reef fronts, lagoons and sheltered back-reef regions, providing different amounts of shelter for fishes, and varying amounts and types of food. Many species of

fishes have evolved to live in quite discrete parts or zones on a coral reef. A sample of fishes collected in six metres of water off the front of a reef, for example, would contain a group of species different from a sample of lagoon fishes. Lagoon species are adapted to quiet water conditions and have plentiful shelter. But the fishes from the shallow fore reef facing the open ocean have to withstand strong wave action, and do not have much shelter because storms break the corals that are then rolled and smashed over the living coral cover, tending to keep it low in profile, and restricted to hardy species. The deeper parts of the fore reef are different again, more fragile species grow, and often there are many sponges and Gorgonian corals – the sea fans and sea whips – and correspondingly different species of fishes. In conditions suitable for very large coral growth, such as the outside of the reef facing the mainland, there are often corals that may be three to

△ The bearded triggerfish (with more of a five o'clock shadow than a beard) lives on the outer reefs and grows to 300 millimetres. Triggerfish are able to lock the first strong spine solidly erect by using the short second spine as a chock. They will race into a hole if chased, and then raise and lock the spine. If predators (or human fingers) reach the trigger's body, they cannot remove it, and the triggerfish is further protected by strong scales.

four metres high, and which are hundreds of years old. Often these corals have eroded bases, and form caverns so large that a person can swim into them. In the dim light of such caves there are other living species, and nocturnal feeders taking shelter through the day.

The many obvious specialisations – the variations in tooth structure for different foods; shapes of body and of heads; size differences; stomachs, intestines

Boxfish, *Ostracion solorensis*

△ *The smaller boxfish may be very colourful and this species has sexes with different colours. The male is brilliant blue and yellow with spotted sides, and the female, left, is paler with reticulated sides.*

Boxfish, *Ostracion solorensis*

and gastric juices to digest various forms of protein, fat and carbohydrate; special behaviour to cope with different environments – and the use of different habitats and times of day and night – show that the potential living patterns, even if not limitless, are nevertheless extremely numerous.

But there could be other factors responsible for the co-existence of so many species. The huge size of the reef, with hundreds of thousands of semi-isolated patches of corals on which species settle in different proportions, and the heavy toll by resident and roving predators, may play some role in reducing competition between species.

▷ Many of the surgeonfish feed in schools, sometimes of more than one species of surgeon, and sometimes even mixing with parrotfish. The blue-lined surgeonfish forms large schools in some places, but in other areas is a solitary species. It is one of the prettiest of surgeons, eagerly sought after as an aquarium species.

▽ The butterfly fish, Chaetodontidae, and the angelfish, Pomacanthidae, are to many the typical fishes of the reef. Brightly coloured and highly visible, they are easily recognisable by strong colour patterns. These black-backed butterfly fish can be abundant on the reefs. They do not seem to be strongly territorial, and may be found singly or in groups of various sizes. This pair are swimming with the regal angelfish. The two groups are closely related, but the angelfish has a strong spine at the corner of the gill.

Blue-lined surgeonfish, *Acanthurus lineatus*

Angelfish, *Pygoplites diacanthus*; butterfly fish, *Chaetodon melannotus*

Emperor angelfish, *Pomacanthus imperator*

Semicircle angelfish, *Pomacanthus semicirculatus*

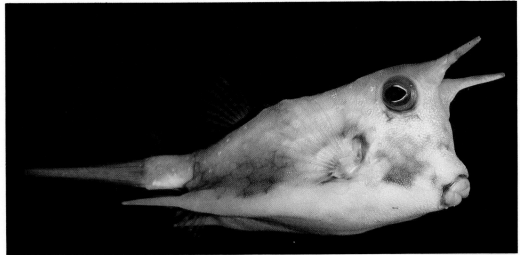

△ The cowfish or boxfish are encased in armour – a set of fused bony plates that is completely rigid, leaving only the fins and mouth movable. They swim effectively, but slowly, with the pectoral or side fins whirring away. This group of fishes produces a toxic mucus from the skin. Strong horns, a box-like body and a skin toxin should make the species safe from predation but these can apparently be overcome by strong stomachs and the long-horned cowfish is sometimes eaten by large predators. A close relative of this species, the thornback cowfish, Lactoria fornasini, has been studied in Japan and has a strange spawning, with the little male having a number of mates, and spawning with all of them each evening in the spring. After the male has raced around a female for a few moments flashing bright colours, the pair swim up close to the surface; then the male hums to the female, with a hum loud enough to be heard by a diver. After a short nuptial song the cowfish spawn.

Long-horned cowfish, *Lactoria cornutus*

Clown triggerfish, *Balistoides conspicillum*

Meyer's butterfly fish, *Chaetodon meyeri*

△ The patterns of the clown triggerfish are so distinctive, and so obvious under water and unlike camouflage, that one can only conclude that the fish is advertising that it is poisonous. The colouring seems amazingly detailed, almost making the triggerfish clown-like but the species name given to this fish would suggest that 'conspicuous triggerfish' would be a better common name.

◁ The adult emperor angelfish, far left, has a striking colour pattern with masked face and longitudinal yellow lines. The colours of the young are quite different, with concentric circles of white and blue. The adult semicircle angelfish has no mask, although it is beautiful with fine spotting over the body and blue-edged fins, gill covers and spines. Semicircle angels, left, are solitary as adults, but the emperor is often in pairs or threes. Smaller angelfish live in harems with one male and several females.

Valentin's pufferfish, *Canthigaster valentini*

△ Meyer's butterfly fish is a bizarre little fish with elaborate stripes. It is not common, but has been found at Heron Island and other places on the reef, in about ten metres of water.

◁ A common but shy fish, Valentin's pufferfish live in small territories that are guarded by the females – a number of which are overseen by a male.

Colour and form
'Like the birds of the air, the coral reef fishes glide over and above their coral caves and turreted coral castles.'

Blue and gold angelfish, *Centropyge bicolor*

Territory and defence

Many coral reef fishes are very territorial. Small fishes, like some of the damsels, will rush at any comers, even large fishes or a diver, and act aggressively to try to keep them off the areas they claim as their own. Usually this is most fiercely done against their own species because members of one species have the same food and space needs.

One of the most interesting examples of territorial behaviour is that of the blue and gold angelfish, *Centropyge bicolor* – a vegetable feeder that lives in groups of four to seven fishes. They prefer portions of reef with algae-covered rubble, and each group has a joint territory that the male defends against other groups. There is usually only one male in this family but when the male dies the largest female changes sex.

While the male's little harem feeds and produces young, he has the task of patrolling the borders of his territory against the surrounding families.

A good strong male can guard enough territory to attract females and keep the group properly fed and therefore reproducing well. Also, weaker males would not be so successful in holding territory and breed less, so that the genes of the stronger males continue in the species, and weak genes disappear. The limited territory defended by the male may be important to the control of population. Instead of sharing food and getting poor nutrition in times of high population numbers, good conditions are provided for the number of fishes the area can feed. Fishes forced into less suitable areas are likely to have poorer nutrition and be more prone to predation and disease. Their family groups could be expected to breed less successfully, reducing the population to a lower level.

△ *The blue and gold angelfish is fiercely territorial to others of its species. The male controls a territory of a few square metres in which he may live with up to seven smaller females. Often there are no other males in his territory, and he rules his small harem like a despot, visiting his females a number of times during the day, patrolling the border of his territory, making sure no surrounding families enter to feed, and preventing any males from capturing or mating with his females. Sometimes his territory may contain a 'bachelor male' who does not breed with his harem. The male mates chiefly in the summer months and, starting 30 minutes before sunset, will usually mate with all the females in turn. If the dominant male is killed (or removed to another spot by a scientist!) the largest female changes sex rapidly, and becomes a fully functional male. If there is a bachelor male, he may take over the harem.*

Black-backed butterfly fish, *Chaetodon melannotus*

◁ *The black-backed butterfly fish seems to show little territorial behaviour and during the day swims over a large area, usually called a 'home range', which it shares with others of the same species. At night it will go to its own resting place deep in the coral, but even here may be near others. This is quite different behaviour from some of its close relatives, such as the strongly territorial chevroned butterfly fish.*

◁ ▽ *The threadfin butterfly fish does not seem to be territorial during the day, but at night expects to sleep in its own spot, and beware any fish that gets in the way. It is able to chase away a medium-sized rock cod (large enough to make a meal of it) by moving backwards into its face with the strong spines of its anal fin erect.*

Black-backed butterfly fish, *Chaetodon melannotus*

△ *A group of black-backed butterfly fish feeds peacefully over the home range. This beautiful creature is common on the Great Barrier Reef.*

Territoriality reduces fighting among the members of species, for the border battles are usually a matter of posturing with no active fighting that could result in injury or death. Each individual knows the borders and will only fight if a neighbour strays into its territory.

All this makes good sense to the individuals concerned in their battle for survival – they each control a set of females by their control of territory, they establish relations with surrounding males which defines their territory without deadly battles or too much waste of energy and there is no surplus of males, for they transform from the females when needed.

Threadfin butterfly fish, *Chaetodon auriga*

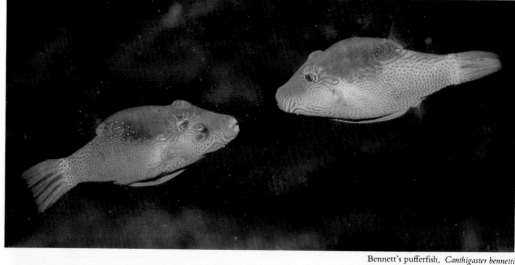

Bennett's pufferfish, *Canthigaster bennetti*

▽ *A few damselfish farm a small territory, removing the larger algae, and leaving the smaller algae that they prefer to eat. This one-spot damsel removes large algae from its 'farm'. The algae it prefers are more productive and more palatable, and its weeding out of the bigger algae increases its food source. This behaviour is amazingly advanced for a fish.*

One-spot damselfish, *Glyphidodontops unimaculatus*

Damselfish, *Glyphidodontops rollandi*

Territoriality, like almost all other behavioural patterns on the reef, is extremely varied. One variation is for females to control their own subterritories within the larger 'family holding' defended by the male. The male patrols the territories of a few females, keeping other males out, and sometimes trying to steal a female and its territory from a neighbour. This happens in the delightful little striped pufferfish, *Canthigaster valentini*. But in crowded areas the territorial system can break down, and the fishes live in a big group where larger fishes are dominant.

Fish farming

Some of the grazing damselfish hold a territory, and actually 'farm' the algae in it. And some species including the damselfish, *Hemiglyphidodon plagiometopon*, defend a small territory that they modify by tearing at the larger tufted algae and removing them from the territory. They also keep out other grazers, and the result is a managed algal turf, kept strictly for the benefit of individuals of one species.

The home range

But territory is not always so clearly defined. Some of the little butterfly fish will travel over an area that may be ten metres in diameter but not defend it in any strictly territorial sense. Other fishes of different species are ignored, and individuals of the same species may not be chased unless they come very close, when usually the larger fish will briefly chase the smaller. These home ranges, as they are called, may be covered many times a day, and the fishes know them well for food and shelter.

Not all butterfly fish have home ranges. A few species actively defend a territory, and this has been tested in a field experiment. If a territorial species is

△ *Two beautiful young damsels face each other in an aggressive encounter over the coral. Many damsels are territorial, and they are most aggressive to their own species – with good reason, for they compete more directly for food and mate with their own kind. Their behaviour is similar to most territorial animals on land and in the sea. Although real fights may occur, once territory is established and boundaries between two territories are learnt, the ritual 'fights' of these little fish are to reconfirm their rights, not to damage each other.*

△△ *Two Bennett's puffers skirmish at the border between their territories, but such fights are more a statement of position than a battle.*

Harlequin tuskfish, *Choerodon fasciatus*

Coral trout, *Plectropoma leopardus*

△ *Two large coral trout communicate closely, but as this species is not strongly territorial the reason is not obvious. This species is known to spawn in groups at particular places on the reef, and it is possible that this confrontation is over an issue of food or space. Individuals of this species may be seen in one area for days or months, and then move off. Tagging has also shown that they may move many kilometres from one reef to another.*

△△ *One of the wrasses, the harlequin tuskfish, strongly states its territorial position. The harlequin has a clearly defined territory, but is tolerant of large human swimmers, and its beautiful colours can easily be closely observed.*

shown its own image it will get furiously excited, so scientists have painted little wooden models with the colours of a strongly territorial species (like the chevroned butterfly fish, *Chaetodon trifascialis*) and species that are not strongly territorial (like the black-backed butterfly fish, *Chaetodon melannotus*). Placed at the end of a perspex rod and moved slowly towards the chevroned butterfly fish, the little fish will make short rushes towards its image, finally striking it repeatedly with lowered head and dorsal fin spines erect. The spines strike the model, and the bumps can be felt by the holder at the end of the rod. The fish is not deterred even if it loses scales in the process. In contrast the black-backed butterfly fish will simply be curious, and a little crowd of fishes will gather around the model, just looking. Another experimental method is to put a fish in a jam jar with a gauze top, and move it closer or further from the fish being tested.

Territorial fishes will attack the jar furiously as it is placed closer to their territory.

Often fishes that are not normally territorial become so during the breeding season. Some of the big triggerfish of the Balistidae family will migrate to the outer edge of the Great Barrier Reef, and in their hundreds will make shallow depressions in which they lay eggs. The nesting site is then fiercely guarded against all comers.

Seeing the differences

Underlying the territoriality is the importance of vision. Individuals of the same species are recognised visually, and presumably the blue and gold angelfish sees the difference between its family group and a neighbour. Recognition may not only be how the other fish 'looks', but also how it reacts and moves. While feeding, two butterfly fish, many of which pair for life, may temporarily lose each other. One will then rise above the coral and its mate will swim rapidly to it. All this is totally visual, although other clues, such as sounds and scents, are probably sometimes involved.

Migratory movements

Many species have large foraging areas, which may vary with time and cannot be called home ranges. Some of the true snappers, like the yellow-banded hussar, *Lutianus amabilis*, will school in the same place each day, and then hunt over wide areas at night, even swimming some kilometres. A large coral trout may stay about an area of coral for weeks, or even months, and then move off somewhere else where the feeding is better. The coral trout seems to be opportunistic, and has no close links to any particular place.

Although little is known about the movements of many species, we do know that larger migrations are common among species such as the 'mackerel' of the genus *Scomberomorus*, including the famous Queensland mackerel, *Scomberomorus commerson* – one of the most sought-after game and food fishes on the reef. Such species may make migrations, presumably for spawning, of hundreds of kilometres. In parts of the world (for example the East African island of Zanzibar), the movements of one of the mackerels is well known to fishermen, who trap them on their migrations.

Off Lizard Island Research Station in the northern Great Barrier Reef there are evenings when a large hammerhead shark, *Sphyrna zygaena*, patrols in shallow water up and down off a particular beach. Its appearance seems to be seasonal, and it has been seen for many years. Little is known about the behaviour of such large beasts but it is possible that they develop regular haunts to which they return again and again.

Long migrations demand good navigation skills, and it seems that fishes that migrate thousands of kilometres may have an ability to use the sun and have the necessary sense of time.

Fairy basslet, *Anthias dispar*

Purple-headed parrotfish, *Scarus*

Blue-barred parrotfish, *Scarus ghobban*

Parrotfish, *Scarus brevifilus*

△ *The blue-barred parrotfish is one of the most widespread species of parrotfish. It exists both in shallow surface waters and in depths of over 50 metres – the young are found in lagoons although adults tend to live in the deeper water off the edge of the reef. It also does not specialise as much as most fishes in its eating – it feeds over sand as well as coral and also eats sea grasses. This initial or 'drab' phase individual is most likely a female, although it could be an immature primary male.*

◁ *One of the most colourful of the fairy basslets, the male Anthias dispar performs a courtship dance and displays to the females in a school nearby. This 'showing off' serves to advertise the male's presence and reinforce the dominance he has over the females. Like most coral reef fishes where the sexes are differently coloured, the males are much more vivid than the females.*

Sex on the reef

Sex is complicated for coral reef fishes – there are males, females, neuters, and many which change from one sex to another.

The parrotfish are splendid examples of this role change. Until recently their identification was confused because what were initially thought to be separate species turned out to be male and female parrotfish of the same species with different colour patterns. Studies have now demonstrated that many species, representing the majority of coral reef fish families, undergo sex changes as part of their normal way of life.

Tropical transsexuals

Hermaphroditism, when both male and female reproductive tissues exist in the same individual, is common among reef fishes. Within different species we may find some or all the individuals starting life as either males (known as protandry; proto – first, andros – male) or as females (known as protogyny) with some or all the individuals changing to the other sex as they grow older. There are species known where no males change to females and no females change to males. Once sex change has occurred in an individual it is not reversible. Very rarely, both ovaries and testes have been found to function in an individual at the same time and although self-fertilisation has been found in a population of small bass (family Serranidae) in the Caribbean, this practice is uncommon.

One of the best-known examples of sequential hemaphroditism is that of the ubiquitous cleaner fish, the blue streak, *Labroides dimidiatus*. These energetic little fishes live in harems containing a male with up to 16 females. Should the male be removed, by predation or old age, the dominant female rapidly assumes his role and within hours is

'The majority of coral reef fish families undergo sex changes as part of their normal way of life. Hermaphroditism, when both male and female tissues exist in the same individual, is also found.'

▽ *The elongated dorsal spines, which are common in adult male fairy basslets, are seen very distinctly in this displaying male.*

Fairy basslet, *Anthias pleurotaenia*

Fairy basslet, *Anthias huchtii*

behaving as a male. Physiological changes start almost immediately and within several days the female has become a functional male.

Only females are born and all females have the potential to change sex. This potential increases with size or age but is kept in check by male dominance and aggression. If the newly transformed male is also removed then the next dominant female undergoes a sex change. Species such as the cleaner fish are known as monandric because all of the individuals are born as only one sex – all the males are derived from females. The fairy basslets of the genus *Anthias* also fit this pattern of sexuality, although their social systems are different as they exist in larger schools feeding on plankton and there may be several males in a group. Experiments on this species have also demonstrated that the removal of a male leads to sex reversal of one of the females in the group – generally the largest.

Primary and secondary

Other fishes that start life as females may have both primary males – those born as males – and secondary males – those derived from females – in their populations. These species are known as diandric. To complicate matters further, in some species these secondary males are derived from females that have not reproduced, although this is not usual.

In most protogynous (female-first) species, there may be two or three colour patterns – mature primary males (born as males) are bright and gaudy, mature females are drab brown, grey or green; and juveniles and immature males are similarly drab. The sexually active secondary males are not as gaudy as the primary males. In protandrous (male-first) species there is little or no colour variation between the sexes.

Among such families as the wrasses, parrotfish,

△ *Fairy basslets school looking for plankton on outer reef slopes or lagoon passes where the water is clear and there are good currents. Like their relatives the grouper and coral trout, these fishes are born female with some later becoming male. The main sexual forms of the fairy basslet are a mature female, a 'changeling', above right, in the process of becoming a male, above, and a sexually active male, right. Schools of fairy basslets consist mostly of juveniles and mature females and only a few adult males. The males spend much of their time 'dominating' the senior females and it is this harassment that keeps the females from changing sex – presumably by keeping the female hormonal balance in check. Should the group grow too large, or some of the adult males die off, the dominant females then change into males.*

Fairy basslet, *Anthias pleurotaenia*

Fairy basslet, *Anthias pleurotaenia*

grouper, cod, fairy basslets, angelfish, some damselfish and gobies it is normal for the females to change sex; while in the flatheads, scorpion fish, bream, hussars, snapper, bass and some anemone fish it is the males that change into females.

Efficient reproductive effort

It would seem simpler to have a strict sexual system as in mammals. But the high diversity and low population numbers of coral reef fishes have brought great evolutionary pressures to develop better ways to maximise reproductive effort.

One of the theories of hermaphroditism is that it gives an individual two chances to reproduce. It can mate and reproduce as it is growing; and, when grown, an individual that has successfully found food, escaped predators and dominated its neighbours is able to change sex, grow larger, and so dominate the fertilisation of the remainder of the group.

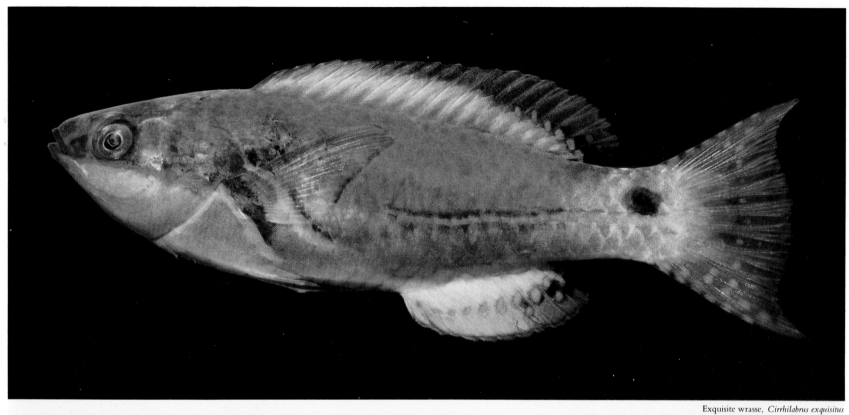

Exquisite wrasse, *Cirrhilabrus exquisitus*

Exquisite wrasse, *Cirrhilabrus labouri*

Fairy basslet, *Anthias tuka*

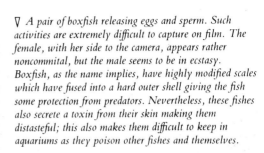

▽ *A pair of boxfish releasing eggs and sperm. Such activities are extremely difficult to capture on film. The female, with her side to the camera, appears rather noncommital, but the male seems to be in ecstasy. Boxfish, as the name implies, have highly modified scales which have fused into a hard outer shell giving the fish some protection from predators. Nevertheless, these fishes also secrete a toxin from their skin making them distasteful; this also makes them difficult to keep in aquariums as they poison other fishes and themselves.*

Fairy basslet, *Anthias tuka*

Boxfish, *Lactoria fornasini*

Δ *This pair of fairy basslets shows the marked difference in colour between the sexes. The male, top, is a bright purple and is displaying his large dorsal fin.*

◁ *Wrasses of the family Labridae are hermaphrodites that start life as females – similar to the parrotfish. The male exquisite wrasse, above left, with the blue colouring has transformed from a female. Pair spawning is also practised in this fish family, as well as group spawning.*

Other advantages of sex change are shown by the small coral associate gobies of the genus Gobiodon. These little fishes are ill-equipped to fend off predators, although they do have toxic secretions that they liberate from their skin when molested. However, as these fishes live in such small groups, the chances of one or other sex being lost, for instance due to predation, would be very high if the sex ratio were equal. Being hermaphroditic overcomes this dilemma as new recruits from the larvae are always female and can turn into males if and when the need arises, thus maintaining a reproductive colony.

One-sex elders
Populations of hermaphroditic reef fishes are thus not evenly balanced in their sex ratios and the larger, older members of the population are predominantly one sex. This has significance in the larger, popular table-fishes like the coral trout. The development of fishery management practices and the right way to exploit these fishes must take this behaviour and physiology into account. The traditional fishery practices 'inherited' from Europe may need revising as they encourage taking the largest fishes and throwing the 'littlies' back. This depresses the age structure of the population and alters the natural sex ratio, with serious effects on the population's ability to reproduce. The result is rapid local overfishing!

The solution may be to reverse this attitude and throw back the very big fishes and concentrate on the small and medium-sized ones. This is now being considered by our government fisheries agencies.

Spawning
It is not known whether fishes get much fun out of the spawning process, but they certainly put a lot of effort into this activity.

▷ *This cluster of several hundred damselfish eggs is attached to a piece of dead coral. Fishes that lay eggs attached to the bottom, that they then look after, produce several clusters, but seldom lay more than a few thousand eggs each year. Broadcast spawners, on the other hand, may release several thousand eggs at a time, and do this repeatedly throughout the year. Obviously, mortality of these eggs and larvae is exceptionally high, but only one or two need to survive to replace their parents and so maintain a stable breeding population.*

Three broad types of reproduction can be found in the fish world: broadcast spawning where gametes are shed into the water and the eggs are dispersed by the currents; demersal spawning where the eggs are laid attached to the coral bottom, perhaps in some kind of a nest; and parental care as in mouth brooding, pouch rearing or even internal fertilisation.

A reproductive orgy

Broadcast spawning is perhaps the more common and certainly the most readily observed by divers. On the outer side of a reef, perhaps near a pass or some promontory where water currents are strong, and in the late afternoons on an outgoing tide in the summer months, a diver may be fortunate to witness a reproductive orgy of parrotfish, wrasses, goatfish and boxfish. These are ideal conditions for fertilisation and for rapidly removing the eggs from the reef where predation on them is intense.

Many of the species that are females before changing sex have group spawning of a single or perhaps a few 'gaudy' males servicing a large number of females. However the 'primary males' – which are often smaller than the secondary males and have the drab colour of the females – may also join in the group spawning activity among the unsuspecting females and hidden from the aggressive males so that they can effectively fertilise some of the females.

A phenomenon which is rarely seen on the Great Barrier Reef is that of the mass spawning aggregations of the large groupers, such as the coral trout. The little information available indicates that many hundreds, and maybe thousands of individuals migrate over tens of kilometres to selected sites during the breeding months of November and December. These sites are generally around the passes of the ribbon reefs where the fishes may spend several days just milling around in the water in a rather docile manner. Biologists studying the commercially important Nassau grouper in the West Indies have observed breeding aggregations of these fishes numbering 30 000 to 100 000 individuals.

Fishermen in the Pacific islands and the Caribbean have learnt of the locations of these spawning aggregations and they have, especially in some Carribean regions, decimated the populations during this period. Fortunately, the Great Barrier

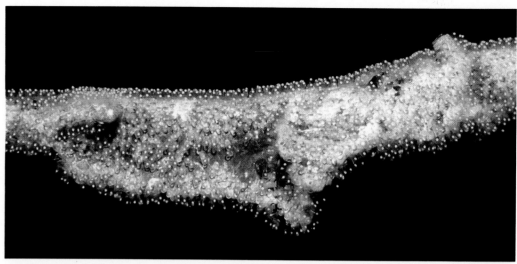

Damselfish eggs

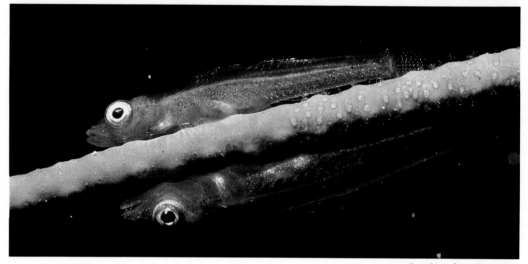

Sea whip gobies, *Tenacigobius*

Reef is vast, and at least in the northern regions, fishing pressures are not great, so that there are only a few of these sites known.

Courting at dusk

Many reef fishes also undergo pair spawning, a behaviour which is common among the angelfish, boxfish, lionfish and some of the wrasses, parrotfish and fairy basslets. The male generally initiates the activity and courts the gravid or ripe females in his territory. Courtship often involves some form of display with fins erect and the male 'showing off' his splendour to the female. This activity is associated with the male nuzzling at the sides or the belly of the female for ten minutes or so, and when they are both ready, a rapid dash is made towards the surface and away from the reef, culminating in the release of sperm and thousands of eggs and a rapid dive back to the shelter of the reef. The eggs

△ *As an alternate to broadcasting eggs in the ocean currents, many species of reef fishes lay their eggs attached to some part of the reef surface. These are called demersal eggs. Nests may be very simple or can be quite elaborate, but the parents generally care for the eggs to some degree. These small sea whip gobies lay their eggs on the sea whip – their eggs can be clearly seen attached, near the tail of the female (on the underside). In some related sea whip gobies, the fish nip the polyps away from the nest area before laying their eggs, which hatch out in about seven to ten days.*

are therefore released away from the reef with its myriad predators, allowing the eggs to drift off into open water. Pair spawning like this generally takes place at dusk.

Nesting fishes

Many reef fishes lay demersal eggs that are attached to the bottom and laid in some form of nest. Perhaps the simplest of these are the pufferfish that lay clusters of a hundred or so sticky eggs on clumps of filamentous algae on the bottom.

Triggerfish make a small depression in the sand by blowing the water with their mouths and physically removing larger stones and lumps of coral. The eggs are laid in this depression by the female, usually at dawn. She then leaves the male to tend the nest, clean the eggs and remove any debris until the eggs hatch in five to seven days.

The behaviour of the damselfish is much more elaborate. Nest sites are generally located among the coral or on clumps of algae, and the fish clean and maintain an egg site which the male, and sometimes the female, busily defends. When they are ready to mate the male performs an elaborate courtship 'dance', swimming up and down in front of the female and leading her to the nest site where she is encouraged to lay her eggs which the male then promptly fertilises.

The anemone fish, which have a very well developed symbiotic relationship with the anemones, choose an area of coral under the protection of the fleshy lobes of the anemone as their nest site. When ready to spawn, the male bites the anemone's tentacles causing them to withdraw and then leads the female to the nest by a series of dances and body nudging. Small clusters of 200 to 400 eggs are laid, that hatch in about seven days. Hatching occurs shortly after dusk, as it does in the majority of the demersal egg-laying species so far studied, and this is presumed to coincide with the period of least predation.

The small sea whip gobies apparently spend their whole lives associated with antipatharian sea whips that provide them with a surface on which to cling and that puts them out into the water currents from where they can dart and catch their planktonic food. At breeding time the gobies clear the polyps from a few centimetres of the sea whip, towards the end, and on this they lay their eggs. After hatching, the egg cases disappear, a fine filamentous growth of algae appears, and then, over the next month or so, the polyps again invade the area and the sea whip is as good as new.

Breeding in burrows

As an alternative to liberating their eggs freely into the water, or laying them in an exposed nest, some fishes have taken to laying their eggs in burrows. This behaviour has been observed in some of the gobies that live in burrows in association with shrimps and in many of the sabre-toothed blennies

Two-lined gobies, *Valenciennea helsdingenii*

Two-lined gobies, *Valenciennea helsdingenii*

Two-lined gobies, *Valenciennea helsdingenii*

Banded damsel, *Amblyglyphidodon curacao*

△ *Gobies are not the only fishes to use sea whips as nest sites as shown by this banded damsel or sergeant-major tending its eggs.*

◁ *Gobies are one of the most diverse families of reef fishes and there is a large group which has a symbiotic relationship with alpheid or snapping shrimps with which they share a burrow in the sand. This pair of two-lined gobies remove algae and pebbles during the maintenance of their burrow. All gobies produce sticky, demersal eggs that are either laid in caves, on the underside of corals, or in burrows. Following spawning, the male tends and guards the eggs. A unique reproductive behaviour has been recently observed at Lizard Island in one of the burrow-living species. The eggs were laid in the burrow and the female sealed the male inside with the eggs. The nest was periodically opened by the female, both parents then cleaned the area, and the male was again sealed inside. After about five days the male stayed outside until finally they opened the burrow when a single, small, sea-living individual emerged. Presumably the larvae fed on energy reserves in their yolk sacs and were possibly cannibalistic. More study is needed to clarify this remarkable activity. The small, coral associated gobies of the genus Gobiodon have been found to be female-first hermaphrodites and live in small groups with one large male, one slightly smaller mature female and the remainder immature females. When nesting time comes, they nip off the polyps and kill a small section on the underside of a branch of coral. A dense mat of algae soon grows on which the eggs are laid.*

'Pair spawning generally takes place around dusk when light levels are low, and the upwards rush to release gametes happens very quickly.'

'To avoid aggression from the older males, the young male parrotfish mingle with the females as transvestites displaying female colour patterns.'

▷ This anemone fish is shown tending a cluster of eggs, a function performed by both sexes. The eggs are fanned and mouthed, and any dead eggs are removed to prevent the growth of fungus and disease. The fish nip the anemone repeatedly to stimulate it to retract away from the nest site where the eggs can be laid. The eggs then receive protection from the anemone.

Anemone fish, *Amphiprion perideraion*

Anemone fish, *Amphiprion perideraion*

△ Anemone fish are among the most hardy and popular aquarium fish and no self-respecting marine aquarist would be without a pair of these brightly coloured fish and their associated anemone. This specialised group of damselfish has evolved an intricate behaviour and dependence on the anemones among the deadly tentacles of which they swim freely, while other fishes that venture too close are instantly paralysed. It has recently been found that these fish are hermaphrodites that are born as males and change to females as the males grow to maturity. A typical group of anemone fish includes a large adult female monogamously mated with a smaller sexually mature male, lower left; the remainder of the group are smaller immature males kept in check by the adult male. Should the female die, the adult male changes sex and the most dominant of the subordinates takes over the role of the male.

that nest in disused worm burrows or holes left by boring sponges. Many damselfish lay their eggs inside dead shells – particularly in dead clam shells. The nests have to be tended, usually by the male but often by both sexes, and dead or unfertilised eggs are removed to eliminate the growth of fungus. There is a lot more energy needed for this type of reproduction than for liberating the eggs freely into the water. To make up for this, the number of eggs released is relatively low, generally only hundreds, compared with the thousands of eggs released by the broadcast spawners.

Male rearing

The final strategy is that of giving birth to juvenile fishes and this has been achieved in many ways. The simplest, from an evolutionary point of view, can be found in the cardinal fish that spawn in pairs. The male gathers up the ball of eggs immediately

they are fertilised and rears them in his mouth. This protects the eggs from would-be predators and ensures a good flow of water over them. In the early days these fish were mistakenly thought to be cannibalistic. The female in some species actively defends the brooding male.

One can imagine an evolutionary sequence leading to the development of this type of behaviour. The physiological energy required to produce eggs is vastly more than that required to produce sperm and in the broadcast spawners one male can satisfactorily service many females thus maximising the number of eggs released. With larger, more developed eggs, fewer can be produced by a female and these need to be protected – the fish cannot afford to waste them. So the male, who has invested less energy in the production of sperm, takes on the role of looking after the nest. As nesting becomes more elaborate, the male becomes

◁ The green puller is one of the most abundant and attractive damselfish on the reef. It swims in large groups hovering about heads of staghorn corals. Should danger threaten, the whole school suddenly darts for cover in perfect unison as if pulled by some unseen puppeteer's strings. This species lays its eggs among the tufts of the green algae, Chlorodesmis. Other species of damselfish make small nests in depressions in the sand.

◁ ▽ There are many species of coral reef fishes that take parenthood very responsibly and 'incubate' their eggs. Incubation is not strictly correct as there is no increase in temperature to help the eggs develop as in birds, but the eggs are given much more protection than they would have if left in an open nest. Among the cardinal fish the male rears the eggs. Pair spawning is practised and, immediately after the female is coaxed into laying a bundle of eggs, the male fertilises them, then takes them into his mouth for safekeeping, where they develop over the next week or so.

Green puller, *Chromis caerulea*

Three-spot damsels, *Dascyllus trimaculatus*

△ Sexuality and hermaphroditism in damselfish is rather confused. One group, the anemone fish, all start life as males, but it seems that a number of other hermaphrodite damselfish species are born as females. The humbug, Dascyllus aruanus, and the beautiful blue devil, Glyphidodontops cyaneus, are thought to be female-first hermaphrodites as no small males and no large females have been found. This pair of three-spot damsels is likely to be hermaphroditic. They also live in association with anemones although they do not appear to be as dependent on them as the true anemone fish. Both sexes tend the eggs, and the darker female can be seen 'mouthing' the eggs to clean them and remove any dead ones. The males generally adopt a lighter colour during breeding and courtship.

Golden-lined cardinal fish, *Apogon cyanosoma*

more involved and the female produces even more well-developed eggs. Finally, the male takes the job of actually nursing the eggs which now needs even more energy, and the female has to help guard the eggs. The eggs hatch into well-developed larvae in seven to nine days.

Another case of male rearing is found in the pipefish and sea horses where the male has a pouch into which the eggs are laid and subsequently hatch. Mating is an intimate affair. The two fish embrace for a while with their heads apparently over each other's shoulders, then the male becomes violently excited and demonstrative, shakes his head and body in a corkscrew fashion and with his snout caresses the female on the belly. The female responds to this and the sequence is repeated several times until, quite rapidly, copulation takes place with the female inserting her anal papilla into the male's pouch to deposit the eggs. It is believed that in some species the male actually nourishes the eggs.

Live birth

Sharks and rays generally give birth to living young through a process called ovoviviparity. In this form of reproduction, the eggs are retained within the female's oviduct and fertilised internally by the male. The males have organs called 'claspers' that in some species are highly evolved with erectile tissues, specialised sensory tissues, glands and special muscles to 'ejaculate' the sperm into the female's cavity, the cloaca, into which the claspers are inserted either singly or, in some species, both together. In several species the eggs receive nourishment from the female, while in some of the sharks one or two of the young cannibalise all the other eggs and juveniles in the oviduct before they are born. These sharks enter the world with a voracious appetite for which they are renowned.

Most of the rays living on the reef, including the giant manta ray, are also ovoviviparous and give birth to live young. Nurse sharks, wobbegongs and whale sharks, however, produce large, well-developed eggs encased in a horny capsule and deposit them among weeds or coral. These eggs are left to develop by themselves and may take a month or more to hatch.

Orphans with a plan

Except in extremely rare cases, reef fishes never know their parents. With only one known exception, the larvae of reef fishes are destined to drift in the plankton away from their spawning site at the mercy of the ocean currents. The ecological significance of this is still not clear and recent studies in the northern reef indicate that the fish larvae are not drifting in a completely passive manner – they appear to have some control over their destination.

It is now possible to count the microscopic daily growth rings in the ear ossicles (similar to the yearly growth rings on trees). Data from these studies show that the time that the larvae are swimming in

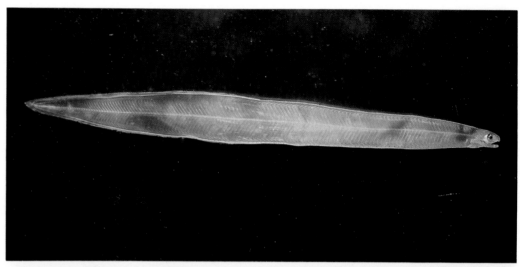

Eel larvae, *Leptocephalus*

Blue eel, *Rhinomuraena quaesita*

the open sea varies from as little as ten to 14 days for some species of sweetlips and sea bream; from three to four weeks for some anemone fish, damselfish and rabbitfish; to as much as two months for some grouper; three months for some triggerfish, surgeonfish and pufferfish; and even nine months for eel larvae.

Once a suitable habitat is located, the larvae settle and metamorphose (transform) very rapidly into the juvenile form. Settling occurs predominantly at night – presumably to minimise predation – but it is known that if a larva cannot successfully settle one evening it can re-enter the plankton and drift further to look for a more suitable location.

Coral reefs occur throughout the vast expanse of the tropical oceans and the same species of fishes are often found as far apart as the Seychelles in the Indian Ocean, on the Great Barrier Reef, and as far east as Tahiti in the South Pacific. The question of

△ *Very little is known of reproduction and breeding behaviour in coral reef eels, or whether they even undergo spawning migrations. However, the blue eel is known to be a hermaphrodite that starts life as a male, which indicates that it may live in small family groups with a close dependence on the reef which they do not leave.*

△△ *In the last century, reproduction in eels was considered a mystery. Adults of the common European freshwater eels would, each year, leave their streams, never to be seen again. Months later tiny eels would return. By following a trail of progressively younger eel larvae from the river mouths out to sea, scientists discovered their spawning location in the Sargasso Sea. The connection between the clear, leaf-shaped larvae and the adult eels was then confirmed.*

'The sea horse shakes his head and body in a corkscrew fashion and with his snout caresses the female's belly.'

◁ *The fabled sea horse, one of the strangest and most appealing of the reef's creatures, is also one of the most specialised. Sea horses have prehensile tails that hold them to seaweeds, sponges and corals, among which they live. They are not commonly seen on the Great Barrier Reef but are occasionally brought to the surface in prawn trawl nets. Sea horses feed on zooplankton, their mouths sucking in unsuspecting shrimps and copepods that drift within range, and with such force that the noise can be heard from some distance. The female sea horse lays her clutch of eggs in a special pouch on the male's abdomen and leaves him with all the responsibility.*

Ghost pipefish, *Solenostomus paradoxus*

Δ *In the rich evolutionary process that led to the present complex assemblage on a coral reef almost everything has been tried. The ghost pipefish are a small family related to the pipefish and sea horses that live in seaweed and sea grass beds. Unlike their relatives – where the males carry the eggs to incubate them – the female ghost pipefish holds the incubating eggs between two skin folds on the belly. The 'paradoxical' shape of the ghost pipefish is superb camouflage. A normal baby shrimp, or other juicy prey, would not expect a mouth at the end of that strange leafy thing. It has different colour forms to fit its background.*

Sea horse, *Hippocampus*

'Eat or be eaten is the rule for survival on the reef. Every kind of offensive and defensive weaponry has been developed to serve these ends.'

▷ *Scorpion fish play the waiting game. Many are predators with the ability to lie absolutely still for long periods, and may be festooned with flaps of skin of different colours to look like a weed-covered rock on the bottom of the reef. But when the strike comes it is startlingly fast. Before the strike there can be some delicate manoeuvring, and a little fish can be put in the right place by a gentle move of a fin that seems to be a seaweed frond. This scorpion fish is obvious against this sponge, but if it were against some coralline algae it would be undetectable.*

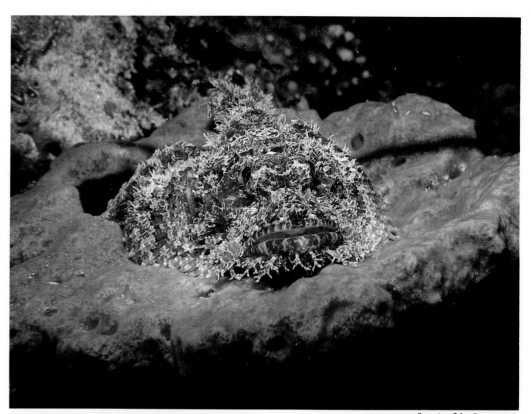

Scorpion fish, *Scorpaenopsis*

Stonefish, *Synanceia horrida*

△ *The stonefish is a close relative of the scorpion fish, and also feeds by hiding and waiting. But although many scorpion fish may have toxic mucus on their spines, the stonefish has developed a pair of poison glands to each of its 13 sturdy dorsal fin spines. It can be fatal to step on the camouflaged fish, for as the sharp spines penetrate the foot, the poison sacs are ruptured and the poison is driven up grooves on each side of the spine by the force of the foot pressing down on the rough outer skin. This would seem a very good protection against predators. Unless its enemy gulped it whole (which would result in appalling stomach pains or death), it would be likely to get away for the predator's mouth could be pierced when it took the first bite. Some islanders eat the stonefish and consider it delicious, calling it 'chicken of the sea'.*

◁ *Lizard fish do not seem to be willing to wait for their prey, but are active hunters, moving frequently between raised pieces of rock, from which they scan the surroundings for small fishes. When the lizard fish spots a prey, its raised head is immediately lowered, and the fish hugs the bottom, making some short stalking moves, or it may wait for the prey to approach. When it is close enough the lizard fish strikes, but only about one in ten strikes is successful, and on average only two or three fishes are taken every day. A missed fish would successfully reach shelter, and would be out feeding again within 30 minutes. Then it would seem to be left alone by the lizard fish – as though once a small fish was aware of the predator, it would not fear being caught. Small gobies that spot a lizard fish bob up and down letting the lizard fish know that it has been seen and are not attacked, presumably because once they knew the predator was there they would be able to leap away before the strike. Harassment by larger fishes, by damselfish pressing their fins into the face of the lizard fish and by labrids rushing at and biting the lizard fish, can be common. Life is clearly not easy for a small predator, but in very stormy weather, when small fishes are swept about the coral by heavy surges, lizard fish have been seen to feed repeatedly and successfully on juvenile fishes.*

Lizard fish, *Synodus variegatus*

Striped catfish, *Plotosus lineatus*

how these species maintain genetic continuity is one of the most fundamental but still unsolved puzzles of the coral reef.

One can imagine a larva, drifting in the ocean for three weeks, at say 20 nautical miles a day, in which time it could travel 644 kilometres – more than the distance separating most coral reef regions. But there is little food and no shelter in the open sea, although some larvae are known to shelter beneath debris floating on the surface. Evidence now shows that behind reefs and islands there exist complicated eddy currents; and that spawning is timed and located to maximise the retention of eggs and larvae in these eddies and return them to the parent reef, or perhaps another reef in the neighbourhood. Spawning also occurs during the months when winds become variable, and ocean currents reverse so that larvae lost downstream may be returned when the currents change direction.

It is possible that the larvae of most reef fishes that appear on a reef were probably spawned not too far away.

Caring parents
The grey and white puller, *Acanthochromis polyacanthus*, is the only coral reef fish actually known to nurse its young. The adults watch over the school of juveniles until they are old enough to fend for themselves and shepherd them into the protection of the coral as soon as danger threatens.

△ *The striped catfish schools so tightly when young that the Japanese call a school a 'catfish ball'. The dorsal and side (pectoral) fins have strong venomous spines, and a very tight school must present a formidable front to an intending predator. Sometimes a school may be many metres long and a metre or more thick, looking like some strange sea serpent.*

Predators and prey
Eat and be eaten is the pattern on the reef. A school of 50 young fishes will settle on a coral patch after their brief larval floating life. They swim slowly because of their small size, have no strong fin spines to act as a deterrent and are not yet used to the nooks and crannies of their chosen home that will later offer them protection from predators. They are very vulnerable and many will be eaten. A severe storm at this stage increases their losses drastically, for as they are swept about the coral in the surges, hungry predators such as lizard fish find them easy prey. The school is lucky if by the end of one year it has a few adults left to breed. But there is much variation on the reef, and those on the next coral head might do better. Losses on one reef may be made up by more successful survival and breeding on the next.

Life seems precarious, and species do become extinct both locally and sometimes totally, but the sheer numbers of species on the average reef mean

▽ *Small tasty prey fishes, like these young ones in a cave entrance, find some protection in a school because fast predators like trevally, Caranx species, do not find it easy to take a fish from the school by rushing into it. The school surges away from the attack, and the predator is apparently confused by not being able to follow an individual – and the rush usually fails. But if the predator can separate one individual from the school the game is over, for it follows relentlessly with its superior speed and finally catches the small fish. A cruder technique is used by the garfish, Tylosurus, which races with its fast, slim body straight into the school, mouth open, striking by chance more than by skill. One way or another there is constant feeding where there are large schools of small fishes, and they help to supply some of the energy that drives the reef system.*

Ransonnet's bullseyes, *Parapriacanthus ransonneti*

that most species survive to the next breeding cycle.

The larger fishes are safer and the giants on the reef, the huge mantas, sharks and rock cods, patrol majestically as if they had no predators at all; and this is probably true unless they are weakened.

The waiting game
Many predators patiently sit next to or on a coral waiting for a fish to come within reach. The stonefish with its wicked poisonous spines is one of these, and a fish coming over a semi-buried stonefish is watched carefully. At first the only movement the stonefish makes is with its eyes – fixed unwinkingly on the small fish and following its every movement. Then a slow roll of head to get the fish in its strike zone; a wait as the little fish swims closer; sometimes even a wily wiggle of the dorsal fin to manoeuvre the fish (still unable to recognise the camouflaged outline). Then the

▷ The trumpet fish is a creature of strange shape and bizarre behaviour. It is elongated with the head extended into a long trumpet-shaped snout, but with only a small flap-like mouth at the trumpet's end. It is a relative of the shrimp fish, pipefish and sea horses, Syngnathiformes, but is more fish-like, lacking the hard outer skeleton possessed by most members of this order of fishes. It seems comfortable lying in the water at any angle, and at night is commonly seen vertical among the sea whips, or against sea fans, not looking at all edible. In the day it can be found on many reefs. It will lie on another fish, usually a grazer like a parrotfish, but sometimes a predator like a rock cod. The trumpet fish (below right) uses a puffer fish as cover and will drift along with it until some small creature comes too close. The prey would not expect the large puffer to bother them as it is slow-moving and does not normally feed on fishes. The trumpet fish then streaks out and makes its strike, sucking in small fishes or crustaceans with the tube-like mouth. Occasionally it will choose quite a small fish as camouflage, and will overhang its 'protection' fore and aft, looking odder than usual.

Trumpet fish, *Aulostoma chinensis*

Trumpet fish, *Aulostoma chinensis*; puffer fish, *Arothron stellatus*

stonefish strikes. Its mouth simultaneously shoots up and sucks in the fish – so quickly that the prey has no time even to begin to flee. A scientist, timing the strike with photography, found it to be fifteen thousandths of a second. During the long wait crustaceans and molluscs will crawl over the stonefish with impunity.

The search

Other predators busily search through the coral all day, hunting with sharp eyes and often long probing snouts for small crustaceans, worms and molluscs crawling around the bases of the living coral and in the algal turfs. Sometimes an individual will develop a 'search pattern' for prey of one species, and only that species will be found in its stomach, while another predator of the same species feeding in the same area will have fed on a different prey.

It seems that feeding is faster and more effective when one kind of shape is looked for over and over again. The predator can then change to another when the first kind of prey becomes rare. Other predators will work over the sand flats, some by day and some by night, hunting for creeping molluscs, or a crab on its own nocturnal food search. Some, like the spangled emperor, will hunt in the lagoon in the hours about dawn and dusk.

The chase

The most exciting to watch are the predators that chase schooling fishes. Elongated long toms with their alligator jaws open will race through a school at high speed, perhaps hoping to strike a fish accidentally. The trevallies use a more common technique, and will try to separate one fish from the school. As they do this the school billows away from them – all the small fishes straining to keep together and the multiple images confusing the predator. Once a fish has been cut off from the school it will twist and turn frantically but it will almost certainly be caught by the pursuing trevally.

One of the smaller predators that chases its prey is a sand-dwelling lizard fish, *Synodus englemani*. This fish moves across the bottom about every four minutes throughout the day, and averages nearly two attacks on prey in an hour. Only about one attack in ten is successful, and the lizard fish has two to three successes a day, eating on average about a tenth of its body weight. This seems hard work, but there are occasions when schools of small fishes are about, and then the mode of feeding of the lizard fish changes. It becomes more active – and much more successful.

Quite often a fish predator is more subtle in its hunting. A large coral trout may play a game more like the waiting stonefish. It will move slowly over the coral among the brightly coloured small fishes, apparently lazing and not thinking of feeding, until the surrounding fishes are lulled into complacency. But when an unwary fish allows the trout to come too close, it will gently move to get the fish in its strike zone, and then pounce upon it with extraordinary speed.

The chase of the trumpet fish is a strange variation. An elongated fish, 300 to 500 millimetres long, its jaw bones are lengthened into a trumpet shape. It is a fish with bizarre habits, sleeping vertically in sea whips at night, and during the day it may swim close to the back of a larger fish like a parrotfish or a rock cod as though attached. As the larger fish moves slowly, hoping for a small fish, or perhaps just resting, the trumpet fish on its back is waiting to rush at anything close by. This could be the very fish the rock cod was preparing to strike at, in which case the trumpet fish is really a parasite. When swimming close to a grazer like a parrotfish the trumpet fish uses the large fish as a foil – the prey fish will not expect a fatal strike from behind a harmless parrot scraping the bottom. In doing this the trumpet is not a parasite but uses the larger fish for camouflage. It seems likely that the larger fish is being unwillingly used and gains nothing.

The hunted
Through the millions of years that fishes have lived on this planet, the struggle of the smaller fishes to avoid predation has been an important evolutionary development. The unsuccessful have become extinct, and the successful have developed speed, or manoeuvrability, or spines, or unpalatable flesh, or camouflage, or a combination of these to stay alive

to slip around and every hole to race into, to avoid hungry predators. If a fish is carefully taken to another coral head and released, its chances of survival as a newcomer without knowledge are extremely slim.

Food chains of the reef
On the land it has been said that 'all flesh is grass', and the basis of the food on the reef is also photosynthesis. Algae and some flowering plants in the form of sea grass found between reefs are the seas' equivalent of the grass on land. The algae grow very fast in the warm clear water of the reef. If a cage is placed over a piece of algal-covered rock in shallow water and protected from grazers, a thick fur of algae will develop in a few days – showing that almost daily grazing by fishes and shellfish is the rule. Most algal growth occurs on the reef, but there is also a constant drift of microscopic algae and

faster. The vacuum cleaner animals that pass the sand of the lagoon floor through their guts, such as the sea cucumbers, are taking organic debris – broken bits of algae, faeces of many different animals, dead planktonic animals and plants – but this is covered in the bacteria of decay, and the animals may derive much of their nutrition from the bacteria, rather than the organic debris.

Very few animals eat the corals because they have powerful stinging cells in the tentacles that make them highly unpalatable. But some fishes seem immune. Some butterfly fish will delicately nip the polyps of a coral, and in their stomachs a mush of polyps can be found, including, of course, the one-celled symbiotic algae, zooxanthellae. Some of the porcupine fish and filefish will bite off the twigs of branching coral, and parrotfish often make great scrapes on a living coral head. The parrots' normal feeding pattern is to scrape algae from coral rock.

Thorny ray, *Urogymnus africanus*

Wrasse, *Xyrichthys*

and breed. Some have sought protection through the stinging cells of others, as in the anemone fish and the many species that shelter under the large jellyfish in the open ocean. Others, being tasty to predators, have copied in fine detail the colouring of unpalatable species. Some find protection in schools and even copy each other in colouring, so that larger schools of more than one species are formed.

Fishes are surprisingly adaptable. They perform their daily rounds by instinct but are able to learn about different environments. Most coral reef fishes have good eyesight, and good colour vision, and are able to remember and avoid unpalatable food such as a brightly coloured nudibranch, after having eaten one. As in all vertebrates, and invertebrates, behaviour is a blend of the instinctive and the learned. A fish in a coral head knows its enemies, its hierarchical position in its own species group, and has developed a detailed knowledge of every coral

animal plankton that has grown in the waters surrounding the reef, or has been swept in from the Coral Sea.

The three primary sources of food are plankton; attached algae that make a thin cover over dead coral and the larger, more plant-like species; and also the microscopic algae found in the cells of corals, molluscs and many other animals. But the food chains that lead from these sources to the many fishes and other animals that are seen on the reef may be complex and strange. They are more webs than chains, for a predatory fish may eat many different species, each with varied sources for *its* food. Simple 'A eats B eats C' food chains are rare in such a complex community as a coral reef.

The fishes themselves may provide a source of food for the corals. When food is passed through a fish's gut it still has much nutritive value, and where fishes school over a coral area, the corals grow

△ *This small wrasse burrows in the sand for protection. It swims clear and hunts smaller animals over the sand surface, but is able to dive into the sand quickly if a predatory fish or a diver comes near.*

△◁ *The thorny ray is common on the reef. Rays have small ventral mouths with tightly packed rows of teeth, sometimes with small sharp cusps, but more often flattened to form a crushing pavement. Food is usually sought by digging in the sand, and molluscs and crustaceans are easily crushed with the strong tooth plates. Unlike most of the rays (stingrays, eagle rays) the thorny ray does not have a pungent spine on the tail, and is quite harmless.*

Coral scrapings may supplement the diet with animal flesh, or the parrots may be after symbiotic algae in the coral cells or the algal filaments that underlie the living corals, boring into their translucent calcium carbonate skeletons as deep as the light penetrates.

A typical food chain would start with an algal territory of a small grazing damselfish. The small fish might be careless, and be eaten by a Moses perch, *Lutjanus russelli*, of half a kilogram in weight. In time the Moses perch might be taken by a large turrum, *Caranx ignobilis*, weighing 15 kilograms. The chain has only three links so far, but already it has reached one of the larger reef fishes. Next, the turrum could be a little off colour, perhaps due to a parasitic or bacterial infection, and be caught and eaten in its turn by a hammerhead, a species commonly feeding at dusk. The hammerhead is nearly four metres long and weighs over 100 kilograms. The top of the chain is now reached and has four links. The hammerhead is likely to escape any larger shark predator, and when it dies will be nibbled at by smaller fishes, and be broken down by bacteria. A food chain is therefore seldom longer than four to six links, although some marine systems may have longer ones.

The energy of the original algae trapped from the sun was used up in keeping the bodies of the 'links' alive and was finally dissipated as heat. The essential minerals for life, however, that were absorbed by the algae and became part of each of the animal links passed back into the water with the bacterial breakdown, available for re-absorption by growing algae to complete the cycle.

Living together

Within the teeming diversity of plants and animals that cohabit on a coral reef there are myriad examples of animals and plants that have together evolved intricate relationships and interdependencies. Coral reefs owe their existence to the symbiotic relationship between the stony corals and the single-celled algae called zooxanthellae that live within the coral's tissues.

One of the most common and most interesting ways in which organisms coexist on the reef is the mutually benefiting relationship of symbiosis. Other relationships are also common in coral reef waters, such as parasitism, where one organism may harm or even kill the other, known as the host, and commensalism, where one organism lives on or inside another, to its own benefit but without apparent harm to the host.

The dancing cleaners
Within the fish world there are many good examples of symbiosis. In tropical waters there are countless minute organisms which live in – and on – fishes and there is a guild of other fishes, and shrimps, which have evolved as 'cleaners'.

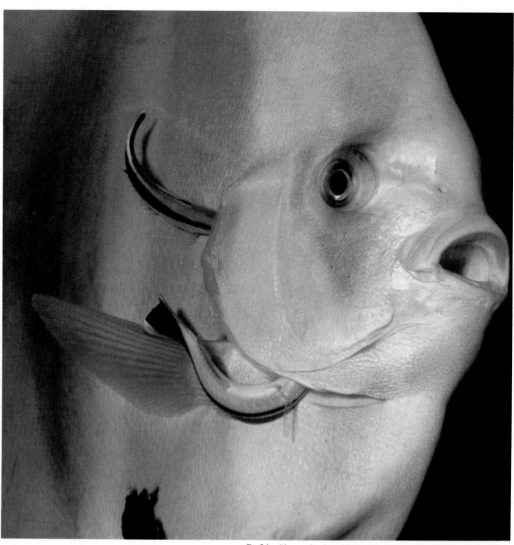

Batfish, *Platax orbicularis*; blue-streak cleaner wrasse, *Labroides dimidiatus*

△ *The cleaner wrasse has evolved a habit of taking parasites off the skin of other fishes. A large fish, such as this batfish, will seem quite relaxed as the cleaners pick over its skin and teeth and poke about in its gills.*

▷ *This blue-streak cleaner is emerging from the mouth of a grey sweetlips where it has been acting as 'dentist', removing parasites, growths and food scraps from its teeth and pharynx. Although cleaner fish forage for shrimps and worms among the coral, a good proportion of their diet consists of parasites of other fishes, dead scales and tissues, and fungus growths. They perform a valuable service and seem essential to the health of a coral reef fish community. All coral reefs have cleaners of some variety, and where the cleaners have been experimentally removed other resident fishes have either moved away or died, and those that remained became diseased.*

Cleaner wrasse, *Labroides dimidiatus*; sweetlips, *Gaterin pictus*

A small, elongated blue and white wrasse can often be seen dancing and gyrating in the water over some prominent landmark. Known as cleaners, these fish have specialised in removing growths and parasites from the skin, mouth and gill chambers of other fishes. The special swimming motion serves to identify them and to advertise their presence.

The area where they perform their trade is known as a cleaning station and fishes that live in the locality, ranging from the small gobies to large grouper and even giant manta rays, will visit this locality periodically to be serviced. The relationship between the cleaners and their 'hosts' is highly evolved as the host completely turns off any predatory instincts allowing the cleaner to swim unharmed into the mouth and gill chambers – a quick snap and it could be a tasty morsel. The cleaners are obviously performing a valuable service as fishes are known to travel considerable distances, perhaps a couple of kilometres, to attend these cleaning stations. Some experiments have indicated that the removal of the cleaners soon leads to a noticeable drop in the abundance and richness of the fish community of an area, and those fishes that remain are often badly infected with fungal growths, ulcers and frayed fins.

In the Caribbean Sea, the dominant cleaner is a small blue and white goby of the genus *Elacatinus* and, interestingly, aquarium fishes collected from Pacific reefs instantly recognise this Caribbean cleaner and solicit its services – cleaning symbiosis has obviously been around for a long time.

A number of coral reef shrimps have also formed a guild of cleaners and advertise their presence by waving their long white antennae from the entrance to their caves. Fishes seeking their service come and 'present' themselves and, as in their relationship with the cleaner fish, allow the shrimps to enter their mouth and gill chambers free of any risk of predation. The shrimp nimbly skips over the fish removing parasites and fungus from the scales, gills and around the teeth of the host.

Cheeky clowns

The clown fish on the Great Barrier Reef are happy little fellows that flaunt their presence with a gay swimming dance as they search for planktonic food in the water passing over the reef. But at the first hint of danger they dart rapidly for safety into an anemone from where they grin cheekily at a would-be predator suddenly confronted by a barrage of deadly stinging tentacles.

There is a group of 27 known species of such damselfish that live on Pacific coral reefs in association with poisonous anemones. These anemone fish belong to a sub-family of their own known as the Amphiprionidae and are usually orange or red in colour with white or blue stripes. They acquire immunity from the otherwise deadly stinging cells in the anemone's tentacles by slowly covering themselves with a layer of mucus from the

Shrimp, *Periclimenes*; cardinal fish, *Apogon*

Δ *The delicate behaviour of the shrimps seems out of character in the 'eat or be eaten' underwater world. But this shrimp is happily cleaning fungal growths from the head of the cardinal fish. These shrimps are very abundant around coral reefs and when not cleaning fishes they are often observed 'hanging about' at the entrance to small caves and holes in the reef.*

anemone. The anemone then assumes the fish is 'self' and the nematocysts, or stinging cells, do not fire automatically on contact. With the water movements continually jostling the anemone's tentacles against themselves, the anemone would soon run out of ammunition if it were always stinging itself.

Fishes isolated from their host anemone for a day or so lose their immunity. This must then be reacquired by a slow process starting with the briefest of contacts, usually tail first. The anemone fish then gradually increases the amount of contact until the fish can again bathe freely among the anemone's tentacles.

Although generally referred to as symbiosis, this relationship is one-sided in the fish's favour. While the anemone can exist without its clown fish associates, clown fish have never been observed living without an anemone.

Apart from the obvious protection from predation, the anemone also provides a protected 'nursery' for the clown fish to lay their eggs, and at least some clown fish are known to eat shed surface tissue, mucus and dead tissues from their host's tentacles. The main benefit to the anemone is that it may be cleaned by its partner. By way of reciprocity, it has been suggested that the clown fish bring food to their anemones, although this behaviour has only been observed in aquariums and not in natural conditions.

The only other reef fish known to have an intimate relationship with anemones is the three-spot damsel, *Dascyllus trimaculatus*, and small groups may occasionally be seen sharing an anemone with a family of clown fish. This behaviour is more common with juveniles and the adults range widely from the anemone's protection.

'Fishes have thousands of scales for "things" to get under and create annoyance, but no fingers with which to scratch.'

A protected haven

'At the first hint of danger the clowns dart for safety into an anemone from where they grin at a would-be predator suddenly confronted by a barrage of deadly stinging tentacles.'

▷ *This pair of anemone fish are the true 'clown fish' and have a very distinctive waving, dancing, swimming motion. The purpose of this advertising display is still unclear; however they seldom venture far from the protection of their anemone, into which they quickly retreat at the first sign of danger.*

Anemone fish, *Amphiprion chrysopterus*

△ *Anemone fish are among the most strikingly coloured and interesting of coral reef fishes. Although members of the large family of damselfish, Pomacentridae, the anemone fish have evolved the distinctive ability to nestle with impunity among the otherwise poisonous tentacles of sea anemones. This anemone fish is completely unharmed by the stinging cells of the* Radianthus *anemone in which it is nestling – but another fish would be stung to death.*

Clown anemone fish, *Amphiprion percula*

Clown anemone fish, *Amphiprion percula*

△ The distinctive colour pattern and swimming motion of the clown anemone fish make it one of the most noticeable of the fishes on the reef.

◁ This anemone fish is very common and is usually found with the large anemone, Radianthus rilleri. If the anemone is disturbed sufficiently, it will retract all its tentacles and close tightly; the fish will try to escape this potential threat, while keeping a wary eye open.

◁◁ If the anemone is further distressed it will close completely, thus excluding the anemone fish which show distinct signs of distress. Not good swimmers, they quickly fall prey to larger predators when removed from the anemone's protection. Anemone fish are never found without an anemone, but anemones are often found alone.

Anemone fish, *Amphiprion perideraion*

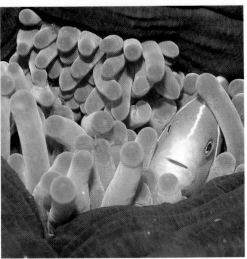

Anemone fish, *Amphiprion perideraion*

> ▷ This adult pair of gobies and an alpheid shrimp can be seen at the entrance of a large burrow among coral rubble. The gobies have good vision and are very alert. The shrimp, however, has poor vision but maintains continual contact with one or other of the fish by means of its long antennae. Should danger threaten, the fish indicates this to the shrimp and all three will rapidly disappear down the burrow. In return, the shrimp does most of the making and maintenance of the burrows using the heavy front claws or chelipeds as a bulldozer blade with which it can push quite large pebbles out of the way.

Gobies, *Cryptocentrus cinctus*; shrimp *A*…

Golden trevally, *Gnathanodon speciosus*

△ As these juvenile trevally grow, they become too large for the jellyfish in which they shelter and some take on the colour patterns of pilot fish and attach themselves to large sharks and manta rays. This juvenile golden trevally has left its manta ray host.

Freeloading pilots

A similar relationship exists between the young of jacks or trevally. These find shelter in the tentacles of jellyfish such as the blue-bottle or Portuguese man-of-war. Young pilot fish especially make a habit of this and apparently acquire immunity to the stinging cells in a similar way to the clown fish. As they grow, young pilot fish leave the protection of their coelenterate host and take up with a larger roving fish or shark. It was long thought by naturalists that these 'pilot' fish were leading their hosts around, and they were revered by early seafarers in the belief that they would lead their ships to safety. It is now known that they are freeloaders riding on the pressure wave of any large object moving through the water, and are also being given protection because few predators would snatch them from their position in front of the jaws of a large shark or grouper.

Another well-known relationship is that between the burrow-dwelling gobies and the alpheid shrimps. Soft, sandy lagoon floors are often littered with tiny burrows occupied by a pair of gobies and a pair of shrimps. The relationship appears to be mutually dependent as neither pair has been observed in isolation.

The gobies use the burrow for shelter during the day and as a sleeping place at night. The shrimps are apparently not gifted with good vision and maintain contact with the gobies with their long antennae. When danger threatens, the goby signals

Pope's damsel, *Pomacentrus popei*; fish

△ *Clingfish have modified pelvic fins on their bellies that act as suckers, similar to those of gobies which they superficially resemble but to which they are not even closely related. This clingfish uses its sucking disc to cling to the arms of a* Comanthus *feather star and is superbly camouflaged by its longitudinal stripes and background colour patterns which blend perfectly with that of its host. These fish are predators on other feather star symbionts – they eat worms and shrimps and occasionally some of the host's tissues.*

◁ *Fish doctors make fishes sick, not better! In fact they are parasites and often lead to the death of their hosts. Why they are called 'doctors' is unclear, unless perhaps it is because of their blood-sucking behaviour which was considered analogous to the supposed benefit from using leeches for blood-letting in medieval times. The larvae of these isopod crustaceans, of the family Cymothoidae, swim away and attach themselves to their host where they can insert their jaws under the scales and into the tissues to suck the host's body fluids. This Pope's damsel appears to be coping for now but will probably succumb as the parasite grows larger.*

the shrimp with a flick of its tail and both fish and shrimp disappear down the burrow.

Hidden pearls

Pearls are held to be symbols of purity and virtue but pearlfish, although translucent and milky in colour, do not fit that image. They live inside the guts of other animals. This relationship appears to be one of commensalism, that is, the commensal needs the host, but the host does not benefit, nor is it apparently harmed by its companion. The fish uses the host as a home during the day, from which it can venture to feed on detritus under cover of darkness. Pearlfish commonly live in the mantle cavity of large molluscs such as the black-lipped oyster and also inside the gut of holothurians or sea slugs.

Parasitic doctors

Fish doctors might be though of as being of benefit to fishes but such is not the case. Fish doctors are isopod crustaceans and are parasitic on fishes. They attach themselves to the fish's body on the fins, under the scales or in the gills and suck their host's blood, often leading to the death of the host.

Luminous devils

Diving off the front of an outer reef at night, without a torch, is the only way to find flashlight or devilfish which have recently been discovered on the Great Barrier Reef. These fish of the genus *Anomalops* have specially developed glands under the opercular or cheek bones, richly supplied with blood, in which they harbour a culture of luminous bacteria. These bacteria are fed on secretions from the fish and produce special enzymes which give off light. The fish thus have their own little indicator lamps, which they can control by rotating the opercular bone down, turning the light off when required. The lights are thought to be used for feeding, communication and avoiding predators.

Colour and camouflage

Coral reef fishes are perhaps so beautiful because they see and respond to the wonderful colour patterns around them. Tropical coral reef waters are exceptionally clear and it is possible to see for greater distances on a coral reef than in some land habitats such as tropical rainforest – and on the reef there is no foliage to get in the way! It is not surprising that vision plays an important role in the lives of coral reef fishes, and their eyesight is generally very well developed.

The eyes of all vertebrates, including humans, are similar in structure, and are remarkably like those of squids and octopuses, which also have good vision. Light passes through the cornea, its amount being controlled by the pupil. It is focused by the lens, and then falls on the light-sensitive tissues at the back of

Magnificent goby, *Nemateleotris magnifica*

△ *These two spectacular gobies, above and above right, are, unfortunately, seldom seen by divers. The magnificent goby and the decorated goby are very shy and live in relatively deep water off the front of reefs from 25 to over 70 metres depth. As a diver approaches they dart rapidly for cover into their burrows in the sand. After a few moments, however, they will reappear and if the diver remains still they will resume their feeding on the plankton in the water. As the natural light has lost a lot of the reds and yellows at these depths the fish do not appear nearly so colourful as they are when photographed with artificial light.*

the eye called the retina. Unlike land animals, the corneas of fishes have the same refractive index as water, so they have no need for goggles. And focusing is achieved not by changing the shape of the lens as land animals do, but by moving the lens in and out of the eye.

Fishes do not have necks and cannot turn their heads (except perhaps for the remarkable sea horses) and they live in a three-dimensional world where danger can threaten from any direction. Consequently, they have protruding eyes that are placed on the sides of the head. Each eye can see through about 180 degrees, with a blind area behind the fish and a portion of the visual field overlapping in front, giving better vision where it is most needed – for catching food, or avoiding obstacles.

Coral reef fishes not only have good eyesight but the majority have the ability to see colours as well. There are two sorts of cells in the retina, called rods

and cones. The rods are most sensitive to light and can detect images in low light intensities but do not discriminate between colours; the cones are selective to colours but need brighter illumination. Fishes active during the day generally have a higher proportion of cones in their retinas and have better vision in good light. Nocturnal fishes have more rods and can see better in dim light. The sharks and rays are exceptions as they have only rods and see in monochrome which may partly explain why they are not also brightly coloured like the bony fishes.

Species recognition

Many behaviourists, evolutionists and ecologists have attempted to explain why coral reef fishes are so colourful. Species recognition is clearly one of the most important reasons. With the thousands of species of fishes living on a coral reef, many of them quite closely related and having similar shapes and

Decorated goby, *Nemateleotris decora*

places of living, there have been strong selection pressures to enable the different species to tell each other apart. Evolution is very hard on individuals that waste their reproductive effort on other species. Many reef fishes also have home ranges, or territories which they defend, and it would be a waste of energy to terrorise a fish that was not related and was therefore not a threat.

It is also obvious that a good many species, especially those that live in family groups or harems, can recognise each other as individuals – each one has a unique colour pattern, much like humans have unique features and fingerprints. Males and females are often differently coloured, so that the sexes can be easily identified and the appropriate behaviour pursued. And the colouring of juveniles is often quite different from adults because they are of no ecological threat and need not be confused with other adults competing for the same resources. Different species have basic colour patterns which are genetically controlled, but there is also some ability to change this pattern during the night or day, during breeding, or to blend in with the animal's surroundings.

Changing colour patterns

The colour of fishes is produced by the colour cells or chromatophores in the skin: some cells have black or brown melanin pigments; other cells have red, orange or yellow pigments; and a third type have opaque white granules of guanine. The colour of each cell is under both nervous and hormonal control. Another type of cell, an iridocyte, is responsible for the iridescent colours of fishes,

◁ *The bicolour dottyback is a common fish found typically on vertical reef faces and in caves. It lives in small family groups although there is no discernible difference in colour pattern between the sexes. Underwater, the brilliant purple appears as a royal blue, as the red wavelengths have been filtered out of the water. The most striking aspect about this shy and rather timid fish is that there is a small bass which lives in the Caribbean with an identical colour pattern – purple front half, yellow rear half and clear fins. And the fishes are not even closely related!*

Bicolour dottyback, *Pseudochromis paccagnellae*

'Coral reef fishes with their well-developed underwater vision can see the full beauty of their extraordinary habitat.'

▽ The saddled butterfly fish is more commonly found in lagoons and its longer snout enables it to pick small shrimps and invertebrates from within the crevices of corals. There have been many theories about why coral reef fishes are so colourful. They need not be all exclusive, and one of the more likely reasons is that the individuals within a species can easily recognise their own kind from among the bewildering diversity of similarly shaped fishes.

Saddled butterfly fish, *Chaetodon ephippium*

Ornate butterfly fish, *Chaetodon ornatissimus*

especially the bright blues and greens. Some fishes have the ability to change not only the shade or intensity of their colours, but also the pattern; such changes take place in a matter of minutes.

One of the simplest functions of colour patterns is that of counter-shading in fishes inhabiting the open sea such as sharks, silversides and trevally. The top half of the fish is coloured dark blue, green or grey, while the underside is pale or white. Seen from above the fish is hard to distinguish from the background of water, and seen from below the fish blends in with the lighter water surface and with the sky above.

Disruptive colour patterns are found among many reef fishes. The humbug, *Dascyllus aruanus*, lives in small groups among the branches of *Acropora* corals and when viewed from a distance blends imperceptibly with the background of the coral and the reef behind.

Bright colours for breeding

Within the really diverse groups such as the butterfly fish, angelfish, damselfish and gobies, each species has a distinctive colour pattern. Species recognition is most important during the breeding period, and colours become brighter and fins are erected to display even more dazzling colours and sometimes false eyes.

False eyes may be important in breeding displays and territorial encounters. Eyes are important signalling devices and have been symbolised in courtship in other animals, a well-known example being the peacock which has dozens of 'eyes' on the tail feathers.

A distinctive colour pattern seems necessary for recognition by a friend or a potential mate. Conversely, being conspicuous if you are tasty carries a strong disadvantage. No wonder some fishes change colour.

△ The ornate butterfly fish frequents outer reef slopes and surge channels and is often encountered in small groups. Although omnivorous, the ornate butterfly fish tend to concentrate on filamentous algae for food, for which their bristle teeth (from which their scientific name is derived, chaeto = bristle and dontum = teeth) are ideally suited.

△ ▷ Butterfly and angelfish hold a special appeal for many divers on coral reefs; this blue-girdled angelfish must be one of the most spectacular of coral reef fishes. They are large fish, growing to a length of 250 millimetres, and are found singly or in pairs only in areas of rich coral growth and in depths from three to 30 metres.

Blue-girdled angelfish, *Pomacanthus navarchus*

Imperial angelfish, *Pomacanthus imperator*

Imperial angelfish, *Pomacanthus imperator*

◁ *Five angelfish species are known in which the juveniles are similarly coloured – having quite distinctive blue bodies and a series of white concentric circles or wavy lines. The adult colour patterns, however, are not only different from the juveniles (far left) but also distinctly vary between the adults of the five species. Quite surprisingly, two of these species are of a different genus to the other three. There can be two explanations for this – either the taxonomy is incorrect and they all share a common ancestor and are closely related, or they have evolved to look alike and have found that there is an advantage in such a colour pattern for the juveniles, though what this could be is unclear.*

Lunar-tailed cod, *Variola louti*

Giamard's wrasse, *Coris giamard*

Lunar-tailed cod, *Variola louti*

Giamard's wrasse, *Coris giamard*

◬ The lunar-tailed cod grows to a length of 800 millimetres; as a juvenile , above, up to about 100 millimetres in length, it has a very distinctive white belly and median stripe over the head.

▷◬ Colour patterns of reef fishes change dramatically with growth. These two photographs of Giamard's wrasse show the bright red and white juvenile, top, which is surprisingly easy to see as it flits among the coral rubble in lagoon back-reef habitats. As the fish grows, the red colour becomes dull, then transforms into a bluish-green background until finally the adult colour pattern with the brilliant blue spots and yellow tail evolves when the fish has reached a length of about 150 millimetres.

▷ The predatory, deep water hawkfish is generally found on outer reef slopes at depths of 40 metres or more in association with soft corals with which its colour pattern blends.

Deep water hawkfish, *Oxycirrhites typus*

Spangled emperor, *Lethrinus nebulosus*

Chameleons of the reef

The chameleon is held as the epitome of adaptive colour change but its ability to change colour is far surpassed by fishes such as soles and flounders (although they too are surpassed by the squids, cuttlefish and octopus). Soles can not only alter the colour and shade of their skins to match the background, but can control the actual pattern of colours on their skins. Soles settling on uniform sandy bottoms will have a fine, uniform, speckled appearance; but should they swim off and settle among some rubble, they quickly assume a blotchy skin, with the size of the blotches matching the size of the coral rubble in which they settle. As the eyes of the sole are on the top side of the body, the fish had to get an impression of the bottom before it settled, then control the myriad colour cells on its back to make the change – a remarkable achievement. Colours are changed not only to match backgrounds, but an angry, disturbed or frightened fish will change colour pattern, perhaps to show aggression to a competitor, or perhaps to warn others of a perceived danger. A variegated emperor, uniformly coloured as it feeds below, will change to a strong mottled pattern when hauled on deck at the end of an angler's line. The red bass has two distinct silver-white spots on each side, but can turn these on and off seemingly at will. Their use may be a signal of some sort – they must be of some value – but their use by the fish is unknown.

Spangled emperor, *Lethrinus nebulosus*

'Many fishes use colour as camouflage; pigment cells called chromatophores allow them to change their skin colour to match the background.'

Spangled emperor, *Lethrinus nebulosus*

Lemon-peel angelfish, *Centropyge flavissimus*

Lemon-peel angelfish, *Centropyge flavissimus*

Orange epaulette surgeonfish, *Acanthurus olivaceus*

△ False eyes are common forms of defence in juvenile fishes (and in butterflies) but are generally located near the tail end of the animal. The reason for this is supposed to be to direct a predator's attack to the fish's rear end where it 'thinks' the head is, thus allowing the fish to escape, often with no more than a few torn tail filaments. But the juvenile lemon-peel angelfish, top, has the false eye in the middle of its body and there is no satisfactory explanation for this paradox.

▷ The orange epaulette surgeonfish has a bright yellow juvenile, above right, that is presumed to be a mimic of some of the yellow angelfish that have tougher skin than surgeonfish and a strong spine on the cheek to deter would-be predators.

Orange epaulette surgeonfish, *Acanthurus olivaceus*

Black and white sea perch, *Macolor niger*

△ *Sea perch, snappers and bass do not often noticeably change colour as they grow but there are two exceptions. One is the red emperor that is generally reddish pink all over but bright red and white as a juvenile, when it is known as the government bream. The other is the black and white sea perch. The juvenile is attractively dressed in a black and white suit which is replaced in the adult, left, by a speckled grey and white pattern, becoming almost sooty grey depending on the fish's mood.*

Black and white sea perch, *Macolor niger*

Changing identity

'Each species of fish has a colour pattern, as unique to that creature as our faces and fingerprints are to us.'

Weedy scorpion fish, *Rhinopias frondosa*

△ *Although distantly related to the stonefish, this weedy scorpion fish, as its scientific name implies, relies on its imitation fronds as camouflage for protection. It is also quite likely that this camouflage helps it to sneak up on unsuspecting prey which it then engulfs with a rapid suction caused by quickly opening its mouth. The jaws and sharp pointy teeth are well suited to its carnivorous ways. The related lionfish also feeds in this manner. The two white spots on the cheeks of the weedy scorpion fish look like eyes when the fish is seen head-on; the real eyes are the little black specks above these white spots.*

Green leatherjacket

◁ *Camouflage is essential for the survival of many fishes – especially the young that are less able than adults to defend themselves or escape predators. Smaller individuals will always have more potential predators than larger ones. Many have therefore evolved both colour patterns and special shapes to blend with their surroundings. The juvenile filefish or leatherjacket is green with a circular shape that makes it appear very similar to a blade of seaweed – which can be seen below and to the left of the fish. The skin is also covered with fine projections of a grey colour which copy the filamentous algae and sediment attached to the seaweeds.*

▷ *Many fishes mimic weeds, leaves and other fishes, but few actually mimic the corals in which they live. The exception is the coral blenny that lives among* Pocillopora *corals and feeds on filamentous algae.*

Peacock sole, *Pardachirus pavoninus*

◁ *The peacock sole, like most of the flat fishes of the sole family, is a master of camouflage, and can change its colour to match its surroundings, and its pattern to match the type of sea bed on which it likes to settle. The camouflage is enhanced by the practice of fluffing up some of the sand when it comes to rest, as the sand then drifts back over the fish making it almost invisible. These little fish have still another trick. At the base of the spines of the dorsal fin are numerous glands which secrete a milky toxin which is ejected if they are eaten. Experiments with sharks in the Red Sea have shown that this secretion is extremely distasteful to the sharks which spit out the fish before any harm has come to it. Scientists are now investigating the possibility of using this as a natural shark repellent for human use.*

Anglerfish, *Antennarius*

△ *This anglerfish lives among sponges. Its pectoral fins are modified into little walking legs and its first dorsal fin spine is elongated with a tassel on its end looking like a worm. This fishing rod and lure is dangled in front of the mouth to entice unsuspecting fishes to come to examine the bait – and suddenly find themselves inside its mouth.*

Coral blenny, *Exallias brevis*

The ultimate mimics

'Fishes may imitate weeds, stony algae, coral or each other to survive. Juveniles of two species may be look-alikes and school together, and their adults be different and live apart.'

'Many fishes camouflage themselves by appearing similar to some inanimate or unpalatable object.'

▷ *Apart from looking like a piece of dead weed or a leaf, the cockatoo waspfish rolls its body over from side to side as if being passively washed by the surge. Many insects practise this form of deception but it is not common in coral reef fishes. There was no wave action when these three photographs were taken.*

Cockatoo waspfish, *Ambliapistus cristigalli*

Deceptive tassels and twigs

Where fishes are constantly threatened by predators, many species camouflage themselves by appearing similar to some inanimate or unpalatable object. This practice is known as deceptive resemblance, and often involves the evolution of strange shapes, tassels and projections to assist in the illusion. It is also much more common in juvenile fishes than in adults, as juveniles are in greater need of protection from predators.

Dead leaves and twigs are common models for fishes. Young garfish, *Hemiramphus*, and young barracuda may copy twigs and bits of stick, and even swim in jerks as if they were being washed by wavelets at the surface. The young of batfish, *Platax*, copy dead mangrove leaves and float at the surface bent up like a leaf. The blenny, *Exallias brevis*, copies a lump of coral, while one of the anglerfish attempts to look like a sponge and a juvenile leatherjacket imitates fronds of algae.

Another deceptive trick practised by many fishes (and which is commonly practised also by land animals) is the presence of false eyes, generally on the rear-end of the body. These false eyes seem to serve to direct the attack of a predator to the tail end of a fish, in the belief that they are aiming at the head. The impression is further enhanced in many cases by having the real eyes camouflaged by dark patches or bands as in the butterfly fish, *Chaetodon melannotus*. The fish then finds it easier to escape and at most loses a few tail filaments.

Cockatoo waspfish, *Ambliapistus cristigalli*

The mimic and the model

True mimicry is when one edible species copies another animal that enjoys some degree of immunity from predation because it is either poisonous, distasteful or protected in some way from its predators. This is known as Batesian mimicry. Mullerian mimicry is where two or more species that are both toxic evolve looking similar to

Cockatoo waspfish, *Ambliapistus cristigalli*

Scorpion fish, *Scorpaenopsis*

each other. Batesian mimicry is the more common and not only does the mimic resemble the model, it may also behave and swim in a similar fashion.

Two 'classic' examples of Batesian mimicry are found on coral reefs. One involves the poisonous pufferfish or striped toby, *Canthigaster valentini*, and its mimic, a small leatherjacket, *Paraluteres prionurus*. This mimicry relies on predators learning that the model is not edible and therefore leaving it alone. The mimic must be rare relative to the model otherwise predators would get confused and neither species would benefit – although the model would always have a greater survival rate than the mimic. The mimic therefore controls its population numbers, though how this is achieved is not known. The similarity between the two species is so close that in many museum collections throughout the world both species can be found in the same bottle with the same label – even the experts are fooled!

Barber and butcher

The cleaner fish, *Labroides dimidiatus*, although edible, is virtually immune from predation because of its help to other fishes. But it is also hampered in its activities by an impostor: one of the blennies, the false cleaner, *Aspidontus taeniatus*, which not only looks like the true cleaner but swims in the same dancing manner and even uses its pectoral fins for propulsion like the cleaner rather than its tail, like most blennies. The true cleaner has a small mouth at the tip of its snout and eats small crustaceans and parasites from the skin, teeth, mouth and gills of other fishes. The false cleaner has an underslung mouth with long canine teeth and feeds on the skin and scales of other fishes that it approaches by pretending to be a cleaner. It bites flesh, fin edges and scales, chiefly from naive young fishes. After being bitten many times, older fishes learn the differences between barber and brutal butcher.☐

△ *Scorpion fish are often mistaken for related stonefish. They look quite similar and are well armed with spines although none of them is venomous. This scorpion fish, like most, hunts by stealth and lies among the corals, perfectly camouflaged, waiting for some unsuspecting prey to pass close enough to grab. This confusion with stonefish is unfortunate because many visitors to the reef see these fish and, thinking they are the deadly stonefish, get the impression that the reef is full of dangerous animals. Stonefish, however, are not usually found in coral habitats where the water is clear and coral growths are luxuriant. Their preferred habitats are further inshore where sediment and weed predominate.*

Fairy basslet, *Anthias*

△ *In this example of mimicry between a fairy basslet and a hawkfish, right, the fairy basslet is not poisonous or toxic but has some degree of protection from predation because of its schooling behaviour. The hawkfish joins in with these schools hovering off the front of reefs and has adapted its feeding to be like that of the fairy basslets, eating plankton rather than feeding on invertebrates from the bottom of the sea like most other hawkfish.*

A clever copy

'In many museum collections throughout the world a fish and its mimic can be found in the same bottle with the same label – even the experts are fooled!'

Hawkfish, *Cyprinocirrhites polyactis*

Striped toby, *Canthigaster valentini*

Pearl-scaled angelfish, *Centropyge vroliki*

Surgeonfish, *Acanthurus*

Leatherjacket, *Paraluteres prionurus*

△ There are several examples of juvenile surgeonfish mimicking angelfish. The pearl-scaled angelfish, top, is the model for the juvenile surgeonfish of an unknown species.

◁ Toadfish and pufferfish, belonging to the family Tetraodontidae, are among the most poisonous of all marine creatures. They possess a powerful nerve poison called tetraodotoxin that is toxic to other fish predators and may produce a rapid and violent death in humans. The little striped toby, above left, is one of the more common puffers to be found around coral reefs, and is almost indistinguishable from its leatherjacket mimic. The similarity in colour patterns is perhaps the best example of mimicry in the fish world. The leatherjacket is not in the least toxic. The only successful way to tell them apart is by the shape of the soft dorsal fin – the striped toby has a short stumpy dorsal fin placed well down on the back, while the leatherjacket has a long transparent dorsal fin along most of its back.

Marine reptiles: creatures of habit

Reef turtles

There are few more memorable events in nature than the laborious egg-laying ritual of the sea turtles that nest in great numbers on islands of the reef.

During the peak breeding season, from October to February (and less frequently at other times of year), the female turtles come ashore to lay their eggs while the males cruise offshore in the hope of mating with the females in transit. The patterns of egg-laying behaviour vary in subtle ways between the six species that breed in reef waters. Three of these – the green turtle, *Chelonia mydas*, the loggerhead, *Caretta caretta*, and the hawksbill, *Eretmochelys imbricata* – nest mainly on coral cays. The flatback turtle, *Chelonia depressa*, nests principally on several continental islands and

sometimes, like the green turtle and loggerhead turtle, on the mainland. The leatherback or luth, *Dermochelys coriacea*, seldom nests in Australia, although it sometimes passes along the reef in its southward migration. The Pacific ridley, *Lepidochelys olivacea*, is a rare visitor to reef waters.

All six, however, have much in common, especially the lumbering emergence of the female from the sea and its exploration of the beach above high-water mark. There the turtle may make several false starts at nest building, leaving behind a series of large depressions in the sand. When it has settled on a suitable site the turtle hollows out a depression in the sand by gradually pivoting its body while using its flippers, mainly the front ones, to throw sand aside in a seemingly haphazard way. Eventually, the

whole body lies within this large hollow. With cupped hind flippers the turtle then carefully scoops out a hole about 200 millimetres in diameter and 400 millimetres deep, in which is laid – varying with the species – from about 50 to 150 round, soft-shelled eggs that closely resemble ping-pong balls. The female turtle may deposit three to five such clutches in any one season. When each egg is laid it has a shallow depression in one side that rounds out in a few days as quite a strong pressure develops in the egg. After egg-laying the turtle fills in the nest and, moving forwards, throws sand about with its front flippers to obscure the site.

On many islands this process is undertaken by dozens or even hundreds of turtles in a single night. On uninhabited islands, however, the numbers may

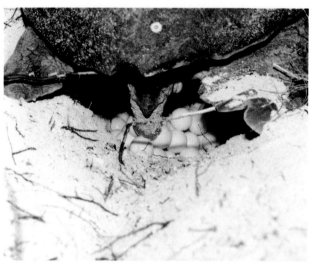

Turtle egg chamber

△ *The back of an egg chamber has been dug away to reveal the eggs being laid. The number of eggs in a single clutch may range from 50 to 150, the higher numbers usually being laid by larger, older females nesting for the first time in a season. The eggs in a single clutch are not laid continuously, but in small groups over a period of up to about half an hour.*

▷ *On the way from their nest to the sea these newly hatched green turtles run the risk of being eaten by predatory ghost crabs. The distinctive colour pattern – black above and white below – will soon change to the beautiful variegated pattern characteristic of the adult green turtle, while the shell, which is soft and leathery at hatching, will quickly harden.*

Green turtle, *Chelonia mydas*

Loggerhead turtle, *Caretta caretta*

Female turtle track

△ *The track of a female turtle is distinctive. Emergent and return tracks can be identified by the position of the sand that piles up behind the flippers, and by the central tail track that tends to be continuous on the return (downhill) run to the water but appears as a series of finger-like depressions on the emergent track where the tail is pushed into the sand.*

△ ◁ *A female loggerhead turtle makes a nesting hollow. The front flippers have been used to excavate the hollow by throwing sand backwards in wide arcs, while the turtle turns its body and moves forward to increase the size of the pit. When this is done the turtle uses its hind flippers to excavate a smaller hole for the eggs.*

be much greater: more than 10 000 female turtles have been recorded emerging to nest in a single night on Raine Island in a good season. The numbers may be greater than an island's capacity to hold them, and the only way the turtles can find a nest site is to dig up an existing nest. Equally large numbers of turtles may nest nearly every night for weeks at a time.

Researchers differ in their estimates of how long it takes before a female turtle is sexually mature and lays her first clutch of eggs. For the green turtle, estimates range from ten to more than 40 years.

Survival of the hatchlings

After they have been laid the eggs develop over the next six or seven weeks until the fully formed babies almost completely fill the eggs. At this stage their shells are soft and their bodies are folded in the middle, so that they are rolled up rather like an armadillo. The eggs in the nest tend to hatch at about the same time, except those that are infertile or fail to develop. When hatching occurs during the day, the young usually remain within the nest until dark. They then scramble up through the sand and set off for the sea. Their sense of direction can be upset by distractions such as lights from buildings or beacons, but their ability to home in on the sea, even when it lies behind sand ridges or can't be heard, is usually unfailing and has for a long time confounded biologists.

On their way to the water's edge the baby turtles run the gauntlet of predatory crabs. If, by some error of judgement, the turtles emerge during the day, then seagulls and other birds swoop on many before they reach the water. Hatchling mortality is greatest on mainland beaches where other predators, especially foxes, pigs and goannas, abound. Even when they reach the safety of the sea, few baby turtles will ever reach maturity.

Incubation and sex

Recent research indicates that the incubation temperature affects the sex of turtles. Previously, the sex of each embryo was thought to be genetically predetermined, until it was found that clutches of eggs incubated at different temperatures could produce either all males or all females. Further experimental work has shown that nests incubated at an average temperature of about 30° Centigrade produce approximately equal numbers of males and females. As the incubation temperature drops towards 26° Centigrade, males predominate, while above 30° Centigrade females begin to outnumber males. Within this temperature range various proportions of males and females are produced.

Slow and steady travellers

Over the past 20 years thousands of hatchlings and adults on the Great Barrier Reef have been tagged. This has provided much information on the distances turtles travel – sometimes over 1000 kilometres in a single year. But because researchers have ready access to turtles at only two stages of their life cycle – when they hatch and when adult females return to island beaches to lay their eggs – knowledge of their life histories is fragmentary. Little is known about what turtles do between hatching and maturity. And because male turtles do not leave the sea, most of our information about turtles is based on females.

All of the available evidence suggests that turtles generally return to breed on the islands where they were born. Turtle canneries that operated in Queensland earlier this century made inroads into regional breeding populations of the green turtle. More recent attempts to 'farm' turtles in

Green turtle, *Chelonia mydas*

Torres Strait, while politically popular, have been an ecological failure. Today, turtles can be taken for food only by Aborigines and Torres Strait islanders, and are otherwise protected by law from man.

Vegetarians and carnivores
Of the six species of sea turtles found in Great Barrier Reef waters, the green turtle of turtle soup fame, and the less common loggerhead, are found throughout the world's tropical seas. The green turtle is largely vegetarian as an adult, feeding on a variety of marine plants, while the more heavily built loggerhead is carnivorous, feeding mainly on molluscs and fishes.

The only sea turtle confined to the Australian region is the flatback. Its shell is more flattened than in other species, usually with the edges turned upwards in adults. It, too, is carnivorous with crustaceans favoured as food.

Although very common throughout the reef, and the smallest of our marine turtles, the hawksbill breeds mostly on only a few northern islands. Also a carnivore, its shell was once highly sought after to be polished and made into combs and jewellery. As its name implies, the hawksbill turtle has a projecting, parrot-like upper jaw.

While more commonly encountered elsewhere in Australia, two other turtles are occasionally seen in Great Barrier Reef waters. These are the Pacific ridley, which superficially resembles the flatback, but with a higher shell, and the giant leatherback or luth. The luth reaches nearly two metres in length and may weigh as much as a tonne. Whereas other sea turtles have a continuous bony carapace with a horny covering, the shell of the luth consists of numerous small polygonal bony plates imbedded in a leathery skin. Despite its enormous size it feeds mainly on jellyfish and salps.

△ *An adult green turtle swims over a reef, where it forages for sea grasses and algae. Although green turtles surface about every ten to thirty minutes for air, they can stay submerged for many hours at a time if necessary and will often rest underwater in crevices or below overhanging coral shelves.*

Crocodiles and sea snakes
While turtles are by far the most common marine reptiles encountered on the Great Barrier Reef, two other reptilian groups – crocodiles and sea snakes – may sometimes be seen. The saltwater crocodile, *Crocodylus porosus*, does venture out to sea and may arrive at a Great Barrier Reef island, but this happens so rarely that visitors to the reef need not feel at risk. Sea snakes are much more likely to be seen by people snorkelling or scuba diving.

Sea snakes are by nature shy and inoffensive in the water but have acquired a fearsome reputation from their aggressive behaviour when they have been dragged from the water in a net or on a fishing line. One sea snake in particular – the olive sea snake, *Aipysurus laevis* – seems to have an innate curiosity that often brings it into contact with a diver. Unlike other sea snakes, which will usually ignore or move away from an approaching diver, the olive sea snake will sometimes head straight for a diver, twining itself about limbs, body or speargun. This can be a terrifying experience; the snake's venom is lethal and in attempting to dislodge the snake a diver runs the risk of making it bite. Fortunately, the fangs of the olive sea snake, like those of most sea snakes, are quite short and only the largest specimens can bite through a wet suit.

Sea snakes have been found to possess some of the most potent animal toxins known, although there is much variation between species. One snake that is common in Great Barrier Reef waters, the turtle-headed sea snake, *Emydocephalus annulatus*, has evolved the habit of feeding only on fish eggs and in the process has virtually lost its fangs, teeth and venom glands. Some other sea snakes feed exclusively on burrowing eels and have evolved a body that allows them to reach deep inside burrows for their prey; the head and front third of their bodies are thin and eel-like, whereas the hind part of the body is much deeper.

Most sea snakes, however, feed on a variety of fishes – some even eat poisonous fishes. About 12 of the 30 species of sea snake found in Australian waters are found on the Great Barrier Reef. All share a number of features that are wonderful adaptations to life in the sea. They have paddle-shaped tails to help propel them through the water and valved nostrils that seal their air passages when they are submerged. Sea snakes are air-breathing reptiles and must come to the surface to breathe. Most replenish their air supply about every 20 to 30 minutes, but if necessary can stay submerged for up to an hour or more.

The potent neurotoxic venoms possessed by many sea snakes have probably evolved in response to the special conditions of life in the sea. Land snakes can use their outstanding olfactory powers to follow the trail of an animal which, having been bitten, moves some distance before dying. But unless a fish bitten by a sea snake dies almost instantly, it may escape into a coral crevice, or be eaten by another animal. In the meantime, the moving water prevents the snake from picking up the victim's scent.

Externally, female sea snakes are usually indistinguishable from males. In most species, however, the females have shorter tails, and in those species with rough or spiny scales the spines are much better developed in the males.

Most sea snakes in Australian waters belong to a group in which between two and ten live young are produced at sea. Most are helpless on land, with only a few species coming ashore, and then only to bask on mud flats or among mangroves. Occasionally, however, one may come across a sea krait, *Laticauda*. The sea kraits are found on many Pacific islands, as well as in New Guinea and countries of Southeast Asia. They are not livebearing, but produce eggs; they are usually brilliantly marked with alternate black and pale blue bands, and move about easily on land where they also lay their eggs.

Sea snakes are common in some areas but rarely seen in others, although the reasons for their patchy distribution are not fully understood. There have been a number of unconfirmed reports throughout the tropical Indo-Pacific region of large groups of sea snakes forming floating islands of thousands of intertwined individuals.□

Turtle-headed sea snake, *Emydocephalus annulatus*

△ A brilliantly banded specimen of the turtle-headed sea snake, a harmless species that feeds only on the eggs of burrowing blennies and gobies. Most species have far less colour, usually being black or dark brown with only a few pale spots or blotches. Like all of the true sea snakes, it bears live young in the sea.

◁ The olive sea snake is one of the most common sea snakes encountered in clear, shallow reef waters, where it is often attracted to divers, much to their consternation! It is highly venomous, its bite quickly immobilising the fish on which it feeds. However, it is not aggressive, and it will rarely bite a swimmer or diver unless molested.

Olive sea snake, *Aipysurus laevis*

Humpback whale, *Megaptera novaeangliae*

Marine mammals: gargantuan yet graceful

Whales and dolphins

No one can fail to be awed by the gargantuan might of a whale or captivated by the agile grace of a dolphin. Yet the whales and dolphins of the Great Barrier Reef are a paradox. Although this group includes the largest and most popular animals that occur in reef waters, very little is known about them. It is also ironic that this knowledge has come mostly from the study of the sometimes putrid carcasses of animals that have been stranded on beaches, have been accidentally drowned after becoming tangled in nets, or have been killed by man for oil, meat and other products.

Whales and dolphins are warm-blooded and belong to the order Cetacea which is divided into two distinct subgroups: Mysticeti, commonly known as baleen or whalebone whales, and Odontoceti, the toothed whales. The baleen or whalebone whales strain their small prey from the water by means of horny 'whalebone' plates called 'baleen' which fringe the upper jaw. In contrast, toothed whales are active predators that catch fishes, squid and other prey and swallow them whole.

Ancestral whales evolved from land-dwelling mammals that are thought to have entered shallow seas to take advantage of rich fish stocks. Deposited in river sediments about 53 million years ago, the skull of *Pakicetus*, the oldest whale yet discovered, has teeth that are not only similar to those of primitive whales, but also resemble those of mesonychid Condylarthra, strange, hooved, wolf-like terrestrial mammals that are now extinct. The skull of *Pakicetus* indicates that it was not fully aquatic because its earbones have features of both terrestrial mammals and modern whales, whose hearing systems have been modified through evolution to pick up sounds travelling through water.

Today's whales and dolphins are highly adapted to spend their entire lives in the water. Typical mammalian features that were not useful or essential in their aquatic environment – such as a lot of hair, a fully mobile neck, most of the pelvic girdle and the hind limbs – have disappeared. Whales and dolphins have a streamlined fish-like shape and move rapidly through the water propelled by the vertical strokes of their powerful tail flukes; their forelimbs have been modified as paddle-shaped flippers. Many species have a dorsal fin that is important for both control of movement through the water and temperature regulation, especially in the smaller species. Because whales and dolphins are warm-blooded they must maintain their core body temperature within narrow limits. They must also come to the surface to breathe, and in the process of evolution their nostrils have moved to a position high on top of the head to form a single or paired blowhole.

Probably because they are such mobile animals the range of most cetacean species extends over a huge geographical area. Not surprisingly, most of the species that have been recorded in Great Barrier Reef waters are those that are known to occur in relatively shallow, tropical, warm temperate seas for at least part of the year.

The long-distance swimmers

The largest of whalebone whales are the Balaenopteridae or rorqual. Rorquals have long grooves along their throats which enable them to fill their mouths with huge amounts of water from which the whale sieves planktonic crustaceans or small fishes (depending on the type of whale). The rorqual's soft fleshy tongue is well adapted for licking food from the filtering baleen.

All six species of rorqual have been recorded off the Queensland coast and all are believed to pass through Great Barrier Reef waters. However,

◁ *Humpback mother and calf simultaneously raise their tail flukes as they dive together in the Whitsunday Island area. These whales, photographed in late September, were probably heading south to the Antarctic to spend the summer feeding. Between 1952 and 1962, commercial whaling reduced the population of humpback whales migrating along Australia's east coast from approximately 10 000 to about 200 animals. Recent studies estimate the present number to be about 600 whales and indicate that the population is slowly recovering. However, sightings of humpbacks are still comparatively rare, a far cry from pre-whaling days when fishermen claimed that winter sightings were commonplace in Great Barrier Reef waters.*

▷ *The giant humpback whales, which may grow to over 15 metres, seek the best of both worlds by wintering in the tropics and spending the summer feeding in Antarctic seas. To do this they must migrate thousands of kilometres each year. The Australian east coast humpbacks travel through southern and central Great Barrier Reef waters to unknown tropical breeding grounds. Because humpbacks are known to breed in sheltered waters around reefs and islands in other parts of the world, some scientists now consider it likely that humpbacks breed in Great Barrier Reef waters.*

Humpback whale, *Megaptera novaeangliae*

except for the more coastal species – the humpback and the minke – these giant animals are reported very rarely in the area. Blue, fin, sei and humpback whales migrate regularly, forming large summer feeding schools in Antarctic waters and moving north to breed in warm waters in winter. The humpback whale passes close to the eastern Australian coast on its way north. Bryde's whale appears to be a warm-water species that rarely moves north or south. The minke whales seen in Great Barrier Reef waters during the winter months are distinct from the substantial populations seen in the Antarctic during summer and may belong to a warm-water race.

Whalebone whales are usually sighted alone or in small groups, and the only social unit that has been established definitely is a mother and her calf. However, it is possible that the low-frequency sounds produced by whalebone whales may help to

group includes oceanic species such as pilot whales, beaked whales, killer whales and spinner dolphins, which usually travel some distance from the coast but occasionally come close inshore and may become stranded. The second group consists of three inshore species that frequent bays and estuaries: the bottlenose dolphin, *Tursiops truncatus*, the Irrawaddy River dolphin, *Orcaella brevirostris*, and the Indo-Pacific humpback dolphin, *Sousa chinensis*.

Sociable, toothed whales

On the whole, toothed whales are more gregarious than whalebone whales but there is a wide variation in the social behaviour of different species. The inshore species are usually seen in small groups of up to a dozen animals. In bottlenose dolphins, these groups are aggregations of stable subgroups, composed of two to six dolphins of the same age and sex. Associations between subgroups are fluid,

examined. It was found in the Somali Republic of East Africa. No one is yet certain that they have seen this species alive.

It is not only rare species that are little known. The Irrawaddy River dolphin is common inshore north of Mackay. Although well known to locals, this species was not recorded officially in Australian waters until an American scientist recognised the skulls of two dolphins that had been eaten by Arnhem Land Aborigines in 1948. It was not reported in reef waters until the 1960s.

Identifying cetaceans at sea is often difficult, even for experienced observers. But with the growing interest in whales, more amateur observers are recording, photographing and reporting their sightings, and knowledge of these creatures is increasing gradually. As humpback whales recover to their pre-whaling numbers, watching whales is becoming a highlight of winter visits to the reef.

Minke whale, *Balaenoptera acutorostrata*

Irrawaddy River dolphin, *Orcaella brevirostris*

maintain contact between animals situated quite a distance from each other.

The most vocal whalebone whale is the humpback, whose repertoire in its tropical habitat is a complex, repeating song. Some studies indicate that humpbacks sing mainly in or near their tropical breeding areas and may be largely silent at other stages of migration. However, along the east coast of Australia, singing humpbacks have been recorded at Coffs Harbour, in New South Wales, at least 1000 kilometres south of their breeding grounds.

The 16 species of toothed whales that occur in the waters of the Great Barrier Reef range in size from the giant sperm whale, the males of which average 15 metres in length, to slender dolphins less than two metres long. The sperm whale is an oceanic species that prefers deep water while the small whales and dolphins form two groups on the basis of their broad ecological requirements. The first

while the composition of each subgroup can remain constant over long time periods. In contrast, breeding schools of some oceanic species, such as sperm whales, pilot whales and killer whales, are believed to consist primarily of stable groups of closely related females and their young.

Experiments with several species of captive toothed whales suggests that they can detect prey by echo location. Echo-locating animals scan their environment acoustically by emitting intense series of high-frequency clicks and interpreting the time and direction of their return. Only some of these clicks are audible to the human ear.

Longman's beaked whale, *Indopacetus pacificus*, a toothed whale first discovered in Great Barrier Reef waters, is probably the rarest whale in the world. This species was described from the skull and jaw of a specimen found near Mackay, Queensland, in 1881, and since then only one other skull has been

△ *Irrawaddy River dolphins are often mistaken for dugongs. Both species occur in the coastal waters of the Great Barrier Reef region. The mistake probably arises because Irrawaddy River dolphins, usually less than three metres long, lack the typical beak of better-known species such as the bottlenose dolphin. The easiest way to distinguish an Irrawaddy River dolphin from a dugong is to look for a dorsal fin, which a dugong does not have.*

△ ◁ *Minke whales visit the reef each winter. They are often inquisitive and appear to inspect boats and divers. Swimming with a minke is an exciting experience; however, it is comforting to remember that minke whales, which grow up to ten metres long, have no teeth. Unlike the minkes seen in Antarctic waters each summer, the minke whales that visit the reef waters have distinctive white markings on their flippers and shoulder regions.*

'Dolphins must come to the surface to breathe, and in the process of evolution their nostrils have moved to a position high on top of the head.'

Spinner dolphin, *Stenella longirostris*

◁ *Schools of spinner dolphins, like this one bow-riding a boat on the outer Great Barrier Reef, are common worldwide in warm seas. The spinner dolphin is so-called because of its habit of spinning around on its tail up to four times in the course of a single leap. Some scientists believe that this is done to make noise and may be an important means of communication, especially when animals are dispersed. An oceanic species, the spinner dolphin is slim-bodied and reaches at least two metres in lengh.*

Bottlenose dolphin, *Tursiops truncatus*

△ *Recent research suggests that dolphins swimming near the surface at high speed save energy by leaping. These bottlenose dolphins, photographed leaping in the waters between Townsville and Wheeler Reef, are the species most often kept in oceanaria. Bottlenose dolphins are distributed widely in coastal waters of the Pacific, Atlantic and Indian Oceans and they are common in reef waters where they are often seen riding the bow waves of boats. Adult bottlenose dolphins grow to three metres.*

Indo-Pacific humpback dolphin, *Sousa chinensis*

◁ *The Indo-Pacific humpback dolphin is a rather slow-moving coastal species that is common inshore in Great Barrier Reef waters. It tends to occur in small groups of about six that may spread out to hunt fishes. Humpback dolphins can enter very shallow water and have been observed feeding within a few metres of shore. Adult humpback dolphins are about two metres long.*

Dugong, *Dugong dugon*

△ *Dugongs feed mainly on sea grasses, although algae are often eaten incidentally as well. In Great Barrier Reef waters, dugongs prefer to feed on soft and delicate sea grasses, presumably because they are more nutritious than fibrous species. The whole plant, including the roots and rhizomes, is dug up leaving a serpentine feeding trail in the sea grass bed. The dugong's upper lip area, covered with sensory bristles, is a versatile and complex structure used to grasp the sea grasses and convey them to the mouth. An adult dugong can eat up to 40 kilograms of sea grass a day.*

'The only sounds that have been recorded from captive dugongs are bird-like chirps, rather like those of a budgerigar.'

Dugong, *Dugong dugon*

Dugongs: shy sea cows

The dugong, *Dugong dugon*, is one of only four surviving species of sirenians or sea cows. Its closest relative, the giant eight-metre Steller's sea cow, was exterminated by man in the 18th century. The only other surviving sirenians are the three species of manatee that occur in the Caribbean region, the Amazon and West Africa respectively. Depending on the species, manatees usually spend some or all of their lives in fresh water, whereas the dugong is the only herbivorous mammal that is strictly marine.

Like whales and dolphins, dugongs spend their entire lives in the sea and their bodies show similar adaptations to a life of swimming and diving. Dugongs grow to about three metres and from a distance look rather like dolphins with their fish-like shape, whale-like tail fluke and paddle-shaped flippers. Unlike dolphins, however, dugongs are not active predators. They feed instead on sea grasses that grow in warm, sheltered, shallow inshore waters. As a result, dugongs tend to be bulkier, less streamlined and slower moving than dolphins. They have sparse body hair apart from thick sensory bristles around the mouth; these are believed to be important for detecting suitable food plants.

Unlike cetaceans, dugongs do not seem to be able to communicate over long distances or to echo locate. The only sounds that have been recorded from captive dugongs are bird-like chirps, rather like those of a budgerigar!

Historically, the dugong occurred throughout the tropical and subtropical coastal and island waters of the Indian and west Pacific oceans from East Africa to the Solomon Islands. It is now considered to be rare in most of these areas and vulnerable to extinction. Aerial surveys conducted since the mid-1970s, however, have shown herds (sometimes numbering more than 100 dugongs) in the shallow seas of northern Australia, and it is likely that this region now harbours most of the world's dugongs.

Dugongs occur along the coast or on large flat reefs such as Corbett Reef in Princess Charlotte Bay where they can feed on sea grasses. Up to 600 dugongs have been seen from the air near the mouth of the Starcke River north of Cooktown, making this the most important dugong habitat yet identified in the world.

The age of a dugong can be determined by counting the growth layers in its tusks, which are laid down like the growth rings of a tree. Dugongs live for up to 70 years and females do not bear their first calf until they are at least ten years old; one calf is produced at intervals of three to seven years. Calving, which has been observed only rarely, takes place in very shallow water with the mother aground but in the wash of the waves. The cow-calf bond is well developed, and calves remain with their mothers for at least two years.

Dugongs have long been prized for their delicious meat (which has been likened to veal, beef and pork) and for the medicinal value of their oil. In the 1920s Aborigines netted dugongs in the Starcke River area to obtain oil that was then supplied to Aboriginal communities throughout Queensland.

The dugong was the basis of the whole culture of the sandbeach tribes whose territories extended from Princess Charlotte Bay north almost to Cape York. The dugong hunting practised by these people has been described as undoubtedly the most spectacular occupation of any Australian Aborigine.

Dugongs are now protected in Australia except for subsistence hunting by Aborigines and Torres Strait islanders living in native communities. These people, who usually hunt from an outboard-powered aluminium dinghy, using a harpoon with a detachable head called a *wap*, still regard the dugong as a very important part of their traditions.

The dugong is very vulnerable to over-exploitation because it is such a slow breeder. A major threat to dugongs in Great Barrier Reef waters is their tendency to drown after becoming tangled accidentally in fishing nets. Marine parks and other sanctuaries from which net-fishing is banned, and in which native hunting is regulated, need to be established in important dugong areas; the first of these has been declared at the Starcke River. Without such properly enforced protection the dugong faces extinction.☐

◁▽ *Although about the size and shape of a rotund dolphin, the dugong is more closely related to the elephant. Adult dugongs are between two and a half and three metres long and weigh from 250 to 400 kilograms. Their skin is very thick and smooth and is often heavily scarred. The nostrils, which are covered with valve-like flaps when the animal is submerged, are close together and situated near the front of the snout so that the dugong can breathe with most of its body below the surface. Dugongs are quiet, gentle animals and because they often occur in muddy waters they are rarely seen by the casual observer.*

▷ *The bond between the female dugong and her calf is strong and long lasting. A single calf is born and may be suckled for up to two years, although it usually starts eating sea grass soon after birth. The mother has two mammary glands, one under each flipper, a position similar to that of human breasts. Despite legendary sailors' tales claiming that the female dugong suckled her calf while upright and half out of the water, modern research has shown that the calf suckles while the mother swims or feeds, apparently taking little notice.*

Dugong, *Dugong dugon*

Rhizophora stylosa

Mangroves: life in a harsh environment

The forest of the sea

Mangroves have been called the forests of the sea because they inhabit tidal swamps, muddy areas of silt at the mouths of rivers and other low-lying areas that are regularly inundated by water. By the standards of land plants, mangroves live in a harsh environment. Their roots are in saline, waterlogged soils where conditions fluctuate between high and low tides, and for a considerable time their lower branches and leaves are submerged in sea water. Seedlings must become established under these difficult conditions, despite disturbance by currents induced by the rise and fall of tides. Yet mangroves are the most widely distributed plant community in Australia and the tropics, and an important part of the northern Great Barrier Reef.

△ *Where rainfall is low or highly seasonal, high salt levels in the soil may inhibit mangrove growth in the upper tidal areas and extensive vegetation-free salt flats may occur. Such salt flats are common around Gladstone to Rockhampton, around Ayr to Townsville and in parts of the Gulf of Carpentaria.*

◁ *Estuaries and river deltas are the major mangrove environments on the mainland. Silt and nutrients, washed seawards by the rivers, provide the conditions for luxuriant mangrove development.*

Unlike other plant communities, mangroves grow at the interface between land and sea, where tides and coastal currents bring unremitting variation, and where plants and animals must adapt continually to changing physical, chemical and biological conditions. Many species use the environment dominated by mangroves for food and shelter during part or all of their life cycle, so there is a constant movement of living and non-living matter into and out of the mangrove community. Yet the mangroves give the appearance of great stability and seeming changelessness. To some extent they are unchanging, for when compared to the land plants of the coral cays, those advance troops of other areas, the mangroves are the home guards of their intertidal realm.

What are mangroves?

The term 'mangrove' is generally well understood, but it is difficult to define exactly what a mangrove is. Mangrove communities consist of plants belonging to a number of different genera and families, many of which are not closely related to each other. What these species do share, however, is a number of adaptations, such as salt tolerance, modified root structure, and large, often viviparous, fruits or seeds. In Australia, about 30 species of trees and shrubs, belonging to 14 families, are generally considered to be mangroves. None of these species is restricted to Australia, and many occur widely throughout the Indo-West Pacific region. Several species, however, including *Bruguiera exaristata, Osbornia octodonta, Camptostemon schultzii* and *Rhizophora stylosa,* are best developed in Australian mangrove communities.

Lianas (creepers and vines), epiphytes (ferns, lichens and orchids), or under-storey vegetation make up another 10 species from eight families in Australian mangrove flora, and a further 10 to 15 species are occasionally associated with mangroves, but they normally occur in other communities as well. A large number of species of algae, sea grasses, fungi and lichens have also been recorded from mangrove communities. Although many of them play important roles in the mangrove communities, most are not restricted to mangrove habitats.

The diversity of mangroves and associated plants is greatest on the northeastern coastline of Australia. The three main reasons for this are: first, the region was the centre of origin and dispersal for mangroves into and out of Australia by virtue of its land connections with Southeast Asia when sea levels were lower than at present; second, that the climate of this area is similar to that under which mangrove vegetation first developed; and third, the coastline of this area, with its numerous estuaries, generally sheltered

▽▽ *Mangrove-lined estuaries, such as that of the O'Connell River near Proserpine, with regular fresh water inputs and large areas of shallow sheltered waters, are prime habitats for commercial species of fishes and prawns, providing the bulk of the commercial and amateur catch. It is also in those areas with a continuous supply of fresh water that the most luxuriant mangroves grow.*

▽ *The availability of fresh water also influences the type of mangrove community. At Repulse Inlet, where runoff from the Conway Ranges occurs throughout the year, the mangrove vegetation extends to the limit of tidal influences and adjoins freshwater swamps of* Melaleuca leucodendron, *as can be seen in the foreground.*

Melaleuca leucodendron

by the Great Barrier Reef, provides large areas of calm, shallow waters suitable for mangrove colonisation and growth.

What mangroves need

Several prerequisites, however, must be satisfied for a mangrove community to develop on any particular section of coastline. Most essential is an adequate supply of water, but a source of nutrients and a shoreline sufficiently stable to allow seedlings to become established are also important.

Most mangrove plants and animals can use sea water as their main water supply. Where there is no freshwater input, where tidal inundation is infrequent, and evaporation is high, however, salt can build up in the top soil layers to produce an environment unsuitable for the growth of plants. In these situations, only a narrow band of mangroves

Cottonwood or river mangrove, *Hibiscus tiliaceus*

Δ *Distributed throughout the tropics, the cottonwood or river mangrove is the most widespread. It prefers the margins of mangroves, where fresh water is abundant, and it can extend up estuaries to the limits of tidal influence. This species has the most spectacular flower of all the mangroves, but it rarely lasts more than a day. The large heart-shaped leaves are dark green and glossy on the upper surface, but the under surface is densely covered with white, very short, star-shaped hairs, which give it a grey appearance. This hairy layer apparently reduces the water loss from transpiration through the stomata, thereby conserving precious fresh water in a habitat abounding in salt. This adaptation is important on low-wooded islands, where there are virtually no freshwater flows.*

◁ *Tall forests of* Rhizophora stylosa *occur on the shores of Princess Charlotte Bay, where the shoreline is being built up rapidly by the silt brought down by the rivers during the annual wet season floods.*

Rhizophora stylosa

occurs on the coastline, and the upper tidal areas, inundated by spring tides, are salt flats, bare of vegetation.

The most luxuriant mangroves are found where there is a continuous input of fresh water to the upper tidal areas. This occurs where rainfall exceeds evaporation throughout the year, where freshwater swamps provide seepage water, or where large catchment areas – those surrounding rivers and bays from which rainwater drains – and heavy seasonal rains cause flooding and dilution of nearby sea water. The fresh water leaches salt from the soil and prevents the build-up of toxic salt levels.

Adapting to the environment

Growing with their roots in sea water largely overcomes the water supply problem for mangroves, but it brings two problems: excess salt and a shortage of oxygen around the roots. Mangroves have three ways of preventing the build-up of high salt levels in their tissues. Salt may be filtered out of sea water, stored in leaves, or excreted through salt glands. Some mangroves use only a single mechanism to avoid salt build-up, but most use two, and species of *Sonneratia* use all three.

Some genera, such as *Rhizophora*, *Ceriops*, *Sonneratia*, *Avicennia*, *Osbornia*, *Bruguiera*, *Exocoecaria*, *Aegiceras*, *Aegialitis* and the mangrove fern *Acrostichum*, have an ultra-filtration mechanism that excludes a proportion of the salt from the water taken up by the roots. Genera such as *Exocoecaria*, *Lumnitzera*, *Sonneratia* and *Xylocarpus* store excess salt in older leaves, which increase in size owing to water retention and are discarded with their salt load after essential nutrients, such as phosphorus and nitrogen, are withdrawn by the plant.

A few mangroves have salt glands in their leaves; the glands can pump a concentrated salt solution onto the leaf surface, where it can be washed away. These salt glands, which are known to occur in *Avicennia*, *Sonneratia*, *Aegiceras*, *Aegialitis* and *Acanthus*, consist of numerous secretory cells situated over a single large basal cell, and their openings are level with the upper or lower leaf surface. The leaves of these plants often have a coating of crystalline salt.

Anchored in mud

The adaptations that enable oxygen diffusion into the roots are usually obvious; an array of root modifications effectively overcomes the problem of soils lacking in oxygen and of anchoring the plants in a semi-fluid material.

Most mangroves have a system of laterally spreading cable roots with smaller, vertically descending anchor roots, which in turn bear fine nutritive roots. This root system is generally shallow, less than two metres deep, and taproots – large, single roots that grow vertically downwards – are not developed. Despite such a shallow root system, the amount of plant material below the

The variety of root systems

Mangroves have developed different root systems to ensure that the plant gets enough oxygen and that it will stand up in the mud in which the mangroves usually grow.

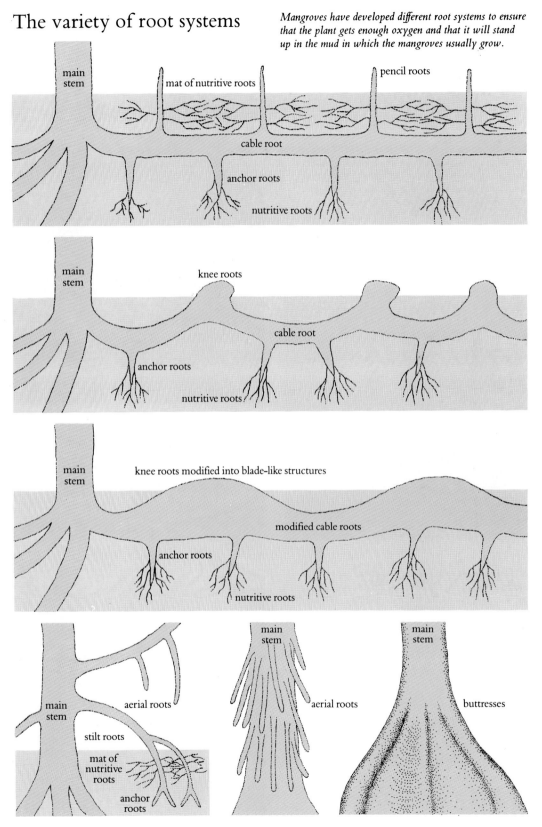

'Mangroves give the appearance of great stability and seeming changelessness, despite unremitting variation in their environment.'

▷ *Most people are familiar with the arching stilt and aerial roots of mangroves, which loop and twine to form a seemingly impenetrable thicket of roots. This* Rhizophora stylosa, *on Howick Island, probably provides the best example of this root system. The internal anatomy of these aerial and stilt roots changes radically on penetrating the sediments. The greatest change occurs in the development of air spaces within the tissues: the aerial root normally has only approximately 5 per cent gas space before entering the sediments, compared with about 50 per cent after penetration.*

Rhizophora stylosa

Avicennia marina

△ *Above-ground roots reflect the different ways the mangroves overcome the problems of anchoring the plant and providing the roots with an adequate oxygen supply. Pencil roots are upward-growing roots rising from the cable root system; by following the lines of pencil roots, the location of cable roots can be traced. Pencil roots occur in* Sonneratia, Xylocarpus australasicus *and* Avicennia marina.

▷ *Knee roots, as in* Bruguiera gymnorhiza, *are modified sections of the cable root that have undergone a short period of upward and then downward growth. Where they project above the surface a swelling occurs, which makes the root look like a bent and knobby knee. Similar knee roots also occur in* Ceriops *and* Lumnitzera.

Bruguiera gymnorhiza

Xylocarpus granatum

surface in mangroves is much greater than that above the surface. Such a distribution of plant material does not occur in other vegetation types, and it is probably this that helps mangroves remain upright in the soft muds where they usually grow.

A few species of mangroves only possess the basic root system (for example, *Aegialitis annulata* and *Excoecaria agallocha*), and these species tend to be found on less waterlogged or coarser, more porous sediments, where salts can be fairly rapidly leached. Other species have highly modified root systems that include pencil roots, knee roots, stilt roots, buttress roots and various types of aerial roots descending from the trunk to lower branches. All of these modified roots are exposed to air at some part of the tidal cycle. The roots have spongy, gas-filled tissues (aerenchyma) and numerous pores, called 'lenticels', in their outer layers, through which oxygen can enter the root tissues. The way oxygen

is taken up has only been studied in a few species, but it seems that, while the roots are submerged by the tide, the gas pressure falls within the aerenchyma as the oxygen held there is used up by the plant. A strong negative gas pressure develops and, during exposure at the next low tide, air is drawn into the root tissue through the lenticels to replenish the internal oxygen store.

Fruits and seeds that float

Given such adaptations, a suitable source of fruits and seeds is still required before a mangrove community can become established, and this is the area in which the mangroves excel. The fruits or seeds of all mangroves are buoyant, and some can survive in sea water for up to a year. The ability to float may be due to the roots of the developing seedling, the seed coat or the cotyledons – the first

△ *A modified form of knee roots in* Xylocarpus granatum *occurs because the upward-growing sections of the cable root do not remain cylindrical; instead, they expand to form blade-like structures that meander over the surface. This upward expansion dramatically increases the surface area available for oxygen uptake.*

two leaves produced by a seedling – within the seeds, and changes in any of these features may alter the seed's buoyancy. The seeds of *Avicennia marina*, for example, sink after shedding their seed coat, but the time it takes for the seed coat to be shed depends on the temperature and salt content of the water. In water of either high or low salinity, seed-coat shedding is slow, but in brackish conditions it is rapid. Seeds in brackish water will, therefore, float for a shorter time and disperse over shorter distances than those in high-salinity or low-salinity water. As

Rhizophora stylosa

Avicennia marina grows best in brackish water, this mechanism increases the likelihood of the seed settling in a favourable habitat.

Precocious seedlings

In many mangroves, the seeds actually begin to develop while still attached to the parent tree. These species really produce a floating seedling rather than a seed. Two forms of this development are known. In one, the viviparous species, the seedling begins to grow and enlarge while still on the parent tree, rupturing the seed coat by developing a primary root which, in genera such as *Bruguiera* and *Rhizophora*, reaches a considerable length. The other group, called 'cryptoviviparous', has seedlings that develop within the seed coat, but they do not grow sufficiently to rupture it until after they leave the parent tree. *Aegialitis, Acanthus, Aegiceras* and *Avicennia* genera are cryptoviviparous.

△ *The stem of* Rhizophora stylosa *elongates slowly, and as these specimens, which are about one year old, show, for a considerable part of their initial development all leaves are submerged at each high tide.*

△ ▷ Rhizophora stylosa *is the most widespread species of Rhizophora in Australia, and it is particularly abundant on low-wooded islands. Seedlings take about 12 months to mature. The developing ovary ultimately becomes a mature, pear-shaped fruit, with one seed. The fruit remains attached to the tree. Here the seeds in two fruits have begun to grow, and the embryonic root and stem can be seen protruding to different lengths from the tips of the fruits. The calyx, which remains when the petals and stamen fall from the flower, can be seen at its other end. When fully elongated, the seedling is released, leaving the calyx, cotyledons and fruit wall behind on the tree. The floating seedling can remain viable in sea water for up to a year.*

▷ *Wind affects mangrove communities in several ways. Currents and wave action are modified by wind. Wind can increase evaporation and soil salt levels, cause physical damage to canopies, and increase water loss from the leaves. But some mangroves make use of the windy conditions of their habitat for several vital processes. For example,* Excoecaria agallocha *is wind-pollinated, producing flowers in long catkins. Male and female flowers are produced on separate plants; the males generally flower a month or so before the females. This species stores excess salt in the leaves, which are shed at the end of the dry season. At the onset of the wet season, but before new leaves appear, flowering occurs, so when the male flowers are present the tree is virtually leafless, allowing efficient wind-dispersal of its pollen.*

Rhizophora stylosa

Mangrove fern, *Acrostichum speciosum*

△ *Like all ferns, the mangrove fern has a complex life cycle in which spores develop on the undersides of the fronds, forming a brown felty coating. When mature, the spores are dry, and they are dispersed by wind. The spores develop into minute plants called 'prothalli', which bear the reproductive structures, but fertilisation requires the presence of water. The mangrove fern thus possesses two means of dispersal: a water-dispersal mechanism for the prothalli over short distances, and a long-distance wind-dispersal mechanism for the spores.*

Excoecaria agallocha

Excoecaria agallocha

▷ Crabs of the genus Uca are among the most colourful inhabitants of mangroves. Males have one outrageously enlarged claw – either right or left – which is held across the front of the body in a horizontal position, resembling a fiddle in both its shape and jerky movements. Both claws of the female are small and used for feeding; the male can only feed with its one small claw. The large claw is used as a warning device, for fighting with other males, and as a sexual status symbol in the courtship display. At low tide, the crabs emerge from their burrows and the males use their small claws to clean the larger one. They feed on the organic matter and plankton deposited on the sediment surface, retreating to their burrows at the slightest sign of danger.

▷▽ Numerous worms live on and in the mangrove sediments but this species, up to 200 millimetres long and with long, flowing golden bristles, is one of the most conspicuous. It is common among coral rubble but it also occurs among mainland mangroves, particularly where gravelly sediments predominate. A sluggish carnivore, this species defends itself by erecting its long bristles; these are brittle calcareous tubes filled with a poison capable of inflicting considerable pain.

▽ The salt-water crocodile, here a shadowy shape covered by vegetation, was formerly to be found in all river systems of northern Australia, as far south as Broome in Western Australia and Maryborough in Queensland. Today, however, it is common only in a few remote river systems. The crocodiles construct large nests of plant material at the landward margins of mangroves, particularly where these grade into freshwater swamps. About 60 eggs are laid at the beginning of the wet season, and they hatch after about 90 days. The female excavates the nest to release the young. Feeding among mangroves on the rising tide, the juveniles prey on crabs, prawns, mudskippers and other small fishes. Adults generally feed on large mud crabs and fishes, birds and mammals.

Fiddler crab, *Uca tetragonum*

Salt-water crocodile, *Crocodylus porosus*

Worm, *Chloeia flava*

A few mangroves, including *Excoecaria*, *Heritiera*, *Xylocarpus* and *Osbornia*, have non-viviparous seeds which, like the seeds of land plants, pass through a dormant stage before they germinate. As vivipary and cryptovivipary are so common in the mangroves they probably represent some form of adaptation that aids mangrove dispersal and ultimate establishment. A number of reasons for vivipary and cryptovivipary have been suggested, including the ability of these seedlings to float and to root rapidly when stranded. Or this seedling development may simply be a way of increasing seed size which, in turn, is likely to increase the chances of survival. Tidal buffeting and floating objects pose a threat to seedlings during establishment, and the smaller their size, the greater the threat. Most of the non-viviparous mangroves have large seeds, possibly for the same reason.

Shaping the coast

Once the seedlings have become established in suitable habitats and the prerequisites for growth are met, the next phase in the development of a mangrove community may take place.

Mangroves provide a shaded and moist habitat under their canopies and they help shape the intertidal area on which they grow. By sheltering the near-shore zone at high tide from the effects of offshore winds, the mangroves are able to trap and fix sediments that might otherwise remain mobile. Suspended matter brought down by rivers becomes trapped among the mangroves. This material contains not only clay, silt and sand particles but also organic matter, which is rich in nutrients such as phosphates and nitrates. Most of these nutrients would, without the mangroves, be simply washed out to sea. Instead, they are trapped in the sediments, taken up by the mangroves, incorporated into their leaves, and then returned to the surface of the sediments, where they can be used again.

Living in the mangroves

Mangroves provide shade, trap and stabilise sediments, and recycle important nutrients through leaf litter, making the areas they inhabit favourable and productive habitats for a variety of animals. This fauna is diverse and specialised in its muddy, intertidal existence. Crabs are abundant among the mangroves, and provide a variety of colourful and amusing displays. Molluscs are conspicuous on mangrove roots; other species leave tracks meandering over the mud surface. The insect and spider faunas are obvious, diverse and sometimes annoying. Even the vertebrates, living permanently among the mangroves, have adapted their life styles. Mudskippers, for example, walk on their fins over the exposed mud, build mud houses, and carry their own water supply in their gill chambers.

Although there is some doubt as to how many of these animals live only in the mangroves, they constitute such a characteristic suite of species as to warrant the term 'mangrove fauna'. Three major groups can be recognised: animals associated with the sediments; those that occur in the waters around and within the drainage channels of the mangroves; and those that live on the trunks or in the canopies of the mangroves.

Retreating from the tide

Most of the sediment dwellers, be they crabs, molluscs, worms or mudskippers, reflect the rhythmic dominance of the tides in their behaviour. Many are active on or just below the surface at low tide and retreat from the incoming tide into protective holes in the ground, towards the shore, or into the mangroves above high-water level. The entire group virtually disappears from ground level at high tide; at this time, the second group of animals, the aquatic ones, roam over these grounds in search of food.

Animals of the sea

Sea water is an important component of the mangroves, flowing freely in and out with the tides. In addition to the waters throughout the mangroves at high tide, channels and creeks with connections to the sea always contain water. As a result, many marine species are to be found within the mangrove community, particularly at high tides. Although some of these species are incidental visitors – belonging to the tides rather than the mangroves – others, such as shrimps, prawns, fishes and jellyfish, are highly dependent on the mangroves in some way, even though not all of them spend their entire life cycle in this habitat. Many of these species find food in the nutrient-rich sediments; others find shelter from predators among the contorted root systems; still others, such as mullet, *Liza dussumieri*, and barramundi, *Lates calcarifer*, use this favourable environment as a convenient assembly ground prior to their seaward breeding migrations. Spawning in most of these species occurs at sea, but the juveniles use the salinity gradients as chemical road maps to find their way back to the mangroves for their early development.

The mangrove nursery

Many commercial and recreational fisheries depend on the 'nursery' characteristics of mangroves; perhaps as much as 75 per cent of the present commercial catch is derived from the mangroves. The leaf litter produced by the mangroves provides the basis of this nursery value. Most of the litter is colonised and partially broken down by bacteria and fungi. These micro-organisms enhance the food value of the litter by converting carbohydrates to proteins, increasing the protein content by up to four times. The enriched leaf particles may then be consumed, recycled and recolonised by micro-organisms and detrital feeders

Mudskipper, *Periophthalmus*

△ Mudskippers, although they rarely exceed 80 millimetres in length, are highly aggressive predators, feeding on spiders, insects, isopods, amphipods, worms, molluscs and crabs. Their aggressiveness can be recognised by energetic posturing and flagging of their dorsal fins. Most species are not strictly territorial, but their aggressive attitude keeps neighbours at a proper distance. The mudskippers' eyes protrude from the top of their head and give a wide-angle view from the mud surface. They also serve as periscopes when these fish swim just below the surface of mangrove-lined creeks.

such as amphipods, prawns and mullet. This cycle of enrichment and consumption continues until the litter is exhausted. The highly efficient utilisation of mangrove litter provides the rich food source, which together with the shade and shelter of the mangroves, creates the nursery effect.

Canopy-dwellers

The canopy of the mangroves is essentially a terrestrial habitat and, with few exceptions, the species associated with it are terrestrial by nature. The species living in the mangrove canopy are mainly insects, spiders and birds, although at certain localities bats, reptiles and even possums are abundant. Although not exclusively dependent on the mangroves, most of the animals use this habitat for feeding, nesting and roosting.

Mud whelk, *Pyrazus ebeninus*

Mud creeper, *Telescopium telescopium*

Soldier crab, *Mictyris longicarpus*

∆ The large mud creeper, common in the mangroves of northern Australia, is a member of the same family as the mud whelk. It also feeds on surface algae and detritus, but it is rarely found in large numbers. Dead shells of this species are commonly inhabited by hermit crabs, which betray their presence by abrupt movements rather than the smooth glide of the mud creepers.

∆ ∆ The mud whelk was one of the half dozen shells collected at Botany Bay by the naturalists accompanying James Cook in 1770, reflecting this species' abundance and wide geographic range. Extremely gregarious, the species is common in mangroves and mud flats from southern Australia to Cape York. Mud whelks feed on surface algae and detritus, and their meandering tracks form characteristic patterns in the soft sediments. A favourite item in east coast Aboriginal diets, the shell of this species is very common in coastal middens, the eating places where Aborigines threw the remains from a meal.

∆ Immense numbers of soldier crabs congregate in dense masses and wander over tidal flats in apparent formation. The military appearance is enhanced by their uniform blue. And unlike most crabs, which walk sideways, soldier crabs walk forwards. If they are chased, however, any military resemblance vanishes, for the soldier crabs will flee or rapidly burrow into the sediments in typical corkscrew fashion. The escape response is an essential survival mechanism, for many species prey on them, including toadfish, ghost crabs, ibis, herons and mangrove kingfishers. As they feed on organic matter and minute organisms in the surface sediments, the soldier crabs are important in recycling mangrove litter and minute algae.

Animals that follow the rhythm of the tides

'The crabs, mud whelks and mud creepers, active beneath the water's surface at low tide, retreat into their burrows, towards the shore or up into the mangroves themselves as the tide rises. It is then that the aquatic animals roam over the area in search of food.'

Grapsid crab, *Metopograpsus frontalis*

Grapsid crab, *Sesarma elongata*

△ Crabs of the family Grapsidae are more soberly coloured and shyer than the fiddler crabs. Like the fiddlers, they build permanent burrows, but they use them quite differently. When the tide comes in and the fiddler crabs are retiring underground, most grapsid crabs emerge from their burrows and climb into the vegetation to avoid the water and its marine predators. The burrows are largely used as dining-rooms; most of the grapsid crabs are omnivores, concentrating on plant material, so fallen leaves are collected from the mud surface and carried into the burrows to be eaten there.

Upside-down jellyfish, *Cassiopeia*

Bracket fungus, *Phellinus lloydii; Rhizophora stylosa*

△ *Fungi have an important role in mangrove communities for, with bacteria, they are responsible for the rapid initial breakdown of leaf litter, twigs and wood that provide nutrients for plants. Although much of this decay is achieved by microscopic fungi on the ground, some species attack dead and living wood while it is still on the tree. Because of their size and colour, the bracket fungi are the most conspicuous of these. This one normally lives in the dead heartwood, which it reaches through wounds. It can occasionally become parasitic and invade living cells of the sapwood, which it may destroy. The outer yellow bracket seen here is the external reproductive structure of this species.*

Periwinkle, *Littorina scabra*

△ *Periwinkles inhabit the leaves, branches and trunks of mangroves. This colourful species ranges from yellow to red and dark brown with mixed patterns of these colours. The colour and pattern of the shell are genetically controlled, but different colours are more common at various stages of the life cycle because different colours are more susceptible to predators in different locations. Adults live mostly in the canopies while the juveniles frequent the lower parts of mangroves. Fish predation is heavy on yellow juveniles, as they are obvious on the dark background, so yellow juveniles are rare. But in the light green foliage, darker adults are more obvious and are preyed on by birds.*

△ ◁ *The upside-down jellyfish is common around mangroves in northeastern Australia. Although capable of sustained swimming, it is typically found inverted on the sea bottom, in the manner of anemones. Small animals trapped on the surface of the jellyfish's frilly oral arms are carried through the many small mouths and a complicated canal system into the stomach. The jellyfish also contains symbiotic algae (zooxanthellae) in its tissues.*

▷ *One of the largest members of the family Neritidae, the herbivorous* Nerita lineata *feeds on algae or algal slime on rocks or mangrove trunks and roots. It is common around the northern Australian coastline, but its brown to slate grey colour and its nocturnal feeding mean that it is often overlooked. During the day it can be found in logs, under rocks and in depressions on mangrove trunks, in the shade of the mangrove canopy.*

Periwinkle, *Littorina scabra*

Nerita lineata

Life in the mangrove roots

'The mangroves create an environment that houses a diverse and specialised fauna, from the jellyfish that lurks on the sea bottom to the animal that shelters in the canopy at high tide.'

Rhizophora stylosa

Harengula

◁ *Unlike most mangroves, members of the genus* Rhizophora *do not have laterally spreading cable roots. Rather they have prop and stilt roots that arch from the main trunk and end in clusters of support roots. Arches may form on existing arches, seen here at Low Isles, a feature which gave rise to the mistaken belief that mangroves could actually creep seawards.*

Saccostrea cucullata

△ *Low tide is a good time to inspect the* Rhizophora *root system, for with little perseverance a feed of oysters can always be found. Several species of barnacles and oysters are invariably associated with* Rhizophora; *they filter-feed on the minute organisms brought in by the rising tide. The commercial oyster shown here is widely cultivated from spat – newly settled juvenile oysters – collected on mangrove wood.*

◁ *At high tide, the roots of* Rhizophora *form the feeding grounds of numerous marine creatures. Schools of small fishes such as pilchards, sardines and sprats can feed here with some protection from their larger predators. A school of herrings can be seen in the clear waters of the reef, moving among the prop roots in search of food.*

△ *Two species that regularly use the mangroves of northeastern Australia, but which are not mangrove specialists, exemplify different patterns of mangrove usage. Banded finches are seed eaters and feed outside the mangroves; however, they frequently build both breeding and roosting nests in mangroves, particularly in Ceriops.*

▷ *The brown honey-eater, unlike the finches, rarely nests in mangroves, but it commonly feeds on their nectar and on insects living in their outer foliage.*

'Over 200 bird species have been recorded from Australian mangrove communities; 14 are found only in the mangroves.'

White ibis, *Threskiornis molucca; Avicennia marina*

Mangrove heron, *Butorides striatus*

Many of the mangroves have developed a relationship with these canopy-dwellers. For example, nectar-feeding birds are largely responsible for pollination in the large-flowered species of *Bruguiera* and in the red-flowered *Lumnitzera littorea*, and species of *Sonneratia* are generally pollinated by bats. With the exception of the wind-pollinated species of *Excoecaria* and *Rhizophora*, the remaining mangroves are pollinated by bees, moths and drosophilid flies.

Weaver ants, *Oecophylla smaragdina*, weave leaves into nests within the mangrove canopy and, in turn, provide some protection to the mangroves by preying on leaf-eating insects and biting human intruders. Large colonies of nesting birds, with their common habit of continually pecking at the young leaves within reach, appear at first glance to be rather destructive users of the mangrove canopy. But the droppings from these birds are rich in those nutrients (phosphorus and nitrogen) that are often in short supply in the mangroves; the droppings fertilise the area, enhancing plant growth.

Mangrove settings

Along the northeastern Australian coastline, mangroves occur in three major settings: estuaries, sheltered bays and inlets on continental islands, and the low-wooded coral islands of the reef.

The richest and most diverse mangrove communities are to be found in coastal estuaries, where abundant fresh water and flood-deposited silts provide a fertile and favourable environment. Dense and luxuriant mangrove forests occur, in some instances reaching more than 30 metres in height, particularly in areas where the annual rainfall exceeds 1800 millimetres.

On the continental islands, where the rainfall and nutrient levels are generally lower, the mangrove

◁ △ *White ibis feed in shallow water and marshes, both freshwater and tidal. They nest in rushes and trees near water throughout northern and eastern Australia, but their largest nesting aggregations occur in the mangroves of northern Australia. Here they build massive nests from twigs pruned from the top of the mangrove canopy, in this instance* Avicennia marina.

◁ *The mangrove heron is common in the mangroves from Shark Bay in Western Australia, and around the northern coastline as far south as Sydney in New South Wales. It nests exclusively in mangroves and feeds on fishes and crustaceans from the mud banks and sea grasses around the mangroves. This heron has two colour-phases: a grey one, shown here, and a brown one. Both phases blend well with the grey-brown muds of its habitat.*

Amyema mackayense

Bruguiera gymnorhiza

Mistletoe, *Lysiana subfalcata maritima*

Bruguiera parviflora

△ *Mistletoe is widely distributed in Australia but only a few species are confined to mangroves. These parasitic plants have normal leaves, but they tap into the water-conducting tissue of their host plant for their water requirements. They have no contact with the soil and their root system is virtually eliminated, being reduced to a penetrating structure termed a 'haustorium'.*

△△ *The mistletoe bird,* Dicaeum hirundinaceum, *is largely responsible for pollinating the flowers and it feeds on mistletoe fruit. The fruits have laxative properties and the undigested seed falls onto the branch on which the bird is perched. A sticky layer on the seed coat cements it to the branch, where it germinates. The emerging root forms a sucker pad, which becomes attached to the host and develops a haustorium to link up with the host's water-conducting tissues.*

△ *The five Australian species of* Bruguiera *illustrate well the different methods of pollination.* Bruguiera parviflora *has colourless flowers clumped together, with two or three to each stalk. The sepals are short and widely spread, aiding pollination by insects.*

△△ Bruguiera gymnorhiza *is pollinated by birds, particularly by the yellow-breasted sunbird,* Nectarinia jugularis, *and silver-eyes,* Zosterops *species. Its flowers are large and red, and they occur singly on each stalk. As buds, the sepals are tightly closed around the petals which, in turn, enclose the stamens. When the sepals open, the petals remain closed, but because of a thick ridge on the outside, they spring apart when gentle pressure is applied. The birds probe the flowers to gather nectar. If the flowers are mature, the petals open suddenly and release the stamens, together with a puff of pollen that covers the head of the bird and can then be transferred to other flowers.*

communities may still be extensive, but they often lack the luxuriance of their mainland counterparts. Nevertheless, the larger islands close to the mainland with sizeable elevation, such as Hinchinbrook Island, still display a richness comparable with that of mainland sites.

Low-wooded islands

It is on the low-wooded islands that mangrove communities form an intimate part of the Great Barrier Reef. Often referred to as the 'carbonate' setting, it differs from the other two environments in a fundamental feature: the sediment of the islands is derived directly from the reef, either from nearby coral growth or from the deposition of imported carbonate particles, rather than from the land. This fine sedimentary material forms a thin veneer over consolidated, fossilised corals. In contrast with the mainland and continental islands, the carbonate setting is characterised by generally low nutrient levels and, because of the small catchment areas involved, by meagre amounts of fresh water. As a result, mangrove communities of this setting are restricted to coral islands where the annual rainfall exceeds 1200 millimetres.

The region where low-wooded islands occur is dominated by southeast trade winds which blow constantly between March and November. Consequently, a sand cay generally develops on the leeward, or northwest, side of the reef platform, while a shingle rampart of coral debris and gravel forms on the windward, or southeast, side. The depression or moat between them is colonised by mangroves, although the extent and exact location of mangroves varies with the size of the reef platform, its history and its topography.

Even on the windward sides of these ridges, or ramparts, as they are known, several species of mangroves commonly occur, including *Avicennia marina* and *Aegialitis annulata*, but instead of forming a continuous community, they occur as dwarf shrubs in discrete patches. Similarly, on the crests of the ridges, patches of mangroves occur, mostly *Osbornia octodonta*, *Excoecaria agallocha*, *Pemphis acidula* and *Thespesia polulnea*.

On the leeward side of the ramparts, the mangroves are often divided into two communities. Mature woodlands occur on the higher, more protected sediments, with mixed group of species including *Rhizophora stylosa*, *Bruguiera gymnorhiza*, *Ceriops tagal*, *Avicennia marina*, *Xylocarpus* species and *Lumnitzera racemosa*. These woodlands are often dense and up to eight metres high. Less than one metre below the surface, a dark brown to black, organic-rich mud with calcareous sediments occurs.

Further towards the leeward reef flat margin, a woodland of *Rhizophora stylosa* occurs, with occasional specimens of *Sonneratia alba* and *Avicennia marina*. These woodlands may be up to 17 metres tall, although at the reef margins the mangroves rarely exceed five metres. Ground material varies

Low Isles

Low Isles

from mud near the centre of this community, to living corals near its periphery. Some of these corals have a characteristic radial growth form resembling miniature coral atolls, so these coral colonies are termed 'micro-atolls'. As the corals colonised by mangroves generally belong to the genus *Porites*, they are referred to as '*Porites* micro-atolls'.

Because of the high salinity levels associated with this environment, several mangrove species that require reduced salinities are absent from these communities, although they are common on the adjacent mainland. These include *Acanthus ilicifolius*, *Scyphiphora hydrophyllacea*, *Acrostichum* species, *Camptostemon schultzii*, *Cynometra iripa*, *Heritiera littoralis*, *Bruguiera sexangula* and *Sonneratia caseolaris*.

High salinity also reduces the number of estuarine animal species in these communities, but this is largely offset by the many marine and coral rubble species that do not occur in mainland mangroves,

△ *The most studied of the low-wooded islands with their sand cays and mangrove woodlands is undoubtedly Low Isles. It was chosen as the site of the 1928–29 Great Barrier Reef Expedition, which spent a year investigating the coral reef, sea grasses, mangroves and the cay of this island. The mangrove communities of Low Isles have been resurveyed since then in 1945, 1954, 1965 and in 1973, and over that time the area of the Rhizophora woodland has increased considerably. Other low-wooded islands, resurveyed in 1973, showed different patterns, and it seems that the mangroves may be rapidly expanding on some reef tops but not on others. Reef-top topography and the extent of micro-atoll formation appear to be the main factors in the rate of mangrove development, although destruction by cyclones can hold some reef tops at the same stage of mangrove extension for considerable periods.*

such as encrusting sponges, *Jaspis* species, soft corals, *Lobophyton* species, hermit crabs, *Dardanus* species, and tube worms, *Reteterebella queenslandica*. The canopy-dwellers are similar in abundance and diversity to the mainland communities. Some species, such as Torres Strait pigeon, *Myristicivora spilorrhoa*, and the noddy tern, *Anous stolidus*, nest in the mangroves of some low-wooded islands but do not inhabit the mainland mangroves.

Young mangrove communities

On a geological time scale, the mangrove communities of the low-wooded islands are very young. Sea levels are stable now, and as upward coral growth is inhibited by the water surface, horizontal and radial extension occurs, with extensive development of micro-atolls on the reef flat. These fields of micro-atolls are suitable for mangrove establishment, and they occur at a suitable level in relation to the tides for subsequent mangrove growth. Similar fields of micro-atolls have been found under the mangroves on the low-wooded islands, which range in age from 5000 to 6000 years, suggesting that the mangrove communities that we see today have developed over no more than the past 5000 to 6000 years, and that the formation of micro-atolls appears to be a prerequisite for mangroves to colonise a reef top. This connection between coral growth and mangrove establishment suggests also that the reef itself, with its micro-atolls, shingle ramparts and carbonate sediments, provides the right conditions for mangroves to develop. The mangroves, in turn, enrich the reef with a range of habitats and species that would otherwise be absent.☐

◁ △ *Where shelter is provided by rock, as on Turtle Island, less stunted specimens of* Aegialitis annulata *may occur.*

◁ *Coral ramparts to windward of low-wooded islands protect mangrove woodlands from excessive wave action. A few species of mangroves can grow on the seaward side of the ramparts. Patches of dwarfed* Avicennia marina, Rhizophora stylosa *and* Aegialitis annulata *occur on the exposed side of the ramparts on King Island.*

▷ *Although the ramparts protect the mangrove woodlands from wave action, they rarely provide much shelter from the prevailing winds. As a result, pruning by wind of the mangrove canopy is a common feature on the windward shores of the low-wooded islands. The progressive dieback, shown on King Island, can also result in a windward zone of dead bushes. In this way there may be a gradual retreat of mangroves on the windward side, while at the same time the mangroves on the leeward side may be advancing onto the reef flat.*

Aegialitis annulata

Avicennia marina; Rhizophora stylosa; Aegialitis annulata

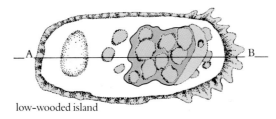

low-wooded island

Changes in landform and plants

This section through a low-wooded island shows the changes in landform and plants from the leeward to the windward side. On the northwestern side, the prevailing southeast trade winds encourage the development of a sand cay, and on this more sheltered side, mature mangrove woodland can develop. On the southeastern side, shingle builds up to form a ridge or rampart, and here the mangroves grow only as dwarf shrubs.

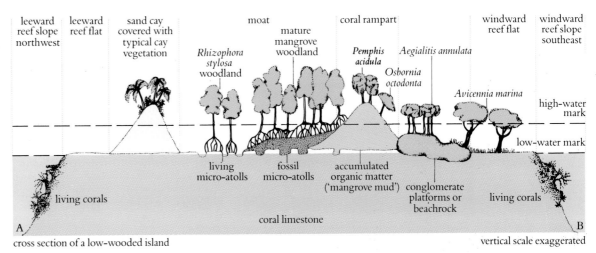

leeward reef slope northwest | leeward reef flat | sand cay covered with typical cay vegetation | moat | *Rhizophora stylosa* woodland | mature mangrove woodland | coral rampart | *Pemphis acidula* | *Osbornia octodonta* | *Aegialitis annulata* | *Avicennia marina* | windward reef flat | windward reef slope southeast

high-water mark

low-water mark

living corals — living micro-atolls — fossil micro-atolls — accumulated organic matter ('mangrove mud') — conglomerate platforms or beachrock — living corals

coral limestone

cross section of a low-wooded island

vertical scale exaggerated

Pemphis acidula

Rhizophora stylosa

▷ *Several species of corals can form micro-atolls, but this one appears to have a decisive role in the colonisation of reef tops by mangroves. Living micro-atolls occur on the leeward side of the* Rhizophora *woodland, which can be seen in the background. Seedlings from these mangroves, particularly from* Rhizophora stylosa, *can establish on the outlying micro-atolls and thereby enlarge the mangrove area. Fossil micro-atolls among the mangrove woodlands suggest that micro-atoll development has gone hand in hand with earlier colonisation by mangroves. In other words, where mangroves occur on a reef top, micro-atolls will be found.*

△ △ *On King Island, coral ramparts are well developed.* Pemphis acidula *is one of the characteristic species growing on, often confined to, the tops of the ramparts.*

Porites andrewsi

Island plant and animal life: biological microcosms

Feast and famine

From the air one sees a chain of emeralds, narrowly fringed by a filigree of brilliant foam, bejewelling the turquoise velvet of the sea. These are the coral islands of the Great Barrier Reef. Their gem-like quality is not destroyed by closer inspection. The warm, smooth beaches, cool vegetation and mild breezes have an appealing quality that evokes romantic images, idyllic dreams and a timeless mystique enjoyed by few other environments.

Repeatedly, writers at a loss for more imaginative phrases return to the hackneyed but apt designation of them as 'tropical paradises'. So they are, but they are much more. They are microcosms of terrestrial life, with all the dramas of the hunter and the hunted, birth and death, and the never-ending quest for food, shelter and mates that characterise all biological systems.

Island life, however, is not just another example of ecology in action; islands have unique features that make them very special to the naturalist and scientist. Their isolation and small size impose conditions not found elsewhere, which sometimes make life precarious for their inhabitants.

Coral islands are 'paradises' only in certain moods. Anyone weathering a severe tropical storm and experiencing the violence of shrieking winds and pounding surf would choose other adjectives. To many of the island-dwelling species, the islands are never a paradise, but rather a harsh environment of little water, much salt and constant danger. To fully appreciate the islands of the Great Barrier Reef, one must view them, not only from the point of view of humans on holiday who have access to restaurants, bars, sun-creams and pleasant companions, but also perhaps from that of a seedling struggling for survival in the hot, shifting and nearly waterless sands of the beach or of a starving earwig enduring famine, waiting for a dead fish to wash up on the beach to supply, for only a short time, a feast – before it must endure yet another famine.

High and low islands

There are two main kinds of islands on the Great Barrier Reef. Continental islands were connected to the mainland during periods when the sea level was lower, or before the intervening land of the continental shelf subsided. That is, they were once hills or mountains that became islands when sea water flooded the lower ground, leaving isolated peaks protruding above the sea. Continental islands are composed primarily of rocks similar to those on the mainland; their vegetation is also similar to that of mainland coasts.

Coral cays differ from continental islands in two important ways: they are formed from materials of the reef itself, and they have never been connected to the mainland. They are relatively young and were formed after submergence of the reefs on which they occur. On the Great Barrier Reef the oldest ones are probably no more than about 4000 years old. Cays are more directly related to the reef, both physically and historically, than continental islands and they are a product of the reef.

Coral cays are themselves of diverse types. Some are mere sand bars protruding above the surface of the sea, small and entirely devoid of terrestrial

Heron Island and Wistari Reef

◁ *In the north the Great Barrier Reef is narrow and ribbon-like with fewer gaps than in the south, where it becomes a scattered group of patches. Heron Island, a forested coral cay, lies on Heron Reef just beyond Wistaria Reef, in the Capricorn group.*

◁ ▽ *Erskine Island is a two-hectare vegetated cay of the Capricorn group. Its vegetation consists of shrubs, screw palms and stunted pisonia trees.*

▽ *Continental islands were once hills or mountains of the mainland that became islands when sea level rose, or the level of the land subsided, flooding the valley and leaving them isolated. Lizard Island, background, is a continental island that is permanently inhabited and has a tourist resort, a marine research station and an airfield. Two other continental islands of the Lizard Group, Palfrey or Saddle Island, centre foreground, and South Island, right foreground, are uninhabited.*

Erskine Island

Lizard, Palfrey and South Islands

Masthead Island

Hook Island

△ One of the larger coral cays of the Capricorn group, Masthead Island is a forested sand cay.

◁ Many of the continental islands are large, high and forested and look similar to the mainland coast. Hook Island, of the Whitsunday group, has an underwater observatory, seen extending from the peninsula in the middle of the photograph.

'On the Great Barrier Reef the oldest coral cays are probably no more than 4000 years old.'

▷ *When coral cays begin to form they are devoid of vegetation. They are small and scarcely protrude above high water. Most are unstable, and wind and water action may change their shape and even location. Here common noddies in the foreground, and crested terns, in the background, can be seen.*

▽ *One Tree Island, a shingle cay in the Capricorn Group, has very complex vegetation. Near the centre is a forest of pisonia and screw palm trees, and other light green patches of pisonia forest occur elsewhere. An incomplete ring of Argusia shrubs grows around the edge. Most of the island is covered by a low herb flat. Around the small brackish pond near the centre is a mat of succulents. The ecology of this island was studied for ten years; three years were devoted to study of the vegetation, land birds, sea birds, insects, spiders and centipedes, the soil and fauna, and how these were affected by weather, immigration, colonisation and extinction.*

One Tree Island

Common noddy, *Anous stolidus*; crested tern, *Sterna bergii*

plants. Others have vegetation, of low creeping plants, shrubs, or even forests, and still others consist of mangroves. Some islands have a combination of several types of vegetation, which in some cases may be quite complex.

Coral cays are made up of different materials, depending on the way the cay was formed; sand is the most common building material. Sand cays are formed from particles of shell or foraminiferans or bits of coral abraded from the reef and then deposited on the reef flat. Where waves of sufficient energy to carry these fragments converge at the edge of a reef, sand is deposited and a cay gradually builds up. At low tide, when the sand is exposed, wind may help pile it into dunes. Gradually, cays are built up until they are above the water at all states of the tide.

Other coral cays are formed from coarse pieces of coral, called shingle or rubble. Storms tear off pieces

of coral from the reef and heap them on to a sand cay or a reef flat. Later storms add to these piles of broken coral, and eventually a cay of considerable size may be formed. Sometimes the individual contributions of successive storms are identifiable as concentric ridges, the older ones towards the centre of the island and the younger ones at the edge.

A third type of material on coral cays is beachrock, which often occurs around the edges of cays. It forms under sand by the binding together of sand grains into a cemented mass. When the overlying loose sand is washed or blown away, beachrock remains. Finally, some coral cays have phosphate rock or cay rock. Although similar in appearance to beachrock it originates in a different way. Sand grains are bound together by phosphate deposits from bird droppings.

Colonising a coral cay

When a coral cay first develops, it is above water at low tides but covered or awash at higher ones. Under such conditions, no terrestrial life is present, and the cay is more a part of the marine than the terrestrial environment. Later, however, as sand or shingle accumulates and the island builds up, some of the terrestrial plants and animals that arrive become established, and the island becomes clothed in vegetation and populated by animals of different kinds. As some of the cays are extremely small and

quite remote from the mainland, it has been a marvel to naturalists that so many species have found their way there.

How do they get there? St Augustine, in the 5th century, was one of the first persons to be perplexed by this problem. He suggested that in addition to swimming and being carried by humans, perhaps angels under divine command transported organisms to remote islands. Today, more realistic explanations are available.

Travelling plants

Plants travel by several means. One common way is by flotation of seeds. Although most species of terrestrial plants have seeds that either sink in water or are killed by exposure to the high salinity of the ocean, others have special adaptations that permit their dispersal by sea currents. Many common plants of beaches and islands have seeds that are buoyant because of air-filled sacs or light materials surrounding them. Some remain afloat for months, and consequently when they are washed from a beach into the sea, they can be carried long distances by oceanic currents. The seeds of many island plants are resistant to sea water and are not killed by it. In some cases, sea water inhibits germination and the seeds are dormant during the long period they are afloat. When washed ashore, however, and soaked by rainwater on the beach, they germinate.

One of the best examples of a water-dispersed

'Sometimes cays move progressively across a reef by having sand washed away on one side and deposited on the other.'

Heron Island

◁ The larger, more stable coral cays have well-developed vegetation. Looking northward on Heron Island a dense forest of pisonia trees can be seen on the western part of the island, and a more open, darker green parkland on the eastern side. A tourist resort is visible on the northeastern tip.

Heron Island

△ Beachrock, such as this example on Heron Island, forms under sand on coral cays by the cementing together of sand grains. When the overlying sand is subsequently removed by erosion, beachrock remains as a pavement that looks like the surface of the moon. Such exposed areas of beachrock mark the location of previous sand accumulations and the former location of sand cays.

◁ Coral shingle or coral rubble consists of large chunks of coral that have been torn from the reef by storms. Some cays are composed entirely of shingle, and on some others the beaches are a mixture of shingle and sand, like Wilson Island in the Capricorn group.

Wilson Island

Argusia argentea

△ Argusia *is one of the most common shrubs on the Great Barrier Reef; its buoyant, salt-resistant fruits are dispersed by sea. It usually occurs on the upper beach where it may form a partial or complete shrub ring around the periphery of islands.*

▷ *The beach morning glory is a pioneer, salt-tolerant species that invades unconsolidated, sandy beaches and begins the process of stabilising the sand. Its seeds, which are resistant to sea water and able to stay afloat for long periods, are dispersed by sea currents. It is rapidly gaining a foothold on the shifting sands of Fraser Island.*

Beach morning glory, *Ipomoea pes-caprae*

plant on the Great Barrier Reef is Tournefortia, *Argusia argentea*, a large, silvery-leafed shrub. Its seeds remain alive in sea water with no loss of germination ability for at least 120 days and maybe much longer. They have a buoyant, cork-like layer around the fruits and have been reported to stay afloat for up to a year. The species is widespread, occurring from east Africa through the Australasian Archipelago, to Taiwan, the Ryukyus, the Philippines and most of Polynesia. It is the only terrestrial plant established on Ducie, east of Pitcairn Island, the most remote coral atoll in the world. It is curious that this plant has been dispersed over many kilometres of open ocean, yet once on land it seems unable to disperse for more than a few metres. It usually inhabits only the outer edge of the upper beach, although it grows well when planted further inland by humans.

Some plants on coral islands are dispersed by sea

Chaff flower, *Achyranthes aspera*

Tar-vine, *Boerhavia diffusa*

△ *Tar-vine in flower on One Tree Island. It produces sticky fruits that are dispersed by clinging to the feathers of sea birds.*

▷ *The large-leaved, luxuriant pisonia tree is one of the most common trees on forested coral cays of the Great Barrier Reef. The branches form support for nests of the black noddy, nesting at Heron Island, and its leaves and twigs provide nesting material. The noddies provide guano, necessary as fertiliser for the tree, and the birds disperse its sticky fruits, which become attached to their feathers.*

◁ *The chaff flower has long spikes of hooked fruits that attach to objects brushing against them. This species is dispersed from island to island by clinging to the feathers of sea birds.*

birds, many of which fly long distances during certain times of year, so they are good dispersal agents. Again, special adaptations of the plants facilitate transport, such as seeds or fruits with hooks or adhesive projections that attach them to objects that brush against them.

One of the common plants dispersed this way is the chaff flower, *Achyranthes aspera*. It fruits in long spikes, with rows of fruits, each containing a recurved spine that attaches it to objects with which it comes into contact. This plant reaches remote cays on which birds nest. Another species that also reaches newly formed, unstable cays inhabited by sea birds is *Boerhavia diffusa*. Its fruit has small projections, each of which oozes a thick, sticky fluid that adheres it to anything it contacts.

The pisonia tree, *Pisonia grandis*, has large leaves and spongy, sappy wood. It is common on forested cays and has a special relationship with the black noddy, *Anous minutus*. Pisonia trees grow best on soil enriched with bird guano and seldom occur in places lacking this natural fertiliser. When a coral cay first forms, the soil is low in organic content and nutrients, but as sea birds of various kinds nest there and deposit their guano and sometimes their dead bodies, the soil becomes enriched. Subsequently the pisonias become established.

The carrier birds

Once the soil has been prepared in this way, a chance visit by a noddy carrying pisonia seeds attached to its feathers may introduce this species of tree to the island. Once trees become established, they provide a favoured nesting place for the black noddy. The close contact between nesting noddies and pisonia trees means that opportunities for picking up seeds and dispersing them are numerous. Thus, the noddy not only fertilises the soil in which its nesting tree grows, but it also distributes its seeds widely. Both species benefit from their association.

Although a number of plants are dispersed on the Great Barrier Reef by attachment to the bodies of birds, it is not the only way in which birds transport seeds over water. Land birds, and even some sea birds, deposit them in their faeces.

Dispersal of seeds to islands is only the first requirement for colonisation. A new arrival must survive and reproduce, and not all immigrants can do that. The beaches of tropical islands are littered with seeds of species of plants that do not grow there. Some of the seeds probably died during the sea voyage, others simply did not find conditions suitable for germination. Occasionally seeds will sprout and the young plant will grow for a short time but die before reaching maturity.

Pisonia tree, *Pisonia grandis*

▷ *An immigrant seedling of the silverbush shrub makes a brave start in life beside an Argusia on One Tree Island. Although the silverbush is abundant on nearby Masthead Island, this plant was the only representative of its species on One Tree. It never flowered and died shortly after this photograph was taken.*

▷ ▽ *A small nightshade plant growing on One Tree Island. The seed was probably brought to the island in the intestinal tract of gulls, and the plant became established. It was eventually exterminated by a beetle that also immigrated; the beetle became extinct when it had demolished its sole food source, the nightshade. Both green fruits and the ripe, purple ones appear on this plant.*

In a similar way, stray animals may reach an island and survive there for a time, but unless they find a mate, they will die without offspring. Very mobile animals, such as land birds, butterflies or dragonflies, may merely touch down on an island and rest there momentarily, or remain for a few days if appropriate food is present and then fly on again. On Heron Island, when the wind blows from the mainland, many species of moths and other airborne insects, not usually found on the islands, appear briefly.

None of these organisms are truly part of the biota, or plant and animal community, of an island, although they may have a brief impact on the more permanent residents. They are transients that never become established. These transients include solitary seedlings or saplings that have never matured; land birds represented by a single individual on many islands; and a butterfly on a small, remote sand cay in the Coral Sea on which there was no vegetation at all. These are conspicuous examples; there are probably many more among the less conspicuous animals, such as the insects, that would go completely undetected.

Transient species
Intermediate between the categories of permanent residents and unestablished transients are the species that become established as breeding populations and maintain themselves for a time but eventually become locally extinct. They are breeding residents but not permanent ones. It is surprising just how many species fall into this category. Sometimes, the permanent residents among the above-ground arthropods, such as insects, spiders and centipedes, account for only about seven per cent of the total number of species, and more than half of the species present at any one time may be transients.

One example shows how the process of

▷ *Plants from the herb flat hanging over a sea-eroded bank on Bell Cay, Swain Reefs. Because of the erosion, between 1981 and 1983 two species of plant growing only on the periphery of the island were lost entirely.*

Silverbush, *Sophora tomentosa*; *Argusia argentea*

Nightshade plant, *Solanum nodiflorum*

Bell Cay, Swain Reefs

colonisation and extinction occurs. A small nightshade plant, *Solanum nodiflorum*, is a rather conspicuous herb that grows up to 50 centimetres high, produces flowers similar in appearance to those of the tomato plant, and has a fleshy purple fruit somewhat smaller than a gooseberry.

Except for one plant in the centre of the island, which was collected before it was realised that it might be the only plant of its kind there, nightshade was not known on One Tree Island in the early part of a three-year study. Later, however, a few plants appeared on the beach at a spot where silver gulls, *Larus novaehollandiae*, habitually roosted. These gulls are known to be fond of nightshade berries, and they fly back and forth between Heron Island (where nightshade is abundant) and One Tree Island. The plants were probably brought to One Tree as seeds in the digestive tracts of gulls and deposited where the birds roosted. These few plants matured and fruited, and the patch increased in size and spread progressively from the gull roost over a larger area until, four months later, it covered most of the island and accounted for six per cent of the weight of herbaceous plants there. Gulls and a small land bird, the silver-eye, *Zosterops lateralis*, were observed feeding on the berries, and their faeces were stained blue and contained whole seeds. These birds probably assisted the rapid spread of the plant throughout the island.

At that point, a small blue beetle, not previously present on the island, appeared. It ate nightshade leaves and nothing else. The beetle was brightly coloured – a condition that, among beetles, usually means they are bad tasting, bad smelling or otherwise noxious to predators, and they are only eaten by animals specially adapted to handle their unpleasant properties. No specialised predators were on One Tree Island, and the beetle population increased rapidly and eventually completely defoliated many of its food plants and severely damaged the rest, finally grazing the nightshade into local extinction. Then, lacking its only source of food it also disappeared. The beetle was on the island for a little more than a year before it ate itself out of food. With both plant and beetle extinct, the cycle ended.

Four years later the nightshade again appeared on the island, but the beetle had not yet returned. How many times the cycle of immigration, establishment, and extinction has occurred for this plant and beetle can only be guessed.

Local extinction
Extinction is common on islands, and the smaller an island the more likely are its species to become locally extinct. There are several good reasons for this. First, small islands are unstable. Some of the very small sand cays may only last a few years before being washed away by storm seas, or being gradually eroded by wave action. Often sand is redeposited and a new cay may form. Thus, even

entire islands may come and go. On Swain Reefs, several cays have disappeared and others have been severely eroded in less than a decade. Sometimes cays move progressively across a reef by having sand washed away on one side and deposited on the other. Shifting cays do not provide enough permanency for many species of plants to become established indefinitely. Also such shifting soils do not mature and they often are highly saline, which makes them less conducive to the establishment of some varieties of plants.

Even islands that are somewhat larger and remain on the same part of the reef for long periods are not completely stable. Beaches erode and are redeposited, so the peripheral parts of the island are undergoing continual change. Water-dispersed species wash up on beaches and become established, only to be lost again by erosion. The centre of the island, however, is more stable, and it may maintain some species for quite a long time. Such islands can be thought of as similar to hoola-hoops: a central area is maintained in a more or less stable manner, but around it there is an area of continuous movement and instability.

Weather extremes

A second reason for extinction on cays is changing weather. Droughts occur on islands; so do unusually wet, or hot, or windy conditions. On the mainland during periods of weather extremes, there are nearly always special refuges, such as protected valleys or gullies and sheltered sides of hills or mountains, where the effects of the physical environment are not so severe. Here some species can survive until more favourable conditions return, even though most die almost everywhere else. On a very small island such refuges are rare or non-existent, and bad weather can cause the elimination of a species. The island must wait until that species is replenished through dispersal from elsewhere, rather than relying on repopulation from a surviving remnant of the original population. A severe drought on One Tree Island in late 1968 caused massive extinction among the insects and spiders. The number of established species remaining after the drought was half to three-quarters that of more favourable conditions. Droughts are not uncommon on Great Barrier Reef islands: at One Tree they occur at intervals of four to five years. Storms may have similar effects and probably other extreme weather conditions do too.

A third reason for extinction is the nesting habits of sea birds. Some sea birds favour small cays where they are isolated from many of the mainland predators, but they have a marked effect on the plant life. While they provide fertiliser in the form of guano, too much may create an unfavourable environment for some plants, or even kill them. In addition, sea birds trample vegetation, and some species pluck it for use as nesting material.

Continued nesting by heavy concentrations of sea birds may virtually destroy the above-ground parts of the low vegetation on some small islands. The sea birds may then move elsewhere for nesting, returning only when the vegetation recovers. Thus, a kind of cycle is generated. Even on islands with lower population densities, sea birds may markedly influence the vegetation that becomes established.

A fourth reason for extinction on islands is that some biological restraints may be missing. On small islands with a restricted flora, species that on mainlands may aid in regulating other species may be absent. A good example is the one described earlier, of the beetle that grazed on nightshade. There was no predator to control its numbers, and it was thus able to deplete its own food supply and thereby become extinct. A predator might have kept the beetle population low enough to prevent it entirely consuming its food plant, and all three species – plant, grazing insect and predator – may have persisted indefinitely.

One Tree Island

The fifth reason for extinction is chance. Very small populations are more likely to become extinct than are larger ones. The smaller the island, the smaller are its populations of organisms, everything else being equal. Chance alone, on a very small island, may cause insufficient offspring to be produced in one season to guarantee the extended success of that species on the island.

Clearly, the structure of life on small islands, such as the cays of the Great Barrier Reef, is one of instability, uncertainty and dynamism.

Island survival

Existence for an island plant or animal is precarious. How, then, do they cope with the demands that island habitats make upon them? Not all species respond in the same way. There are certain characteristics that are useful in such an environment, but not all species have all of them.

Three main categories seem to be important: the ability to tolerate harsh conditions; the ability to wait out unfavourable periods; and the ability to move to new places and to exploit favourable conditions rapidly.

Many of the plants on the cays of the Great Barrier Reef are halophytes, or species that can tolerate high levels of salt either in the water surrounding their roots, or as salt spray on the shoots and leaves. Some of them tolerate high salt levels within their own tissues. A few are known to be able to take up water more easily than most plants. Another drought-resistant measure is the closure of the pores (stomata) in the leaves during water shortage, thereby reducing the amount of water lost through the leaves by evaporation. On One Tree Island, over half of the established species of plants are salt-tolerant.

Waiting out unfavourable conditions can be

One Tree Island

△ *The herb flat on One Tree Island is lush and healthy when there is no drought.*

△ ◁ *The herb flat on One Tree Island during a severe drought. Many of the low plants are dead or dying.*

'St Augustine, in the 5th century, suggested that in addition to swimming and being carried by humans, perhaps the heavenly angels under divine command transported organisms to remote islands.'

achieved in a number of ways. Seeds may lie dormant for long periods and germinate only when conditions become favourable. In a sense, this happens during dispersal by sea currents; the seeds do not germinate while in contact with sea water and do so only when fresh water, in the form of rain, reaches them on some beach.

Another strategy for survival is storing food and waiting for better conditions. Some plants form large roots that store food. Even if the green parts are killed or trampled by birds, the root remains alive, and it can send up shoots when favourable conditions prevail. A good example of a plant with large storage roots is *Boerhavia diffusa*, a small herbaceous plant with white flowers. It has a long, fleshy taproot that can not only store food, but also reach down to the deeper layers of soil where water is more likely to be found during periods of drought. The plant succeeds on small islands and,

Tar-vine, *Boerhavia diffusa*

△ *A common plant of herb flats of coral cays on the Great Barrier Reef, the tah-vine has a long, thick taproot which stores food and reaches water deep in the soil. These roots, exposed as a result of shifting sand on Frigate Cay, Swain Reefs, persist for long periods even if the green parts of the plant are destroyed by sea birds.*

'A new arrival on a cay must first of all survive and then reproduce.'

once well established, survives for extended periods even if its green parts are repeatedly destroyed by sea birds. There are many species, from both island and mainland habitats, in which seeds may be dormant for long periods.

The ability to move to new places is an obvious advantage in an unstable environment. Many island plants have this characteristic to a remarkable degree. Responsible for their dispersal to islands in the first place, the same attribute continues to permit their colonisation of new islands as they become available and as the one they occupy becomes untenable.

The ability to exploit new habitats quickly is a feature of weedy species, whether insular or not. A species that can colonise a new habitat as soon as it becomes available, grow rapidly, produce seeds early and in large numbers, exploit a temporary, unstable surface, and move on to another when the first one becomes uninhabitable has a decided advantage on islands.

How a coral cay forms

Some changes in the vegetation and animal life of coral cays occur for reasons other than instability of the islands. Even on relatively permanent, immobile islands, the composition of the flora and fauna alters with time. There are several reasons for such changes. One is that during the continual cycle of immigration and extinction, by chance different species reach an island at different times, and they remain there for different lengths of time. Thus, the composition alters.

There is more to the story than just the vagaries of dispersal and extinction, however, and the process does not seem to be completely haphazard. Whether a particular species can become established is determined by whether it fits into the total food web of the community. For example, for a predator to become established, suitable prey species must be present; for a nectar-feeding bee to survive, appropriate flowers must occur. In general, it seems that if a particular kind of feeder, perhaps a predator, is represented by too few species on an island, an immigrant species in that category can become established more easily than if the category is over-represented. Species in over-represented feeding categories are also more likely to become locally extinct than those in under-represented feeding categories.

For a given type of island and stage of development, there seems to be a nearly constant proportion of predators, grazers, seed-eaters, flower feeders and scavengers. These proportions remain stable at a given stage of island development, but over time, they shift the balance to favour some kinds of food habits at the expense of others. Progressive stages in the development of islands often have different proportions of species in the various feeding categories.

Island development

There seem to be definite patterns of life that an island goes through in its development, but the sequence is unexpected. One could reasonably predict that once a sand cay is formed, the first invaders would be plants, followed by animals that feed on plants (herbivores) and then by predators that feed upon herbivores. This does not often seem to be the case. The reason is that young islands are greatly affected by the life of the sea. Dead fish and other marine animals wash up on the beach before green plants become established. Any scavenger that arrives has a ready source of food and may become established, whereas a herbivore that arrives would be unsuccessful. Sea birds and perhaps intertidal organisms assist the establishment of a scavenger industry by depositing guano, food scraps and, upon their death, carrion. Predators that arrive at this stage have scavengers to eat.

Although all food ultimately originates from green plants, in the case of bare islands it is the plants of the sea that provide food. It is then consumed by marine animals, which in turn are either washed up dead on the beach or are eaten by sea birds or intertidal animals that indirectly transfer this material from sea to land as guano or carrion. A number of cays without vegetation in the Great Barrier Reef region have been examined and many have only scavengers as terrestrial animals or a combination of scavengers and predators.

Eventually green plants do invade and become established. They produce food and supplement that transferred from the sea. Herbivores can arrive and, following them, a greater number of predators as well as parasites; the proportion of animals in the various feeding categories gradually shifts.

The first plants that become established are hardy, pioneer species that can contend with the harsh, unstable conditions of their islands. They hold the sand together and begin to stabilise the soil. With the advent of these plants and their production of food directly on the island, organic matter accumulates and, along with sea bird guano, enriches the soil sufficiently for the establishment of plants that require more stable, more mature soils. Low herbs, grasses and vines are followed by shrubs and eventually trees. Finally, delicate plants that require shade, shelter from wind, and a richer, moister soil can become established under the protective canopy of developing forests.

The change from bare sand through various stages to forest is called ecological succession. Each cay goes through an ecological succession during its development. It is not an inevitable progression, however, because of that characteristic feature of islands already mentioned – instability. Storms, erosion, drought, dense populations of nesting birds and other environmental influences destroy or injure vegetation and animals, or impose harsh conditions that set back succession to earlier stages.

In extreme cases, an island can be denuded entirely and the succession must start again. Where there is great instability, especially on small islands, development may be halted at an early stage. Where stability is greater, as on larger islands, the final stage of forest in some cases may be reached and maintained indefinitely.

Growing in shifting sands

Even on the most stable islands, however, there are areas of instability. The peripheral areas are more subject to erosion, the effects of salt spray and wind, and are less stable than the interior. Consequently, the beaches and adjacent zones often have shifting sands and harsh conditions and only pioneer species can grow there. Further inland occur the plants characteristic of a later stage of succession, and in the interior, more stable areas, is the forest. In this way different vegetation zones occur on islands.

Younger or less stable islands have vegetation types characteristic of early successional stages, and older or more stable ones have a variety of zones. Here the plants characteristic of a late stage in the succession occur in the centre with a grading through intermediate ones to the vegetation characteristic of early succession on the periphery. Local environmental conditions can alter the general pattern, but it applies well to many of the cays on the reef. And the major kinds of vegetation that occur on cays are common to most of them.

Strand vegetation

Strand vegetation consists of the pioneer, salt-tolerant, drought-resistant species that invade shifting mineral sands and begin to consolidate them. Such plants are the first to appear on newly deposited sand cays and are characteristic of the least stable parts of older vegetated islands. These are the plants of the open beach and usually they are distributed sparsely. In addition, they are often creepers, such as the grass *Thaurea involuta*, the beach morning glory, *Ipomoea pes-caprae*, and the beach pea, *Canavalia rosea*.

Shrub rings

Many islands have a ring of shrubs around the periphery just at the edge of the upper beach, behind the strand vegetation. The ring may be nearly complete, or may be broken by gaps. Sometimes shrubs may extend further inland to contribute to the vegetation of other zones, but often the shrub ring is distinct, sharply defined, and only one or two shrubs wide.

The most characteristic species in shrub rings on cays of the Great Barrier Reef is *Argusia argentea*, and often the shrub ring is composed of only that species. Other species sometimes encountered are the fan-flower, *Scaevola taccada*, and the silver bush, *Sophora tomentosa*. Sometimes the casuarina, *Casuarina equisetifolia*, forms a ring, much like the shrub ring, but comprised of taller plants.

Herb flats

On many islands, the vegetation lying inside the shrub ring consists of a dense meadow of low herbs, grasses and vines – the herb flat. It includes a large variety of species, and the composition varies from island to island. Some of the common species occurring are tar-vine, *Boerhavia diffusa*; caltrop, *Tribulus cistoides*; lantern flower, *Abutilon albescens*; a daisy, *Melanthera biflora*; and the grasses *Stenotaphrum micranthum* and *Lepturus repens*.

Succulent mats

On a few of the Great Barrier Reef cays, there is a special kind of meadow made up of low succulent plants. This lush carpet is formed mainly of two species, sea purslane, *Sesuvium portulacastrum*, and pigweed, *Portulaca oleracea*.

Forests

In some cases, the shrub ring gives way to forest rather than meadow. On the Great Barrier Reef the primary tree in such forests is *Pisonia grandis*, a luxuriant, large-leaved species that often forms a closed canopy providing dense shade. Other trees, such as the casuarina, *Casuarina equisetifolia*, and the sea trumpet tree, *Cordia subcordata*, are also sometimes components of forest. Casuarinas are most common on the edge of the forest near the beach.

Mangroves

Under special conditions, mangrove trees may form dense tidal forests, either as entire islands or as parts of other islands.

In addition to these major vegetation types, there are some that are less clearly defined and take on characteristics of two different zones. For example, shrubs may invade a herb flat, there may be small clumps of forest surrounded by herb flat or there may be open patches in forests.

Coastal parkland

One common intermediate type is a savanna-like parkland of trees and shrubs with a rather open canopy and a ground layer of species characteristic of the herb flat. Such parkland includes species of shrubs and trees from the shrub ring and forest, such as *Argusia*, *Scaevola* and *Pisonia*, as well as species that seem to be especially characteristic of parkland, such as screw palm, *Pandanus* species, the fig, *Ficus opposita*, and *Casuarina equisetifolia*.

The zones occur in different combinations. Typically, there is a zone of strand vegetation, followed by a shrub ring, inside of which is either herb flat or forest. But shrub rings may be missing entirely, with the strand vegetation grading directly

◁ *A canopy covers a stream running through a rainforest at North Point, Lizard Island. Vegetation in the interior of continental islands is more similar to that of the mainland than it is to coral cays.*

Lizard Island

Coral cays and continental islands

△ *Islands are of various kinds; some are vegetated coral cays, like the cay with beach vegetation in the foreground, others are coral cays with no vegetation, as the tiny sandy island in the left background, and still others are continental islands with vegetation resembling the mainland, as in the right background.*

▷ *Strand vegetation is capable of surviving on shifting surfaces of high salinity and low water content. It is the first kind of vegetation to colonise new coral cays and persists along the beaches of stabilised ones, as at Frigate Cay, Swain Reefs. The birds are sooty terns among a mixture of pioneer herbs and grasses.*

Sooty tern, *Sterna fuscata*

into herb flat. The shrub ring may not be well developed, and parkland sometimes begins at the edge of the upper beach, often with no peripheral zone of strand vegetation. Almost all possible combinations occur, yet there seems to be a general progression in succession from strand vegetation to shrubs or herb flat or both to parkland to forest, with succulent mats and mangroves constituting special situations.

Human interference

Human activities have affected the vegetation of many coral cays. Early disturbances included guano mining for fertiliser. At the turn of the century, a number of islands were inhabited by Chinese or Malay guano miners who stripped off the vegetation and mined the rich soil. Regeneration has occurred to varying degrees since cessation of mining, but the islands that were stripped nearly to the bare

Daisy, *Melanthera biflora*

'Many islands have a ring of shrubs around the edge of the upper beach, and within the ring often lies a dense meadow of herbs, grasses and vines.'

◁ *This daisy is one of the common species of plant in herb flats on coral cays. It is replaced by more drought-resistant species during dry periods.*

Daisy, *Melanthera biflora*

Sea purslane, *Sesuvium portulacastrum*

Fan-flower, *Scaevola taccada*

△ *A daisy in yellow flower dominates an island herb flat. In the background is a shrub ring and in the far background, continental islands. Many coral cays of the Great Barrier Reef have a meadow of herbs, vines and grasses called the herb flat. Different species occur in islands herb flats, and the composition varies from island to island.*

▷ *One of the more showy of the plants in the herb flats of coral cays is the caltrop. The fruits have heavy spikes that aid dispersal by sea birds.*

△ *A common shrub on Great Barrier Reef coral cays is the fan-flower. It often forms part of a shrub ring. Here a bumblebee pollinates one of the plant's distinctive flowers.*

◁△ *Sea purslane, in flower on One Tree Island, is a salt-tolerant species that commonly makes up a great proportion of the succulent mat on coral cays. The succulent mats do not occur on all coral cays, but where they do, they form a lush carpet.*

Caltrop, *Tribulus cistoides*

The ecological sucession

'Once the pioneer species have colonised an island, they help create the conditions that allow herbs and grasses, then shrubs and eventually trees to become established.'

Pisonia forest

▷ *The pisonia forest on Lady Musgrave Island forms a dense canopy that provides a cool, moist, shaded environment. Under the canopy, leaf litter accumulates, but few under-storey plants occur.*

Sea purslane, *Sesuvium portulacastrum*; pigweed, *Portulaca oleracea*

Δ *The brackish water pond on One Tree Island, Capricorn group. In areas of high soil salinity, a lush mat of succulent vegetation occurs, composed chiefly of pigweed and sea purslane.*

▷ *Islands are unstable habitats. An ancient casuarina tree leans seaward, tenaciously clinging to the land by the few remaining roots not exposed by beach erosion.*

Casuarina

Screw palm, *Pandanus*

△ The screw palm, delicately balanced on its stilt roots, is a characteristic of open parkland on islands.

◁ A pisonia tree, gnarled, broken and stripped of some of its leaves, stands at the edge of an encroaching beach and guards a view of a distant continental island.

Pisonia tree, *Pisonia grandis*

△ *The barren landscape of Lady Elliott Island, Bunker group, is the result of guano mining at the turn of the century and the ravages of goats for several decades. The goats have been destroyed, and the vegetation restored. Seabirds have returned to nest. It is truly a conservation success story.*

△ ▷ *An open parkland sometimes develops on islands of the Great Barrier Reef. The tree canopy is not closed and the plants represented are a mixture of forest species (such as the pisonia tree), a variety of shrubs and trees characteristic of parkland (such as the clump of screw palms in the centre), and an under-storey of low plants characteristic of herb flats. Parkland appears to be a transitional stage between herb flat and forest.*

'The results of guano mining and goat raising were ecological disasters for many of the islands of the Great Barrier Reef.'

limestone still show the effects and will do so for many years to come. Islands that were mined include Lady Elliott, North West, and the eastern cay on Fairfax Reef in the Bunker-Capricorn area, and Bird Islet from Wreck Reef.

Goats were also brought to coral cays until recent decades, to provide food for future shipwrecked sailors. The result was an ecological disaster and the vegetation of a number of Great Barrier Reef islands was severely disrupted. Lady Elliott, Lady Musgrave, the eastern cay of Fairfax, and North West islands all had goats at one time or another. By the early 1940s, most herds had been destroyed, and at present there are no free-roaming goats on any of the coral cays.

Many other animal species have been introduced, either inadvertently or intentionally, on to the coral islands of the Great Barrier Reef. Rats are easily transported by ships and have been on some of the islands for a long time. Thriving populations of feral cats and chickens live on North West Island; the chickens are of considerable scientific interest, because they resemble the wild ancestors of domestic breeds.

Ornamental plants have been brought to the islands to beautify the gardens around lighthouses and resorts. Some of these have escaped from cultivation and have established wild populations. Others have arrived perhaps as seeds in supplies or attached to clothing and have become established.

Pisonia tree, *Pisonia grandis*; screw palm, *Pandanus*

On some islands, like Heron Island, where many people visit and a large volume of supplies and materials is brought in, the number of introduced plants may reach as high as 33 per cent of the species, even if planted ornamentals are not included. Indeed, none of the islands of the Bunker-Capricorn Group has its vegetation in its original state.

Introduced plants

Some of the plants are pests. For example, the burr grass, *Cenchrus echinatus*, was inadvertently introduced on to Heron Island, and has spread naturally to a number of the nearby islands. This species produces a spiked fruit that injures bare feet, so it is clearly undesirable on resort islands. Yet it is likely to remain a part of the permanent flora of a number of these coral cays.

Perhaps the most interesting of the introduced plants is the searocket *Cakile edentula*, a species that was originally found only along the sandy beaches of eastern North America. It arrived, probably as seeds in the ballast of American sailing ships, some time prior to 1863 in the vicinity of Melbourne. It has buoyant, salt-resistant fruits, and it spread by natural means around the coast of eastern Australia, reaching Heron Island some time before 1958. It then spread among the islands of the Capricorn-Bunker Group, and in the early 1980s reached some of the cays of the Swain Reefs, about 150 kilometres northeast of Heron Island. Once established on an island, it grows well and persists. This species will probably become one of the very common plants of the islands of the Great Barrier Reef.

The development of resorts, lighthouses, research stations and other facilities also affects the island environment. Destruction of vegetation to provide space for buildings, paths and sport facilities, and disposal of rubbish, garbage and sewage, are problems that have been inadequately assessed, and very little realistic planning has been carried out. Campers have littered many islands, chopped down trees for firewood and built rough, aesthetically unpleasing shelters. Construction of channels and coastal 'improvements' in some cases have resulted in alteration to the erosion pattern, and facilities have been threatened by severe beach erosion.

With ever-increasing tourism on the reef, the undesirable influence of humans on coral cays is likely to increase unless forward planning, unbridled by short-sighted policies motivated by immediate economic gain, can be carried out and sound management principles established. Despite the recent zoning by the Commonwealth Government of parts of the Great Barrier Reef as marine parks, attention to islands has been woefully inadequate, and the scientific base so necessary for establishing management policies is still lacking.

It is important that tourism be developed and that as many people as possible be provided the exquisite privilege of experiencing a coral cay. But at present there is often conflict between environmentalists and developers, with neither side prepared to yield. Scientific studies leading to better understanding of management procedures may provide a means of safeguarding the environment and at the same time permitting its reasoned exploitation.

Island vertebrates

Sea birds and sea turtles (see Marine Reptiles, page 294) are the most conspicuous vertebrates on coral islands. In addition there are some land birds and a few species of lizards and snakes, and occasionally introduced rats and mice. By contrast, continental islands have quite a varied vertebrate fauna including mammals, frogs, birds and reptiles. Their faunas resemble mainland fauna to varying degrees, depending on the size and distance of the island from the mainland.

Land birds

Birds are a prominent feature of many islands, and, as already mentioned, they play important roles in dispersing plants, providing fertiliser and trampling vegetation. The continental islands have a wide variety of land birds living in habitats similar to those they occupy on the mainland. The larger the island and the closer it is to the mainland, the more closely its bird life, or avifauna, resembles that of the adjacent mainland. Coral cays, by contrast, have

Searocket, *Cakile edentula*

△ *The searocket is native to North America. It was introduced into Australia and has spread to many islands of the Great Barrier Reef, and it is still spreading. Its fruits are dispersed by sea and it is salt tolerant.*

fewer habitats and their land bird fauna is more limited in number of species. Many of the land birds observed on cays are transients: birds that are lost, blown offshore by storms, or merely passing through during migration. They are there temporarily and do not breed on the island. Often only one individual is present. There is a surprising number of such transient individuals. For example, during the study of One Tree Island only three species of land birds were resident, yet 18 species have been sighted as transients.

Some species of land birds, however, are frequently found on cays, and they occur as permanent breeding populations. The silver-eye is abundant on Heron Island and on some nearby wooded cays. It is the only species of land bird that is represented on the islands of the Great Barrier Reef by a different subspecies than that on the mainland. The bar-shouldered dove, *Geopelia humeralis*, is commonly found on coral cays throughout the Great Barrier Reef. Perhaps the most characteristic land bird on the island is the buff-breasted rail, *Rallus philippensis*. This species

is distributed throughout the islands and coastal regions of Australia, the eastern Indian Ocean and the southwestern Pacific Ocean. It occurs on many islands, even tiny ones as small as five hectares, as well as on mainlands. It nests in burrows or depressions in the ground, and it is probably susceptible to mainland predators from which it is isolated on islands. Torresian imperial pigeons, *Ducula spilorrhoa*, migrate to the northern parts of the Great Barrier Reef and nest in dense colonies among mangrove trees. They make daily trips to the nearby mainland in search of fruit in the tropical rainforests.

Sea birds

Sea birds are more numerous and conspicuous on cays than are land birds. They include gulls, terns, gannets, shearwaters and frigate birds, that feed at sea on fishes and other marine life.

Twenty-nine species of sea birds from seven different families are distributed broadly throughout the Great Barrier Reef region. Of these, 19 species breed there, with colonies occurring on at least 78 different islands. Some of these colonies are large: 20 000 sooty terns, *Sterna fuscata*, nest on Michaelmas Cay and 10 000 on Raine Island (along with 12 other species); 70 000 black noddies, *Anous minutus*, nest on Heron Island and 160 000 on North West Island. In addition, 8000 common noddies, *Anous stolidus*, nest on Michaelmas Cay and 6000 on North Reef Cay, Frederick Reef; and 750 000 wedge-tailed shearwaters, *Puffinus pacificus*, nest on North West Island.

Some islands are more important as breeding sites than others. The ten most important ones, in descending order, are Raine, Bramble, Michaelmas, Swain Reefs, Masthead, North West, One Tree, Wilson, Pipon, and Fairfax. Also important are Hoskyn, Tryon, Heron, Bird, Pandora, Booby, Bushy, Wood, Claremont, Ocean Creek and Sand Cay. A number of these cays are in the Capricorn Group of islands, and that region is extremely important: including non-breeding birds that use the islands for roosting, as well as the breeding populations, it has been estimated recently that there are 1.5 million wedge-tailed shearwaters, half a million black noddies, more than 3000 each of crested terns and bridled terns and 2000 each of black-naped terns and roseate terns in the Capricorn area.

Breeding habits

Some sea birds, such as the black-naped, roseate, crested and lesser crested terns and the masked gannet, nest on bare sand or rubble, whereas the sooty tern requires low vegetation and the black noddy requires shrubs or trees in which to nest. Consequently, different species of birds nest on islands at different stages of development and as an island goes through ecological succession, not only

Silver-eye, *Zosterops lateralis*

△ *An adult silver-eye feeds a fledgling in a pisonia tree on Heron Island. The silver-eye is one of the numerous small land birds found on wooded coral cays of the Great Barrier Reef.*

▷ *The buff-breasted rail is one of the most characteristic land birds on islands. It breeds even in habitats as small as five hectares. It is distributed throughout the islands and coasts of Australia, the eastern Indian Ocean and the southwestern Pacific islands.*

Buff-breasted rail, *Rallus philippensis*

'Many of the land birds seen on the cays are transients – birds that are blown offshore by storms, or passing through during migration – but the reefs and beaches provide important habitats for the feeding and roosting of shore birds or waders.'

Terns

◁ *A mixed flock of terns on the beach of Gannet Cay, Swain Reefs. Terns of various species occur on many cays in very large numbers and are often the most conspicuous life on such islands.*

Bar-shouldered dove, *Geopelia humeralis*

◮ *The bar-shouldered dove is a land bird frequently encountered on islands of the Great Barrier Reef. It nests in low shrubs or mangroves and feeds mainly in pairs or small flocks.*

◁ *A flock of black noddies feeds on a school of small fish. These birds breed on reef islands, building untidy nests of leaves and sea weed mixed with droppings.*

Black noddy, *Anous minutus*

ISLAND PLANT AND ANIMAL LIFE 341

does its vegetation change, but at the same time its bird population changes too.

The silver gull, *Larus novaehollandiae*, one of the most common island sea birds, has a broad diet. It is a scavenger, feeding on refuse on the beach, but it also eats insects, fruits and almost any foodstuffs discarded by humans. It has a taste for eggs, and when nests of other sea birds are left unattended, even briefly, the silver gull will dart in, break the eggs and consume them. Consequently, any disturbance to sea bird colonies that causes the parent birds to leave nests unattended usually results in destruction of many of the eggs, and even young chicks, by the gulls.

Protecting the nest

Important breeding colonies are now closed to humans during breeding seasons, a wise policy indeed in view of the predatory habits of gulls and the inadvertent assistance in raiding nests that people give them. Under most other conditions, at least one parent bird attends the eggs and young chicks.

The gulls are very protective of their own eggs, screaming and swooping upon a person who approaches the nest. They repeatedly wheel into mock attacks as long as anyone remains in the vicinity. They have dark eggs, which usually are laid near some prominent object, such as a piece of coral, a plant, or debris that has washed ashore.

▷ *A black noddy and its chick on Heron Island. The nest is constructed of pisonia leaves.*

▷ ▽ *A black noddy perched on a twig of shrub. About half a million black noddies may inhabit the Capricorn Bunker area.*

▽ *A group of black noddies with white caps preen as they sun themselves on the beach.*

Black noddy, *Anous minutus*

Black noddy, *Anous minutus*

Black noddy, *Anous minutus*

Muttonbird, *Puffinus pacificus*

Muttonbird, *Puffinus pacificus*

△ *An adult muttonbird or wedge-tailed shearwater. The nocturnal serenades of these birds during the breeding season and their burrowing habit for nesting have made these birds unpopular with island developers.*

▽ *An egg of the black-naped tern laid in the open on bare rubble at One Tree Island. Many terns nest on bare sand or rubble without the aid of a nest constructed of softer materials, or of the shade of plants.*

Black-naped tern egg, *Sterna sumatrana*

△ *A fluffy muttonbird chick. Muttonbirds remain in the underground burrows dug to contain the eggs until they are ready to begin to fly.*

The young continue to beg food from the parents even after they are quite capable of obtaining their own. They adopt a crouched position and appeal for food in a most piteous manner. One could be misled easily into believing that the plump, healthy chick was starving.

Graceful gliders

The frigate birds are perhaps the most accomplished aerialists of any of the sea birds. They soar in circles for hours on end, seldom flapping their wings, and appear to glide effortlessly except for the occasional steering movements of their forked tail. These birds are often pirates. They soar above other birds and carefully watch their activities. When another sea bird has caught a fish they relentlessly pursue it, eventually causing it to drop the prey, which they then dive upon and swoop up in midair. They nest in colonies on islands.

There are two species, the great frigate bird, *Fregata minor*, and the lesser frigate bird, *Fregata ariel*. The former usually nests in shrubs or trees. The males have large red sacs on their necks, which they inflate during courtship. The lesser frigate bird nests in shrubs or on the ground. The ungainly, somewhat rumpled chicks have rusty red heads and develop the sleek black and white plumage of the adult when they are ready to fly. Repeated nesting, year after year, at the same place results in damage to the vegetation, and dead or dying vegetation can

be seen around the rookeries of ground-nesting frigate birds.

Several species of gannets are found on the Great Barrier Reef. They combine grace and harmonious efficiency in the air with comic clumsiness in landing and taking off. They flap laboriously and heavily when trying to get aloft, and often nose-dive and fall on landing, but in the air they glide and wheel as they search for fishes, which they catch by performing nearly vertical dives to the sea.

From egg to hatchling

The chicks are bare, grey-skinned and ugly when hatched. Usually two eggs and hatchlings are produced, but seldom do both survive to the fluffy awkward stage of the older hatchling. Nests are attended until the chicks are large enough to be immune from gull attacks and capable of withstanding the hot sun. The parents bring fishes which they regurgitate for their young to eat.

The different species of gannets have different nesting habits. The masked gannet or masked booby, *Sula dactylatra*, a handsome white and black bird, usually nests on bare, fine sand in the open,

Lesser frigate bird, Fregata ariel

▷ *The rusty head, hooked beak and beady black eye of a young lesser frigate bird. The ungainly, fluffy appearance of the chicks gives way to the sleek plumage of the adult when the birds are ready to fly.*

▷ ▽ *Where sea birds nest in large numbers, trampling and heavy concentrations of guano may kill vegetation. Chicks of the lesser frigate bird at Bell Cay, Swain Reefs have caused the death of the plants (mainly caltrop and Boerhavia diffusa) around their colony.*

Great frigate bird, Fregata minor

△ *The male great frigate bird inflates a brilliantly coloured throat sac as part of its elaborate courtship ritual to attract the female.*

'The frigate birds are perhaps the most accomplished aerialists of any of the sea birds. They soar in circles for hours on end, seldom flapping their wings, and appear to glide effortlessly.'

Lesser frigate bird, Fregata ariel

Masked gannet, *Sula dactylatra*

◁ *The masked gannet usually nests on bare sand without constructing a nest. Parents guard a chick that will come to appear larger than them, because of its fluffy down, before it grows sleeker feathers. The chicks are fed on fishes regurgitated by their parents.*

◁ ▽ *Brown boobies nestle with their white fluffy chicks among grasses of the herb flat.*

Brown booby, *Sula leucogaster*

Silver gull, *Larus novaehollandiae*

and away from vegetation or large objects. By contrast the brown booby, *Sula leucogaster*, usually nests on small, cleared patches in low vegetation. When no vegetation is present, they often adorn the nesting sites with small objects such as shells, seaweed, flotsam, or even dead, dried sea snakes. In contrast to these two ground nesters, the red-footed booby, *Sula sula*, often nests in shrubs.

The tropic birds, *Phaethon* species, are not as common as other sea birds, and usually only a few nests are found on any one island. They hide their nests among rocks, coral or other debris.

Wedge-tailed shearwaters nest in large numbers on some of the coral cays. They dig burrows in the soil in which they lay their eggs. The chick remains in the burrows until time to fledge. By day these birds are not conspicuous, as they remain inactive underground, and, indeed, a visitor to an island may never become aware of their presence until his foot

Brown booby, *Sula leucogaster*

△ *The nest of a silver gull beside an old boot washed up on Gannet Cay, Swain Reefs. The silver gull likes to build a nest in which to lay its eggs and usually locates it near some prominent object. Silver gulls are very protective of their eggs, and they will wheel into mock attacks if anyone approaches the nest. But they have a great taste for the eggs of other sea birds.*

◁ *Brown booby chicks are ugly and nearly helpless when hatched. Usually two eggs are laid but seldom does more than one chick survive beyond the very early stages. The nests, made on small patches of low vegetation, are attended until the chicks are large enough to be immune from gull attacks.*

suddenly breaks through the roof of a burrow. At dusk and dawn the birds fly out over the sea in search of food.

The courtship ritual

During the breeding season they spend much of the night calling to each other as part of the courtship ritual. The sound is an insistent, yet mournful moaning, which is as disturbing to the sleep of some tourists as it is pleasant to the naturalist. These serenades and the potential effect of their burrowing in undermining runways have not made them popular with developers of tourist facilities on islands. Their nesting areas were bulldozed during the breeding season on one island, and lighthouse keepers were asked to destroy their eggs prior to construction of an airfield on another.

Each of the many species of terns has its own kind of nesting site. The black-naped tern, *Sterna*

Brown booby, *Sula leucogaster*

△ *A brown booby at Northeast Cay, Saumarez Reef, on a nest constructed of feathers, corals, sponges, calcareous algae and a dried sea snake. When plant material is not available, almost any object is used to make a nest.*

▷ *A female yellow-breasted sunbird peers from its pouch-like hanging nest. This tropical coastal land bird nests on some of the continental islands.*

Yellow-breasted sunbird, *Nectarinia jugularis*

Golden plover, *Pluvialis dominica*

White-tailed tropic bird, *Phaeton lepturus*

△ *A white-tailed tropic bird sits on its nest among rocks on Herald Cay. Tropic birds are among the least common of the sea birds of the Great Barrier Reef, and they are rarely seen, because they hide their nests among rocks, coral or other debris.*

△ *The golden plover, seen here in one of its plumage phases, breeds in northeast Siberia and northern North America but migrates to the southwest Pacific, Australia and South America during the non-breeding season, like many waders or shore birds.*

sumatrana, often nests on bare rubble; the bridled tern, *Sterna anatheta*, usually conceals its nest among or under low plants; and the black noddy, *Anous minutus*, builds nests which are constructed from dead leaves, in trees.

All the ground-nesting terns nest in colonies, often of hundreds of pairs, with the nests placed closely together. Although the colony breeds repeatedly on the same island, it moves the exact nesting site almost every year. For those that nest in vegetation, this habit means that their intensive use of an island will not cause long-term damage, as plant life in particular places can recover during years when the colony has moved its nesting area to a different site.

Although dead birds, both young and adult, are a common feature of most sea bird colonies, some tern populations have unusually high mortality. For example, on one occasion on North Reef Cay, Frederick Reef, over 7000 dead common noddies, *Anous stolidus*, were found. The cause of such a heavy death toll is not known. Perhaps a contagious virus persists in the soil and re-infects the nesting birds each season.

Shore birds

A number of other species are closely linked with the sea and yet are not usually considered as true sea birds; they include sandpipers, curlews, whimbrels, tattlers, a sanderling, a turnstone, plovers and dotterels. Collectively they are called shore birds or

'Birds are a prominent feature of many islands; they play important roles in dispersing plants, providing fertiliser and trampling vegetation.'

waders. The reefs and beaches of some of the Great
Barrier Reef islands have become important habitats
for feeding and roosting of shore birds, as estuarine
habitats have become progressively destroyed in
other places and continental shores have been
populated by humans. The oystercatchers are
among the few waders that breed on deserted
beaches of the islands. The sooty oystercatcher,
Haematopus fuliginosus, defends a territory along the
beach where it nests. It lays its eggs in a small
depression just above the highwater mark.

Most waders nest elsewhere, such as in the Arctic
regions of Alaska and Siberia, or other parts of Asia
or America, but migrate during the non-breeding
season to the coastal region of Australia. They are
common, usually in groups, along the beaches of
islands. Unlike the sea birds, which feed in the
ocean, the waders feed along the shoreline
or in shallow water.

Three other kinds of birds frequently associated
with the islands are the reef herons, *Egretta sacra*, the
sea eagle, *Haliaeetus leucogaster*, and the Australian
pelican, *Pelecanus conspicillatus*. The heron comes in
two colour varieties within the same species, a white
phase and a grey phase. It nests in trees and spends
its feeding time on the reef flats looking for small
marine animals. The sea eagles build huge nests on
the ground or in trees or lighthouses. They prey on
fishes, sea snakes and sea birds. The Australian pelican
has traditional breeding colonies in northern parts of
the Great Barrier Reef. One island was named after
this bird by Captain Cook, and it is still inhabited
by a large number of the species.

Land reptiles

Most of the very small coral cays lack land reptiles,
and even many of the larger ones at the southern
end of the Great Barrier Reef do not have these
animals (exceptions are Wilson Island and Lady
Elliott Island). In the north, a number of coral cays
do have lizards. These are primarily of two kinds,
skinks and geckos.

Skinks and geckos
The geckos, of the genera *Gehyra* and
Lepidodaetylus, are adapted to island life. They
often live in close proximity to humans, occupying
crevices in dwellings. They are more likely, as a
consequence, to be carried around by man in

▷ △ *A white-breasted sea eagle in flight. Sea eagles build
huge nests on the ground or in trees or lighthouses.*

▷ *A baby white-breasted sea eagle in a nest on Clarke
Island. Some sea eagles use the same nest year after year.
On One Tree Island a large nest, first seen in 1843 at its
present size of about two metres tall, has been used
intermittently up to the present time.*

White-breasted sea eagle, *Haliaeetus leucogaster*

White-breasted sea eagle, *Haliaeetus leucogaster*

Reef heron, *Egretta sacra*

Reef heron, *Egretta sacra*

△ *A pair of white reef herons perch on the bough of a casuarina tree. These birds nest in colonies, building nests of sticks in trees, on rock ledges or under scrub.*

◁ *Reef herons stalk their prey of small marine organisms in shallow water on the reef flat. Moving in a stealthy crouch, they occasionally plunge on their prey from a tree perch.*

'The voice of the elegant white reef heron is an incongruous hoarse croak.'

The hunters and the hunted

'Few reptiles inhabit the coral cays, but invertebrate life is abundant.'

Sand goanna, *Varanus gouldi*

▷ *A large sand goanna, the species after which Captain Cook named Lizard Island. It occurs on continental islands but not on coral cays.*

Gecko, *Lepidodactylus lugubris*

Δ *A gecko from coral cays. Males of this species are not known and these lizards will reproduce parthenogenetically; that is, females produce eggs without being fertilised by males.*

▷ *The giant centipede is commonly found on coral cays on the Great Barrier Reef, where it may provide an unpleasant welcome for visitors. The creature's bite is painful but not serious.*

▷ ▷ *A locust roosts in a shrub. It blends well with the colour of the leaves of the shrubs and trees on which it feeds. But plagues of this species occasionally defoliate the vegetation on coral cays.*

Giant centipede, *Scolopendra*

Locust, *Valanga irregularis*

supplies and inadvertently introduced to new islands. The species most widespread among the cays of the Great Barrier Reef, *Lepidodactylus lugubris*, lays eggs that are initially sticky and adhere to the sides of crevices in which they are deposited, such as under the bark of trees. They are more easily transported by floating logs or other debris than eggs of most species and are especially suitable for accidental transport by humans in lumber or in cracks in boats. This species is also adapted to island life by being parthenogenetic (females producing young without being fertilised by males). No males are known in the species, and a single female is sufficient to found a new population.

Lizards and snakes

The only terrestrial snake which is common to coral cays, the blind snake, *Typhlina bramina*, is also parthenogenetic.

In all, only a few species of lizards and snakes occur on the coral cays of the Great Barrier Reef and not one cay has all of them. If the continental islands are considered as well, the number of species would be increased greatly, and in addition to small skinks, geckos and blind snakes, most of the families of lizards and snakes known from Australia would be included, even some of the larger venomous snakes, such as the taipan, and the large lizards known as goannas. One species of goanna, *Varanus gouldi*, was sufficiently conspicuous to prompt James Cook to name Lizard Island after it.

Sea snakes are abundant in some parts of the Great Barrier Reef, but absent in others. (See Marine Reptiles, page 294.)

Land invertebrates

The small land animals of continental islands are much the same as those of the mainland, only rather fewer in numbers of species. It is more difficult to describe the invertebrate fauna of coral cays. The main problem is that there is continual change. Species present at one time may be gone the next and may be replaced by others that were not there before. Certain species, however, do occur on coral cays so frequently that they can be considered characteristic of them.

Utetheisa pulchelloides is a spotted moth that is restricted to *Argusia* shrubs. Its food plant is widely distributed, even to remote islands, and so is the moth. The caterpillar eats *Argusia* leaves, and the adult feeds on the nectar of the flowers, perhaps assisting bees and flies in pollinating it. Thus, the

▷ *The St Andrew's Cross spider weaves white strands across the orb of its web to strengthen it. This species is widespread in eastern Australia and also occurs on some of the islands of the Great Barrier Reef.*

St Andrew's Cross spider, *Argiope aetherea*

lives of the moth and the plant are intimately connected. The plant is sometimes found without the moth but never the reverse.

The giant centipede, *Scolopendra* species, is a large yellow-brown centipede that finds its way to many cays where it provides an unpleasant welcome for visitors. It has the disconcerting habit of crawling into sleeping bags. Its bite is painful but not serious. It usually hides under objects such as logs or weathered chunks of coral, from which it ambushes the roaches, earwigs and other animal prey on which it feeds.

The locust, *Valanga irregularis*, blends well with the colour of the leaves of the shrubs and trees on which it feeds. Usually this large locust occurs in low numbers and only the occasional one is seen roosting in a shrub, or munching on a leaf. However, populations can build up to nearly plague proportions and they seriously defoliate the plants on an island. The locust population then crashes and remains at low levels for several years.

Island scavengers
The tenebrionid beetle, *Gonocephalum* species, is a scavenger, and it is one of the first insects to appear on small cays. Sometimes present on cays that lack terrestrial vegetation, it is attracted to dead birds, and both larvae and adults feed on the rotting flesh.

The cricket, *Telegryllus oceanicus*, is a common species on many vegetated islands, even those that are relatively small and remote. It feeds on a variety of foods of both plant and animal origin, so it easily becomes established on the islands it reaches.

The seaside wolf spider, *Lycosa* species, is a large ground spider often found on coral cays. It is one of the more common predators of insects. It lives under objects by day, but at night ranges widely in search of prey. It is characteristic of beach and island habitats on the Great Barrier Reef.

The seaside earwig, *Anisolabis maritima*, is a major scavenger on beaches, including those of coral cays. It lives under objects but especially flourishes on beaches made of coral rubble, as the large pieces of broken coral provide abundant shelter. It crawls under dead fish or other carrion washed up on the beach and eats it from below.

Beach-dwelling hermits
Hermit crabs are usually thought of as being marine, and indeed many species spend their entire life in the water, searching out empty seashells, backing into them and carrying them around as their own protective cover. Some species, however, come out on land after an aquatic larval stage and use washed-up seashells in a similar way to their marine relatives. They can be seen on some islands in large numbers, either sheltering under objects on the beach or ambling along, each with its own shell for protection. When an individual grows too big for its shell, it finds a larger one and transfers to it. If shells are scarce, hermit crabs sometimes fight for

possession of desirable ones. One of the more common species of terrestrial hermit crabs on the beach is *Coenobita perlata*.

These are only a few of the conspicuous invertebrate inhabitants of coral cays. Often many species can be found on the larger, more stable cays. Bees, flies, and butterflies swarm around flowers and partake of nectar; caterpillars, beetles and grasshoppers graze on the leaves; ants scurry to and fro in search of their food; flies, beetles and earwigs congregate around the dead bodies of animals; bugs and beetles crawl deep into the fruits of plants and munch away on seeds; leafhoppers suck juices from their host plants; ticks and mosquitoes lie in wait for warm-blooded vertebrates whose blood they consume; spiders spin webs to trap unwary prey; and a variety of predators like dragonflies, mantids or ground spiders ambush or run down their prey.

In the soil, a host of minute, nearly microscopic

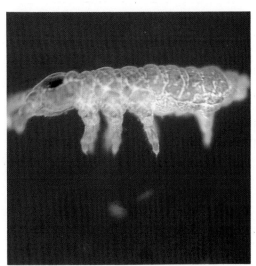

Springtail, *Oudemansia schotti*

animals, such as mites, springtails, and false scorpions, carry on similar dramas undetected by the casual observer walking unknowingly over their subterranean world.

Semi-marine species
In addition to the strictly terrestrial insects and spiders, a few remarkable semi-marine species occur behind the reef rock rim or on beachrock. They are exposed to air at low tide but at high tide are submerged. They are insulated from the water covering them by a thin film of air around their bodies or by pockets of air trapped in crevices of the rock in which they shelter. So far eight such species have been recorded from the Heron Reef: one spider, two springtails, three beetles and two bugs.

Small insects known as springtails or collembolans live in the spaces among sand grains of the intertidal region on some of the coral cays. If

a hole is dug in the sand, as water oozes in these tiny animals float out on the surface. They are scarcely visible to the naked eye, and indeed the members of one species are so small that they were not seen even by the scientist looking for them! They were collected inadvertently while larger species were being scooped up from the water surface. The smaller species were first noticed when the collection was examined under the microscope. Several species of these animals are now known from the Great Barrier Reef. Some are new to science; one had been previously described from one other place – the beaches of Norway!

More remains to be discovered about the life of coral island invertebrates. Many of the species are still undescribed and unnamed, even among the conspicuous species. How many discoveries await the naturalist among the small unobstrusive species can only be guessed.□

Hermit crab, *Pagurida*

Δ *Hermit crabs fight for possession of a desirable shell. These crabs carry empty mollusc shells on their backs for shelter. When the animal gets too big for its shell, it discards it in favour of a roomier one. Some hermit crabs are marine; others are terrestrial in the adult stage.*

Δ ◁ *A small springtail or collembolan seen through the microscope and magnified many times. This tiny, flightless insect lives in the small spaces between sand grains in the intertidal region of coral cays on the reef.*

Dangerous animals of the reef: offensive and defensive

Chemical warfare

There is constant warfare on the reef and some smart technical equipment has been developed for both offensive and defensive tactics by many organisms. Chemical warfare is the chosen defence of a host of animals, for if a poisonous or unpalatable substance can be accumulated in the skin or tissues it can prevent or reduce predation. Bacterial attack can also be countered by the development of bacteriocides. For example, 60 per cent of a large number of sponges tested showed some anti-bacterial activity. This can be very important for an animal sitting on the bottom, straining the water for fine particles, and needing to feed on and not be infected by bacteria.

Offensive weapons are also abundant, and sometimes extremely sophisticated. They are often both mechanical and chemical. The coelenterates, including the corals, hydroids, sea anemones, box jellyfish and the Portuguese man-of-war, have special toxin-loaded cells with needle-sharp barbs at the end of a coiled spring. These fearsome weapons are set off with a trigger that can be brushed by the touch of a prey animal, or a human finger. The stinging cells may be merely an irritant to humans, or may be like those of the box jellyfish, where contact with the long tentacles results in many stings, and can cause death within minutes.

Sharp spines are the stock-in-trade of most fishes and sea urchins, but spines are often made more effective as weapons by a coating of venomous mucus or by associated glands. Sea snakes are also found on the reef. They nearly all have small fangs but deadly venom, although they will not strike unless provoked.

Surprisingly the venom is more dangerous than that of land snakes to humans.

▽ The butterfly cod is from the family Scorpaenidae, which is closely allied to the stonefish. The spines of this cod are very long and coated with venomous mucus. Each spine acts very efficiently as a hypodermic syringe for the injection of venom. A mere brush can cause immediate and intense pain. A number of deep punctures are more dangerous. The symptoms include a sudden rise in temperature followed by a rapid fall. In severe cases this can be followed by cardiac failure.

Butterfly cod or fire fish, *Pterois antennata*

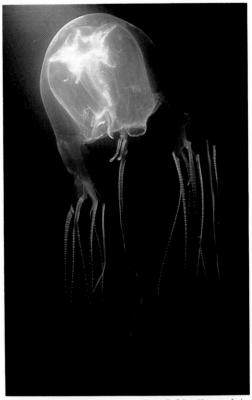

Box jellyfish, *Chironex fleckeri*

△ *The box jellyfish belongs to a group known as Cubomedusae. Its four-sided bell is usually less than 150 millimetres across, but in spite of its moderate size it is among the most dangerous of the stingers. At each of its four corners is a cluster of long trailing tentacles, loaded with batteries of venomous stinging cells, whose touch may be fatal or cause severe injury. It is not normally encountered in the southern part of the reef, or near offshore islands, but during the wet summer it may be found in the north in the muddied waters of the mainland coast.*

△ ▷ *This hydroid is a colonial animal, containing different individuals with various tasks to perform, such as feeding and reproducing. The feeding individuals have stinging cells, called nematocysts, which they fire at their prey in either a lassoing or a harpooning motion. The prey is stunned and drawn back to be consumed. The sting is very painful, but not deadly.*

'The butterfly cod is as bright and conspicuous as its name implies. If one is approached, it will wave its fins and spines in warning.'

White stinging hydroid, *Lytocarpus philippinus*

Four safety rules

Even with these dangers, by observing simple precautions the reef is safer than any city. There are four primary warnings:

1. Don't wander in the shallow water among and between the reefs without wearing a pair of sandshoes with sturdy soles.
2. Swim in bright sunlight and in water where there is good visibility.
3. Don't eat any fish until you have talked to the locals about it. An eating fish in one area may be known to cause ciguatera poisoning in others. You should also beware of pufferfish.
4. Don't pick up cone shells; this harmless-looking and often beautiful shell can be dangerous.

Invertebrates to keep at a distance

Most of the invertebrate animals of the Great Barrier Reef are not dangerous to humans, but it is worthwhile being aware of those that are potentially harmful, or that may cause irritation if touched or handled.

The coelenterates capture their prey by using their stinging cells, and in some of them these are powerful enough to cause pain or injury to humans as well. One of the most notorious is *Physalia*, the Portuguese man-of-war, but it is not common in the waters of the reef. Swimmers and divers are more likely to encounter the stinging hydroids, *Aglaeophenia cupressina* and *Lytocarpus philippinus*. A

brush with either of these can be searingly painful. *Aglaeophenia* is found in the tide pools of the reef flat. It looks like a clump of coarse, sturdy, yellow brown fern fronds. *Lytocarpus* occurs at greater depths and has a finer, more feathery appearance.

The hydrozoan corals are relatives of the hydroids that look superficially like the reef builders because they have hard limy skeletons. The stinging fire coral, *Millepora platyphylla*, lives towards the outer edge of the reef flat.

Among the jellyfish in reef waters, the lion's mane jellyfish, *Cyanea capillata*, is the largest. With its hundreds of long, highly elastic stinging tentacles, it can cause injury to humans. The most dangerous is the box jellyfish, *Chironex fleckeri*, but it usually occurs only in summer in the northern part of the region near the coast.

Fire anemones

The fire anemone, *Actinodendron plumosum*, has stinging cells in its tentacles containing an extremely strong poison that burns painfully if injected into the skin. When expanded, it looks like a tiny conical fir tree, and varies in colour between blue-grey and light brown and the disc around its mouth is speckled with dark spots.

Of the segmented worms, the fire worms ought not to be handled. These polychaetes have long slender bristles that are as sharp as very fine needles. They can easily pierce the skin and, when touched, they tend to snap off, becoming embedded and setting up a fierce local irritation. *Eurythoe complanata* is a common fire worm that lives on the reef flat among the coral rubble and under boulders.

The crustaceans of the reef pose little threat to humans, although the flesh of some of the crabs is known to be poisonous. If molested, the spiny mantis shrimps of the reef flat are capable of inflicting painful stab-wounds with their sharp claws, but they are so swift and wary that they are unlikely to be a hazard.

Among the molluscs, some of the cones are notorious for the toxicity of their venom. These reef carnivores inject poisonous saliva into their prey through sharp grooved teeth at the tip of a retractable proboscis. Harpooned victims quickly succumb. The poisons secreted by fish-eating cones are also toxic to other vertebrates, including humans. The beautiful reticulated and striped geographer cone, *Conus geographus*, has caused fatalities, and the tulip cone, *Conus tulipa*, the striated cone, *Conus striatus*, the magician cone, *Conus magus*, the textile cone, *Conus textile*, the marble cone, *Conus marmoreus*, and the court cone, *Conus aulicus*, are all recorded as being dangerous.

A living cone must be approached with caution and, if handled, should be picked up by the broad, whorled end only. At the same time, a sharp eye must be kept on the slit of the shell, in case the flexible proboscis tube starts to protrude, with its threat of a quick shot of venom. The octopus is another mollusc with a very poisonous bite.

A few of the echinoderms are capable of injuring people. Of these, the crown-of-thorns starfish, *Acanthaster planci*, is widely known for its devastation of reef corals. The upper surface of this large starfish is a bristling mass of stout spines, each coated with a thin layer of skin that secretes an irritant poison. A puncture-wound from the crown-of-thorns' spines is painful, and may become inflamed and swollen. The long, slender, needle-like spines of the sea urchins *Diadema* and *Echinothrix* break off easily and lodge in the flesh. Because of their barbs, they are difficult to remove and the surrounding area may fester.

Another sea urchin that should not be touched is *Toxopneustes pileolus*. It has a spectacular array of densely packed, waving nippers that reach out in every direction. They look like three-petalled flowers, but they are equipped with poison glands and contact with them is dangerous. Holothurians, or sea cucumbers, contain toxins and if they are handled, care should be taken not to let them come in contact with the eyes.

Not to be eaten

The pufferfish of the Tetraodontidae family have two unusual characteristics, one endearing and one unpleasant. They can puff themselves up, often into comical little balls, and they produce a particularly strong poison, called tetrodotoxin. This poison is in the gonads, gut, liver and blood. The flesh is considered a delicacy in Japan (called *fugu* after the Japanese name of the fish), but it is eaten only after a specially trained cook has separated poison from flesh; even then there are fatalities. These quaint and unaggressive fish are best left alone on the reef and thrown back if caught on a line.

It is easy to say that fishes containing the poison ciguatera should not be eaten, but the instruction is difficult to comply with, for the origin of this poison seems to be an alga which is eaten by grazers and passes up the food chain, making it difficult to know which fish has ingested it, or enough of it to affect a human. The concentrations of poison are greater the further up the food chain a fish is. A grazer may feed on ten such fishes and store their poison. When these fishes are eaten by the next predator it will be feeding on fishes that have already concentrated the poison. The older and larger the fish, the more poison it may contain.

So what fishes should be avoided? Luckily, local fishermen usually know which fishes have ciguatera, and their advice is invaluable. The chinaman-fish, *Glabrilutianus nematophorus*, and the red bass, *Lutjanus bohar*, have both been implicated on occasion, as have large individuals of the rock cod genus *Epinephelus*, and large moray eels.

Ciguatera symptoms often start with numbness in the lips, pain in the arms and legs, and nausea. There may be vomiting and diarrhoea, and hot things may feel cold, and vice versa. Recuperation takes a long time, but there is said to be a 90 per cent rate of recovery.

A number of stingrays, Dasyatidae, and eagle rays, Myliobatidae, are common on the reef and have one or more sharp serrated spines on the base of the tail. There are grooves running the length of each spine, filled with glandular tissue secreting venom. Don't stand on these rays, for they can strike rapidly. The wounds are intensely painful and have caused death in rare cases. Some large stingrays come into shallow water to feed at night, so wading carelessly in the dark is not recommended.

Many of the scorpion fish, Scorpaenidae, have strong spines that can give a painful wound, but the aptly named fire fish or butterfly cod, *Pterois*, is

Geographer cone shell, *Conus geographus*

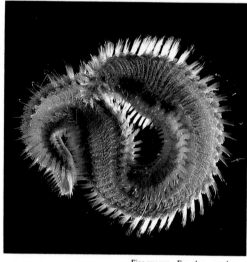

Fire worm, *Eurythoe complanata*

Fire coral, *Millepora*

◬ *The most dangerous of the cone shells are the geographer cone,* Conus geographus, *and the tulip cone,* Conus tulipa. *The first has caused several fatalities and both have inflicted serious injury. The striated cone,* Conus striatus, *and magician cone,* Conus magus, *are also potentially dangerous and it would be safer to avoid touching any of the cone shells. A sting from a venomous cone may affect vision, hearing and speech, and even cause partial or complete paralysis.*

◬ Millepora *is not a true coral, in spite of its heavy, limy skeleton. Closely related to hydroids, it is known as a hydrozoan coral. The polyps have tentacles armed with nematocysts, or stinging cells. When a victim brushes against the tentacles, threads loaded with toxins are fired. The pain is severe but can be helped by applying alcohol, dilute acids or aluminium sulphate.*

◬ ◁ *The fire worm has long slender bristles as sharp as the finest needle. When touched, they pierce the skin, snap off and become firmly embedded, setting up a severe local irritation.*

more dangerous, and the long and colourful fins have very venomous spines. Stabs from this fish are extremely painful, and can be fatal.

The stonefish, Synaciidae, belong to a family closely allied to the scorpion fish, but have a more elaborate and vicious defensive mechanism. The 13 dorsal spines are sharp, sturdy and grooved on each side, and each spine has a pair of poison sacs containing a venom so strong that the pain can drive a victim insane. This is followed by numbness, and sometimes death. The stonefish is well camouflaged, looking very much like a weed-covered stone. The best defence is care when walking in the shallows and the wearing of shoes with strong soles.

Much less dangerous are rabbit fish, Siganus, catfish of the family Plotosidae, and surgeonfish, Acanthuridae. The rabbit fish have strong dorsal spines with a venomous coating and a sting can be painful. Ironically, the fish have been called 'happy moments'! The catfish also have poisonous pectoral spines and spines in the dorsal fin. Surgeonfish have a sharp scalpel on each side of the tail base, movable in some species, large and fixed in others. They should be handled with care.

A number of small blennies found on the reef have large canine teeth and will use them if handled. The sabre-toothed blenny, Plagiotremus, is only a few centimetres long, but has two very long canines in the lower jaw which have grooves that carry venom. A bite can be painful.

Rare or reluctant biters

Many fishes with normally peaceful dispositions, at least towards man, will bite when provoked, cornered or hurt. Moray eels and barracudas have large, razor-sharp teeth. Although they do not normally seem aggressive, they have both done severe damage to divers who have speared them. In other parts of the world there are a few records of attacks by the great barracuda, Sphyraena barracuda. These are not usually considered to be deliberate attacks on humans, but probably a swift rush at something flashing in the water such as a watch or a thrashing arm, or a swimmer carrying a bleeding fish. Occasionally a barracuda will follow a swimmer.

Small and normally harmless reef sharks can sometimes be picked up by hand; but they, too, may object and bite, and some have sharp teeth.

Sea snakes are most commonly seen by divers, not by the tourist. Though dangerous, they do not seem to be aggressive and they have twined around many divers who have gently extricated themselves without being bitten. They are said to be merely curious, but the best approach is to keep clear and not put them to the test!

Sharks

Most visitors to the reef will not be lucky enough to see a large shark, and the chances of being bitten are negligible for the sensible tourist or diver. However,

after dusk the behaviour of many sharks changes, and an angler hooking a good-sized turrum in the fading light can have it viciously attacked by a hungry hammerhead, absolutely determined to get the fish away, and unafraid of torches, yelling anglers, or boats. Some sharks may also feed during the day, and it is advisable to swim in full sun, and in water with good visibility. One is more prone to meet sharks off steep drop-offs on outer reefs, and more care is needed in such places. It is not wise to carry bleeding fishes.

The tiger sharks. Galeocerdo cuvier, hammerheads, Sphyrna, and some of the whaler sharks, Carcharinus, are known to have attacked humans and are found on the reef. The sharks that the visitor is more likely to see, however, are the black-tipped reef shark, Carcharinus melanopterus – a timid shallow-water shark – and the white-tipped reef shark, Triaenodon obesus, a territorial shark that is usually only a little

over a metre long, common around many of the island reefs. Both of these sharks avoid humans. In very shallow water about the corals, and active at night, is the slim little epaulette shark, Hemiscyllium ocellatum, which will bite only if picked up out of the water, and then not very fiercely. The tassellated wobegong, Orectolobus ogilbyi, is a harmless shark sometimes seen in pools on the reef. It rarely swims away, relying on its camouflage, and is tempting to touch. Don't – it has fierce, long sharp teeth.☐

▽ *The wound from a stonefish spine is said to be unbelievably painful by those who have survived the experience; several deaths have been recorded. Bathing the wound in extremely hot water seems to help. A stonefish in coral rubble is difficult to recognise, so when walking through coral or coral rubble, sturdy shoes with thick soles should be worn.*

Moray eel, *Enchelycore bayeri*

Stonefish, *Synanceia horrida*

◁ △ *There are dozens of species of eels on the reef. Most have territories among corals and rubble and are difficult to detect. Generally timid, these eels will only attack if provoked.*

◁ *A sting from this beautiful creature will cause muscle weakness, shock, neurological damage, respiratory distress and sometimes death.*

Flower urchin, *Toxopneustes pileolus*

Mangroves

Part four: humans and the reef

Humans have been involved with the Great Barrier Reef for over 40 000 years. It has been fished for seafoods and searched for shells, and the variety of its marine animals has been wondered at. But as the 21st century approaches our relationship with nature has changed. For the first time our increasing population and our ability to harness huge quantities of energy have enabled us, often not through our own collective wish, to make irreversible changes on a global scale. Will the reef be immune from these changes?

There is no definite answer to this question, but it is likely that the reef will continue to be a 'coral battleground', to use words of the poet Judith Wright. There will be those who will exploit the reef's resources, with no thought for future generations. And there will be those who will strive to keep man away from it altogether, forgetting that it has already come to terms with a thousand generations of humans. Somewhere between these two extremes, man and the reef will eventually achieve a balance.

Early Aboriginal prehistory of the area is still obscure, for much of the archaeological evidence is under reef waters and waits for work by divers. When Europeans first arrived, the Aboriginal coastal people were using huge 20-metre double outrigger canoes in the north of the reef. These were built in Papua and obtained by barter. Further south the Aborigines built smaller canoes, and travelled confidently up and down the reef and to outlying islands. But the early story – lasting tens of thousands of years – will never be fully known. It is likely that those early inhabitants were hardy coastal people, skilful fishermen who caught turtle and dugong as well as fishes and shellfish with fine traps, lines, hooks and spears. In the 18th century there were 40 tribal groups along the coast, living in tune with the coastal and reef environment.

European exploration in the early 19th century started a period of great change, with sailors traversing the intricate coral maze, and the settlement of the north by the new immigrants, spurred on by the discovery of gold. Scores of vessels were wrecked on the reefs until improved charts, towers and lights tamed these waters towards the end of the century.

Conflict was common along the Queensland coast at this time. Murder of Aborigines by whites – with subsequent retaliation – and the spread of European diseases, decimated coastal groups. But Aborigines became an integral part of most maritime industries, including the collecting of shells and bêche-de-mer, and local shipping.

The diving for pearl oyster shells, then later trochus, *Trochus niloticus*, and the green snail shell, *Turbo marmoratus*, all for the making of mother-of-pearl buttons, was an industry occupying many luggers with big crews in the late 19th and early 20th centuries.

Reef use has changed again, and trawl nets are now being used increasingly for prawns, as well as the more traditional handline and trolled lure for fishes. With the growth of tourism, recreational fishermen are now being catered for.

The pursuit of leisure has become the reef's biggest industry, and as this has become more sophisticated, the gentle arts of bird watching, botanising, photography and diving, in order to look and learn, have become popular.

These changes have done little so far to disturb the reef. Perhaps coastal land-use changes and industry may have greater effects in the future, but at present the reef retains a pristine, timeless aura.□

◁ *Mangroves grow in saline soil and adapt themselves to the rise and fall of the tides which submerge their lower branches and leaves in sea water.*

▽ *On 11 June 1770 the* Endeavour *struck a coral reef off the Queensland coast and almost sank. The ship was anchored for repairs in the river now named after it near present-day Cooktown. Two months later, Captain Cook succeeded in sailing through a narrow passage near Lizard Island, only to seek again the protection of the reefs.*

HMS *Endeavour*

Man on the reef: the first arrivals

The end of a long sea journey

Long before the Great Barrier Reef formed in the warm shallow seas that swamped the land between the present coastline and the outer edge of the continental shelf, the Aborigines had discovered, explored and settled Australia. Archaeological investigation over the past 20 years has pushed back the date of the arrival of Aborigines in Australia from 10 000 to 40 000 years ago, and beyond. The earliest Australians must have reached the continent at the end of a long sea journey. Even at the height of the ice age, when sea levels were at their lowest and land masses were more extensive, a voyage of 50 to 100 kilometres would have been necessary to reach Australia from the nearest point in Southeast Asia. These earliest colonists had a knowledge of the sea, rudimentary maritime technology and an economy based on harvesting the resources of estuaries and coastal waters.

One theory about the occupation of Australia suggests that the early Aborigines settled first along the shorelines of the continent, using the technology they brought with them and exploiting the kinds of environments they were familiar with, before venturing inland along the river valleys. If this were so, then the east coast probably was occupied quite early. Archaeological work to test this hypothesis is just beginning in north Queensland, and most sites that have been examined are less than 2000 years old. The Early Man rock shelter at Laura, however, has yielded remains dating from 13 000 years ago. The oldest site so far unearthed, it is in the middle of the Cape York Peninsula, but much older sites may be scattered along the ancient coastline, which was drowned when sea levels rose after 15 000 BC as the ice age drew to a close.

Archaeologists are considering the possibilities of exploring caves deep under the outer reef to recover relics of the earliest societies established along the east coast of Queensland. Such submarine research may eventually provide valuable information about the technology and life of the people who camped in places that have been covered for thousands of years by reef waters. But even the richest archaeological sites cannot recreate the emotional experience of tribes who, for thousands of years and perhaps 400 generations, saw the slow, uneven, but inexorable rise of the sea across favourite beaches and over familiar hunting grounds.

Aborigines of the reef

Generation after generation, coastal Aborigines edged inland or up to the hills that remained above the encroaching tide. These hills became the continental islands that have studded offshore waters for over 5000 years. The memory of the creeping sea probably survived in the legends of tribes whose lands fronted reef waters, legends that were lost in the confusion of European settlement in the 19th century. Until then, the flooded hunting grounds and camp sites were regarded as traditional territory, and the islands remained part of the tribe's economic and ceremonial life, as they had been when they were part of the mainland.

Plentiful food supplies made the Queensland coast a favourable area for Aboriginal settlement; though each tribe's territory – the area needed to support the tribe – was small, tribal numbers were higher than average and life styles were more sedentary than those of inland Aborigines. About 40 tribal territories existed along the coast inside the reef, and most covered coastal hills and valleys, mangroves, beaches and estuaries as well as offshore islands and reefs. Each area provided different kinds of foods, and each was visited at some time during a typical year as clans moved, hunting and harvesting, through tribal territory.

Not much is known about the coastal tribes, and we may never discover how often the Aborigines visited offshore islands and reefs. The casual observations of early European voyagers, however,

'Walter Edmund Roth (1861–1933) was a medical doctor working in north Queensland in the 1890s. He travelled extensively among the Aboriginal tribes of the area, making an ethnographic study and photographing the native people fishing, hunting and at their ceremonies.'

◁ *Dugout canoes with double outriggers were used around the tip of Cape York. The long harpoon was used for spearing dugong and turtle.*

△ *A dugout canoe with single outrigger used along the northern part of Cape York peninsula.*

◁ *Small canoes made of bark stitched with vines were used in all but the roughest weather along the central and southern parts of the reef. The long spears, made by Cape York Aborigines, were traded throughout the Torres Strait islands.*

◁ ◁ *Murray Island, at the top of reef, as depicted by William Westall in the early years of the 19th century. In the foreground is a large dugout canoe with double outrigger acquired from trade with Papua. These canoes, up to 20 metres long, were the largest and most sophisticated vessels used in reef waters. They enabled the Torres Strait islanders to range far from their home islands and visit mainland Australia.*

give us some information about occupation of the islands. Murray Island and Darnley Island at the northern end of the reef had large residential populations – mainly the Miriam people of the eastern Torres Strait – while the major continental islands – Keppel, Whitsunday, Magnetic, Palm and Hinchinbrook – were probably home to clans who spent most of their time offshore, with occasional visits to the mainland for religious ceremonies or hunting expeditions.

Smaller islands were certainly used on a casual basis, as almost every early European visitor, from Captain James Cook onwards, attested. The navigators recorded seeing Aborigines on the islands or sailing to and from the mainland. They noted smoke from Aboriginal fires by day and camp fires flickering in the dark. Abandoned huts and wells were found, as well as the remains of turtle and dugong feasts. In the far north, the Europeans were struck by the dense populations on Murray Island and Darnley Island and the established villages along the coastline.

Splendid sea-faring people

European seamen took a keen interest in Aboriginal canoes and left many descriptions of them, and of their variations in size, structure and seaworthiness. The Torres Strait islanders traded with Papua for large dugout canoes, up to 20 metres long, equipped with double outriggers and sails. These could hold as many as 50 men, and in them the islanders were able to range far and wide through the sheltered waters inside the reef. They visited mainland Australia and travelled along the reef for several hundred kilometres beyond Torres Strait. At the tip of Cape York the Aborigines made double outrigger canoes that may have been modelled on those of the Torres Strait islanders, although they were smaller,

△ *The stone arrangement seen here is the remains of a 'bora' ground, which was the scene for important Aboriginal ceremonies. Bora grounds usually consisted of two stone circles, joined by a path. The outer ring was a public one, where women and children could join in the preliminary part of ceremonies, and the other, secret, ring could be used for further initiation rituals. Bora grounds were usually in remote places.*

△ ▷ *Aboriginal cave paintings in many parts of Australia provide evidence of the European impact. Although horses and cattle are the main subjects depicted throughout the inland, coastal tribesmen around far north Queensland painted the European boats that sailed past their country.*

perhaps eight to ten metres long. South of Princess Charlotte Bay, the dugout canoes had a single outrigger. Aboriginal dugouts were seaworthy enough to take small parties to the offshore islands and to travel up and down the coast for trade, ceremonial occasions or attack and revenge.

South of Hinchinbrook Island, bark was the main material used for canoe construction. Europeans reported craft made from single, double or triple bark sheets sewn together with tough vines and carefully caulked with resin and paperbark. Although smaller and much lighter than the dugouts from the north, the bark canoes of the southern reef waters were handled with great skill and dexterity and used in all but the roughest weather. Even so, it is likely that people often drowned in accidents at sea or were marooned by contrary winds on rocks or sandbanks. In 1848, the *Bramble* and *Rattlesnake* found two men and a boy who had been weather-bound for three days without water on a low, barren island.

Yet despite the dangers of the sea, the sheltered waters inside the reef and the many islands and sandbanks gave Queensland's coastal Aborigines an offshore mobility unmatched anywhere else in Australia. The ocean and the islands were a rich source of food. Studies of coastal tribes in the Northern Territory give some idea of the traditional diet of their Queensland counterparts. A survey of the Wanindiljaugwa people showed that 98 different marine animals and 39 types of crabs and shellfish were included in their diet.

Hunting the dugong

A number of fishing techniques were used in reef waters. Many fishes were caught with long, multi-pronged spears from canoes or convenient rocks. (Fish-bone prongs were quickly replaced by wire after the arrival of Europeans.) Nets of various sizes were used in the shallows, and big fish traps were constructed on both the coast and the offshore islands. But the most dramatic and exciting form of fishing was the dugong and turtle hunt. Both these animals, as well as rays and sharks, were speared with long harpoons that had detachable, barbed heads tied to long coils of bark rope.

An anthropologist who lived with the Kawadji people of Princess Charlotte Bay in the 1920s wrote, after experiencing a dugong hunt:

> *They are splendid sea-faring people – great adventurers and great fighters. In small dugout canoes with only a few inches of freeboard, they make long journeys to the islands and sandbanks inside the Barrier Reef, hunting dugongs and turtle with the long harpoon. Dugong hunting, as it is carried out by these natives, is undoubtedly the most dangerous and spectacular occupation practised by an Australian aboriginal.*

A subtle variation in the hunting of large marine creatures involved the use of a remora or sucker fish, *Echeneis naucrates*, found attached to rocks or to captured dugongs or turtles. The fish was detached carefully and kept in an enclosed pool until it was needed, when a light string was tied to its tail. It was then taken to sea and released over a turtle or dugong. With luck, the remora locked on to the animal, allowing the eager hunters to follow every twist and turn of their quarry until it could be killed and secured. The remora was then detached and kept for further use.

Turtles and dugongs were more than just food. They played an important part in the ritual life of coastal tribes. Early European explorers often found that the Aborigines had hung turtle heads in trees on offshore islands, a practice adopted to ensure an increase in turtle numbers.

Among Princess Charlotte Bay Aborigines the principal event in the life of a young man came when, after years of tuition, he had successfully

harpooned and captured his first dugong or turtle without assistance. The animal was cooked and eaten at a ceremonial feast and dance. The skull of the turtle or the lower jaw of the dugong was painted by the initiate and then hidden in a cave or other secret place.

The sea and sea creatures were central to the life of coastal and island clans. A vast amount of traditional knowledge – about the habits, life cycle and habitats of many sea creatures – was handed on to the children. Time-honoured rituals and ceremonies were performed to ensure the future abundance of the oceans. Mature men learnt magic that they believed could control the weather and ensure calm waters and fair winds – a skill that bolstered confidence on sea voyages in frail craft. Rock art at sites along the coast featured turtles, dugongs and other sea creatures and, here and there, European ships that appear to sail incongruously through shoals of ancient iconography.

From the land of the spirits
The sudden appearance of Europeans was an awesome event in the lives of coastal communities. The white men were considered initially to be people who had returned in strange form from the land of the spirits, usually thought to be beyond the flat oceanic horizon. The colour white was associated everywhere with death, which added weight to the spiritual identification. In many northern languages the word for ghost was applied to early European visitors. Clans living around Cape Bedford believed that spirits travelled east at death, where they entered the bodies of white people. They called Europeans *Ganggal-Naka-Waraigo* or, literally, babies coming from the east.

The young Scottish castaway, Barbara Thompson, who lived with the Kaurareg people of the Prince of Wales Islands for five years in the 1840s, found that it was universally believed among Aborigines and Torres Strait islanders that whites were the spirits of black men come back in a new form. The islanders mimicked the Europeans in what was called the ghost spirit dance. The dancers made face masks from light yellow bark, applied red colouring to the cheeks and used scraps of black cloth for the eyebrows and to outline the mouth. Shirts acquired from passing ships were worn above white pipeclayed legs. The white spirits could either be malignant and dangerous, in which case they were shunned, or if possible killed, or they were greeted as returned relatives and accorded the status of kinsmen. Barbara was recognised by a leading man of the tribe as a reincarnation of a newly deceased daughter and immediately accepted into the kinship network.

A conflict of cultures
Contact between the coastal Aborigines and visiting Europeans was often friendly. Seamen rarely outstayed their welcome and their demands were

△ *Torres Strait islanders and coastal Aborigines were anxious to trade native artefacts for iron and other manufactured goods. An artist on board HMS* Fly *in the 1840s depicted a scene of intense bartering between islanders and the European crew in the shallows close to Murray Island.*

'Aborigines and Torres Strait islanders believed that whites were the spirits of black men come back in a new form.'

limited to water, fresh food and women. Unlike inland pioneers, they did not impinge directly on traditional society or take permanent possession of water holes or hunting grounds. Yet meetings often ended in violence. It could flare up out of chronic misunderstanding or the high tension of such meetings. Cook's experience on the Endeavour River provides an apt illustration. Earlier easy relations soured quickly when the Europeans refused to share the large number of turtles they had caught. From the Aboriginal point of view, this was grossly ill-mannered behaviour, especially for guests, and it led to an attempt to burn the Europeans out.

Increased shipping inside the reef and through Torres Strait led to greater demands on often limited water supplies. Serious conflict flared on Darnley Island in the late 1860s when European seamen washed their clothes in the islanders' major source of water.

Growing demands for Torres Strait and Aboriginal women was another cause of tension. A Queensland Government official who visited Torres Strait in the early 1880s heard insistent complaints about the ill-treatment of island women. In one community, he was told that all the girls and women were taken aside and buried in the sand whenever a sail was seen, and they were left there until the European ships had departed.

Trade was important from the very start of contact – cementing relations here, exacerbating them there. The Europeans' need for fresh water and food was matched by the Aborigines' and Torres Strait islanders' desire for iron, which rapidly replaced bone and stone in spears, harpoons, fish-hooks, knives, and other weapons and implements. At first, any scrap of iron was sought – bolts, nails, wire, rods. Eventually, steel axes became the most desired object of trade.

The Aborigines sought out the Europeans, keeping watch for sails or canoeing considerable distances to meet ships in order to trade turtle flesh or shell, necklaces, traditional implements, or fresh food. Sailors who were close enough inshore often saw Aborigines standing on their beaches making chopping signs in silent appeal for steel axes.

Soon a whole range of European bric-a-brac – iron, tins, bottles, glass, clothing – found its way into Aboriginal trade networks, to be passed inland from the coast, through the hands of people who had never seen the ocean, let alone the large winged ships of the white men. The Aborigines and islanders often didn't understand the source of these European manufactured goods. When Barbara Thompson's clansmen visited the *Rattlesnake*, they were fascinated by the cups and saucers and bottles, but they assumed, not unreasonably, that they were an exotic form of shellfish and wondered why none ever appeared on their beaches.

Navigating the hidden reef

Although early navigators had a wary interest in coastal Aborigines, they were usually preoccupied with the dangers and complexities of navigating sailing ships through waters abounding in hidden or half-concealed reefs. Many who sailed inside the outer reef relived Cook's experience of being, as he put it in 1770, 'barrocaded with Shoals'. His three months spent in reef waters foreshadowed many of the problems of later navigators. After emerging from inside the barrier, through the passage just north of Lizard Island that now bears his name, Cook estimated that he had sailed more than '360 leagues ... by the lead without having a leadsman out of the chains', an experience 'that perhaps never

'A reef such as we have just passed is a thing scarcely known in Europe, or indeed anywhere but in these seas.'

happened to any ship before'. Even then the *Endeavour* ran on to a reef. Sailing at night with soundings of 37 metres and more for an hour, the leadsman had just bottomed his line at 32 metres when the ship hit the coral reef that very nearly destroyed it. European mariners had long known about coral reefs, but Cook and Sir Joseph Banks were both impressed by the uniqueness of the Great Barrier Reef. Just after the *Endeavour* was guided out of a narrow passage in the outer reef and into the surge of the Coral Sea, Banks wrote:

A reef such as we have just passed is a thing scarcely known in Europe, or indeed anywhere but in these seas. It is a wall of coral rock, rising almost perpendicularly out of the unfathomable ocean, always covered at high water ... and generally bare at low-water. The large waves of the vast ocean meeting with so sudden a resistance make here a most terrible surf, breaking mountains high, especially when, as in our case, the general trade winds blow directly upon it.

But the exhilaration of reaching the open sea was short-lived. New dangers confronted the *Endeavour* outside the reef. The wind dropped, the water was far too deep to provide anchorage, and the current carried the ship back towards the awesome line of breakers marking the outer parapet of the reef. After moments of acute danger and high anxiety, a light wind carried the vessel away from the reef. But the

threat of the outer barrier remained, and the following day Cook gratefully accepted the chance of sailing with the tide through a narrow break in the reef which he called Providential Channel. 'It is', he wrote ruefully, 'but a few days ago that I rejoiced at having got without the Reef; but that joy was nothing compared to what I now felt at being safe at an Anchor within it'.

The dangers of approaching the outer barrier reef from the Coral Sea were emphasised by many navigators over the half century following Cook's narrow escape. After anxiously standing off the line of breakers during his epic voyage of 1789, William Bligh was able to guide the *Bounty*'s launch through a narrow passage just south of Providential Channel. Two years later the *Pandora*, returning from the South Seas with imprisoned *Bounty* mutineers, was driven on to a reef by a sudden gust of wind.

'Threading the needle'

Matthew Flinders was fully aware of the dangers of sailing through the outer reef. In October 1802, after sailing along the east coast of Queensland, he wrote in caution that the captain who hoped to sail through the reef:

must not, however, be one who throws his ship's head round in a hurry, as soon as breakers are announced from aloft; if he do not feel his nerves strong enough to thread the needle, as it is called, amongst the reefs, whilst he

directs the steerage from the mast head, I would strongly recommend him not to approach the coast in this part of New South Wales.

Flinders's warning was prophetic. Many ships were lost on the reef during the first half of the 19th century. Almost all surviving accounts of voyages along the Queensland coast during the following 50 years contain descriptions of the remains of wrecked, and often unknown, vessels strewn over the coral. They were grim, sobering reminders of the danger of reef waters.

Despite the hazards of the Queensland coast, however, the attraction of the passage through Torres Strait was sufficient to induce increasing numbers of masters to 'thread the needle'. The importance of Torres Strait was quickly recognised after Cook's rediscovery of it in 1770. It was then, as it remains today, the vital passage between the Pacific and the Indian Ocean, and it was by far the shortest route between Port Jackson and China and India. Despite the problems of navigation in reef waters, the Torres Strait route was often preferred to the alternative of beating westward along the south coast of Australia in the teeth of the relentless westerlies. There remained the question of whether it was safer to take the outer route, in the Coral Sea beyond the reef, or the inner route, between the barrier and the coast. The question was debated in the professional literature of the day, in the colonial papers and over the bars of many waterfront pubs. The outer route promised a comparatively trouble-free run north, but then it presented the problem of discovering the narrow and hazardous passages through the reef. Captain P. P. King, the first surveyor of the inner route, pointed to the dangers in 1820 when he wrote that:

if on approaching the part where it is intended to enter the reefs, the weather should be thick, and the sun too clouded at noon to procure an observation for the latitude, the navigator is placed in a very anxious and a very unenviable situation; for the currents are so strong, that the position of the ship is by no means sufficient known, to risk running leeward to make the reefs.

The inner route had the advantage of sheltered water and anchorages, but until it was fully charted and lit, progress was slow and it was necessary to anchor every night, an operation unattractive to lightly manned merchantmen, who tended to favour the outer route.

Although coral reefs were a constant hazard for ships, the sheltered waters inside the barrier were normally safe for small vessels. From the earliest years of settlement, adventurous colonists explored reef waters but left little record for posterity. But the first party to follow Cook along the Queensland coast was made up of convicts escaping from the infant settlement at Port Jackson in 1792.

Led by William and Mary Bryant, the conspirators pirated the Government cutter and slipped unseen out of Sydney Heads. They made their way along the coast, threading a passage through the inner route, anchoring in the lee of reef islands and off mainland beaches, and going cautiously ashore to supplement supplies slowly stockpiled at the convict settlement. They eventually reached their chosen destination, the Dutch settlement of Coupang on Timor, where their carefully rehearsed story about shipwreck was exposed, and they were returned to England in chains.

Shipwrecks and castaways

Although wrecks were common, the chances of survival were good. Ships often came to grief in clear weather with light winds and moderate seas. In such conditions, vessels could be abandoned in an orderly fashion, and small boats could take survivors off to islands or sandbanks. But while parties survived the immediate trauma of shipwreck, they often faced long voyages with limited food and water and the possibility of Aboriginal hostility when landings were eventually made on the mainland or the continental islands. James Morrell's story illustrates many of these vicissitudes.

Morrell was a 21-year-old English sailor whose ship, the *Peruvian*, was wrecked in the Coral Sea in 1846. Along with 20 other survivors he drifted on an improvised raft for six weeks. The party had

△ *Raine Island was ideally placed at the entrance to one of the safer passages through the outer reef. The tower, built in 1844, enabled captains to approach the outer reef with greater confidence. Twenty convict tradesmen, shipped north in HMS* Fly, *built it from stone quarried and cut on the island, mortar made from local shells and timber scavenged from nearby shipwrecks. It was visible from 13 to 14 km when viewed from the deck of approaching vessels. Some of the convicts carved their names in the stone, below.*

very little water, and only seven members were still alive when the raft reached shore at Cape Cleveland near the future site of Townsville. Of those who stumbled ashore, only Morrell survived to be found by two frontier stockmen in 1863, when the wave of pastoral settlement swept north.

But the dangers of both the inner and outer routes were gradually reduced as the 19th century progressed. The early survey work of Matthew Flinders in 1802–03 and P. P. King in 1819–22 was followed up after 1841 when the Admiralty commissioned a series of surveying expeditions. These were carried out by F. P. Blackwood in the *Fly* and Owen Stanley in the *Rattlesnake* in the 1840s, and by H. M. Denham in the *Herald* in the late 1850s. As the Admiralty charts became available, knowledge of the reef was widely disseminated, augmented by the experience of seamen who passed on their knowledge by word of mouth or privately made charts and diagrams. In 1844, a 12-metre tower was erected on Raine Island to guide ships coming from the Coral Sea through the outer barrier and so ease their journey through Torres Strait. In 1864 a settlement was established at Somerset on the tip of Cape York to provide a port of refuge for crews of ships thrown up on the reefs.

Developments in the second half of the 19th century enhanced the importance of Torres Strait and of the inner route. The introduction of regular steam services and the opening of the Suez Canal saw an increase in shipping along the Queensland coast. Steam solved one of the critical problems of Torres Strait navigation, which was that sailing ships could only travel from east to west through most of the year when the southeast trades were blowing. With the increase of steamer traffic, the Somerset settlement was moved to Thursday Island in 1876 and the island became a major port for coaling vessels. In 1884 the Torres Strait Pilot Service was officially established.

Pastoralists, miners and planters

Linked to the growing importance of Torres Strait for international shipping was the rapid expansion of settlement after the establishment of Bowen in 1861. Pastoralists pushed inland from rudimentary coastal towns or overlanded from the south. Within 20 years they had pushed up into the base of Cape York and wheeled westward right across the Northern Territory to occupy the tropical pastures in the Kimberleys, 3200 kilometres away.

Gold discoveries in central Queensland in the 1850s and 1860s sparked intensive prospecting, both private and official, which culminated in the opening up of many north Queensland fields – especially around Charters Towers and Ravenswood, southwest of Townsville, the Culbert, the Etheridge, the Palmer – in the 1870s and 1880s. Gold lured thousands of people into the remote areas of the north. New steamer services from Southeast Asia enabled Chinese miners to stream into the northern

gold fields. On the Palmer River, north of Cairns, they greatly outnumbered the Europeans.

Once the shallow alluvial deposits were picked over, the ever-restless diggers moved on, 'washing' rivers and creeks in every corner of north Australia. They worked their way to the tip of Cape York, followed the tracks of the cattlemen westwards to the Kimberleys and the Pilbara, or packed aboard small ketches and sailed out of Cooktown, Cairns and Townsville to pursue their dreams of eldorado in the jungles of New Guinea.

In the lush tropical valleys notching the coast, planters established sugar plantations and built crushing mills, drawing their labour from the islands of Melanesia across the Coral Sea. For 40 years the 'blackbirders' sailed their schooners from budding coastal towns out through the reef on recruiting voyages to take islanders to work as labourers. They cleared the coastal rainforest and planted the first sugar cane, pioneering what is still the major rural industry of the north Queensland littoral.

Reflecting the dynamic development of the vast hinterland, the coastal towns boomed and by the late 19th century boasted many of the amenities of urban civilisation. The construction of wharves, jetties and breakwaters facilitated the expansion of coastal shipping services, which were crucial to development until the northern railway systems were linked with Brisbane in 1925.

Australia's Grand Canal

By the end of the 19th century Queenslanders saw the 'taming of the Barrier Reef' as yet another milestone of colonial progress, the maritime equivalent of the 'taming of the wilderness' on the inland frontier. In a major work entitled *The Great Barrier Reef of Australia*, published in 1893, William Saville-Kent celebrated the transformation of the inner route from a dangerous and threatening passage into 'Australia's Grand Canal':

> The linear chain of reefs that form the outer edge of the Barrier, together with the innumerable secondary reefs … constitute a natural breakwater against the ever reverberating surges of the Pacific Ocean, and this converts the Inner Route into a relatively shallow and tranquil inland sea, which the largest ocean steamers may traverse in safety, for the greater part of the year, with open ports and on an even keel.

Yet the confidence was exaggerated. Only a year or so before these words were written, the 3000-tonne passenger steamer *Quetta* struck an unmarked rock in Torres Strait, sinking in three minutes with the loss of 133 lives. Cyclones also continued to present a significant danger in reef waters. In March 1899 over 300 lives were lost and the pearling fleet was almost destroyed by cyclonic winds and tidal surge in Princess Charlotte Bay; in 1911 the *Yongala* went down with all hands in a cyclone off Cape Bowling Green, Queensland.

Scientists and escapists

The problems and potential of navigation were not the only source of interest in the Great Barrier Reef. During the 19th century visitors commented on both its scientific and aesthetic value, and commercial exploitation of the marine resources dates from the 1840s. As early as 1770 Sir Joseph Banks appreciated the scientific significance of the teeming life of the reef. He took a small boat and sailed over a reef just inside the outer barrier and was 'entirely taken up with' his investigation, meeting with 'many curious fish and molluscs', which he sought to classify and place in that obsession of the late 18th century, the great chain of creation. Later naval expeditions carried scientists and artists who made known to a wider world the biological richness of the reef.

Paralleling the growing scientific interest in the reef was a developing appreciation of its physical beauty. Matthew Flinders seems to have been the first European to find pleasure in a coral reef, which he saw when sailing north in HMS *Investigator*, even though he 'could not long forget with what destruction it was pregnant'. Yet he saw the reef with the ordered eyes of the 18th century. Watching the living coral in shallow water he was reminded of a formal floral arrangement, 'the most favourite parterre of the curious florist'. Forty years later J. B. Jukes, the naturalist on the *Fly*, reacted to the reef with all the ardour of the ascendant Romantic Movement. He spent a night camped on a wrecked ship on the outer barrier and was deeply moved by the experience. There was, he wrote:

a simple grandeur and display of power and beauty in this scene, as viewed from the forecastle of the wreck ... that rose even to sublimity. The unbroken roar of the surf, with its regular pulsation of thunder, as each succeeding swell first fell on the outer edge of the reef, was almost deafening, as both the sound and the sight were such as to impress the mind of the spectator with the consciousness of standing in the presence of an overwhelming majesty and power, while his senses were delighted by the contrast of beautiful colours afforded by the deep blue of the ocean, the dazzling white of the surf, and the bright green of the shoal water on the reef.

The idea of the barrier reef islands as the place for romantic escape from urban life received its most articulate and celebrated expression in the work of E. J. Banfield, who as 'The Beachcomber' wrote a series of best-selling books about his reclusive life on Dunk Island between 1897 and 1923. For Banfield, Dunk was 'clean and undefiled', entirely free from the 'mauling paws of humanity'. On the off-shore islands: 'The heat, the clatter, the stuffy odours, the toilsomeness, the fatigue of town life are abandoned; the careless quiet, the calm, the refreshment of the whole air, the tonic of the wide sea are gained'.

A nasty, stinking business

By the end of the 19th century, reef waters were being exploited for pearl shell and bêche-de-mer, an edible sea slug. Their export – the first to London, the second to Singapore and Hong Kong – was a small though still significant aspect of Queensland's overseas trade. Bêche-de-mer had been collected in north Australian waters by Indonesian fishermen since the 17th century. Large fleets of proas came down to the north coast on the northwest monsoon and returned when the prevailing winds shifted around to the southeast in March or April. The Indonesians ventured as far east as the Gulf of Carpentaria, but it is unlikely that they ever passed through Torres Strait.

Australian colonists appear to have become interested in the commercial potential of bêche-de-mer in the 1840s. In 1848 crew members from the *Rattlesnake* stumbled upon the remains of a curing establishment on a remote north Queensland island. Apparently small parties were already sailing north from Sydney to engage in the trade, taking back cargoes of dried and smoked bêche-de-mer for export to Asian markets.

Bêche-de-mer was found along most parts of the reef. It was easily collected at low tide, but to avoid deterioration it had to be processed quickly. It was split open, gutted, boiled and then smoked over open fires. The secret of success was a ready supply of cheap labour both to collect and process the catch, so Europeans established their small curing works on many of the reef islands and used coastal Aborigines to perform most of the operations. It was a small man's industry that needed limited capital and simple technology. John Douglas, the long-time Government Resident on Thursday Island, wrote of the industry:

It is not a nice business. Life on board one of these boats, or at the stations on the islands ... is unspeakably

'Dried and smoked sea slugs, known as bêche-de-mer, the 'worm of the sea', were traded with the Chinese for tea.'

◁ *Between 1863 and 1904 over 62 000 Melanesian labourers were shipped from the Solomons and the New Hebrides to the Queensland coastal ports in schooners like this one, photographed in Cairns harbour in the 1890s.*

'Aboriginal labour was obtained sometimes by kidnapping or trickery, and sometimes by mutual agreement.'

squalid and dirty. For some men, however, it has an attraction, and there is illicit intercourse with native women. It is altogether a nasty stinking business.

The bêche-de-mer captains obtained their Aboriginal labour in a number of ways, ranging from kidnapping or trickery to mutual agreement. Agreement probably became more important than force as the century wore on.

Young Aborigines were often willing to work for specified periods with the Europeans to gain access to European food, tobacco, steel, tools and guns. Yet the industry was pregnant with violence. Many workers were kept virtually as prisoners marooned on offshore islands long after the agreed period of labour. Conflict over women was endemic to life in cramped vessels and small isolated islands. For their part, coastal Aborigines struck back at the bêche-de-mer men, attacking them at their island stations or mutineering while on board, throwing the crew overboard and sailing off with their ships.

Conflict intensified in the late 1880s and early 1890s. In 1890, a Cooktown newspaper estimated that in the previous 16 years at least a hundred Europeans involved in the bêche-de-mer industry had been killed by Aborigines and Papuans. The situation was so serious that, with the exception 'of about a dozen who live in daily and nightly dread of a bloody end, all the 250 men once engaged in the bêche-de-mer industry have been wiped out or driven back upon southern civilisation'. For every European killed and wounded between 1860 and 1890, however, there were probably five to ten Aborigines who died violently.

The tension associated with the bêche-de-mer fishery led to the death of Mary Watson, who became one of the first martyrs of northern settlement. Arriving in Cooktown as a governess, she married a bêche-de-mer fisherman and went to

live at the curing station on Lizard Island. Eventually her husband and his partner sailed north seeking new fishing grounds, leaving Mary and her three-month-old baby, Ferrier, with two Chinese servants. Aborigines from the nearby coast crossed to the island, killing one of the servants and wounding the other. In a desperate bid to escape, Mary and the Chinaman Ah Sam dragged the disused ship's water tank, used for boiling bêche-de-mer, down to the sea and sailed it away from the island and to a horrible death from thirst on a waterless island nine days later.

The last pages of her diary, kept right up until her death, were found a year later with her body and that of her son. In matter-of-fact staccato sentences the tragedy unfolds:

September 3 – Left Lizard Island Sunday afternoon in the pot that the bêche-de-mer are boiled in. Got about three or four miles from the Lizard.

September 4 – Made for the island north of the Lizard, could not, and got on a reef, but do not know which one. Squally weather.

September 5 – Remained on the reef all day looking out for a boat. Saw none.

September 6 – Very calm morning, able to pull the tank up on an island with three small mountains on it. Ah Sam went on shore to try and get water as ours was done. There were natives camped there, so were afraid to go far away. We had to wait the turn of the tide, anchored under the mangroves, got in the reef, very calm.

September 7 – Made for an island about 4 or 5 miles from the one spoken of yesterday, ashore at last. Could not find any water. Cooked some rice and clawfish. Moderate SE breeze. Stayed here all night. Saw a steamer bound north, hoisted Ferrier's pink and white wrapper, but did not answer me.

September 8 – Changed the anchorage of the boat as the wind was freshening. Went down to a kind of little lake on the same island (this done last night). Remained here all day looking for a boat. Did not see any. Very cold night, blowing very hard. No water.

September 9 – Brought the tank ashore as far as possible with the morning tide; made camp all day under the trees. Blowing very hard. No water. Gave Ferrier a dip in the sea; he is showing symptoms of thirst. Took a dip myself. Ah Sam and myself parched with thirst. Ferrier showing symptoms.

September 10 – Ferrier very bad with inflamation. Very much alarmed. No fresh water, and no more milk but condensed. Self very weak. Really thought I should have died last night.

September 11 – Still all alive. Ferrier much better this morning. Still feeling very weak. I think it will rain today, clouds very heavy, wind not quite so high.

The last entry was undated:

No rain, every sign of fine weather. Ah Sam gone away to die. Have not seen him since 9th. Ferrier is more cheerful; self not feeling at all well. Have not seen any boat … No water, nearly dead with thirst.

Dispersal of the coastal clans

Thursday Island came to reflect in its population the fact that it was a focal point of shipping routes. In the late 19th century it was probably the most cosmopolitan community in Australia. Europeans made up about 40 per cent of the population, but· there were small communities of Japanese, Chinese, Filipinos, Malays and other races.

Torres Strait islanders and mainland Aborigines were extensively employed in the pearling and bêche-de-mer boats that came and went from Thursday Island anchorages. In the early stages of the industry their labour was crucial: it was cheap and readily available. But beyond that, the coastal Aborigines brought with them into the maritime industries all the traditional knowledge of the sea

and reefs, of the weather and currents and the life cycle and habitat of the marine creatures. Their gathering skills were invaluable for the bêche-de-mer fishery, and their swimming ability was crucial for pearling before the introduction of the diving dress in the 1880s. Coastal Aborigines were as important for the fisheries as their inland counterparts were for the northern cattle industry.

Yet the coastal clans suffered severely from the impact of the Europeans. Contact along the coast was probably a little less violent than inland. The offshore islands and coastal littoral were bypassed by the main thrust of the squatting movement, and sugar plantations were concentrated in a few fertile river valleys. The notorious Native Mounted Police – a force of Aboriginal troopers recruited from settled districts and then employed in areas where they had no kinship ties and spoke a different dialect – 'dispersed' the Aborigines on Hinchinbrook

Island, although their energies were usually absorbed on the vast inland frontier. But diseases brought back from the pearling luggers and bêche-de-mer stations – tuberculosis, gonorrhoea, influenza and other bronchial disorders – cut a swathe through communities that had little inherited immunity. A taste for alcohol and opium acquired from the Europeans and Chinese assisted in the process of demoralisation and depopulation. Early in the 20th century, the Queensland Government gathered the survivors together on reserves and missions, where children were raised in dormitories away from their parents. In the process, coastal dialects were partially forgotten or lost altogether; with them went that vast storehouse of knowledge about the reef and nearby waters and the legends about the long history of people who may have lived within earshot of the ocean for a thousand generations.☐

△ *The ruins of Mary Watson's stone house can still be seen on Lizard Island. The beach has since been named Mrs Watson's Beach.*

△ ◁ *An etching of Mary Watson, romantically named 'the heroine of Lizard Island'.*

'For every European killed and wounded between 1860 and 1890, there were probably five to ten Aborigines who died, violently.'

Diving and snorkelling: a wilderness adventure

The world of the reef

Since the beginning of time, man has sought new worlds but perhaps one of the strangest to be found is also for many people readily accessible. A journey into the sea requires only a mask and snorkel. With them, one can hover like a bird above the kaleidoscopic pastures of the reef and, for a moment, share that world with its inhabitants.

The Great Barrier Reef is particularly rich and rewarding. It offers the experience of snorkelling in shallow sun-drenched lagoons and the chance to be suspended near a vertical coral wall over waters that drop off to great depths. Colour and drama, movement, contrast, mystery and grandeur are there, but never sameness or boredom. Yet, a visit is not simply an underwater activity: calm turquoise

△ *A reef is more than just a diving adventure; to the underwater photographer, it is an endless array of shapes, colours and patterns that, because of the clear waters, can be captured on film. The camera's flash reveals an extraordinary world of brilliance beyond imagination.*

waters, clear sunny skies, small boats, quiet warm nights amid tropical vegetation, relaxation and a sense of apartness from the daily environment are also what the Great Barrier Reef is about.

Viewing the underwater world of the reef is as easy as floating in a bath. The clarity of the water and the penetration of sunlight ensures that everything there can see the light of day; nothing is hidden or swallowed by the swirling fog of turbid waters.

The shapes are clear and the colours are rich when seen from an underwater observatory or from a glass-bottomed boat. But the true experience of

the reef is a private one. To discover the mystery and excitement of the underwater world one needs to don face-mask and snorkel, and swim down into the silence below; a silence removed from the concrete echoes of the underwater observatory and the squeals from the glass-bottomed boat.

Joining the underwater life

Drifting in the shallows, one can watch the small sand-inhabiting fishes such as flathead, grubfish, gobies, rays and lizard fish dart from their resting places on the sand to settle farther on. Among the corals of the reef flat, the numbers of fishes increase dramatically with blennies, demoiselles and damselfish, and wrasses of all shapes and sizes. The brush-like turtle weed can be seen providing a vivid green home for an equally vivid green crab.

Nearer the reef edge, the profusion increases, seemingly to the point of overcrowding. Large groups of the blue-green pullers shelter in the staghorn gardens, butterfly fish dart to and fro while masses of surgeons, stripey snappers, sweetlips, parrotfish and sergeant majors appear to mill around aimlessly.

With increasing confidence, one can venture down the reef slope, or brave the surf on the windward side of the reef, or dive the reef slope or lagoon at night, when cardinal fish, squirrelfish, moray eels and cuttlefish can be seen on their nocturnal forays. Then, too, other fishes can be approached under ledges or in holes in the reef, or the delicate structure of the coral can be admired or the blinded turtle can be observed at close quarters. The shadowy outlines of even larger predators may also be glimpsed.

Alternately, one can explore a wreck, a slowly dissolving time capsule of a long-gone past, now providing a lodging house for a variety of boarders. Here, one is likely to find pennant coral fish weaving in and out of dark openings, schools of fusiliers hovering above, or large groupers, furtively darting to secret lairs within.

Knowing the reef

These are some of the riches of this underwater world. But the beauty and serenity of the reef can lull the diver into a false sense of security. There are treacherous currents, the coral is sharp, and it is just as easy to be harmed in crystal clear waters as it is in other areas.

Local knowledge is essential for any diving activity on or about the Great Barrier Reef and it is usually freely available. Many island resorts have their own experienced dive leaders and many of them will give instruction in scuba diving and snorkelling techniques. Charter boat captains are also familiar with the reef, know the good dive spots and know the dangers.

Preparing to dive

Careful preparation is vital to diving, and the chief requirement is to be medically fit. Many dive leaders, whether at resorts, on charter boats or with dive tours, insist on evidence of a diving orientated medical examination carried out within the past twelve months before taking that person on a diving excursion.

While the skills for snorkelling are minimal, scuba diving is a highly technical pastime, and it does require initial training in the use of scuba gear. At all resorts and on most charter boats, evidence of having qualified from an accepted scuba course must be shown, or alternately, a basic training course can be undertaken over several days while holidaying on some of the islands.

Scuba gear and safety

After training, equipment is the next priority. Travelling with scuba equipment is often a bother and most resorts and other dive operators carry a range of equipment for hire provided that acceptable diving qualifications are held by the hirer. Awkward tanks and weight belts especially are readily available for hire.

Before leaving home, it is a good idea to check all personal gear, and have the regulator and any other gauges serviced. The Standards Association of Australia covers the manufacture, testing and filling of steel and aluminium cylinders, and these standards are enforced by the Department of Occupational Safety in Queensland.

All diving cylinders must be hydrostatically tested by a Standards Association approved testing station every year, and filling stations generally will not fill a cylinder which is out of test.

Rules of the reef

Knowledge of local rules is extremely important. Throughout Australia the recognised diving flag is the international flag code A, a blue and white swallow-tailed burgee. The size of the diving flag should be a minimum of one metre by one metre so that it can be easily seen. The flag should always be flown when divers or snorkellers are in the water and under local boating regulations this signifies 'I have a diver below – keep well clear at low speed'.

Australia is in the enviable position of possessing the largest marine park in the world. The Great Barrier Reef Marine Park, covering the whole of the reef, has a number of rules that must be adhered to. Local divers will undoubtedly know the local rules but, in some instances, prior permits are required for certain activities or areas. Before camping on one of the islands, ownership should be ascertained. If the island is a private holding, permission of the owner is required. If the island is

crown land, it may be reserved for special purposes such as Aboriginal Reserves or National Parks and consequently there may be permit requirements.

Finally, Australia has a 'Historic Shipwrecks Act' that prohibits diving on any declared historic wreck in Australian waters. Many shipwrecks have occurred along the Great Barrier Reef but only a handful of these have been proclaimed historic. Some of these can be dived but only after a permit has been obtained. Ships from many countries, such as Spain, Portugal, Britain and Holland, have been lost here.

This is not a comprehensive review of the laws and rules relating to diving and associated activities; it must be emphasised that local knowledge can increase awareness of the limitations and restrictions that are placed on all users of the Great Barrier Reef. But diving on the reef is still remarkably easy and must rate as one of the greatest possible wilderness adventures.□

◁ Once underwater, a new world opens up to the scuba diver or the snorkeller. There are endless coral gardens to be explored, thousands of species of plants and animals to be found and photographed. Caves, canyons and vertical drop-offs are there to be investigated, above, each with its own photogenic inhabitants.

'One can hover like a bird above the kaleidoscopic pastures of the reef. Diving here is a rich and rewarding adventure ... and a very private one.'

Island resorts: where to go, how to get there and what to do

Many of the Great Barrier Reef's islands have excellent tourist facilities and are easily accessible from the mainland. Visit these islands and experience at first-hand the beauty and diversity of the reef's flora and fauna. Take a walk through lush, green rainforests. See the sea bird and turtle rookeries, where breeding takes place every year. At low tide, stroll in stout shoes over exposed corals where miniature communities live happily in rock pools. Glass-bottomed boats reveal a magical underwater scene of brilliant colours and fascinating shapes. Learn to snorkel and dive at the island schools and then go 'down under', entering a strange new world of coral gardens, brightly coloured fishes – some tiny and elusive, some aggressive and cheeky – and meadows of sea grass grazed by shy dugongs. Look closely at a coral boulder and see the bizarre spirals of Christmas tree worms and the holes made by boring sponges. And marvel at the tiny coral polyp, more like a plant than an animal, which builds the reef's framework.

Island	Size	Access	Accommodation	Reef-related activities
Bedarra	100 ha. (continental island)	Boat from Dunk Island, no day trips, charter boat from Cairns or Townsville.	Motel-style and cabins (no children under 15)	Reef trips, bush walks, snorkelling, fishing, game fishing, national park.
Brampton	78 ha. (continental island)	Air and boat from Mackay, day trips, charter boat from Mackay.	Motel-style	Reef trips, glass-bottomed boats, bush walks, snorkelling, fishing charters, national park.
Daydream	11 ha. (continental island)	Air and boat from Shute Harbour, helicopter from Proserpine, day trips, charter boats from Shute Harbour, water taxi from Hamilton Island.	Motel-style	Reef trips, glass-bottomed boats, bush walks, snorkelling, fishing, scuba lessons, cruises to other islands, national park.
Dunk	1200 ha. (continental island)	Air from Cairns or Townsville, boat from Clump Point, day trips, charter boats from Cairns or Townsville, water taxi/hovercraft transfers from Mission Beach.	Motel-style	Reef trips, bush walks, snorkelling, fishing, game fishing, cruises to other reefs and islands, national park.
Fitzroy	324 ha. (continental island)	Boat from Cairns, day trips, charter boats from Cairns.	Motel-style and cabins	Reef trips, glass-bottomed boats, bush walks, snorkelling, boating, diving, fishing, cruises to outer reefs.
Great Keppel	1454 ha. (continental island)	Boat from Roslyn Bay boat harbour, air from Rockhampton, day trips, charter boats from Yeppoon.	Motel-style, cabins and camping	Bush walks, snorkelling, diving lessons, fishing, cruises, underwater observatory, sandy beaches.
Green	13 ha. (coral cay)	Daily launch/hydroflite from Cairns, day trips, charter boats from Cairns.	Motel-style	Reef trips, glass-bottomed boats, bush walks, snorkelling, scuba diving, boating, underwater observatory, aquarium, national park.
Hamilton	607 ha. (continental island)	Air from Proserpine, Shute Harbour and Mackay, direct flights from Sydney, Melbourne and Brisbane, Cairns, Rockhampton and Ayers Rock, day trips, occasional charter boats from Mackay, boat from Shute Harbour.	Hotel and motel-style	Bush walks, snorkelling, fishing, flights to reef, boat hire, wildlife park.
Hayman	360 ha. (continental island)	Charter boat from Shute Harbour, helicopter from Proserpine, day trips, launch or helicopter from Hamilton Island. Seaplane from Proserpine/ Shute Harbour or Mackay.	Motel-style	Reef trips, glass-bottomed boat, bush walks, snorkelling, scuba diving, fishing, big game fishing, cruises to other islands.

Island	Size	Access	Accommodation	Reef-related activities
Heron	17 ha. (coral cay)	Boat or helicopter from Gladstone, day trips, charter boat from Gladstone.	Motel-style and cabins	Guided reef and bush walks, glass-bottomed boat, snorkelling, scuba diving, fishing, visits to turtle and sea bird rookeries, cruises to other islands, national park.
Hinchinbrook	642 sq. km. (continental island)	Helicopter and seaplane from Townsville to Cardwell, charter boats from Cardwell and Lucinda, day trips, charter boat from Townsville.	Cabins	Reef trips, rainforest walks, snorkelling, scuba diving, cruises, excursions to mangroves, the reef and other islands, national park.
Hook	2400 ha. (continental island)	Catamaran from Shute Harbour Accessible for coach tour camping trips.	Cabins and camping	Coral and fish viewing from underwater observatory, snorkelling, glass-bottom boat for coral viewing, fish feedling, paddle skis, bush-walking, national park.
Lady Elliott	42 ha. (coral cay)	Air from Brisbane, Maroochydore, Hervey Bay, Bundaberg and Noosa, day trips, charter boats from Bundaberg.	Cabins and camping	Reef trips, glass-bottomed boat, bush walks, snorkelling, diving (including night diving), fishing, visits to sea bird and turtle rookeries.
Lindeman	800 ha. (continental island)	Air from Mackay, Hamilton Island or Proserpine, day trips, charter boats from Mackay and Shute Harbour, boat from Hamilton Island or Shute Harbour daily, helicopter from Proserpine.	Motel-style	Reef trips, bush walks, snorkelling, fishing, flights to reefs, national park.
Lizard	1012 ha. (continental island)	Air from Cairns or Cooktown, day trips, charter boats from Cairns.	Motel-style	Reef trips, bush walks, snorkelling, scuba diving lessons, deep sea fishing, flights to reef, national park.
Long	103 ha. (continental island)	Helicopter from Proserpine, boat from Shute Harbour or Hamilton Island.	Motel-style, cabins and camping (18–35-year-olds only)	Reef trips, bush walks, snorkelling, fishing, cruises, national park.
Magnetic	52 sq. km. (continental island)	Vehicular ferry and daily boat from Townsville, day trips, charter boats from Townsville.	Hotels, guest houses, self-contained flats, cabins and camping	Reef cruises from Townsville, bush walks, wildlife park, snorkelling, camping, aquarium, national park.
Newry	45 ha. (continental island)	Boat from Victor Creek via Seaforth, day trips.	Cabins and camping	Boat trips, bush walks, fishing, national park.
Orpheus	2200 ha. (continental island)	Catamaran from Townsville, air from Townsville or Cairns, no day trips.	Motel-style and cabins	Fishing trips to reef, glass-bottomed boat, bush walks, snorkelling.
South Molle	405 ha. (continental island)	Boat from Shute Harbour and Hamilton Island, helicopter from Proserpine and Hamilton Island, day trips, charter boats from Shute Harbour.	Motel-style	Reef trips, glass-bottomed boat, bush walks, snorkelling and diving lessons, fishing, cruises to other islands, national park.

Conserving for the future: scientific research

An ecological puzzle

Coral reefs are among the world's most diverse and complex ecosystems. Our scientific understanding of how they work is far from satisfactory and is well behind our understanding of all other ecosystems, except perhaps those in Antarctica. This is in part because many universities and other centres of learning are concentrated in the temperate regions of the northern hemisphere, well away from coral reefs.

Early navigators in the Pacific, while surveying in the reef, often reported on the natural history of the region. Many naturalists visited the reef on survey vessels: J. Beete Jukes, who sailed with Captain F. P. Blackwood on HMS *Fly* in 1843, was the first scientific investigator of the Great Barrier Reef. His work was primarily geological and provided evidence for Darwin's theories. T. H. Huxley and J. MacGillivray sailed on HMS *Rattlesnake* in 1852 and were more involved with the reef's fascinating natural history. Towards the end of the 19th century Saville Kent published several reports, at the request of the Queensland Government, on the marine resources and fisheries of north Queensland. Among these was his classical, superbly illustrated volume entitled *The Great Barrier Reef*, published in 1893.

Established research

In 1922, the formation of a Great Barrier Reef Committee within the Queensland branch of the Royal Geographical Society of Australia marked the beginning of concerted research into the reef. Disagreements with the Royal Geographical Society later led to the committee's separation from its parent body. Recently, the Great Barrier Reef Committee has been reconstituted, and it is now known as the Australian Coral Reef Society.

One of the first projects undertaken by the original committee was the drilling in 1926 of a 183-metre bore-hole in Michaelmas Cay, near Cairns, under the supervision of Charles Hedley. A second, 223-metre bore was later drilled at Heron Island in 1937, but neither of these provided information to satisfy the geological questions about subsidence and the growth of coral reefs.

In 1928, the Great Barrier Reef Committee collaborated with the Royal Society of London to co-ordinate the first major biological expedition to the reef. For over 13 months, a team of 23 scientists, led by Sir Maurice Yonge, occupied a small field laboratory on Low Isles, off Port Douglas. The results of their studies, published over several decades by the British Museum of Natural History, are still being used today, although the buildings have long since disappeared.

Since then, four island research stations have been established to support scientific research into coral reefs. Three of these are operated by universities: on Heron Island by Queensland University, on One Tree Island by Sydney University and on Orpheus Island by James Cook University. The fourth is operated by the Australian Museum at Lizard Island in the northern region of the Great Barrier Reef.

In 1972 the Federal Government established a large research centre located 50 kilometres south of Townsville: the Australian Institute of Marine Science (AIMS). The research programs of the Institute are directed towards understanding the key environmental and ecosystem processes of the Great Barrier Reef region. In particular, the focus is on five main areas: the mangrove systems of northern Australia, the near-shore coastal environment within the reef lagoon, the oceanography of the continental shelf of the region, and two programs that attempt to understand and describe coral reef systems.

One of these major programs is designed to gain an understanding of the metabolic process leading to the development, growth and maintenance of coral reefs. The other program covers studies of the nature and extent of the distribution of corals and the associated plants and animals of the reef.

Researchers in Australian universities – notably James Cook University of North Queensland in Townsville and the universities of Sydney and Brisbane – and from overseas institutions, make major contributions to our knowledge of the reef ecosystem. The island research stations and AIMS provide the basic facilities utilised by these researchers. Facilities are now much better on the reef, although there is still a need in the far north. Assistance for all but AIMS is tenuous, however, with no permanent Commonwealth support.

The techniques and equipment used to study the reef are as diverse as the reef itself. In the early days much work was done by remote methods – dredges, nets, bottom grabs and explosive. A major boost was given to marine studies, following World War II, with the manufacture of self-contained underwater breathing apparatus (scuba), which permitted scientists to directly observe the life and behaviour of the reef organisms.

At one end of the scale, biologists are unravelling the mysteries of physiological processes using electron microscopes to 'see' into algal cells, while geologists are using x-ray diffractometers and radiocarbon dating to determine growth rates of corals and clams, which can then be used to date the reef structure. At the other end of the spectrum are the high technology remote sensing devices aboard earth satellites, which can show structures of whole reefs, indicate water-mass movements and determine large-scale patterns of distribution of corals and algae in shallow water.

Direct underwater observation by diving scientists, however, has been the basis of modern reef discoveries. Researchers often spend many hours a day underwater. Records are kept on underwater slates of perspex or polystyrene, and supplemented by underwater photographs. These long-term projects have provided insights into such phenomena as sex reversal in reef fishes, territories and home ranges, and the mass spawning of corals on just one or two nights a year.

The advent of small personal computers is also expanding research. Many studies now generate such vast data banks that analyses can only be performed by computers. Another approach being used at the Lizard Island research station is to take photographs of experimental ascidian colonies from fixed distances, develop and enlarge the photographs by a set amount, then place these photographs directly on a digitiser connected to a computer from which immediate measurements of area, change in area and growth rates of the colony can be obtained. Microprocessors and data loggers are also becoming widely used for continuously monitoring the reef, especially locations that are not safe for humans, such as the reef front during a cyclone.

Where does the water go?

One of the fundamental questions essential to an understanding of many reef processes is that of water movements within the reef province. At what rate is water exchanged between the Great Barrier Reef and the Coral Sea and through Torres Strait? What are the effects of trade or monsoon winds on surface water movements? And where do the deeper waters go? Answers to these questions are important for shipping, and for predicting the progress of pollutants, or of the larvae of reef organisms.

At a more restricted scale there are important questions to be answered to describe the patterns of wakes and eddies that occur in the lee of reefs and islands. Recent work shows that these water bodies are important for maintaining or returning the larvae of reef organisms to their parent reef system.

At the microscopic level we need to know how water passes over a reef and between the actual branches of the corals to carry nutrients and remove waste products from the system.

Another major field of interest is that of the population dynamics of reef organisms. What are the geographical limits of a local population? What are the growth rates of the individuals? What is the carrying capacity of the environment? What impact do man's activities – such as increasing nutrient levels – have on the growth of local populations? When and where does spawning take place? If a local population is overfished or destroyed by a cyclone how long will it take the population to recover, and where will the new population come from? What factors control the populations of crown-of-thorns starfish? These problems are of paramount importance if the living reef is to be managed properly and if the enormous diversity of species is to be retained.

The reef's resources

The Great Barrier Reef region is protected from extensive resource development by the Great Barrier Reef Marine Park Act of 1975, the establishment of the Great Barrier Reef Marine Park, and the 1981 inscription of the Great Barrier Reef on the World Heritage List. The resources that can be exploited in the Park are renewable, 'living' resources and the water itself. The variety of living resources is probably far greater in a tropical reef system than in any other marine habitat. Since the early 20th century – when bêche-de-mer, trochus shells and turtles were exploited commercially – the reef's principal 'living' resource has been food: fishes and prawns from wild stock. In more recent years the Moreton Bay 'bug' has also been fished. A small pearl oyster industry has existed for many years in the far northern Great Barrier Reef and in Torres Strait.

Additionally, there have been small enterprises based on hard coral and shell collecting for the tourist trade, and the trochus shell industry was re-established in the early 1980s on reefs near Mackay and the Whitsunday Islands.

However, in none of these – except the pearl oyster industry – have farming techniques been introduced to guarantee continuity of supply. Until now, the demand for fishes has never exceeded the supply, and therefore little attention has been given to mariculture: farming of the sea. On the Great Barrier Reef, the cultivation of prawns both for stock replenishment and for production to commercial size, is now a priority.

Salt, water and alternative food

Small industries have been established for the recovery of salt from marine waters and, eventually, the recovery of fresh water from sea water may be one of the most important resources in dry, tropical areas.

The reef is also proving to be a rich source of alternative food products and species from which chemicals, biochemicals or polymers can be produced. Marine polymers such as agar, carrageenan and alginates – mainly from seaweeds – are used as gel stabilisers in ice-cream, for the fining of wines, and in cake and pie constituents.

A number of toxic and venomous species of plants and animals occur in the reef region, including various cone shellfish, Conidae; the blue-ringed octopus, *Hapelochlaena maculosa*; the stonefish, *Synanceja trachynis*; the box jellyfish or sea wasp, *Chironex fleckeri*, and the crown-of-thorns starfish, *Acanthaster planci*. The presence of these species has encouraged research into their toxins to test suitability for medical and veterinary use. Bacteria, algae, sponges, hard and soft corals, sea anemones, molluscs and fishes were investigated. Scientists established that the active principle of the blue-ringed octopus's toxin is tetrodotoxin, which is also found in the pufferfish. They also discovered that the infections and ulcerations that follow coral scratches were almost always caused by three closely related species of marine bacteria, which were resistant to penicillin, ampicillin and carbenicillin – the antibiotics often recommended first – but were sensitive to tetracyclin and to erythromycin.

Early adventurers

For many thousands of years, human impact on the Great Barrier Reef was probably restricted to the immediate requirements of a relatively sparse coastal population who did not develop a major seagoing tradition. It was settlement of the Australian mainland by another wave of immigrants about 200 years ago that heralded the beginning of more intensive and widespread use of the natural resources of north Queensland and the reef.

Early commercial users of the reef relied upon coastal shipping and small boats. They sought bêche-de-mer, or trepang, turtle shell and meat, oil from dugongs, oysters, trochus shells and fishes for local consumption. Few areas of the reef were not explored by these early adventurers. Modern motor vessels with freezers, and trawlers have increased the range of both commercial and amateur operations, and proposals have been put forward in other areas, such as tourism and mineral exploration and extraction.

With the growing use of the reef and the slow accumulation of knowledge of some of the physical and biological characteristics of the area has come the realisation that the Great Barrier Reef is not only an area of national significance; it is also the largest system of coral and its associated life in the world. It is a part of the world's heritage.

The question is how, in the face of continually increasing pressures and demands on its resources, do we ensure that this area remains in perpetuity for inspiration, for enjoyment and recreation, and also as a source of livelihood for those who depend more directly on its natural resources? How are decisions to be made on uses that are compatible with its conservation; how are reference areas to be established so that changes due to human activity can be detected above the seasonal and other cyclic changes that may occur naturally, and how are conflicts between potential users to be avoided?

Environmental protection

In the late 1960s and early 1970s there was growing environmental concern in Australia and an

△ *A battery-operated 'wet' submarine allows diving scientists to carry extra tanks or heavy equipment to underwater work sites, or to travel long distances for underwater surveys or to follow large fishes, such as sharks. The submarine is a retreat on occasions when sharks under observation become a little too inquisitive.*

'The biological and geological complexity of the Great Barrier Reef make it the richest marine habitat on earth.'

increasing awareness that the Great Barrier Reef needed protection if its wonderful riches were to be retained. There was an outcry when drilling for oil was to be started on the reef. A great many Australians considered that the area should be totally protected from mining and other development to preserve it in as natural a state as possible. There were, however, established users: a number of people make their living from the area, and it was also considered possible that reserves of oil or other scarce mineral resources may have been present. Some sections of the community thought that serious consideration should have been given to the costs and benefits of extracting those resources.

While a great deal can be achieved by individuals and concerned groups acting to protect areas in which there is an obvious or immediate threat, the conservation and protection of an area as large as the Great Barrier Reef requires a firm basis in the existing framework of government.

The Marine Park Act
Early disputes between the State and Commonwealth governments over control of the sea and seabed off Australia hampered the development of an integrated approach to conservation of the Great Barrier Reef. In 1975, the Great Barrier Reef Marine Park Authority was formed under an Act of the Australian Parliament, which provided for the protection of the area while recognising the need to accommodate reasonable use. (Before 1975, the Queensland Government had also recognised the need for conservation, and had declared the Heron and Wistari Reefs and the Green Island Reef as Marine Parks.) Under the 1975 Federal legislation the one use not permitted is mining for minerals, including oil, except for approved research.

The Great Barrier Reef Marine Park Act provides for extensive public participation. The Act is Commonwealth legislation, but because it has profound implications for the State of Queensland, provision is made for co-ordination between State and Commonwealth interests. One of the three members of the Great Barrier Reef Marine Park Authority is nominated by the Queensland Government. The Authority is responsible to a Commonwealth Minister, who is the convener of a ministerial council made up of two Queensland and two Commonwealth Ministers, intended to co-ordinate the policies of the two governments on Great Barrier Reef matters. Additional advice to the Federal Minister and the Authority comes from a large consultative committee, which receives advice and requests from various government authorities, conservation organisations, tourist, commercial and recreational fishing, and other interest groups.

The major functions of the Authority and its staff are the identification and delineation of areas that are to be included in the Marine Park and the preparation and monitoring of zoning plans.

Because the Act applies only to the waters and seabed of the region, with all islands other than those used for defence or navigational purposes under the control of the Queensland Government, co-ordination of the zoning plans with existing controls on the islands is important. Although the Great Barrier Reef Marine Park Act provides the legislative basis for the care and development of the area to which it applies, it can only function effectively with support from an informed and sympathetic public. Three opportunities are provided for public comment between the declaration of the outer boundaries of a section of the Park and the implementation of a zoning plan.

Some people consider that the term Marine Park for the whole region is a misnomer, as commercial exploitation of natural resources is allowed in extensive areas within the region, although it is controlled by the zoning plan and management practices. They claim that the entire region should be subject to the same degree of protection found in major national parks, with smaller areas identified for commercial and other potentially damaging uses. Others believe that the protection of particularly sensitive areas by zoning and management controls to accommodate a variety of uses will ensure the conservation of the entire area generally accepted as the Great Barrier Reef. The zoning process at present identifies areas within a section in which no extractive or potentially damaging activities are permitted. Areas adjacent to particularly sensitive localities or features may be set aside as buffer zones, providing broader scale protection by progressively excluding activities that may damage the reef and its animals and plants, or by regulating the intensity of those activities.

A long-term reference area
In contrast to terrestrial ecosystems, in which there may be comparatively little import of nutrients and energy, other than those in water and from sunlight, water movement and current systems are extremely important in the maintenance of the reef. We still do not know how large an area of the reef has to be maintained in an undisturbed state to serve as a long-term reference area.

Three main areas are of primary importance: research, to provide the information necessary for good decisions; monitoring, to assess the impact of those decisions; and education, to provide information to the community and to create a climate in which conservation practices are accepted by the reef's users.

The future of the reef

The biological and geological complexity of the Great Barrier Reef make it the richest marine habitat on earth, and it increases in relative value as other areas of coral reef come under stress, often from communities whose needs for the very basics

of life demand reef use. The largest remaining herds of the gentle dugong are in reef waters, the world's greatest mass breeding of turtles occurs on Raine Island and breeding sites of many sea birds are situated the length and breadth of the reef.

However, the living reef can be – and has been – damaged. Its dugongs are easily killed accidentally in fishermen's nets. Its turtle populations can be reduced by the careless use of their breeding islands. Many of the bird populations cannot tolerate human interference at nesting time, and eggs and nestlings may be destroyed by rats introduced with human habitation. The beautifully adapted island vegetation can be transformed by human introductions, deliberate and accidental.

Since the formation of the Great Barrier Reef Marine Park Authority a new perspective of the reef has been formed, much of which bears on how it is to be protected. Whereas the reef was previously regarded as a relatively unchanging system, with stable populations of most species from year to year, it is now known to be highly dynamic. A species that is abundant one year may have a poor recruitment the next year; populations may become extinct on one patch of coral or on a complete reef, and follow this with a number of successful years.

The rise and fall in the numbers of crown-of-thorns starfish were startling because they made severe inroads on the corals on which they feed: the living surface of the reef. But skeletal pieces in lagoon sands have established that even the coral-eating starfish has had population booms before. And the fluctuations noted in other reef species suggest that this behaviour is perhaps not abnormal.

Inshore reefs differ from those near the outer barrier, and researchers have documented changes in the abundance and food sources of fish communities across the reef. Many of the reef's inhabitants produce floating eggs or larvae, some of which float for two to three weeks before settling. The strong currents of the reef may move fish larvae hundreds of kilometres from their parent reef, leaving them little possibility of resettling on it. Oceanographers have discovered that long period waves may generate alternately reversing currents of about 500 kilometres along the southern reef area. These two facts, from different disciplines, have an obvious conservation message – the protection of a reef is pointless if surrounding areas are damaged.

In geologists' terms the reef is young – only about two million years old – and the last low-sea-level period, which lasted 100 000 years, stripped off up to 15 metres of reef surface. The present period of reef growth, building on older reef platforms, has already lasted for 8000 years, but the future may hold another erosional period. In that event people may again be able to walk to the outer edge of the reef, as the early Aboriginal Australians did long ago. For the foreseeable future, however, the reef in its present state is in our hands. □

Glossary of scientific terms

ampullae: the dilated end part of certain ducts or canals.

atoll: a coral reef surrounding a lagoon.

baffle: a spur and groove construction which reduces the power of the waves on the reef front.

baleen: whalebone – horny plates attached to the upper jaws of true whales.

barbel: a long, fleshy projection, usually about the mouths of fishes.

Batesian mimicry: where one species (mimic) evolves to look like another (model), to benefit the mimic.

benthic: living on the sea bottom.

biota: the plant and animal life of a region.

bivalve: molluscs with two shells, such as oysters, scallops and clams.

blue light: light which penetrates deepest into the ocean.

bombies: large heads of coral.

broadcast spawning: gametes shed into the water are dispersed by the currents.

calyx: the outer 'envelope' that protects a flower bud; also, a cup-shaped cavity or structure.

carapace: a horny or bony shield covering the whole or part of the bodies of animals such as crabs and turtles.

carnivore: a flesh eater.

cartilage: tough elastic tissue forming the skeleton in the group of fishes including sharks, skates and rays.

cellulose: the main constituent of plant cell walls.

cerata: long tubular projections on the backs of aeolid nudibranchs. These may be used to store stinging cells collected from prey which are used as the aeolid's own weapons.

chelae: large pincer-like claws of crabs and other crustaceans.

chemoreceptors: an organ, such as a tastebud, able to receive chemical stimuli.

chromatophore: a cell in the skin in which pigment is concentrated and which by alteration of shape causes the animal to change colour.

ciliate: fringed with short threads, cilia; also a common name for the class of single-celled Protozoa called Ciliata.

cirri: finger-like structures.

cloaca: a cavity into which the alimentary canal and genitals and urinary ducts open.

clone: an asexually produced descendant.

commensalism: two different organisms living in close association without either being harmed by it.

continental island: also known as a high island, it is made of rock similar to the nearby mainland, and rises above sea level.

continental shelf: the sea bed surrounding a continent at depths of up to 200 metres, at the edge of which the continental slope drops steeply to the ocean floor.

coral cay: a small low island or bank composed of sand and coral fragments.

coralline algae: organisms that create a thin veneer of calcium carbonate over other surfaces. They need light to grow and create a cementing material between corals.

cotyledon: the primary leaf or leaves of a seed plant found in the embryo.

cryptic: tending to conceal by hiding or by disguising or camouflaging the shape.

Cuverian organs: long white, sticky threads, sometimes poisonous, emitted through the cloaca of some holothurians to entangle a predator.

cytoplasm: the living substance or protoplasm of a cell exclusive of the nucleus.

demersal spawning: eggs are laid and fertilised on the sea bottom.

detritus: an accumulation of dead plant and animal tissue and fine sediment.

dorsal fin: fin on the back of fishes and some other aquatic vertebrates.

ecosystem: a system formed by the interactions between organisms and their environment.

endostyle: a mucus-producing groove on the underside of an ascidian's pharynx.

eversible: capable of being turned inside out.

exoskeleton: the protective or supporting structure covering the outside of some animals, such as crustaceans.

fenestrate: perforated or having window-like openings.

filiform: threadlike.

flagella: whip-like growths used by diatoms and dinoflagellates to move in the water.

flukes: the two lobes of the tail of a whale or related animal; also, the common name for parasitic worms.

foraminifera: a group of single-celled animals (Protozoa) which form shells of lime. Some are microscopic, but some form shells over ten millimetres across.

fringing reefs: the simplest reef landforms built upwards and outwards in shallow seas, beside islands or continents.

gamete: reproductive cell; sperm or ova.

gametogenesis: gamete formation.

genera: the taxonomic groups which contain one or more species of common evolutionary origin.

gills: organs for air exchange (respiration) in water-living animals.

gonads: sex organs – the animal organs in which gametes are produced.

gonopore: external pore through which gametes are released.

haustorium: a small sucker of a parasitic plant, which penetrates the tissues of the host and draws food from it.

herbivore: a plant eater.

hermaphrodite: a creature in which both male and female organs are normally present, as in some molluscs and worms.

hybrid: the offspring of two animals or plants of different species.

invertebrates: animals without backbones.

lignin: a substance in some plant cell walls which makes the plant rigid.

littoral: relating to the shore of sea, lake or ocean.

madreporite: a sieve-like plate in an echinoderm's water vascular system.

mandible: the lower jaw.

mesenteries: vertical sheets of tissue which divide the body cavity in such animals as sea anemones and coral polyps.

modular organisms: a special kind of colonial animal in which a single founder individual divides and replicates itself over and over, repeating its set of vital organs.

monandric: all individuals are born as only one sex.

morphological: concerned with the form and structure of organisms.

moult: to cast or shed the outer covering periodically.

mouth brooding: eggs being kept in the mouth of the parent fish until they hatch.

Mullerian mimicry: where two or more species, which may be toxic, evolve looking similar to their mutual advantage.

necrosis: the death of cells or tissues.

nematocysts: stinging cells used to stun prey.

ocellate: spotted.

operculum: the gill-cover of a fish; the plate which closes the shell aperture of some molluscs.

ossicles: small bones or skeletal calcareous plates.

ovo-viviparity: reproductive system whereby the eggs are retained within the female; fertilisation by the male is internal; and the young are then born alive.

palps: long flat sensory structures associated with the mouth, found in worms and some arthropods.

papilla: a finger-like projection of the body wall.

pedicellariae: calcareous appendages of some echinoderms, tiny pincer-like organs with movable grasping jaws.

pelagic: living in the open sea.

peristaltic: waves of muscular contractions of bodily tubes, such as the alimentary canal, which transports food and waste products.

phylum: the primary taxonomic division of the animals and plants that have the same general plan and are considered to be related.

polyp: an individual of a colonial animal such as in corals.

pouch rearing: the females of fish such as pipefish lay their eggs in the pouch of the male where they subsequently hatch.

proboscis: an extensible, tubular structure used in the capture of prey.

protandry: starting life as male and becoming female later.

protogyny: starting life as female and becoming male later.

raptorial: predatory, or adapted for seizing prey.

reef crest: the highest part of the reef on the windward side.

rhizome: an underground stem putting out stems above and roots below.

rostrum: an elongated beak or snout.

salp: a planktonic animal, related to ascidians, having a transparent barrel-shaped body with openings at either end.

sepals: any of the separate parts of the calyx of a flower.

sessile: sitting directly on the sea bed without support; also sedentary, fixed to one spot.

setae: bristles or hairs.

speciation: the development of a new species by evolutionary processes.

spicule: a small, slender, pointed structure or crystal in the skeleton of sponges, corals and the like.

stamen: the male reproductive organ of a flower.

stigmata: respiratory openings or breathing pores in invertebrates.

stolon: a branch which strikes root at the top, and then develops an ascending growth, which becomes an independent plant, like a strawberry runner.

substrate: the sea bed on which animals and plants live or are attached, including sand, mud, rock and coral.

swimmeret: an abdominal limb or appendage of a crustacean adapted for swimming.

symbiont: one of two organisms which live in symbiosis with each other.

symbiosis: different animals living together, which may or may not be beneficial to one or the other.

test: outer protective 'coat' or covering of ascidians; also, the skeleton of echinoids and other echinoderms.

trophic: of, or pertaining to nutrition.

tubercles: a small rounded protuberance on a bone or the body surface.

ventral fin: fin on the underside of fishes and some other aquatic vertebrates.

vertebrates: any chordate animal of the subphylum vertebrata, characterised by a bony or cartilaginous skeleton including a backbone and a well-developed brain.

viscera: internal organs in the cavities of the body.

viviparous: producing live young.

zooid: term often used in place of 'polyp'; refers to a single animal or one from a colony in invertebrates such as corals and ascidians.

zooplankton: the animal constituent of plankton.

zooxanthellae: symbiotic yellow-brown single-celled algae living in various animals, such as corals and some molluscs.

Index